BECAUSE SOMETIMES YOU
JUST GOTTA DRAW A COVER
WITH YOUR LEFT HAND

Other *Pearls Before Swine* Collections

Larry in Wonderland
When Pigs Fly
50,000,000 Pearls Fans Can't Be Wrong
The Saturday Evening Pearls
Macho Macho Animals
The Sopratos
Da Brudderhood of Zeeba Zeeba Eata
The Ratvolution Will Not Be Televised
Nighthogs
This Little Piggy Stayed Home
BLTs Taste So Darn Good

Treasuries

Pearls Blows Up
Pearls Sells Out
The Crass Menagerie
Lions and Tigers and Crocs, Oh My!
Sgt. Piggy's Lonely Hearts Club Comic

Gift Book

Da Crockydile Book o' Frendsheep

BECAUSE SOMETIMES YOU JUST GOTTA DRAW A COVER WITH YOUR LEFT HAND

A Pearls Before Swine
Collection
by Stephan Pastis

**Andrews McMeel
Publishing, LLC**
Kansas City • Sydney • London

Pearls Before Swine is distributed internationally by Universal Uclick.

Andrews McMeel Publishing, LLC
an Andrews McMeel Universal company
1130 Walnut Street, Kansas City, Missouri 64106

www.andrewsmcmeel.com

12 13 14 15 16 RR2 10 9 8 7 6 5 4 3 2 1

ISBN: 978-1-4494-1023-0

Library of Congress Control Number: 2011932652

Pearls Before Swine can be viewed on the Internet at
www.pearlscomic.com

These strips appeared in newspapers from May 24, 2010, to February 27, 2011.

To Ron O'Neal,
a great salesman,
a great friend,
and yet another
person who didn't
like this cover.

Introduction

Here is the feedback I normally get from my book editors when I turn in a book cover:

'Great!'
'Hilarious!'
'Love it!'

Here is the feedback I got when I turned in this one:

'Strange.'
'Really?'
'We don't like it.'

You see, there's this committee at Andrews McMeel that votes on book covers. And they've voted against this one twice.

I am not sure how many people are on that committee or what the room looks like, but I'm guessing it resembles the Kremlin circa 1979 and Leonid Brezhnev sits at its head (Google him for the full effect).

But I am nothing if not annoying. And so I kept proposing it every time a book cover was due.

I am sure Andrews McMeel thought they could outlast me. But they were wrong. They did not know that in 1982 I was voted the Most Obnoxious Person at Huntington Junior High. They did not know that I won the award again in 1986 at San Marino High School.

Indeed, my obnoxiousness was no fluke.

It was a dynasty.

And so, like the kid in the back seat yelling, 'Are we there yet?', I kept whining, 'Can we do the left-handed one?? Can we do the left-handed one?'

And eventually, they got tired of saying, 'Nyet.'

So here it is, a victory for free speech. Artistic integrity.

And general obnoxiousness.

Stephan Pastis
April, 2012

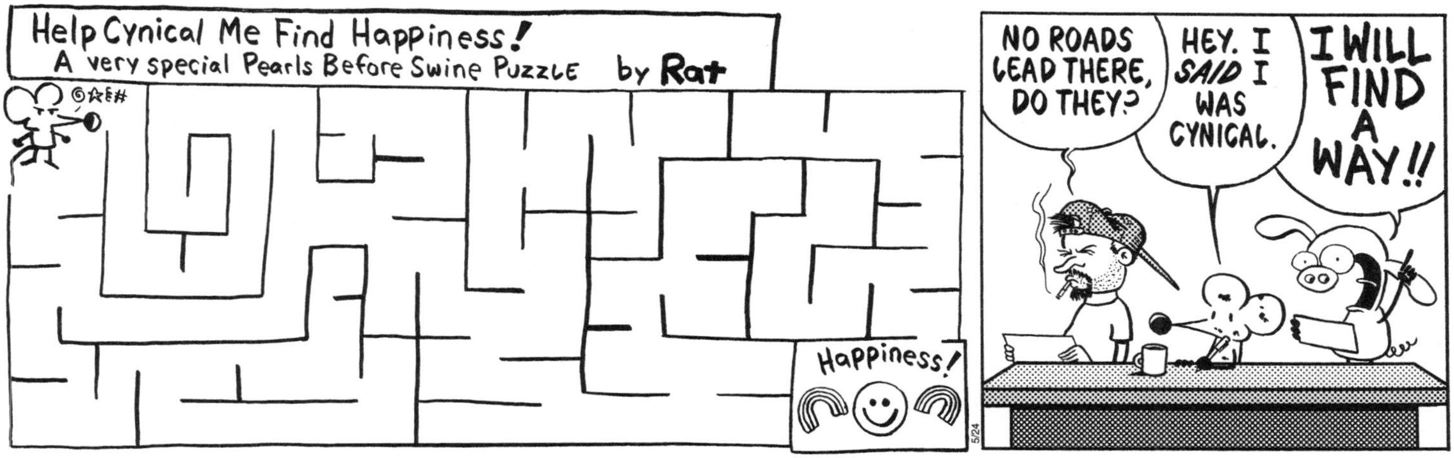

Help Cynical Me Find Happiness!
A very special Pearls Before Swine Puzzle by Rat
Happiness!
NO ROADS LEAD THERE, DO THEY?
HEY. I *SAID* I WAS CYNICAL.
I WILL FIND A WAY!!
5/24

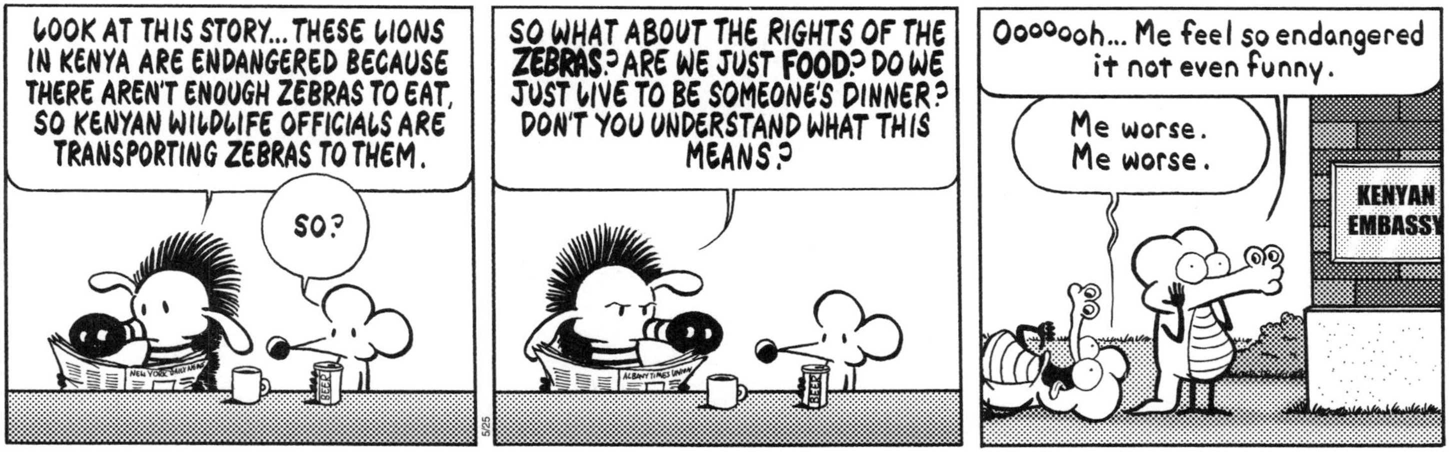

LOOK AT THIS STORY... THESE LIONS IN KENYA ARE ENDANGERED BECAUSE THERE AREN'T ENOUGH ZEBRAS TO EAT, SO KENYAN WILDLIFE OFFICIALS ARE TRANSPORTING ZEBRAS TO THEM.
SO?
BEER
SO WHAT ABOUT THE RIGHTS OF THE **ZEBRAS**? ARE WE JUST **FOOD**? DO WE JUST LIVE TO BE SOMEONE'S DINNER? DON'T YOU UNDERSTAND WHAT THIS MEANS?
BEER
5/25
Ooooooh... Me feel so endangered it not even funny.
Me worse. Me worse.
KENYAN EMBASSY

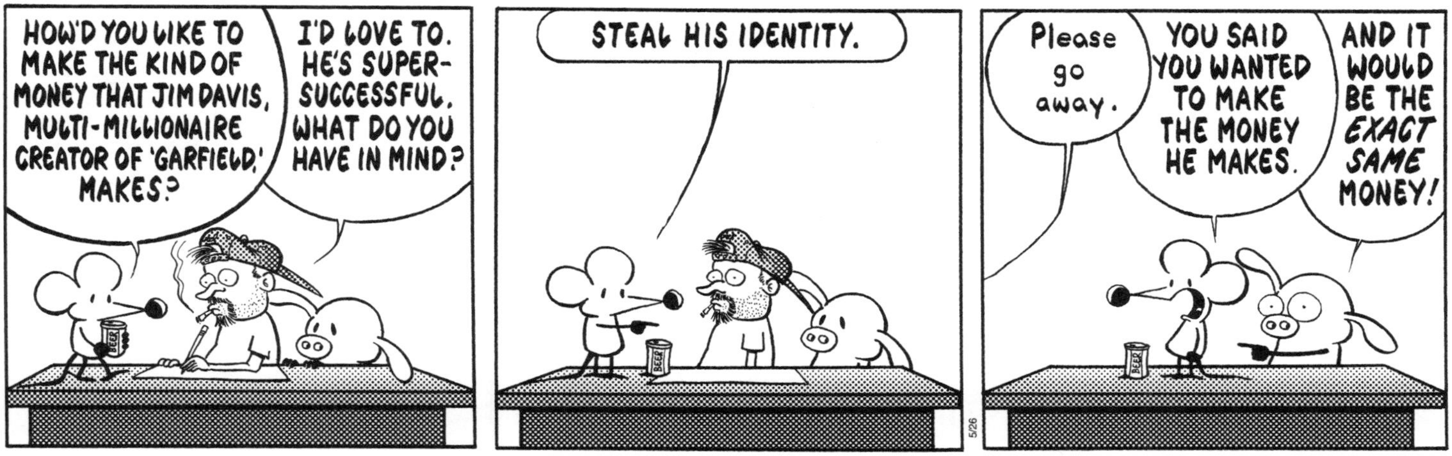

HOW'D YOU LIKE TO MAKE THE KIND OF MONEY THAT JIM DAVIS, MULTI-MILLIONAIRE CREATOR OF 'GARFIELD,' MAKES?
I'D LOVE TO. HE'S SUPER-SUCCESSFUL. WHAT DO YOU HAVE IN MIND?
BEER
STEAL HIS IDENTITY.
BEER
Please go away.
YOU SAID YOU WANTED TO MAKE THE MONEY HE MAKES.
AND IT WOULD BE THE *EXACT SAME* MONEY!
BEER
5/26

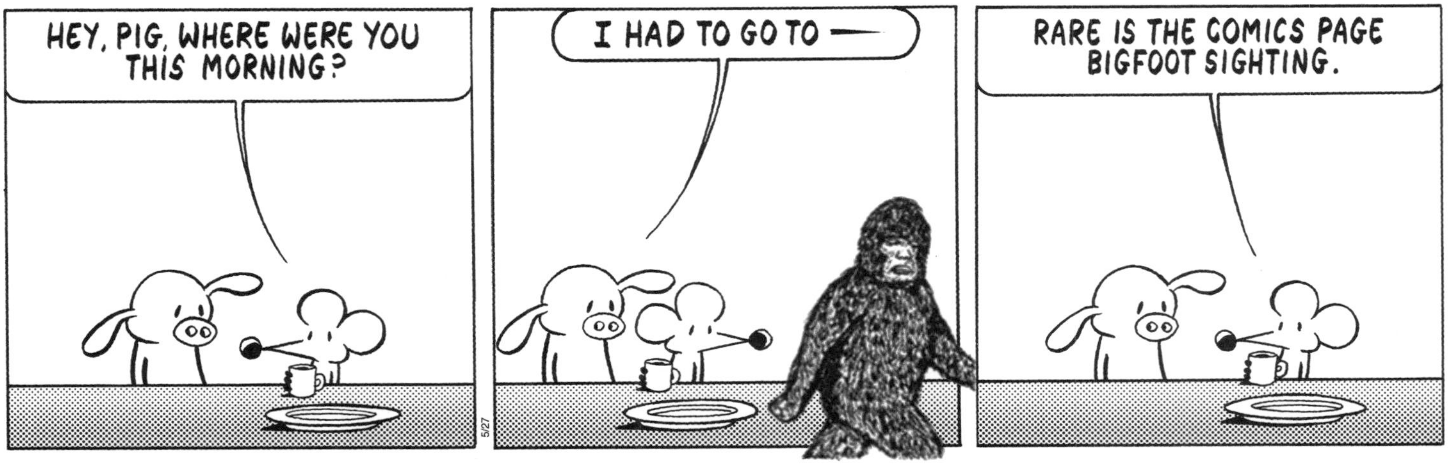
HEY, PIG, WHERE WERE YOU THIS MORNING?
I HAD TO GO TO —
RARE IS THE COMICS PAGE BIGFOOT SIGHTING.
5/27

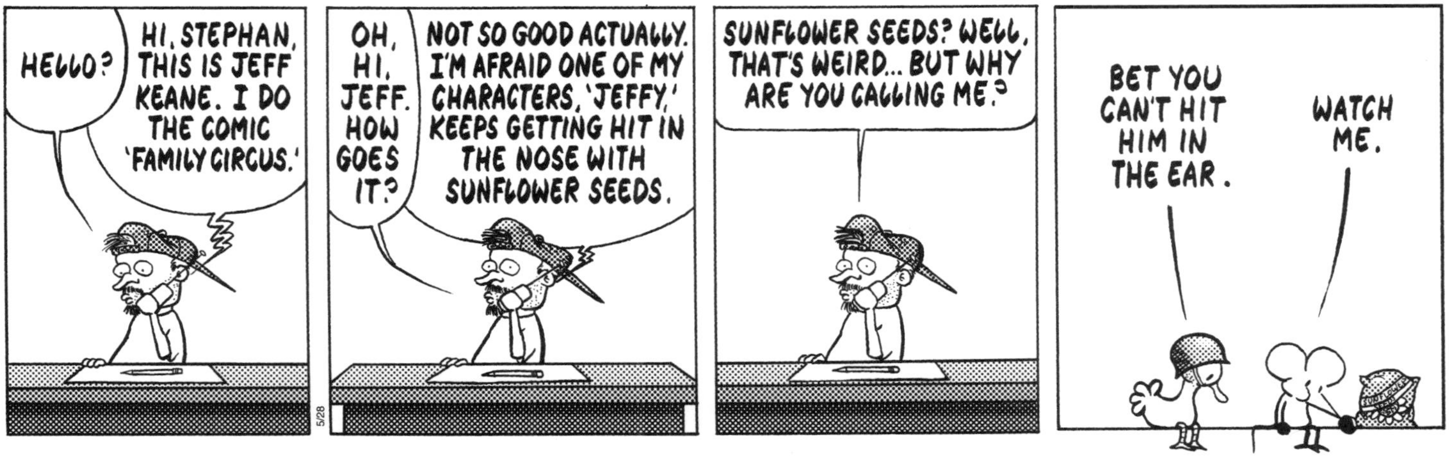
HELLO?
HI, STEPHAN, THIS IS JEFF KEANE. I DO THE COMIC 'FAMILY CIRCUS.'
OH, HI, JEFF. HOW GOES IT?
NOT SO GOOD ACTUALLY. I'M AFRAID ONE OF MY CHARACTERS, 'JEFFY,' KEEPS GETTING HIT IN THE NOSE WITH SUNFLOWER SEEDS.
SUNFLOWER SEEDS? WELL, THAT'S WEIRD... BUT WHY ARE YOU CALLING ME?
BET YOU CAN'T HIT HIM IN THE EAR.
WATCH ME.
5/28

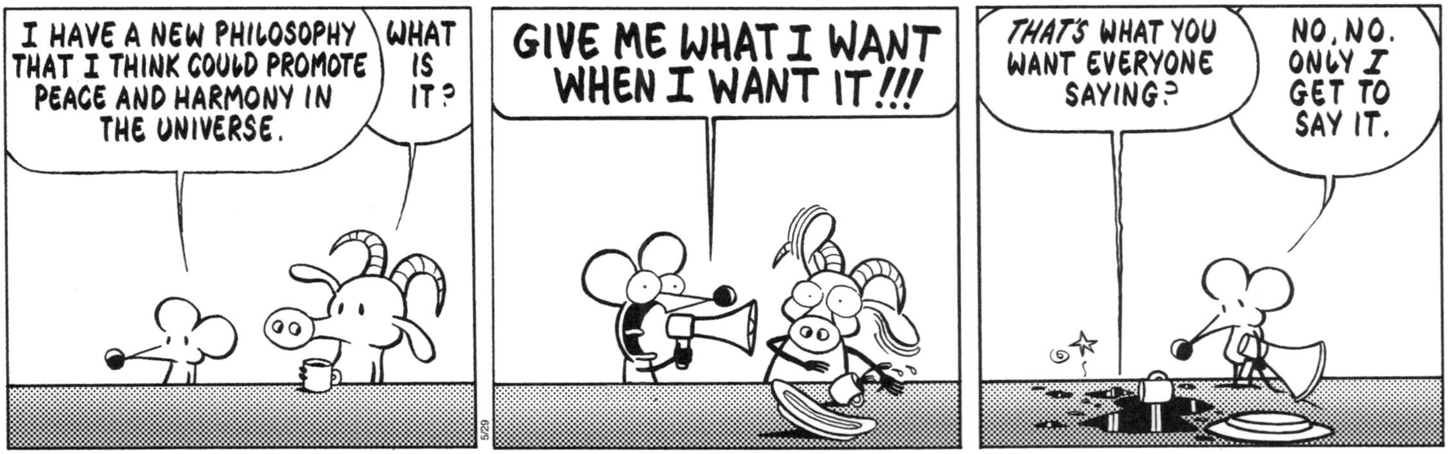
I HAVE A NEW PHILOSOPHY THAT I THINK COULD PROMOTE PEACE AND HARMONY IN THE UNIVERSE.
WHAT IS IT?
GIVE ME WHAT I WANT WHEN I WANT IT!!!
THAT'S WHAT YOU WANT EVERYONE SAYING?
NO, NO. ONLY *I* GET TO SAY IT.
5/29

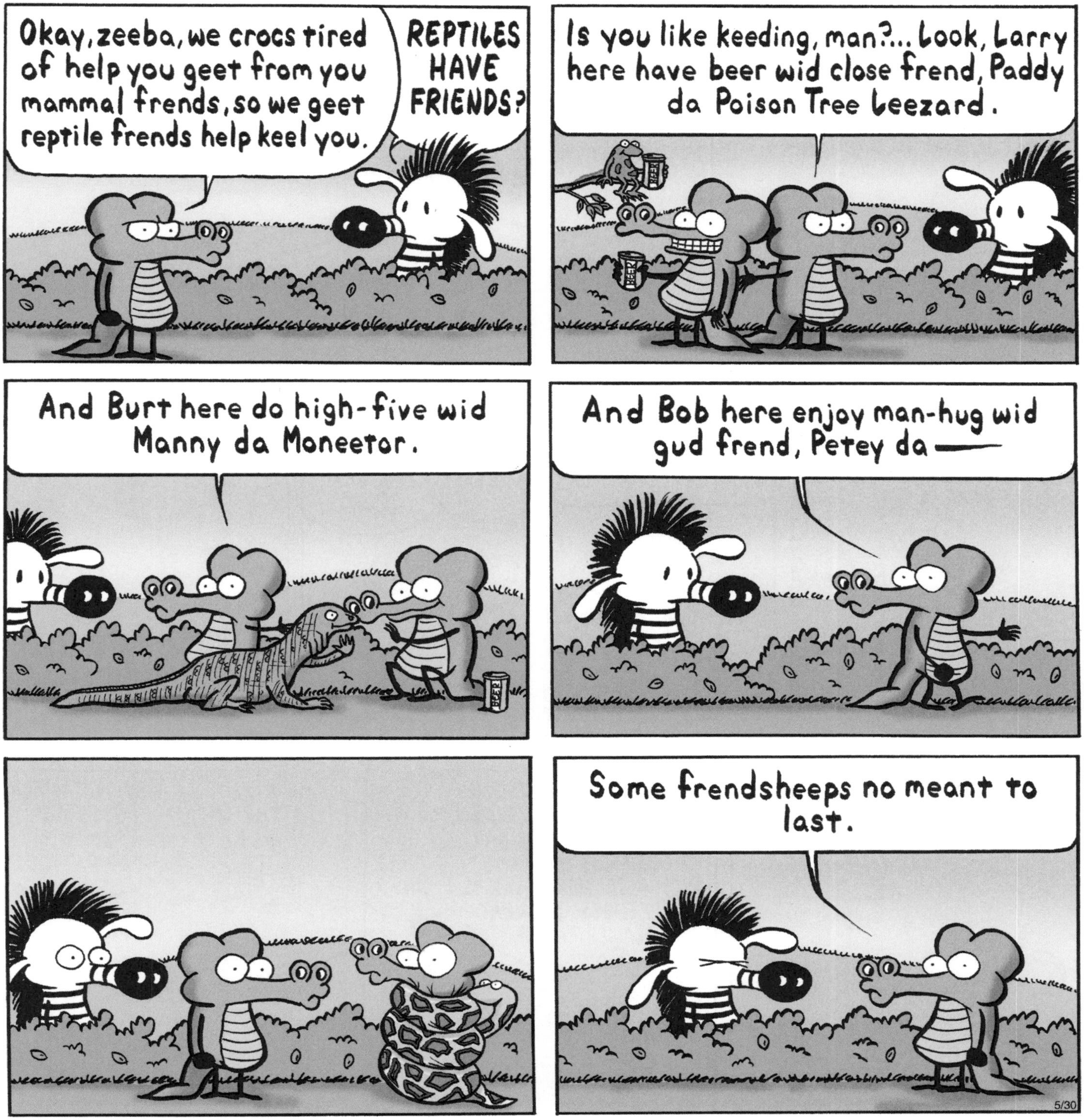
Okay, zeeba, we crocs tired of help you geet from you mammal frends, so we geet reptile frends help keel you.
REPTILES HAVE FRIENDS?
Is you like keeding, man?... Look, Larry here have beer wid close frend, Paddy da Poison Tree Leezard.
BEER
BEER
And Burt here do high-five wid Manny da Moneetor.
BEER
And Bob here enjoy man-hug wid gud frend, Petey da —
Some frendsheeps no meant to last.
5/30

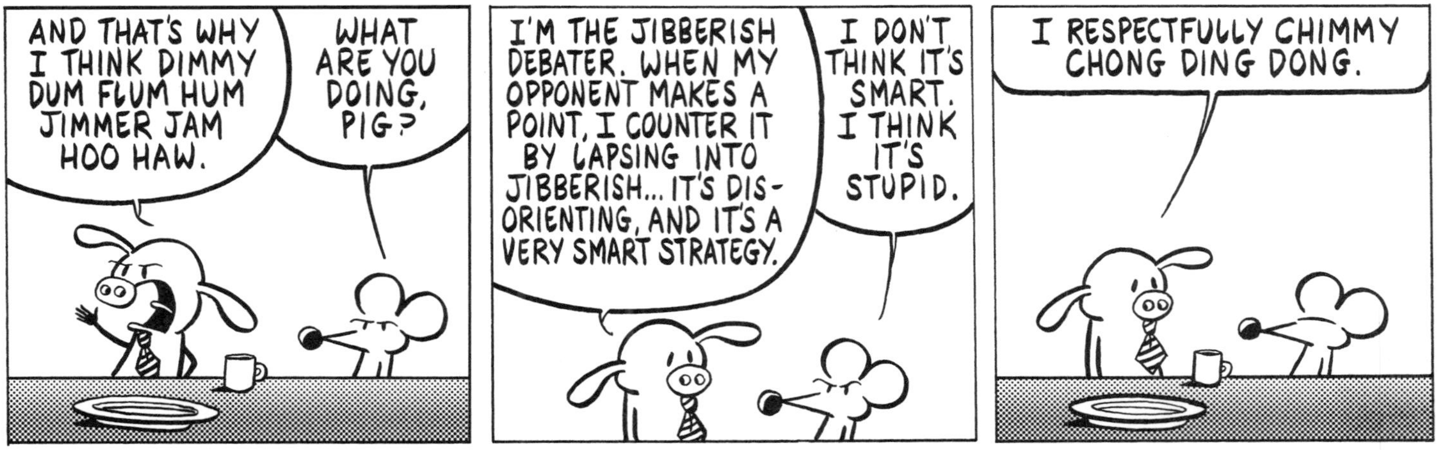
AND THAT'S WHY I THINK DIMMY DUM FLUM HUM JIMMER JAM HOO HAW.
WHAT ARE YOU DOING, PIG?
I'M THE JIBBERISH DEBATER. WHEN MY OPPONENT MAKES A POINT, I COUNTER IT BY LAPSING INTO JIBBERISH... IT'S DISORIENTING, AND IT'S A VERY SMART STRATEGY.
I DON'T THINK IT'S SMART. I THINK IT'S STUPID.
I RESPECTFULLY CHIMMY CHONG DING DONG.

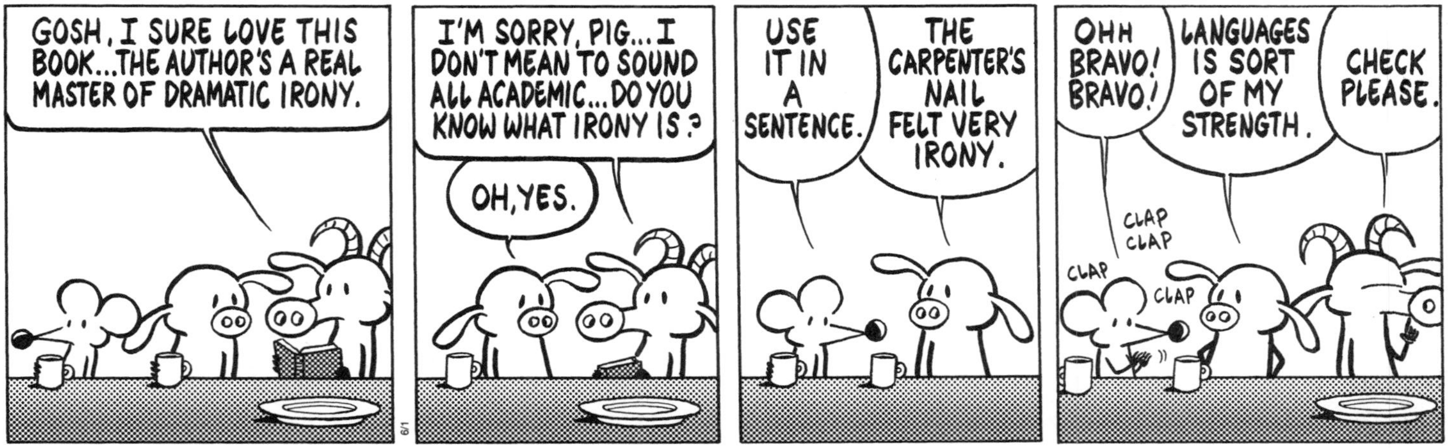
GOSH, I SURE LOVE THIS BOOK...THE AUTHOR'S A REAL MASTER OF DRAMATIC IRONY.
I'M SORRY, PIG...I DON'T MEAN TO SOUND ALL ACADEMIC...DO YOU KNOW WHAT IRONY IS?
OH, YES.
USE IT IN A SENTENCE.
THE CARPENTER'S NAIL FELT VERY IRONY.
OHH BRAVO! BRAVO!
CLAP
CLAP CLAP
CLAP
LANGUAGES IS SORT OF MY STRENGTH.
CHECK PLEASE.
6/1

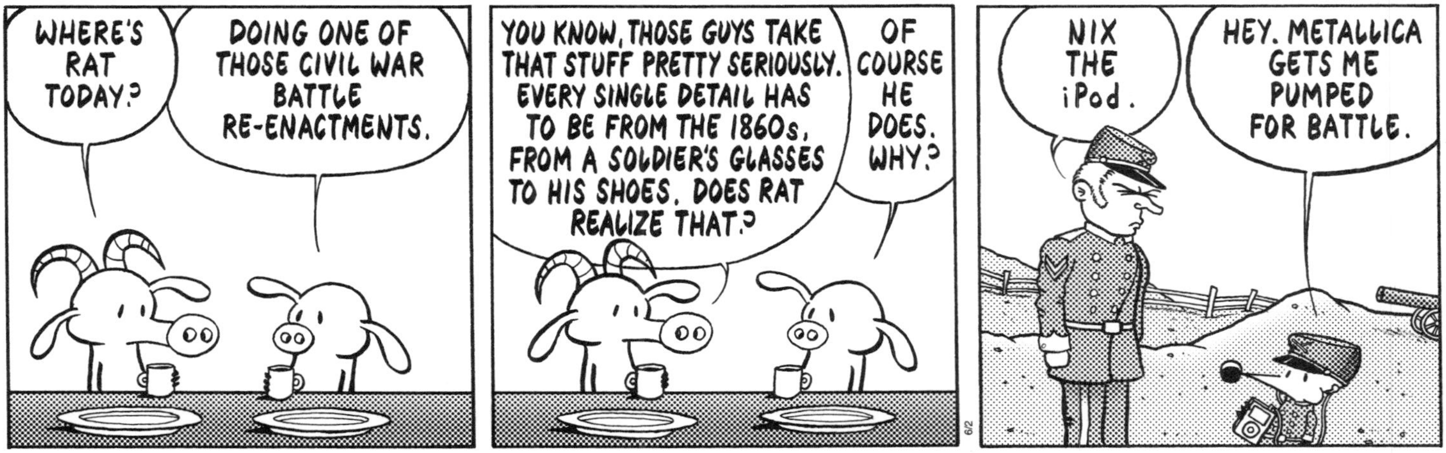
WHERE'S RAT TODAY?
DOING ONE OF THOSE CIVIL WAR BATTLE RE-ENACTMENTS.
YOU KNOW, THOSE GUYS TAKE THAT STUFF PRETTY SERIOUSLY. EVERY SINGLE DETAIL HAS TO BE FROM THE 1860s, FROM A SOLDIER'S GLASSES TO HIS SHOES. DOES RAT REALIZE THAT?
OF COURSE HE DOES. WHY?
NIX THE iPod.
HEY. METALLICA GETS ME PUMPED FOR BATTLE.
6/2

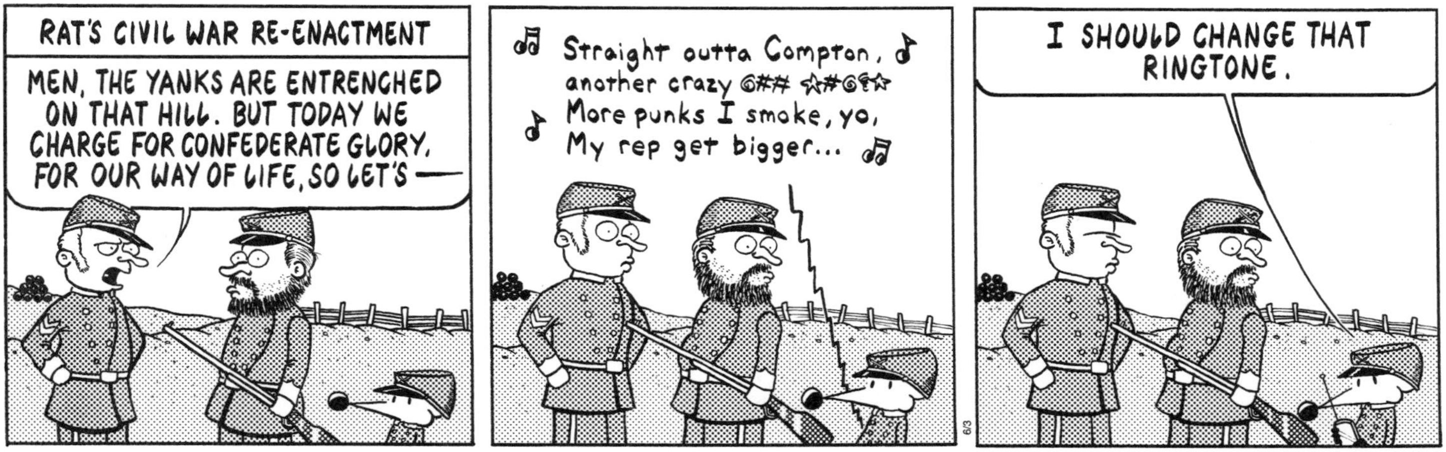
RAT'S CIVIL WAR RE-ENACTMENT
MEN, THE YANKS ARE ENTRENCHED ON THAT HILL. BUT TODAY WE CHARGE FOR CONFEDERATE GLORY, FOR OUR WAY OF LIFE, SO LET'S —
Straight outta Compton, another crazy @## ☆#@$☆ More punks I smoke, yo, My rep get bigger...
I SHOULD CHANGE THAT RINGTONE.
6/3

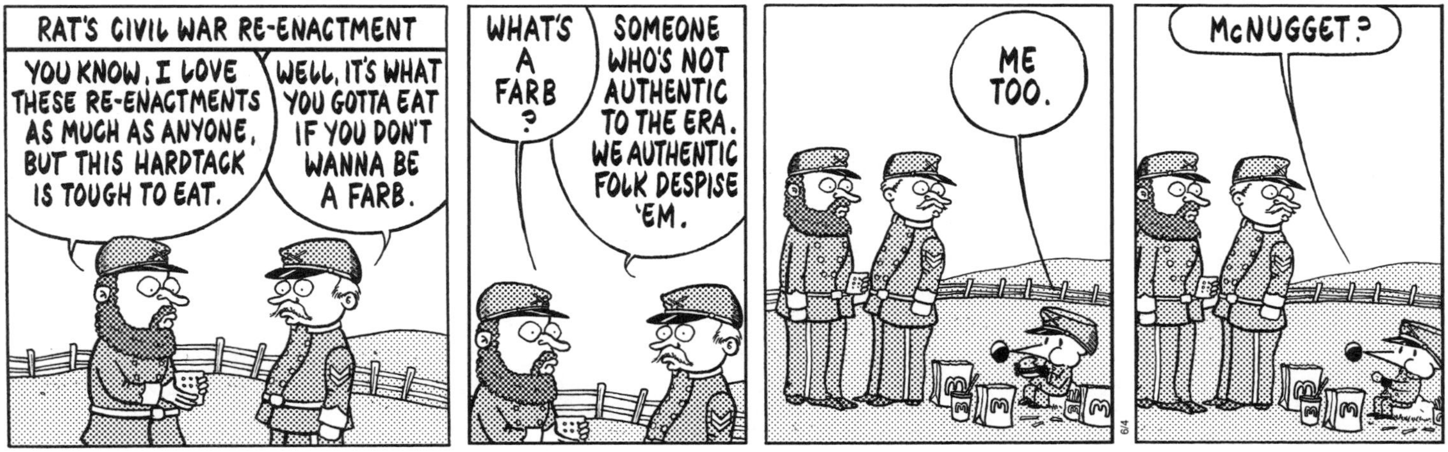
RAT'S CIVIL WAR RE-ENACTMENT
YOU KNOW, I LOVE THESE RE-ENACTMENTS AS MUCH AS ANYONE, BUT THIS HARDTACK IS TOUGH TO EAT.
WELL, IT'S WHAT YOU GOTTA EAT IF YOU DON'T WANNA BE A FARB.
WHAT'S A FARB ?
SOMEONE WHO'S NOT AUTHENTIC TO THE ERA. WE AUTHENTIC FOLK DESPISE 'EM.
ME TOO.
McNUGGET?
6/4

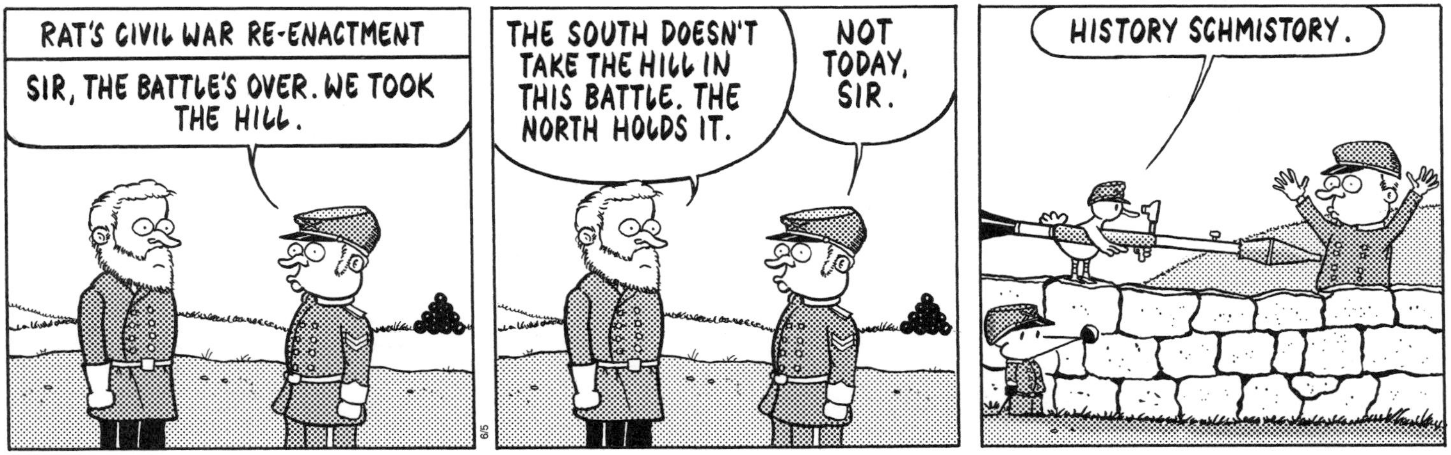
RAT'S CIVIL WAR RE-ENACTMENT
SIR, THE BATTLE'S OVER. WE TOOK THE HILL.
THE SOUTH DOESN'T TAKE THE HILL IN THIS BATTLE. THE NORTH HOLDS IT.
NOT TODAY, SIR.
HISTORY SCHMISTORY.
6/5

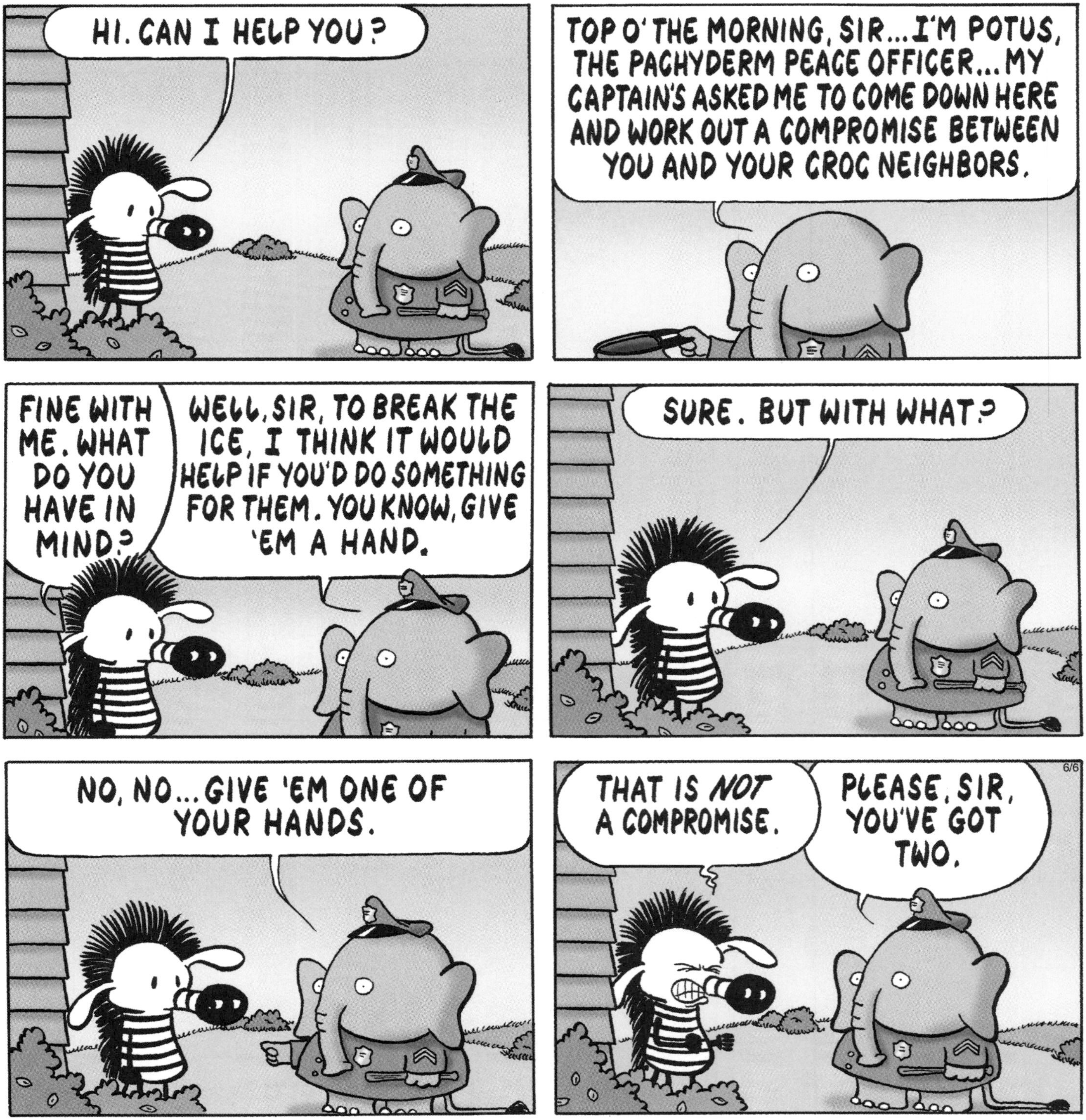
HI. CAN I HELP YOU?
TOP O' THE MORNING, SIR... I'M POTUS, THE PACHYDERM PEACE OFFICER... MY CAPTAIN'S ASKED ME TO COME DOWN HERE AND WORK OUT A COMPROMISE BETWEEN YOU AND YOUR CROC NEIGHBORS.
FINE WITH ME. WHAT DO YOU HAVE IN MIND?
WELL, SIR, TO BREAK THE ICE, I THINK IT WOULD HELP IF YOU'D DO SOMETHING FOR THEM. YOU KNOW, GIVE 'EM A HAND.
SURE. BUT WITH WHAT?
NO, NO... GIVE 'EM ONE OF YOUR HANDS.
THAT IS *NOT* A COMPROMISE.
PLEASE, SIR, YOU'VE GOT TWO.
6/6

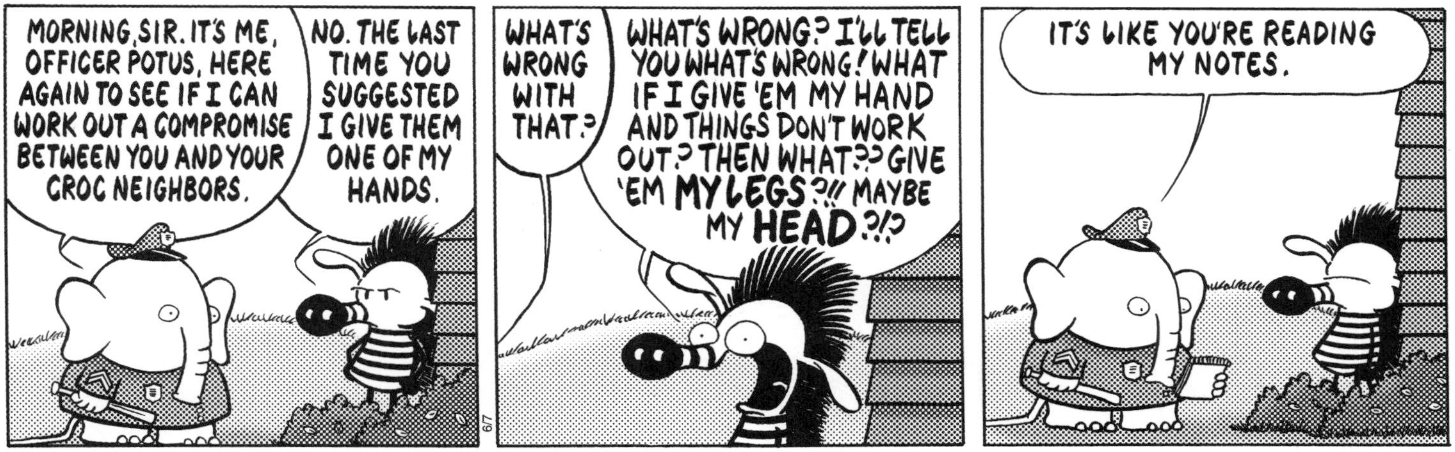
MORNING, SIR. IT'S ME, OFFICER POTUS, HERE AGAIN TO SEE IF I CAN WORK OUT A COMPROMISE BETWEEN YOU AND YOUR CROC NEIGHBORS.
NO. THE LAST TIME YOU SUGGESTED I GIVE THEM ONE OF MY HANDS.
6/7
WHAT'S WRONG WITH THAT?
WHAT'S WRONG? I'LL TELL YOU WHAT'S WRONG! WHAT IF I GIVE 'EM MY HAND AND THINGS DON'T WORK OUT? THEN WHAT?? GIVE 'EM MY LEGS?!! MAYBE MY HEAD?!?
IT'S LIKE YOU'RE READING MY NOTES.

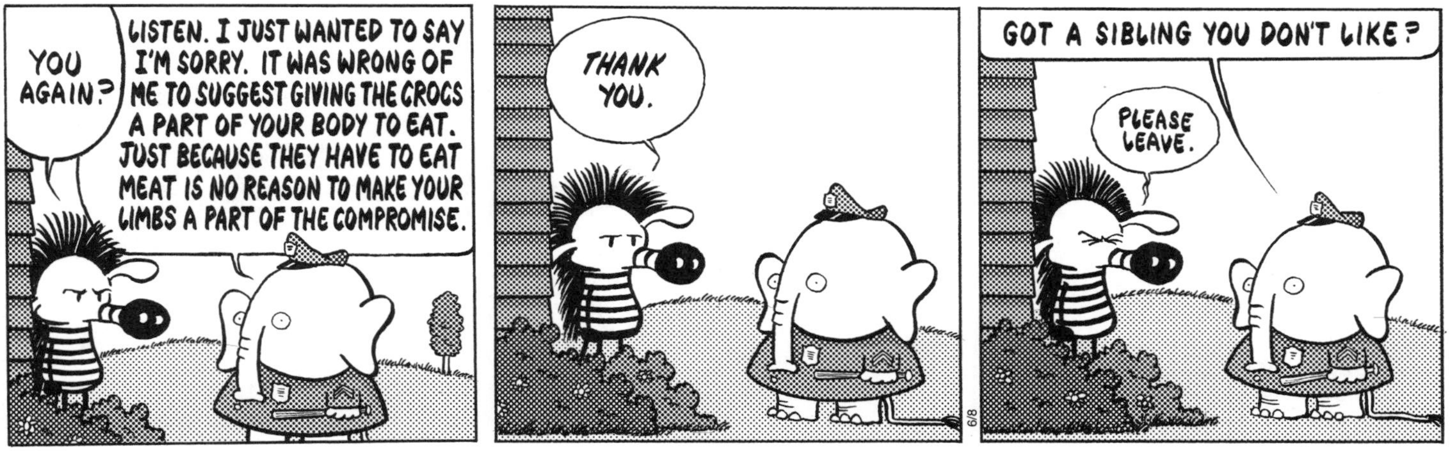
YOU AGAIN?
LISTEN. I JUST WANTED TO SAY I'M SORRY. IT WAS WRONG OF ME TO SUGGEST GIVING THE CROCS A PART OF YOUR BODY TO EAT. JUST BECAUSE THEY HAVE TO EAT MEAT IS NO REASON TO MAKE YOUR LIMBS A PART OF THE COMPROMISE.
THANK YOU.
6/8
GOT A SIBLING YOU DON'T LIKE?
PLEASE LEAVE.

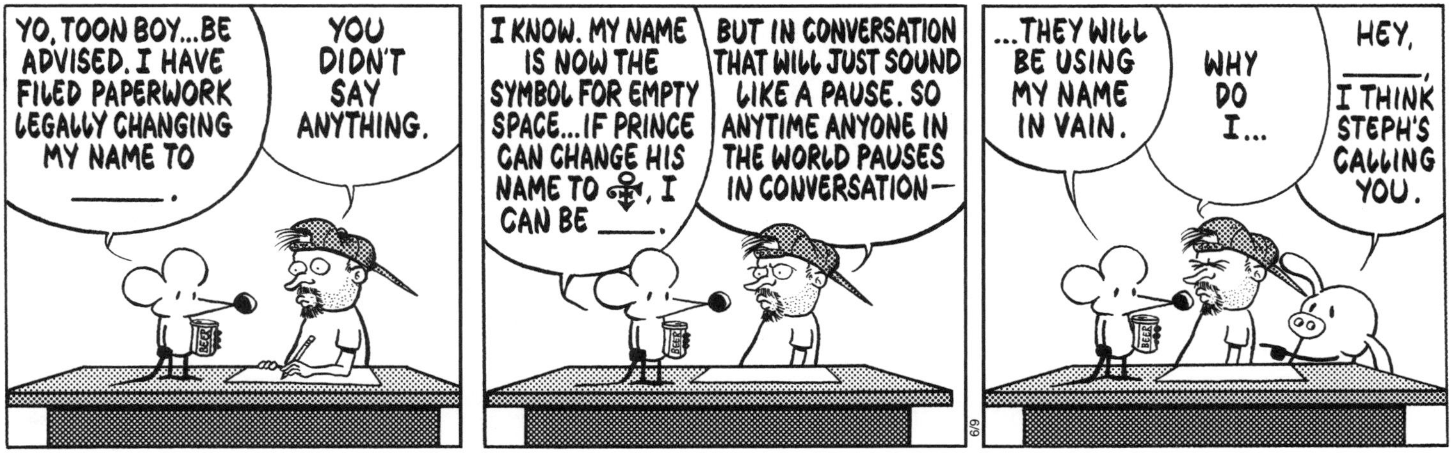
YO, TOON BOY...BE ADVISED. I HAVE FILED PAPERWORK LEGALLY CHANGING MY NAME TO ______.
YOU DIDN'T SAY ANYTHING.
I KNOW. MY NAME IS NOW THE SYMBOL FOR EMPTY SPACE...IF PRINCE CAN CHANGE HIS NAME TO , I CAN BE ____.
BUT IN CONVERSATION THAT WILL JUST SOUND LIKE A PAUSE. SO ANYTIME ANYONE IN THE WORLD PAUSES IN CONVERSATION—
6/9
...THEY WILL BE USING MY NAME IN VAIN.
WHY DO I...
HEY, ____, I THINK STEPH'S CALLING YOU.

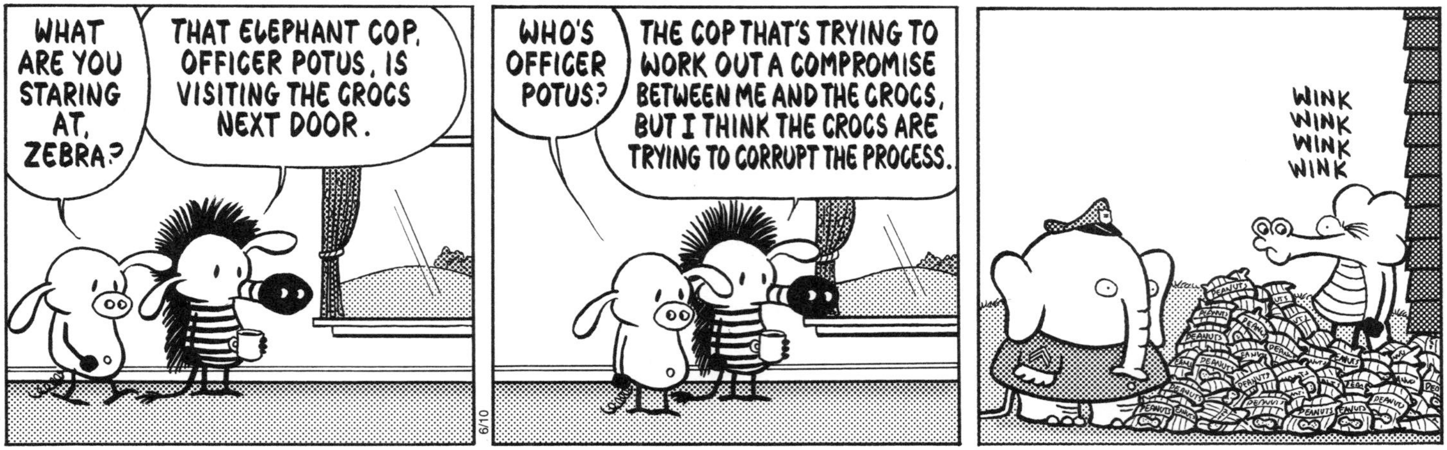
WHAT ARE YOU STARING AT, ZEBRA?
THAT ELEPHANT COP, OFFICER POTUS, IS VISITING THE CROCS NEXT DOOR.
WHO'S OFFICER POTUS?
THE COP THAT'S TRYING TO WORK OUT A COMPROMISE BETWEEN ME AND THE CROCS, BUT I THINK THE CROCS ARE TRYING TO CORRUPT THE PROCESS.
WINK WINK WINK WINK
6/10

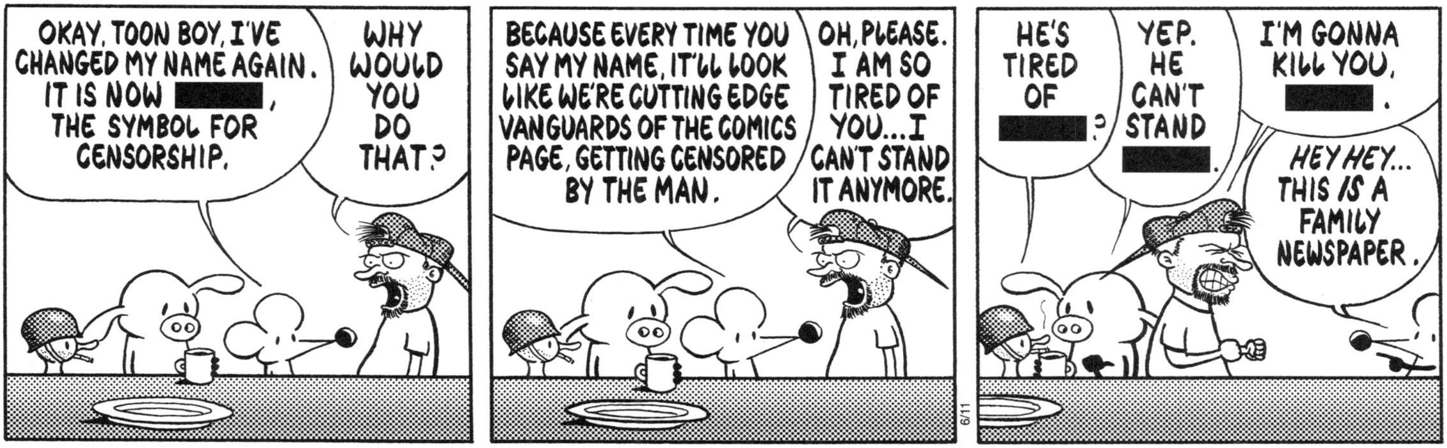
OKAY, TOON BOY, I'VE CHANGED MY NAME AGAIN. IT IS NOW [redacted], THE SYMBOL FOR CENSORSHIP.
WHY WOULD YOU DO THAT?
BECAUSE EVERY TIME YOU SAY MY NAME, IT'LL LOOK LIKE WE'RE CUTTING EDGE VANGUARDS OF THE COMICS PAGE, GETTING CENSORED BY THE MAN.
OH, PLEASE. I AM SO TIRED OF YOU... I CAN'T STAND IT ANYMORE.
HE'S TIRED OF [redacted]?
YEP. HE CAN'T STAND [redacted].
I'M GONNA KILL YOU, [redacted].
HEY HEY... THIS *IS* A FAMILY NEWSPAPER.
6/11

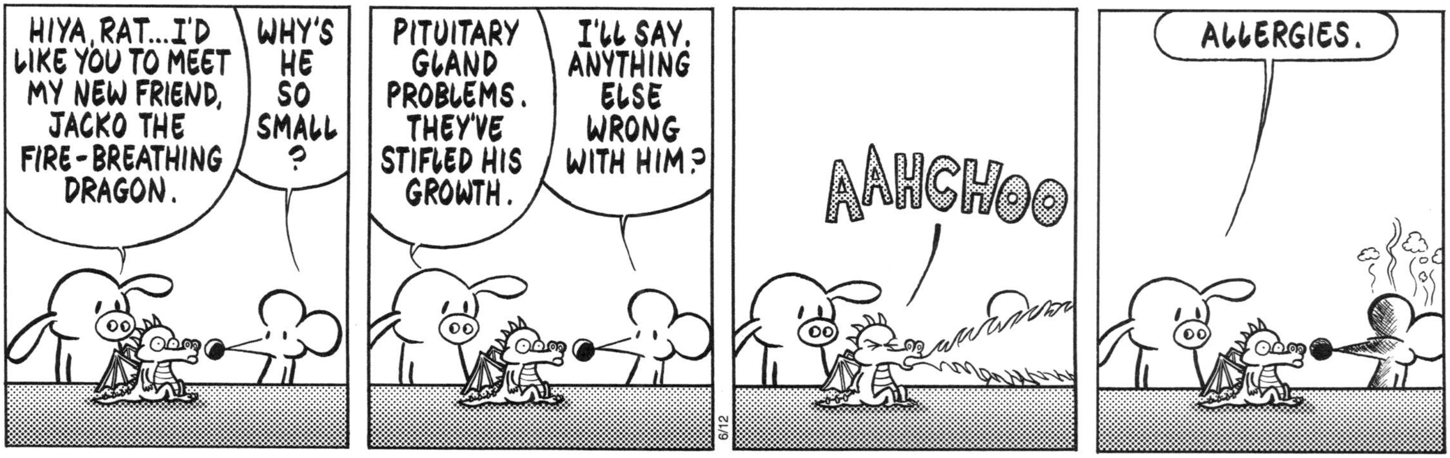
HIYA, RAT... I'D LIKE YOU TO MEET MY NEW FRIEND, JACKO THE FIRE-BREATHING DRAGON.
WHY'S HE SO SMALL?
PITUITARY GLAND PROBLEMS. THEY'VE STIFLED HIS GROWTH.
I'LL SAY. ANYTHING ELSE WRONG WITH HIM?
AAHCHOO
ALLERGIES.
6/12

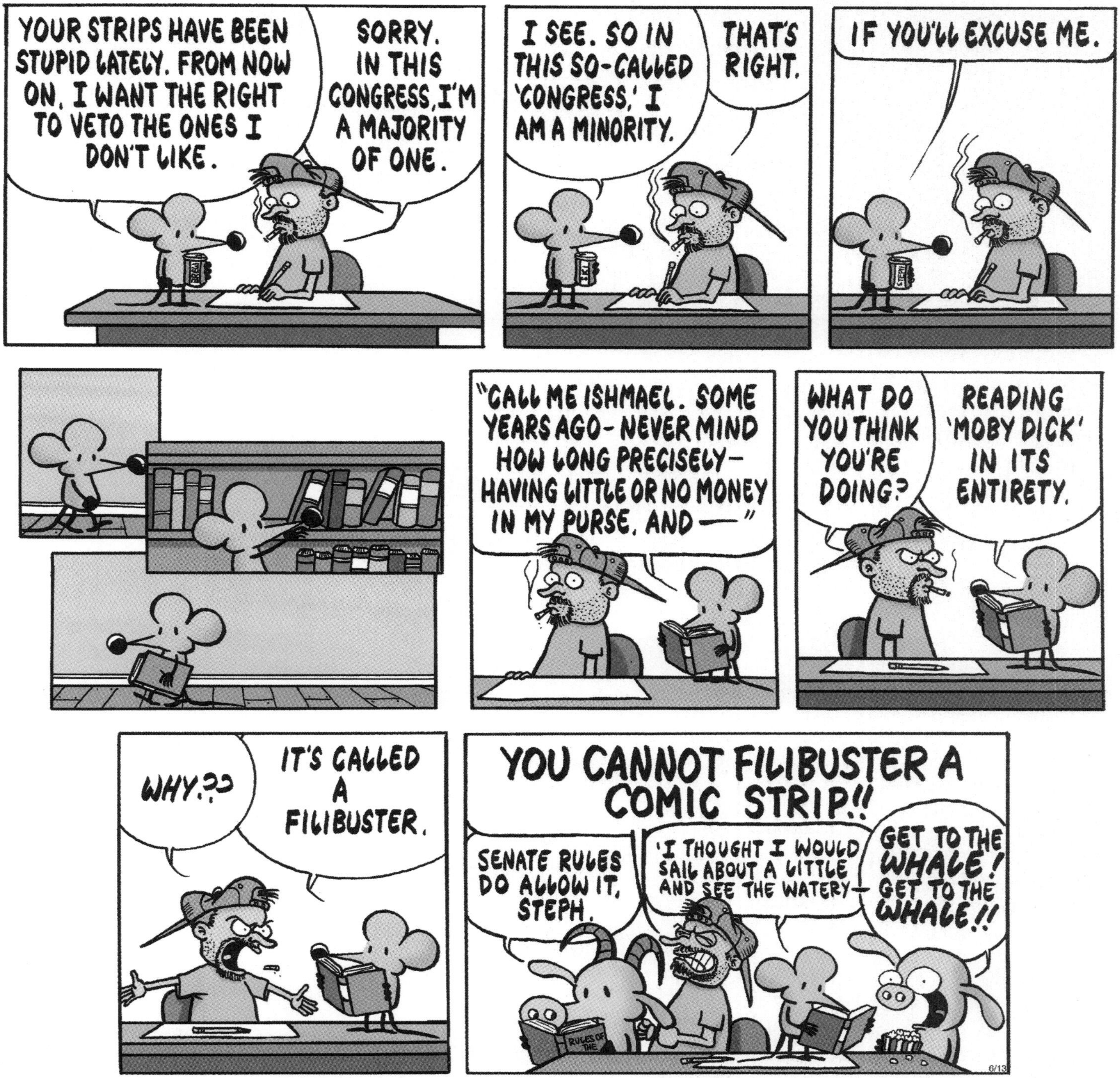
YOUR STRIPS HAVE BEEN STUPID LATELY. FROM NOW ON, I WANT THE RIGHT TO VETO THE ONES I DON'T LIKE.
SORRY. IN THIS CONGRESS, I'M A MAJORITY OF ONE.
I SEE. SO IN THIS SO-CALLED 'CONGRESS,' I AM A MINORITY.
THAT'S RIGHT.
IF YOU'LL EXCUSE ME.
"CALL ME ISHMAEL. SOME YEARS AGO- NEVER MIND HOW LONG PRECISELY- HAVING LITTLE OR NO MONEY IN MY PURSE, AND —"
WHAT DO YOU THINK YOU'RE DOING?
READING 'MOBY DICK' IN ITS ENTIRETY.
WHY??
IT'S CALLED A FILIBUSTER.
YOU CANNOT FILIBUSTER A COMIC STRIP!!
SENATE RULES DO ALLOW IT, STEPH.
'I THOUGHT I WOULD SAIL ABOUT A LITTLE AND SEE THE WATERY—
GET TO THE WHALE! GET TO THE WHALE!!
RULES OF THE
6/13

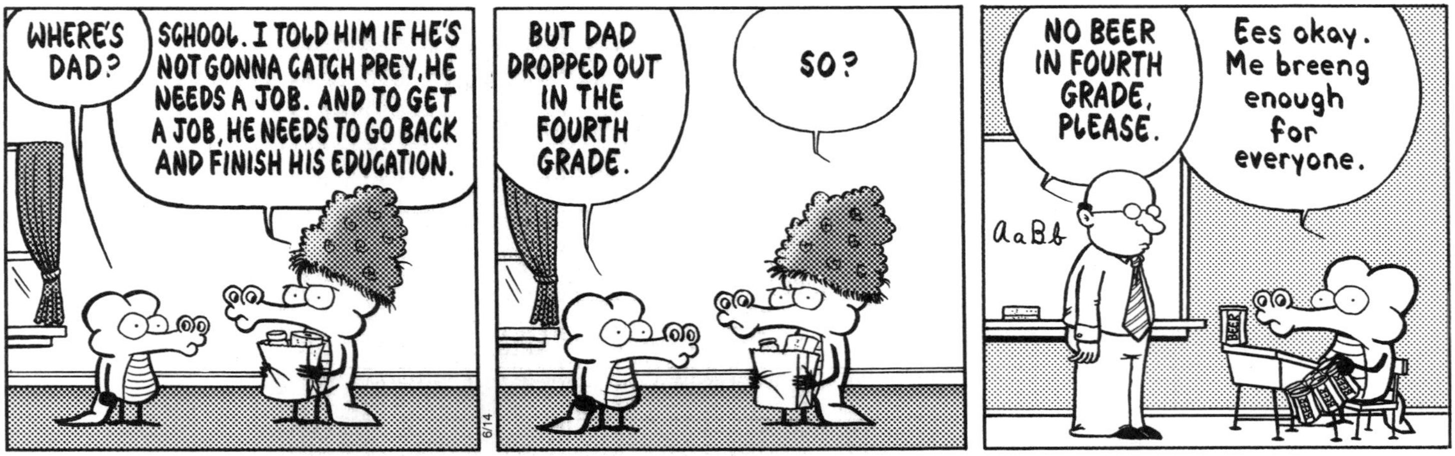
WHERE'S DAD?
SCHOOL. I TOLD HIM IF HE'S NOT GONNA CATCH PREY, HE NEEDS A JOB. AND TO GET A JOB, HE NEEDS TO GO BACK AND FINISH HIS EDUCATION.
6/14
BUT DAD DROPPED OUT IN THE FOURTH GRADE.
SO?
NO BEER IN FOURTH GRADE, PLEASE.
Ees okay. Me breeng enough for everyone.
AaBb
BEER

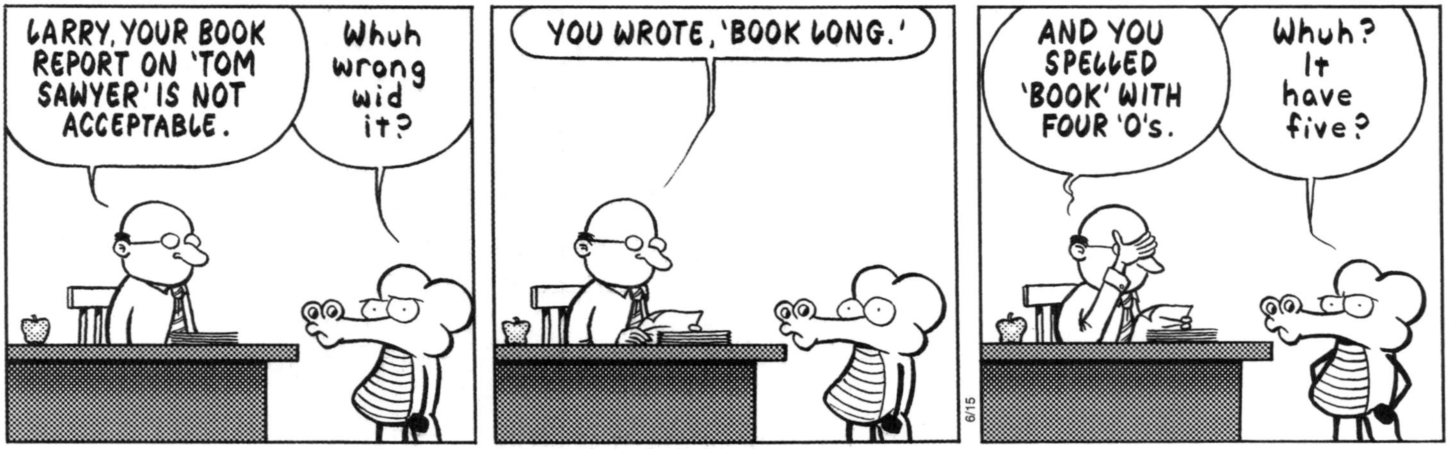
LARRY, YOUR BOOK REPORT ON 'TOM SAWYER' IS NOT ACCEPTABLE.
Whuh wrong wid it?
YOU WROTE, 'BOOK LONG.'
AND YOU SPELLED 'BOOK' WITH FOUR 'O's.
Whuh? It have five?
6/15

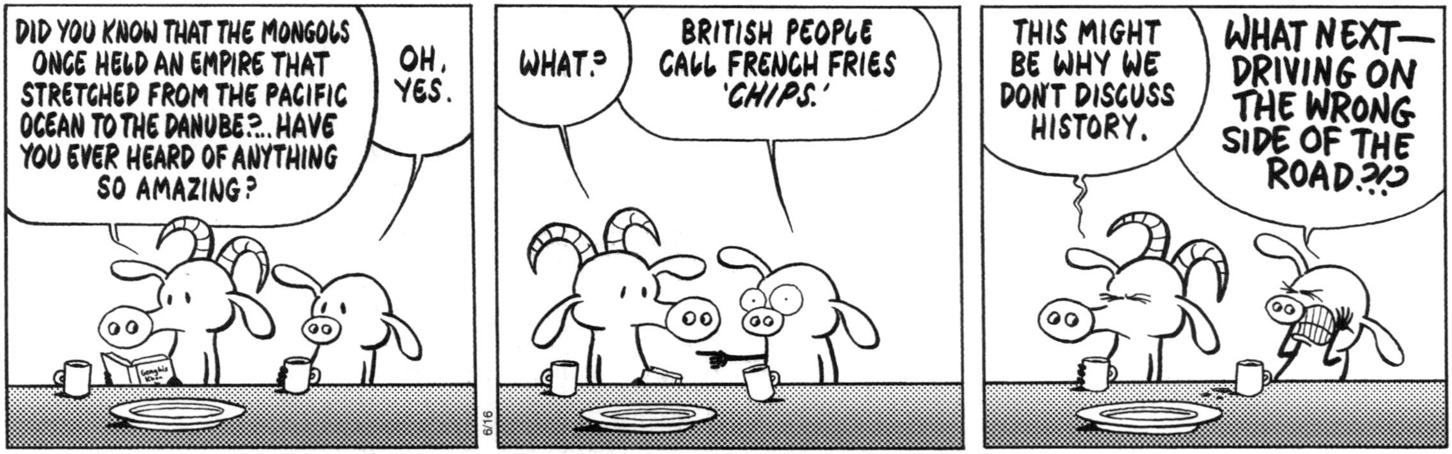
DID YOU KNOW THAT THE MONGOLS ONCE HELD AN EMPIRE THAT STRETCHED FROM THE PACIFIC OCEAN TO THE DANUBE?... HAVE YOU EVER HEARD OF ANYTHING SO AMAZING?
OH, YES.
6/16
WHAT?
BRITISH PEOPLE CALL FRENCH FRIES *'CHIPS.'*
THIS MIGHT BE WHY WE DON'T DISCUSS HISTORY.
WHAT NEXT— DRIVING ON THE WRONG SIDE OF THE ROAD?!?

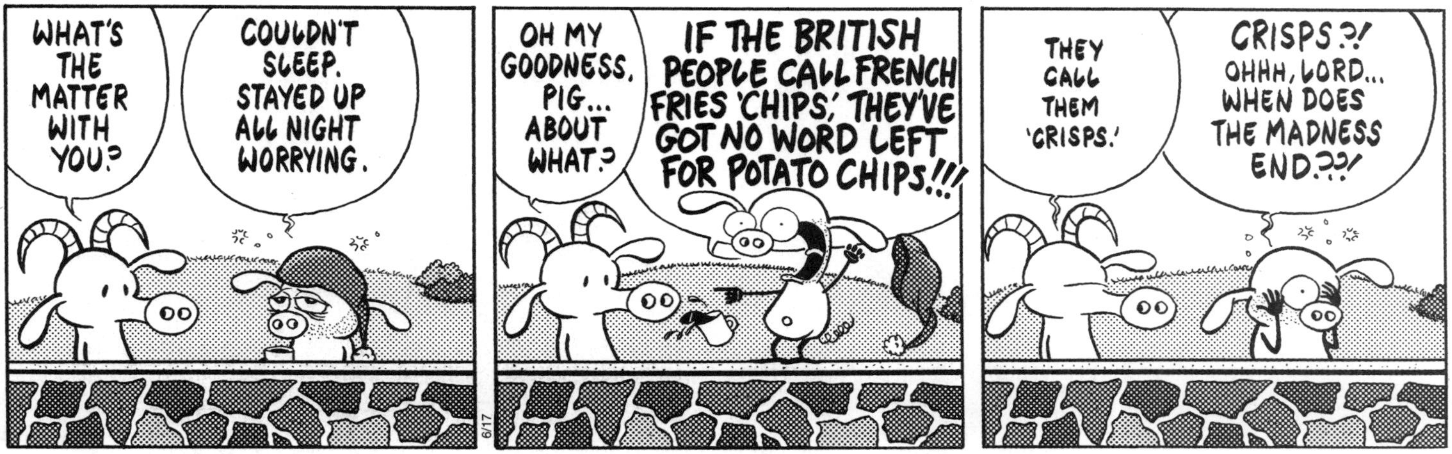
WHAT'S THE MATTER WITH YOU?
COULDN'T SLEEP. STAYED UP ALL NIGHT WORRYING.
OH MY GOODNESS, PIG... ABOUT WHAT?
IF THE BRITISH PEOPLE CALL FRENCH FRIES 'CHIPS,' THEY'VE GOT NO WORD LEFT FOR POTATO CHIPS!!!!
THEY CALL THEM 'CRISPS.'
CRISPS?! OHHH, LORD... WHEN DOES THE MADNESS END??!
6/17

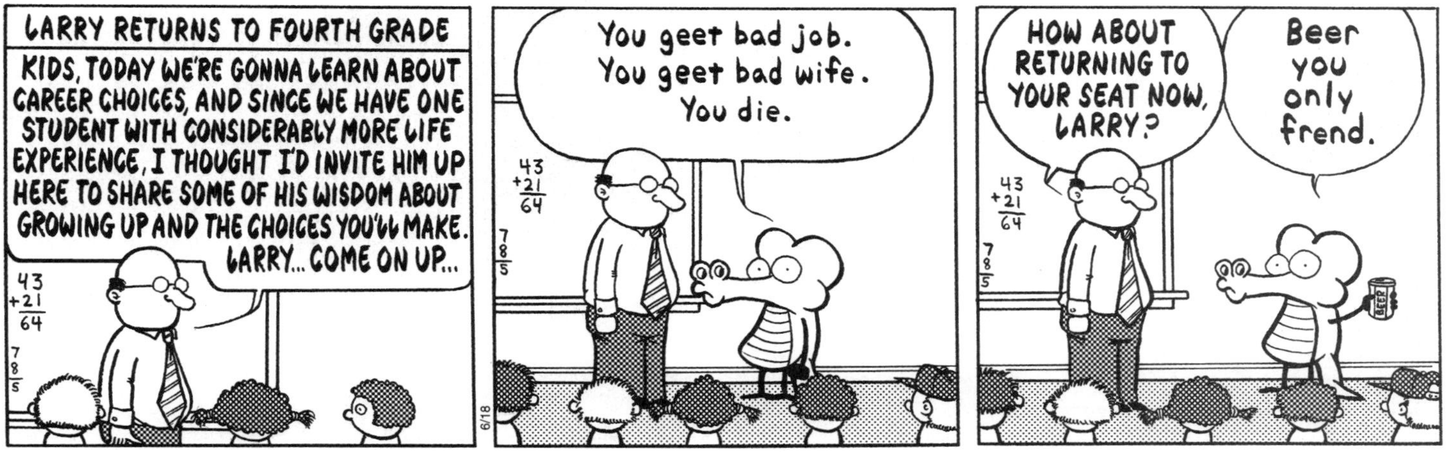
LARRY RETURNS TO FOURTH GRADE
KIDS, TODAY WE'RE GONNA LEARN ABOUT CAREER CHOICES, AND SINCE WE HAVE ONE STUDENT WITH CONSIDERABLY MORE LIFE EXPERIENCE, I THOUGHT I'D INVITE HIM UP HERE TO SHARE SOME OF HIS WISDOM ABOUT GROWING UP AND THE CHOICES YOU'LL MAKE. LARRY... COME ON UP...
You geet bad job. You geet bad wife. You die.
HOW ABOUT RETURNING TO YOUR SEAT NOW, LARRY?
Beer you only frend.
6/18

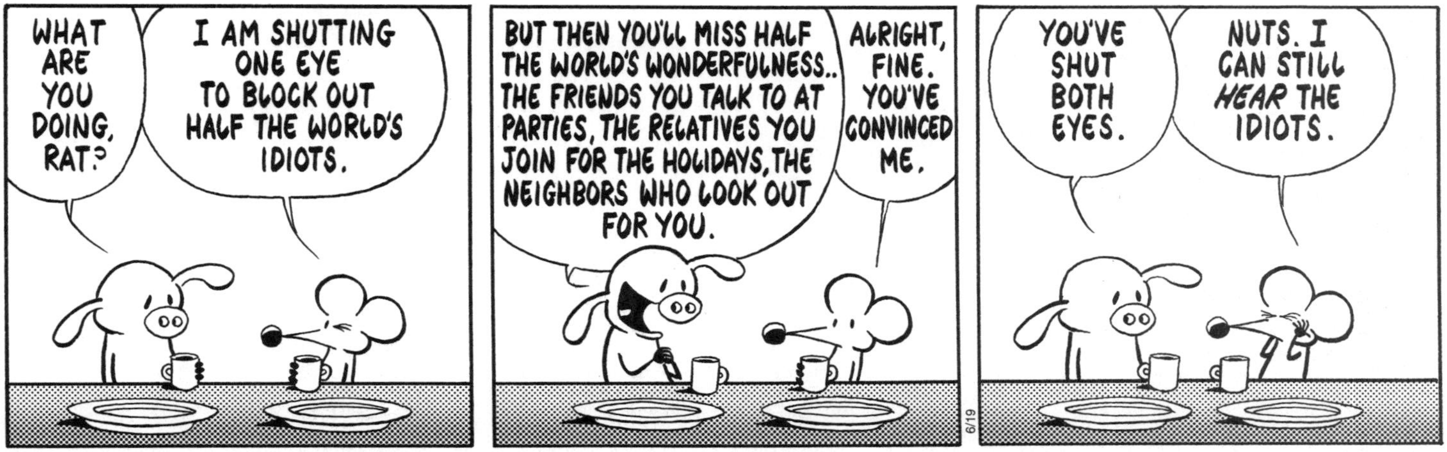
WHAT ARE YOU DOING, RAT?
I AM SHUTTING ONE EYE TO BLOCK OUT HALF THE WORLD'S IDIOTS.
BUT THEN YOU'LL MISS HALF THE WORLD'S WONDERFULNESS.. THE FRIENDS YOU TALK TO AT PARTIES, THE RELATIVES YOU JOIN FOR THE HOLIDAYS, THE NEIGHBORS WHO LOOK OUT FOR YOU.
ALRIGHT, FINE. YOU'VE CONVINCED ME.
YOU'VE SHUT BOTH EYES.
NUTS. I CAN STILL *HEAR* THE IDIOTS.
6/19

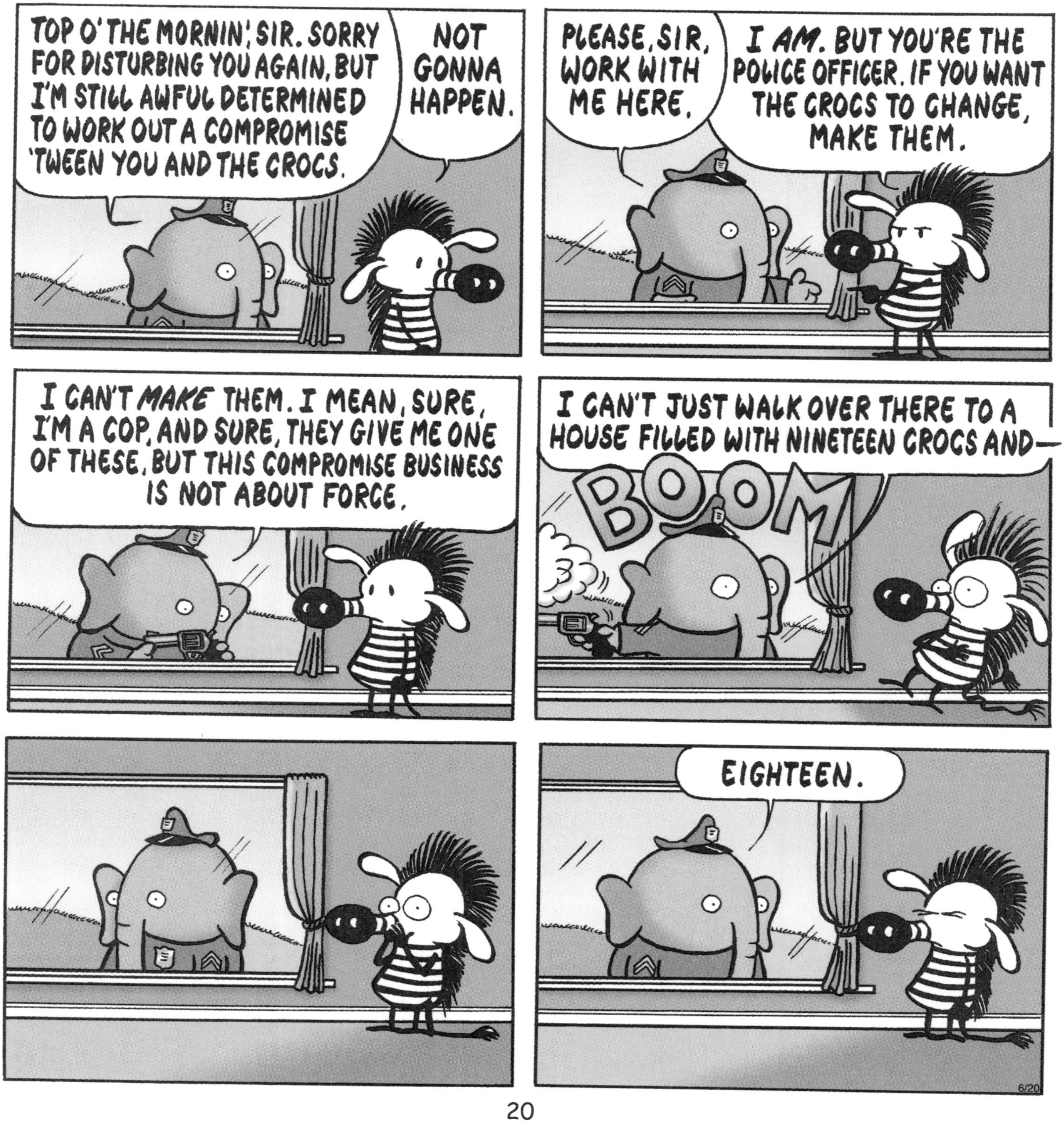
TOP O' THE MORNIN', SIR. SORRY FOR DISTURBING YOU AGAIN, BUT I'M STILL AWFUL DETERMINED TO WORK OUT A COMPROMISE 'TWEEN YOU AND THE CROCS.
NOT GONNA HAPPEN.
PLEASE, SIR, WORK WITH ME HERE.
I AM. BUT YOU'RE THE POLICE OFFICER. IF YOU WANT THE CROCS TO CHANGE, MAKE THEM.
I CAN'T MAKE THEM. I MEAN, SURE, I'M A COP, AND SURE, THEY GIVE ME ONE OF THESE, BUT THIS COMPROMISE BUSINESS IS NOT ABOUT FORCE.
I CAN'T JUST WALK OVER THERE TO A HOUSE FILLED WITH NINETEEN CROCS AND—
BOOM
EIGHTEEN.
6/20

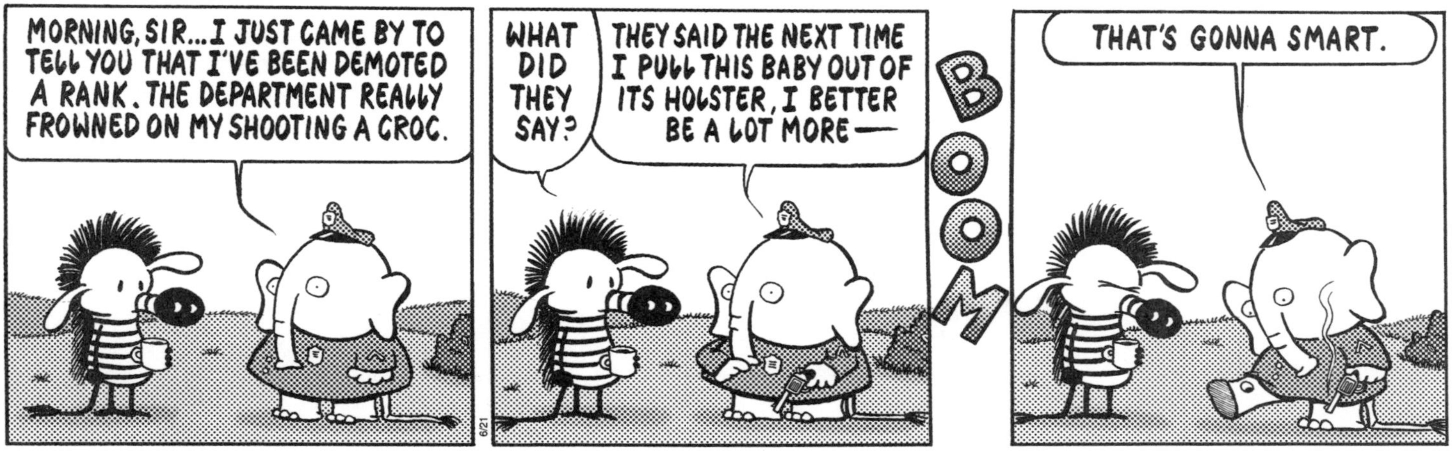
MORNING, SIR...I JUST CAME BY TO TELL YOU THAT I'VE BEEN DEMOTED A RANK. THE DEPARTMENT REALLY FROWNED ON MY SHOOTING A CROC.
WHAT DID THEY SAY?
THEY SAID THE NEXT TIME I PULL THIS BABY OUT OF ITS HOLSTER, I BETTER BE A LOT MORE—
BOOOM
THAT'S GONNA SMART.
6/21

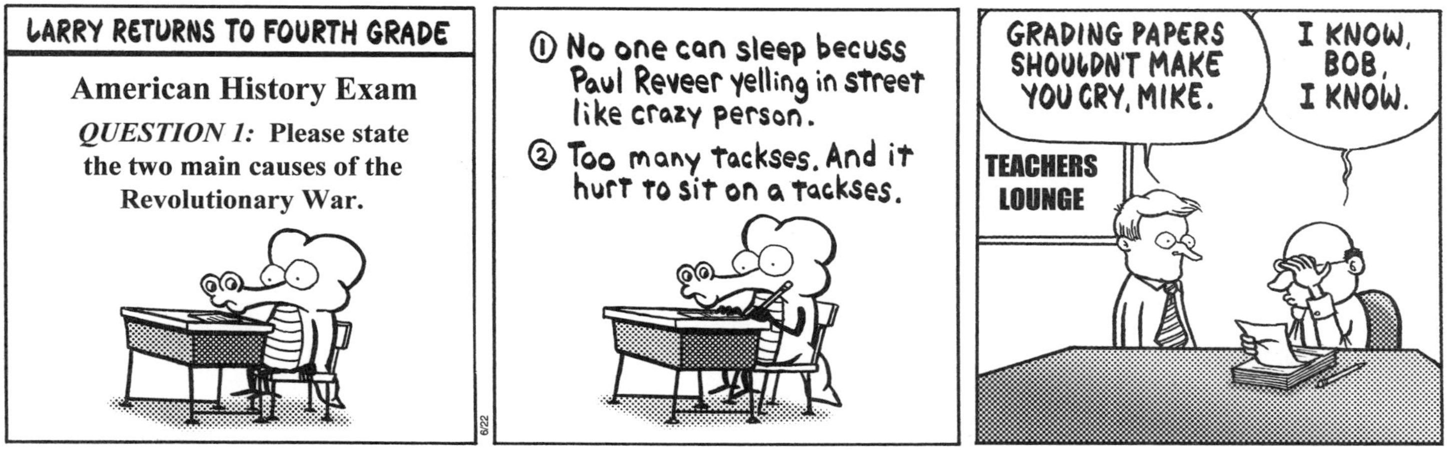
LARRY RETURNS TO FOURTH GRADE
American History Exam
QUESTION 1: Please state the two main causes of the Revolutionary War.
6/22
① No one can sleep becuss Paul Reveer yelling in street like crazy person.
② Too many tackses. And it hurt to sit on a tackses.
GRADING PAPERS SHOULDN'T MAKE YOU CRY, MIKE.
I KNOW, BOB, I KNOW.
TEACHERS LOUNGE

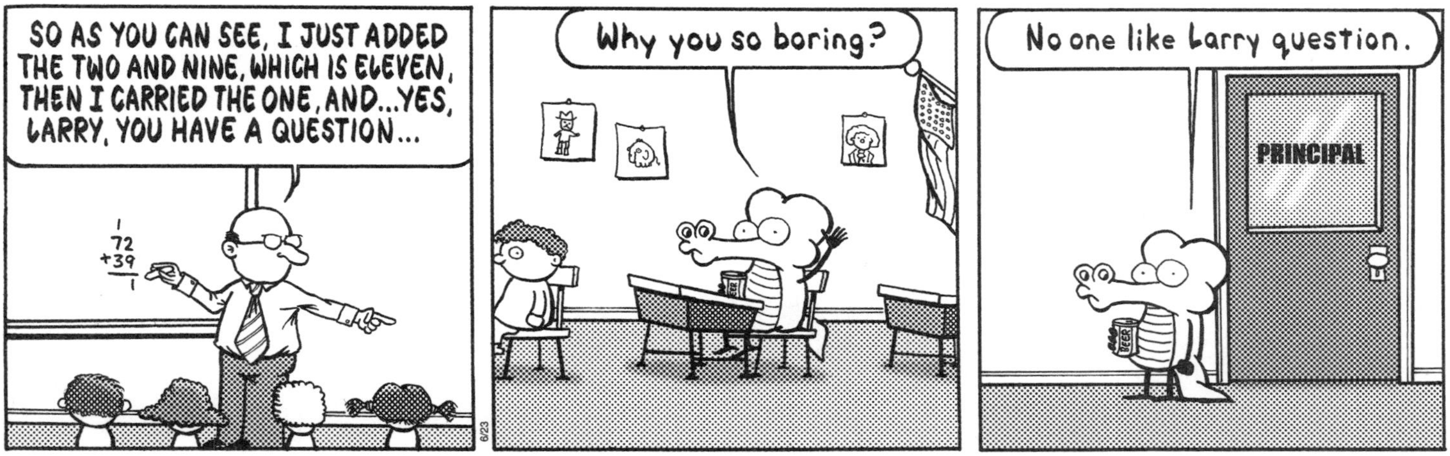
SO AS YOU CAN SEE, I JUST ADDED THE TWO AND NINE, WHICH IS ELEVEN, THEN I CARRIED THE ONE, AND...YES, LARRY, YOU HAVE A QUESTION...
1
72
+39
1
6/23
Why you so boring?
No one like Larry question.
PRINCIPAL

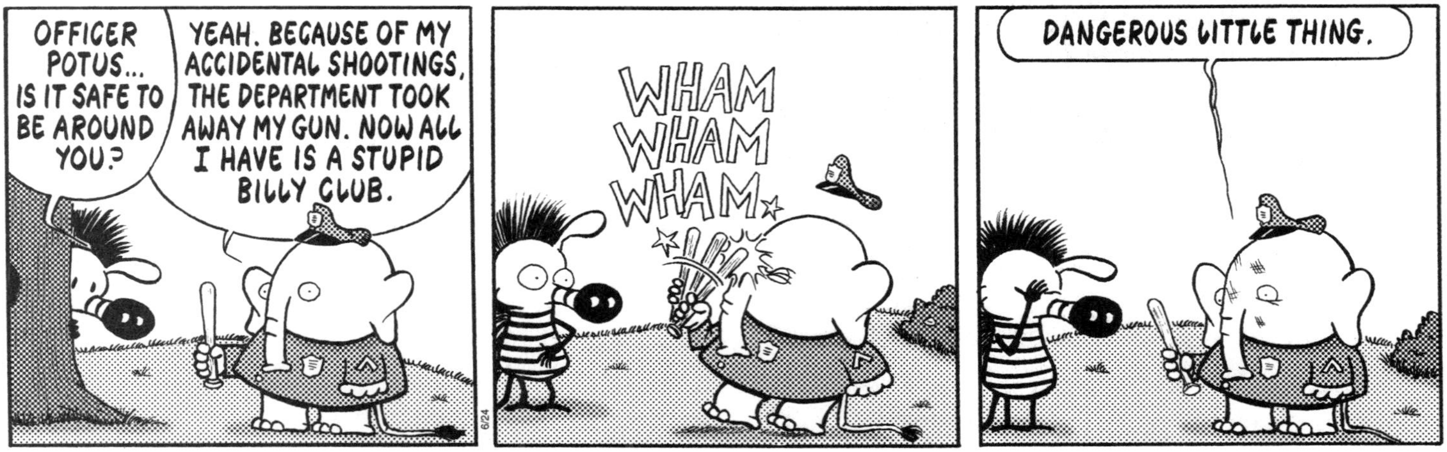
OFFICER POTUS... IS IT SAFE TO BE AROUND YOU?
YEAH. BECAUSE OF MY ACCIDENTAL SHOOTINGS, THE DEPARTMENT TOOK AWAY MY GUN. NOW ALL I HAVE IS A STUPID BILLY CLUB.
6/24
WHAM
WHAM
WHAM
DANGEROUS LITTLE THING.

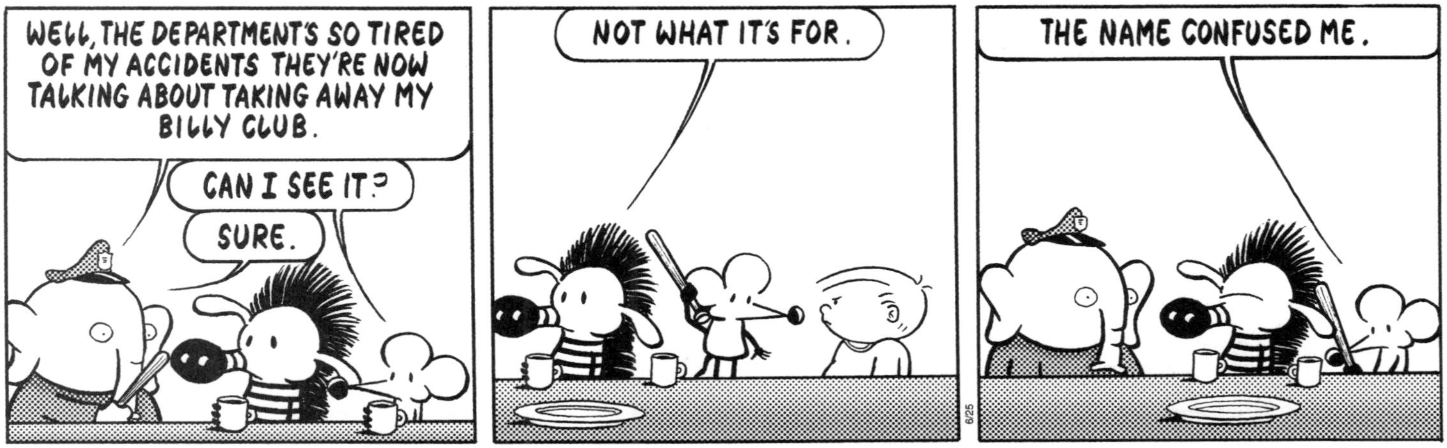
WELL, THE DEPARTMENT'S SO TIRED OF MY ACCIDENTS THEY'RE NOW TALKING ABOUT TAKING AWAY MY BILLY CLUB.
CAN I SEE IT?
SURE.
NOT WHAT IT'S FOR.
6/25
THE NAME CONFUSED ME.

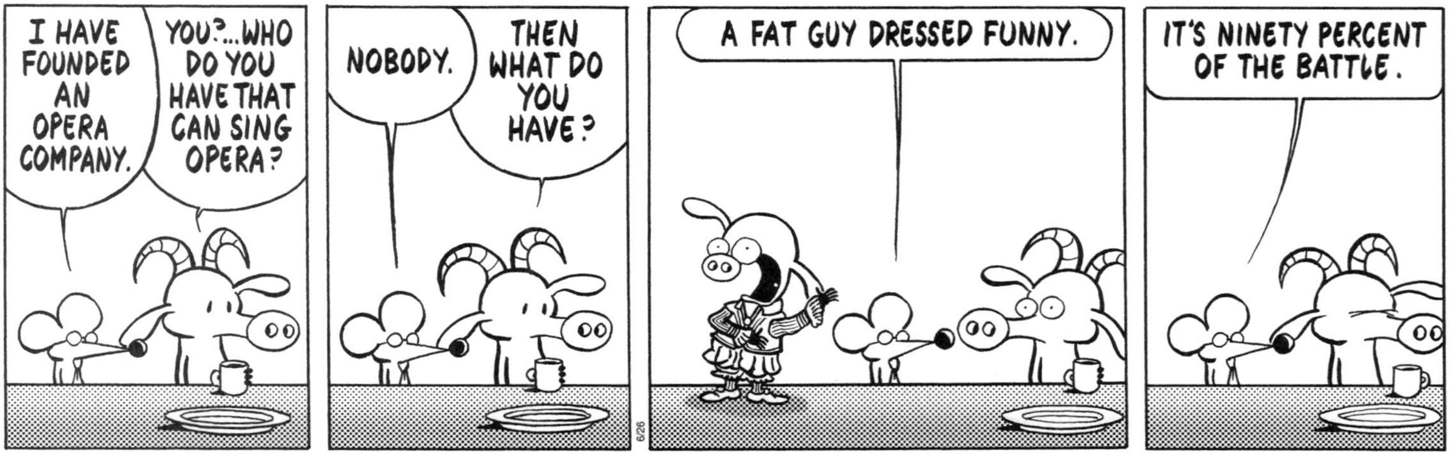
I HAVE FOUNDED AN OPERA COMPANY.
YOU?...WHO DO YOU HAVE THAT CAN SING OPERA?
NOBODY.
THEN WHAT DO YOU HAVE?
6/26
A FAT GUY DRESSED FUNNY.
IT'S NINETY PERCENT OF THE BATTLE.

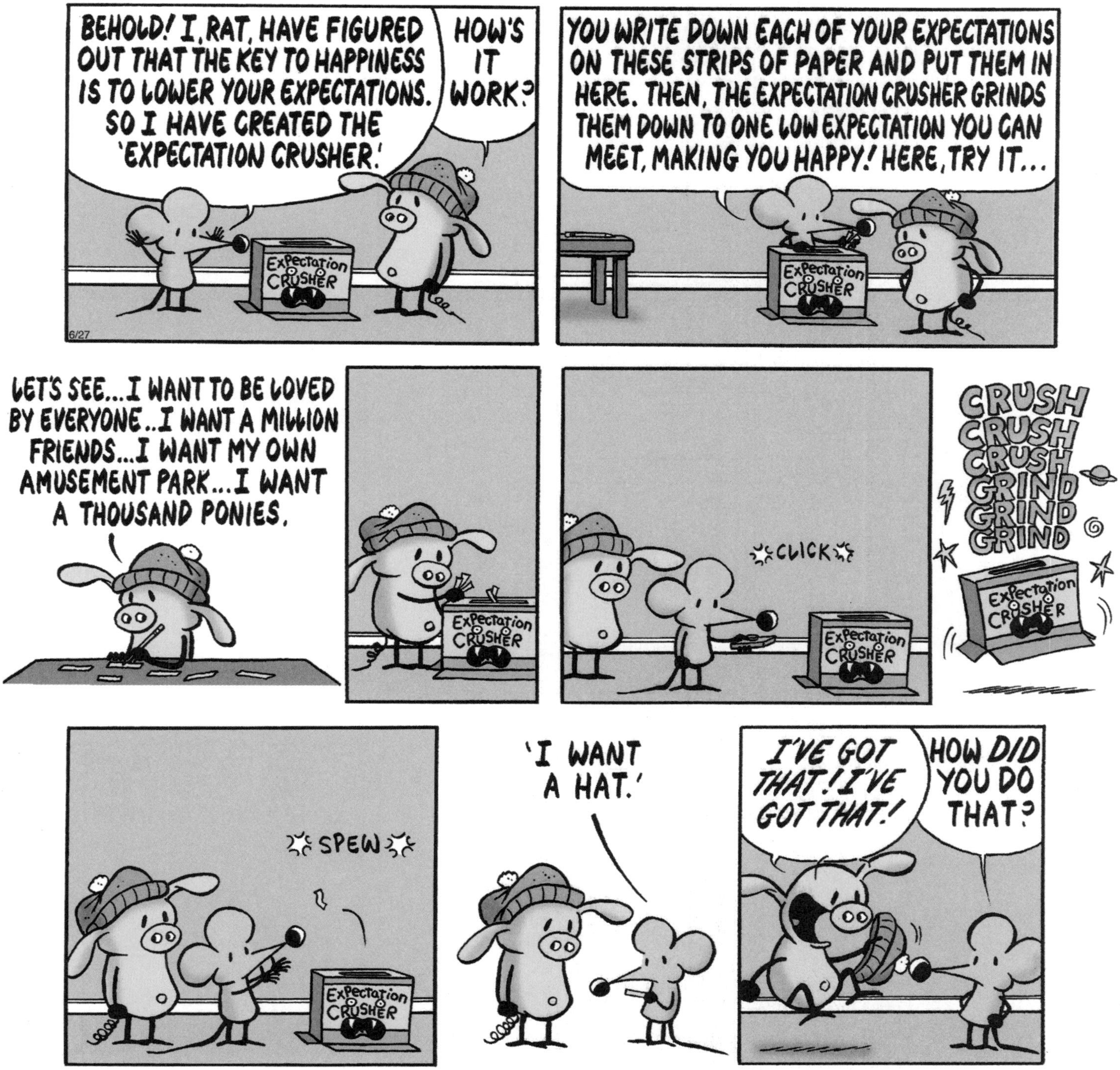
BEHOLD! I, RAT, HAVE FIGURED OUT THAT THE KEY TO HAPPINESS IS TO LOWER YOUR EXPECTATIONS. SO I HAVE CREATED THE 'EXPECTATION CRUSHER.'
HOW'S IT WORK?
EXPECTATION CRUSHER
6/27
YOU WRITE DOWN EACH OF YOUR EXPECTATIONS ON THESE STRIPS OF PAPER AND PUT THEM IN HERE. THEN, THE EXPECTATION CRUSHER GRINDS THEM DOWN TO ONE LOW EXPECTATION YOU CAN MEET, MAKING YOU HAPPY! HERE, TRY IT...
LET'S SEE... I WANT TO BE LOVED BY EVERYONE.. I WANT A MILLION FRIENDS... I WANT MY OWN AMUSEMENT PARK... I WANT A THOUSAND PONIES.
CLICK
CRUSH
CRUSH
CRUSH
GRIND
GRIND
GRIND
SPEW
'I WANT A HAT.'
I'VE GOT THAT! I'VE GOT THAT!
HOW DID YOU DO THAT?

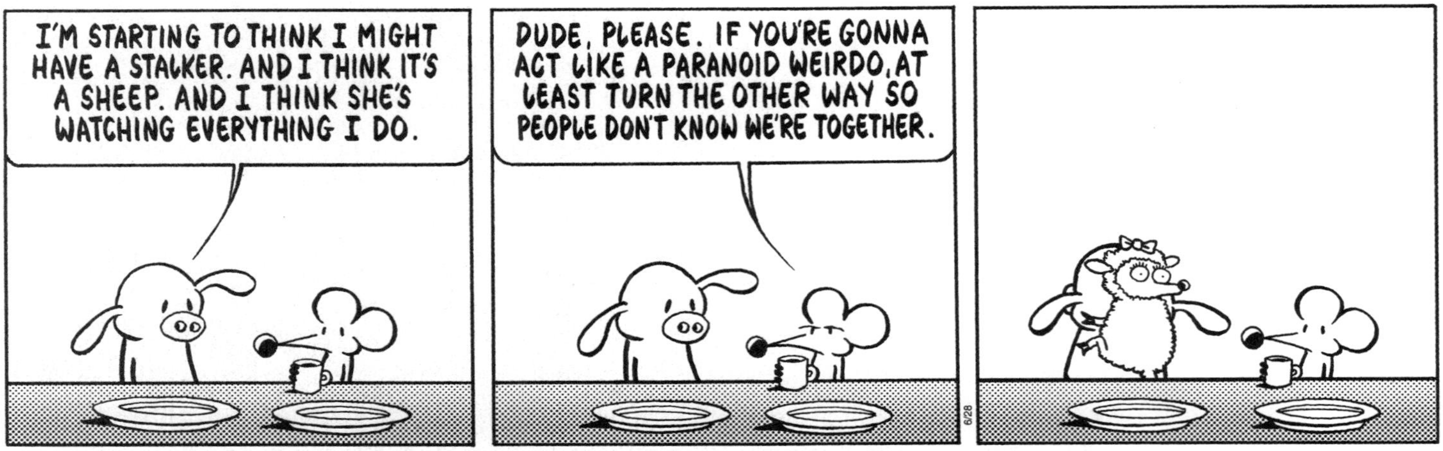
I'M STARTING TO THINK I MIGHT HAVE A STALKER. AND I THINK IT'S A SHEEP. AND I THINK SHE'S WATCHING EVERYTHING I DO.
DUDE, PLEASE. IF YOU'RE GONNA ACT LIKE A PARANOID WEIRDO, AT LEAST TURN THE OTHER WAY SO PEOPLE DON'T KNOW WE'RE TOGETHER.
6/28

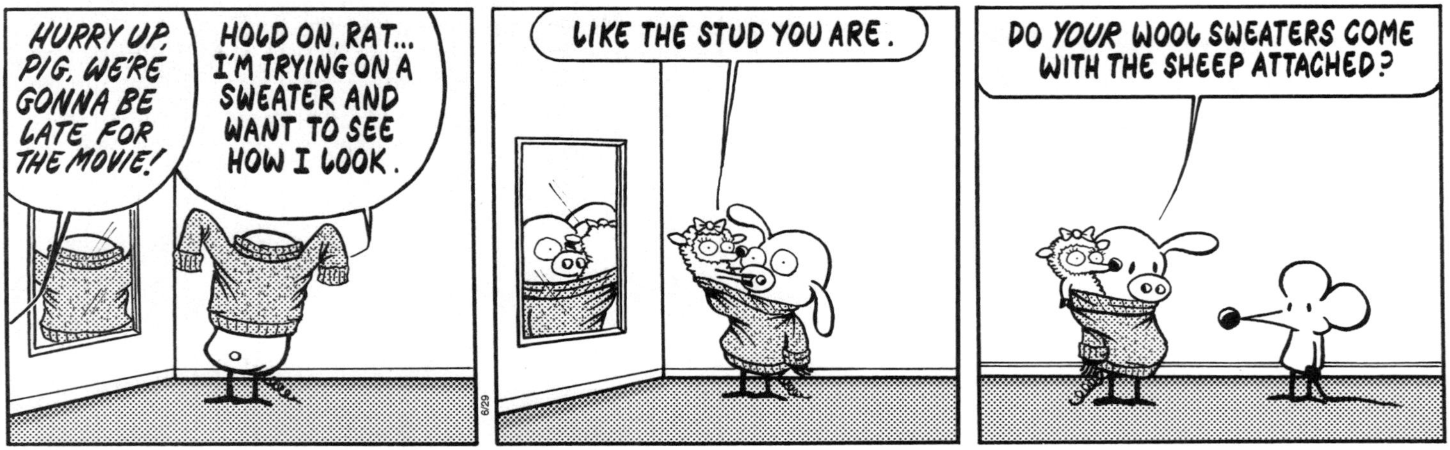
HURRY UP, PIG. WE'RE GONNA BE LATE FOR THE MOVIE!
HOLD ON, RAT... I'M TRYING ON A SWEATER AND WANT TO SEE HOW I LOOK.
6/29
LIKE THE STUD YOU ARE.
DO *YOUR* WOOL SWEATERS COME WITH THE SHEEP ATTACHED?

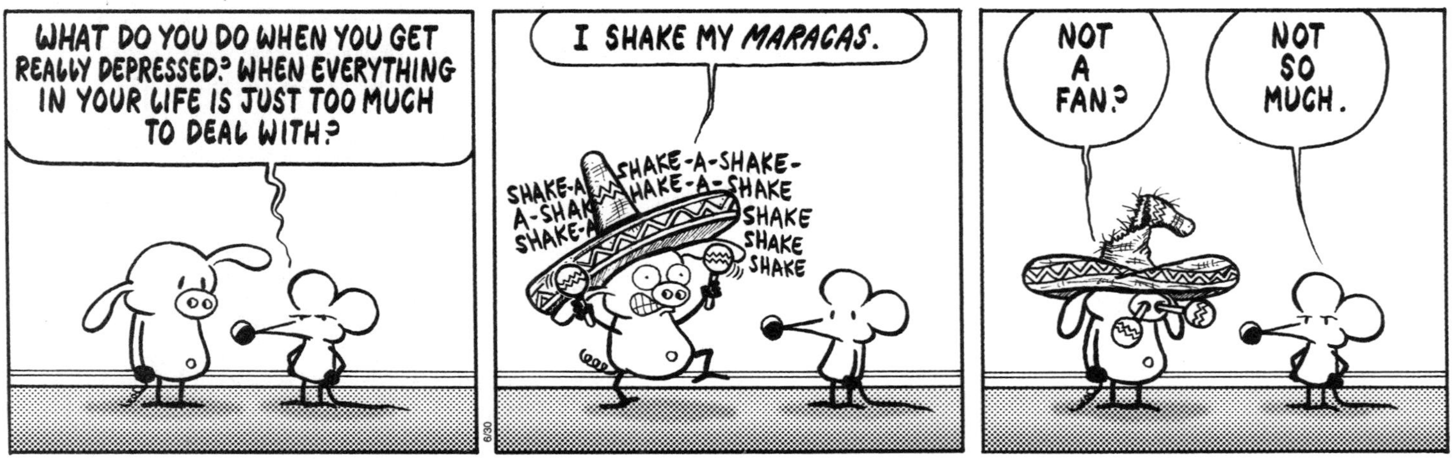
WHAT DO YOU DO WHEN YOU GET REALLY DEPRESSED? WHEN EVERYTHING IN YOUR LIFE IS JUST TOO MUCH TO DEAL WITH?
6/30
I SHAKE MY *MARACAS*.
SHAKE-A-SHAKE-
HAKE-A-SHAKE
SHAKE SHAKE SHAKE
NOT A FAN?
NOT SO MUCH.

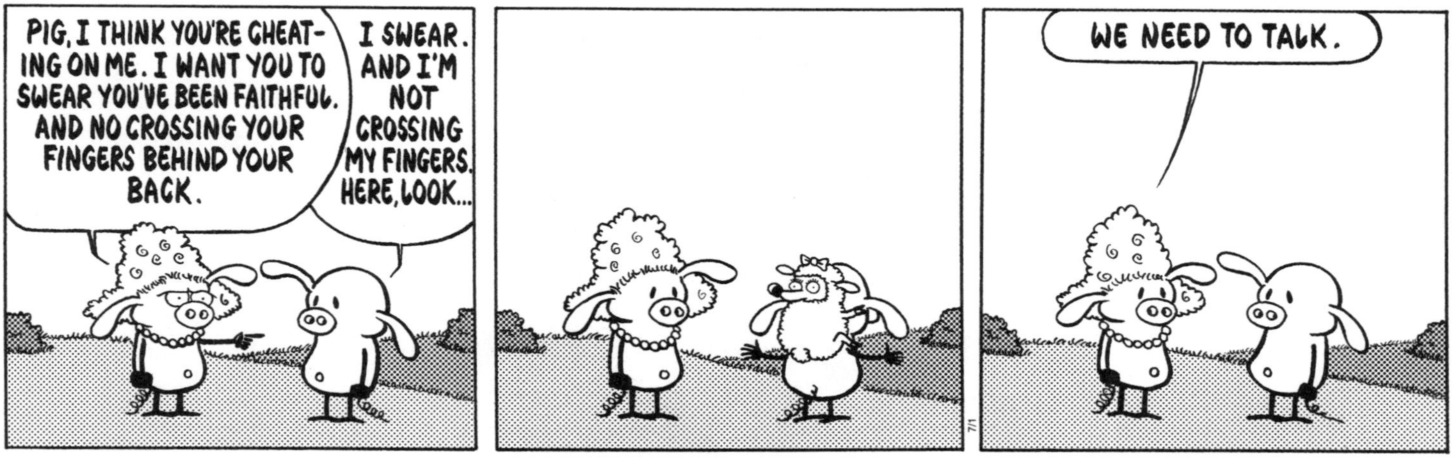
PIG, I THINK YOU'RE CHEATING ON ME. I WANT YOU TO SWEAR YOU'VE BEEN FAITHFUL. AND NO CROSSING YOUR FINGERS BEHIND YOUR BACK.
I SWEAR. AND I'M NOT CROSSING MY FINGERS. HERE, LOOK...
WE NEED TO TALK.

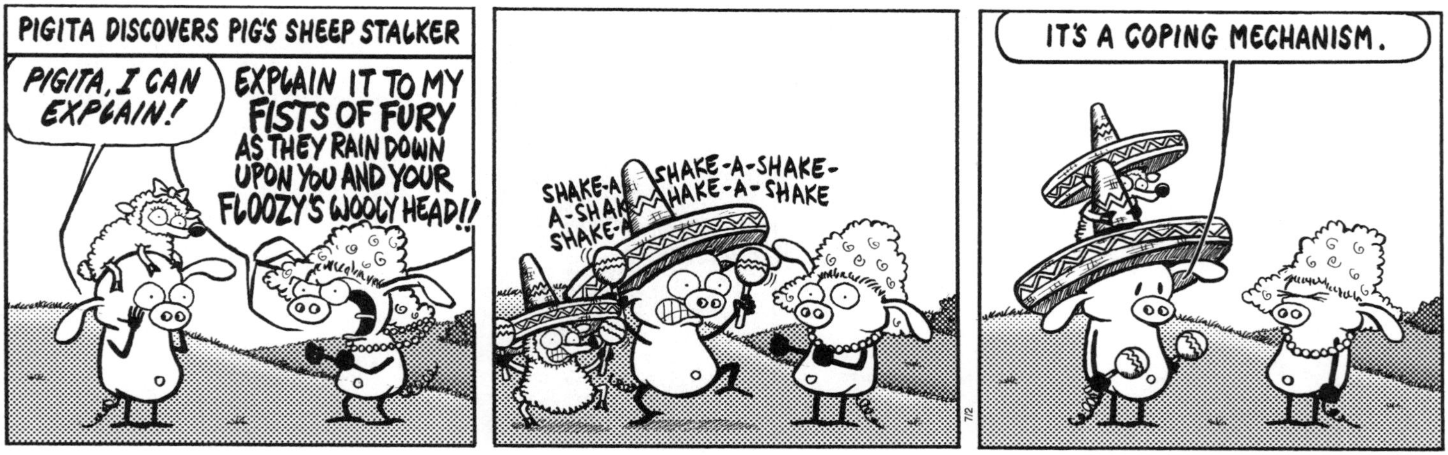
PIGITA DISCOVERS PIG'S SHEEP STALKER
PIGITA, I CAN EXPLAIN!
EXPLAIN IT TO MY FISTS OF FURY AS THEY RAIN DOWN UPON YOU AND YOUR FLOOZY'S WOOLY HEAD!!
SHAKE-A-SHAKE-A-SHAKE-A-SHAKE-A-SHAKE-A-SHAKE
IT'S A COPING MECHANISM.

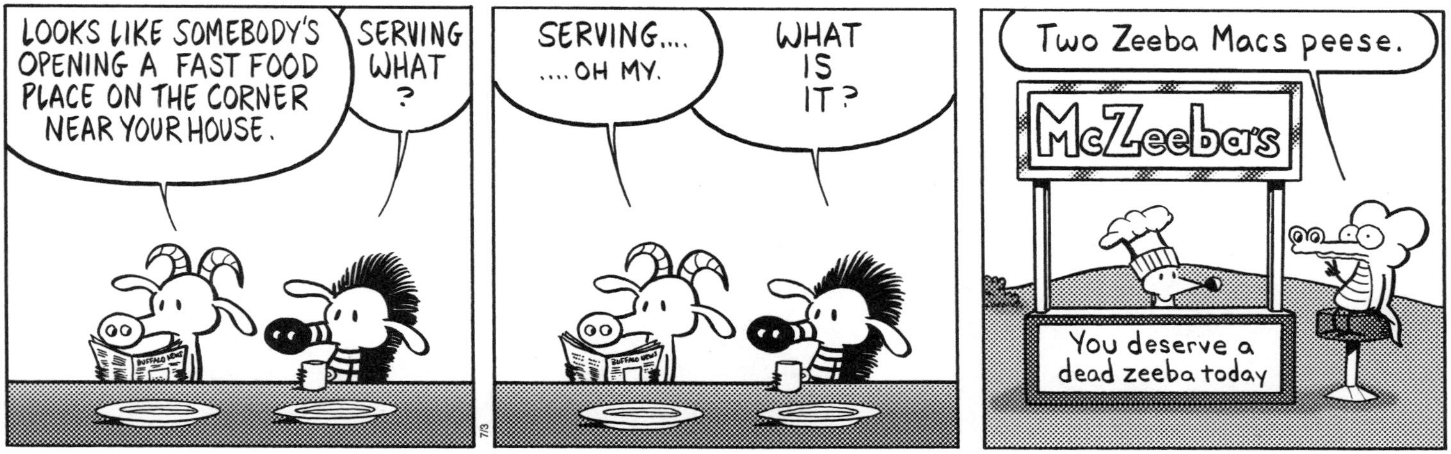
LOOKS LIKE SOMEBODY'S OPENING A FAST FOOD PLACE ON THE CORNER NEAR YOUR HOUSE.
SERVING WHAT?
SERVING.... ....OH MY.
WHAT IS IT?
Two Zeeba Macs peese.
McZeeba's
You deserve a dead zeeba today

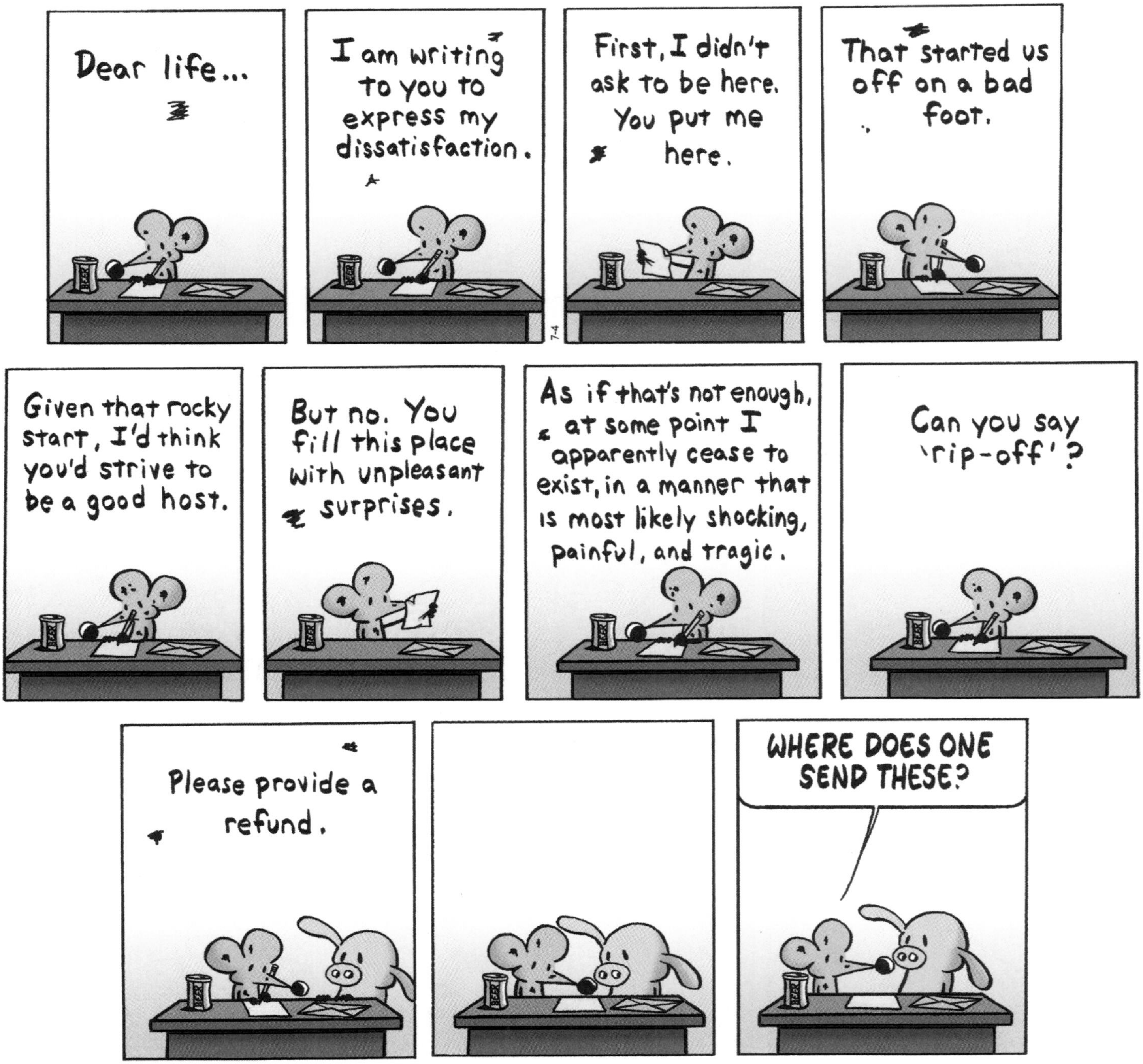
Dear life...
I am writing to you to express my dissatisfaction.
First, I didn't ask to be here. You put me here.
That started us off on a bad foot.
Given that rocky start, I'd think you'd strive to be a good host.
But no. You fill this place with unpleasant surprises.
As if that's not enough, at some point I apparently cease to exist, in a manner that is most likely shocking, painful, and tragic.
Can you say 'rip-off'?
Please provide a refund.
WHERE DOES ONE SEND THESE?

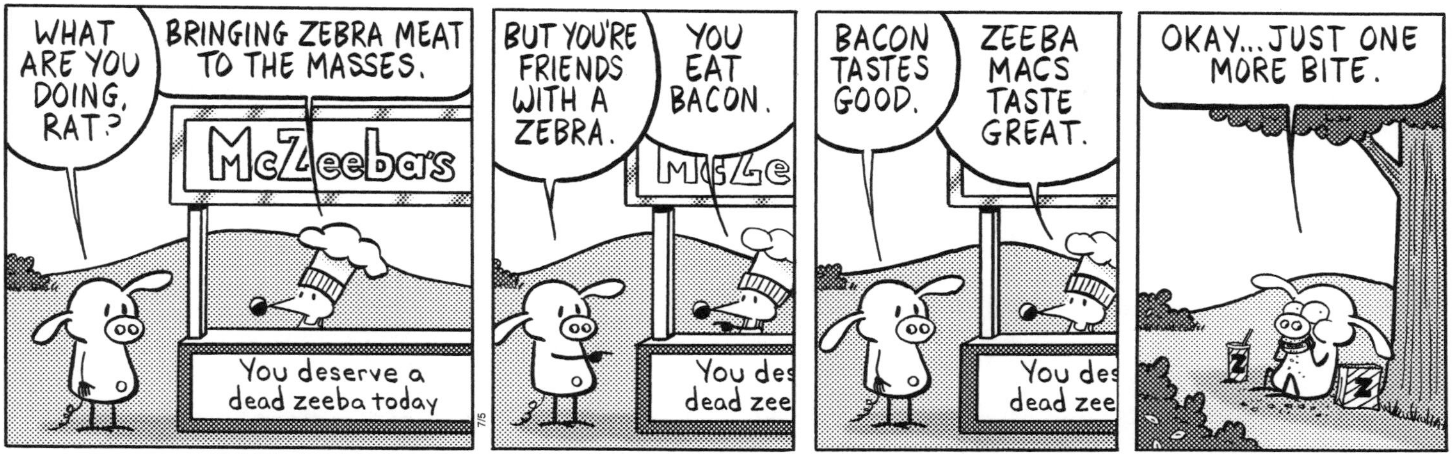
WHAT ARE YOU DOING, RAT?
BRINGING ZEBRA MEAT TO THE MASSES.
McZeeba's
You deserve a dead zeeba today
7/5
BUT YOU'RE FRIENDS WITH A ZEBRA.
YOU EAT BACON.
BACON TASTES GOOD.
ZEEBA MACS TASTE GREAT.
OKAY... JUST ONE MORE BITE.

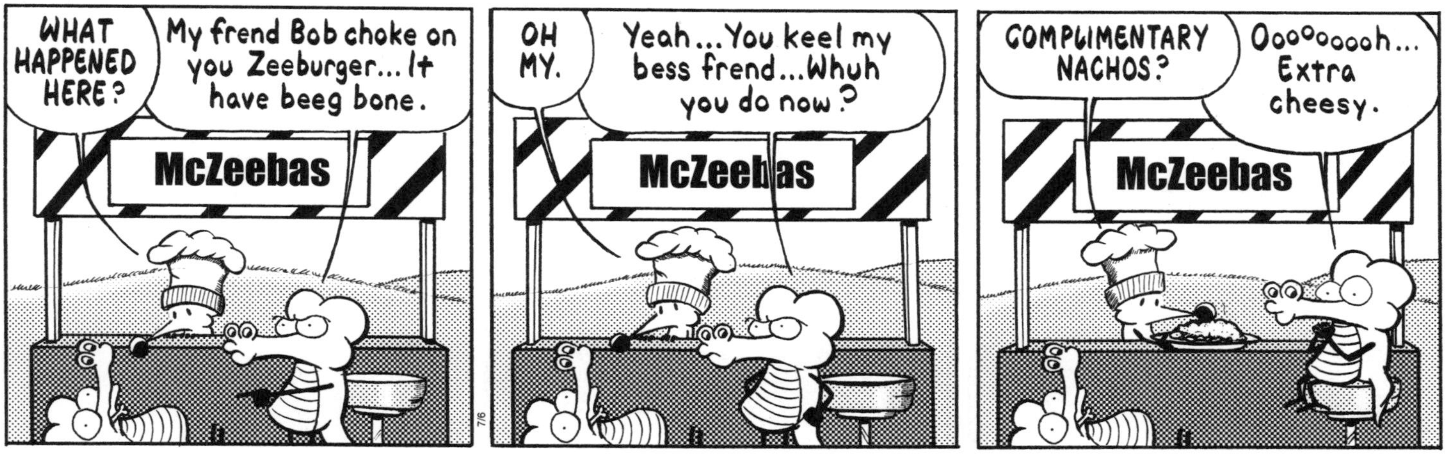
WHAT HAPPENED HERE?
My frend Bob choke on you Zeeburger... It have beeg bone.
McZeebas
7/6
OH MY.
Yeah... You keel my bess frend... Whuh you do now?
COMPLIMENTARY NACHOS?
Oooooooh... Extra cheesy.

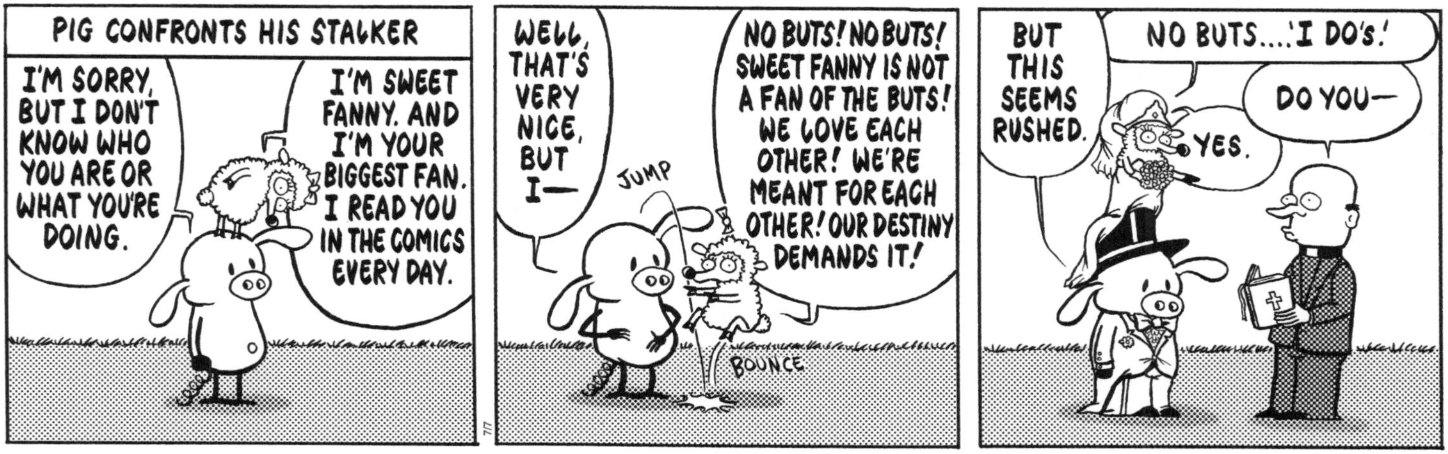
PIG CONFRONTS HIS STALKER
I'M SORRY, BUT I DON'T KNOW WHO YOU ARE OR WHAT YOU'RE DOING.
I'M SWEET FANNY. AND I'M YOUR BIGGEST FAN. I READ YOU IN THE COMICS EVERY DAY.
7/7
WELL, THAT'S VERY NICE, BUT I—
JUMP
NO BUTS! NO BUTS! SWEET FANNY IS NOT A FAN OF THE BUTS! WE LOVE EACH OTHER! WE'RE MEANT FOR EACH OTHER! OUR DESTINY DEMANDS IT!
BOUNCE
BUT THIS SEEMS RUSHED.
NO BUTS....'I DO's.'
YES.
DO YOU—

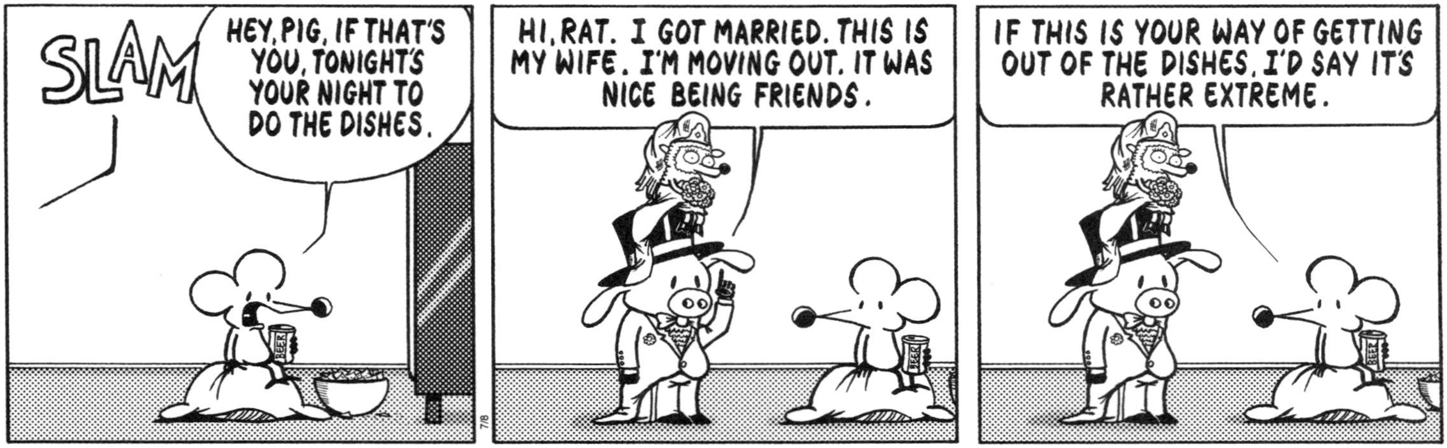
SLAM
HEY, PIG, IF THAT'S YOU, TONIGHT'S YOUR NIGHT TO DO THE DISHES.
BEER
7/8
HI, RAT. I GOT MARRIED. THIS IS MY WIFE. I'M MOVING OUT. IT WAS NICE BEING FRIENDS.
IF THIS IS YOUR WAY OF GETTING OUT OF THE DISHES, I'D SAY IT'S RATHER EXTREME.

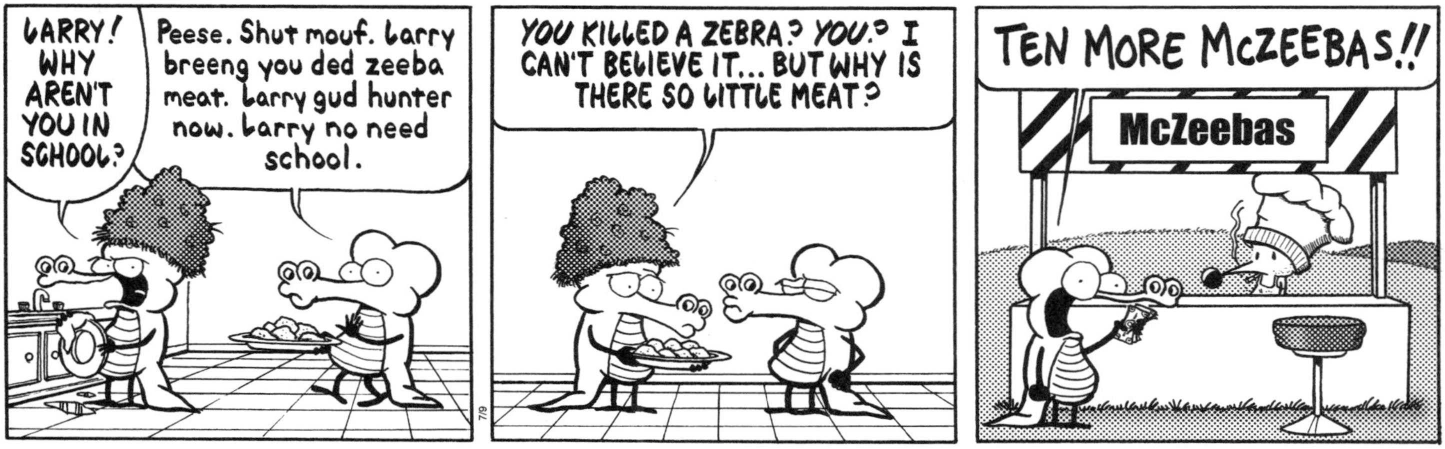
LARRY! WHY AREN'T YOU IN SCHOOL?
Peese. Shut mouf. Larry breeng you ded zeeba meat. Larry gud hunter now. Larry no need school.
7/9
YOU KILLED A ZEBRA? YOU? I CAN'T BELIEVE IT... BUT WHY IS THERE SO LITTLE MEAT?
TEN MORE McZEEBAS!!
McZeebas

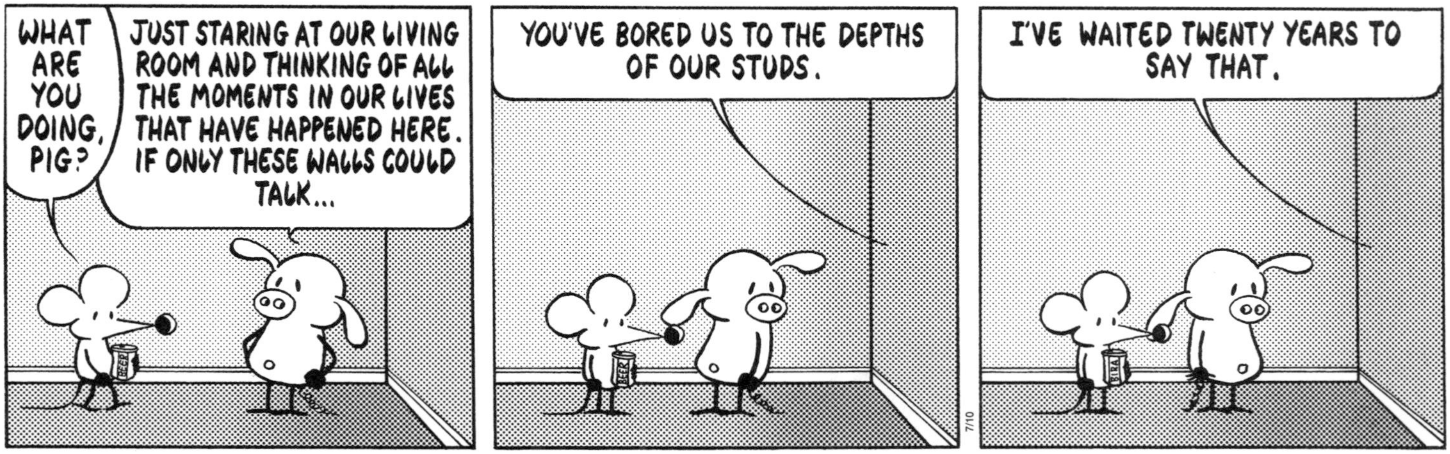
WHAT ARE YOU DOING, PIG?
JUST STARING AT OUR LIVING ROOM AND THINKING OF ALL THE MOMENTS IN OUR LIVES THAT HAVE HAPPENED HERE. IF ONLY THESE WALLS COULD TALK...
YOU'VE BORED US TO THE DEPTHS OF OUR STUDS.
7/10
I'VE WAITED TWENTY YEARS TO SAY THAT.

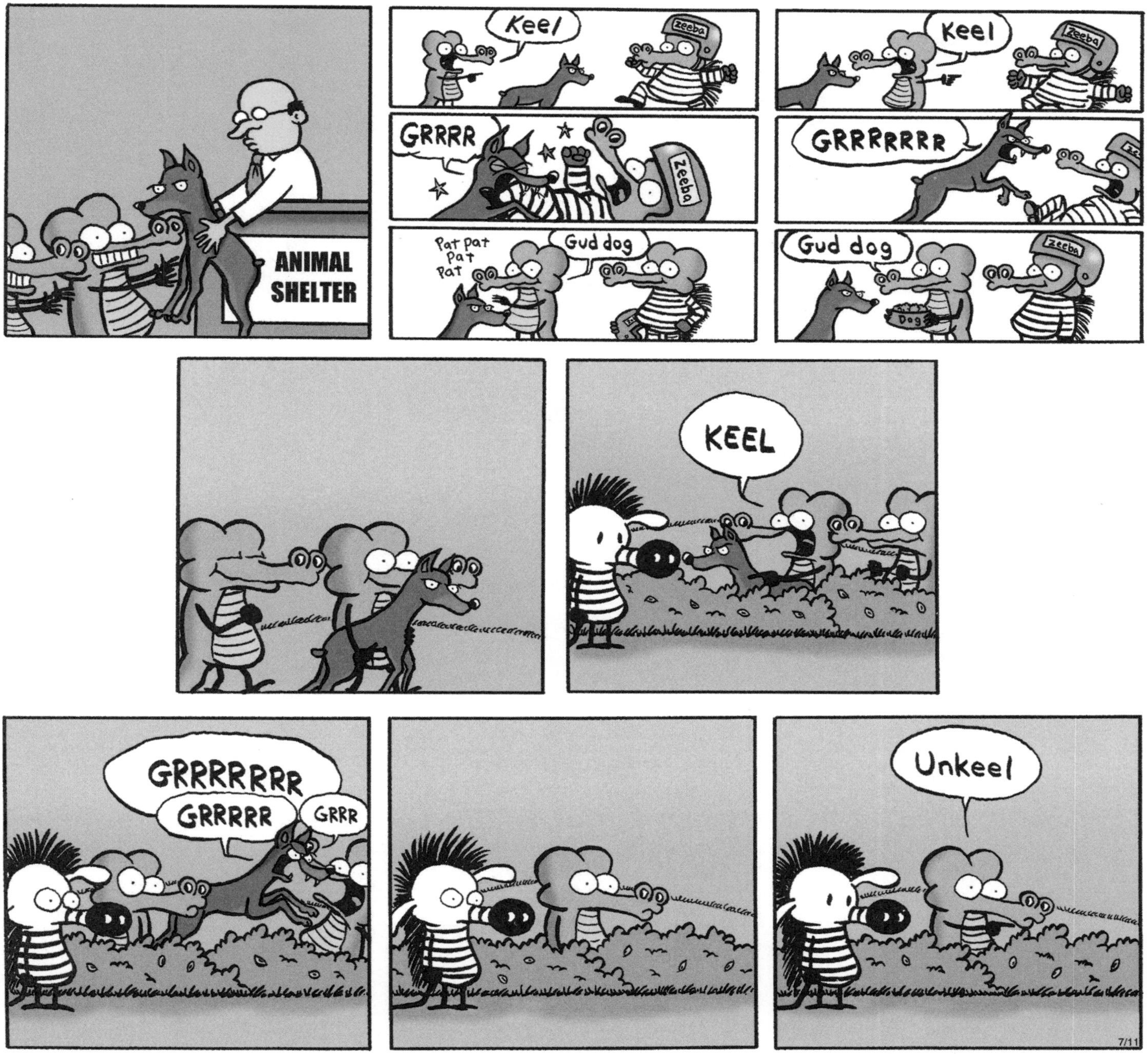
ANIMAL SHELTER
Keel
Zeeba
Keel
Zeeba
GRRRR
Zeeba
GRRRRRRR
Pat pat Pat Pat
Gud dog
Gud dog
Zeeba
Dog
KEEL
GRRRRRRR
GRRRRR
GRRR
Unkeel
7/11

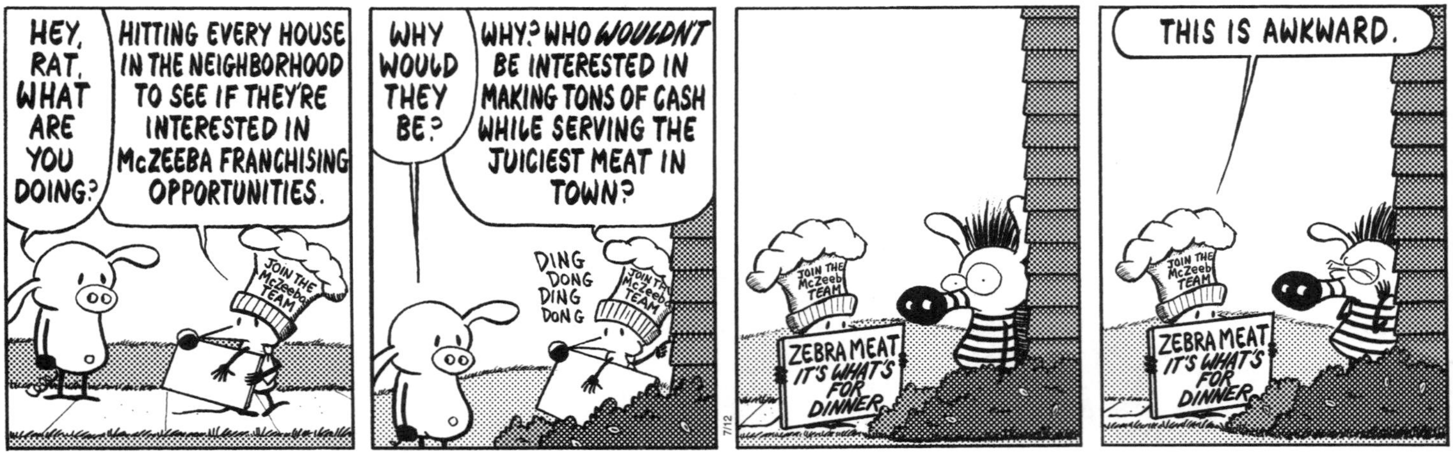
HEY, RAT. WHAT ARE YOU DOING?
HITTING EVERY HOUSE IN THE NEIGHBORHOOD TO SEE IF THEY'RE INTERESTED IN McZEEBA FRANCHISING OPPORTUNITIES.
JOIN THE McZeeba TEAM
WHY WOULD THEY BE?
WHY? WHO *WOULDN'T* BE INTERESTED IN MAKING TONS OF CASH WHILE SERVING THE JUICIEST MEAT IN TOWN?
DING DONG DING DONG
ZEBRA MEAT IT'S WHAT'S FOR DINNER
7/12
THIS IS AWKWARD.

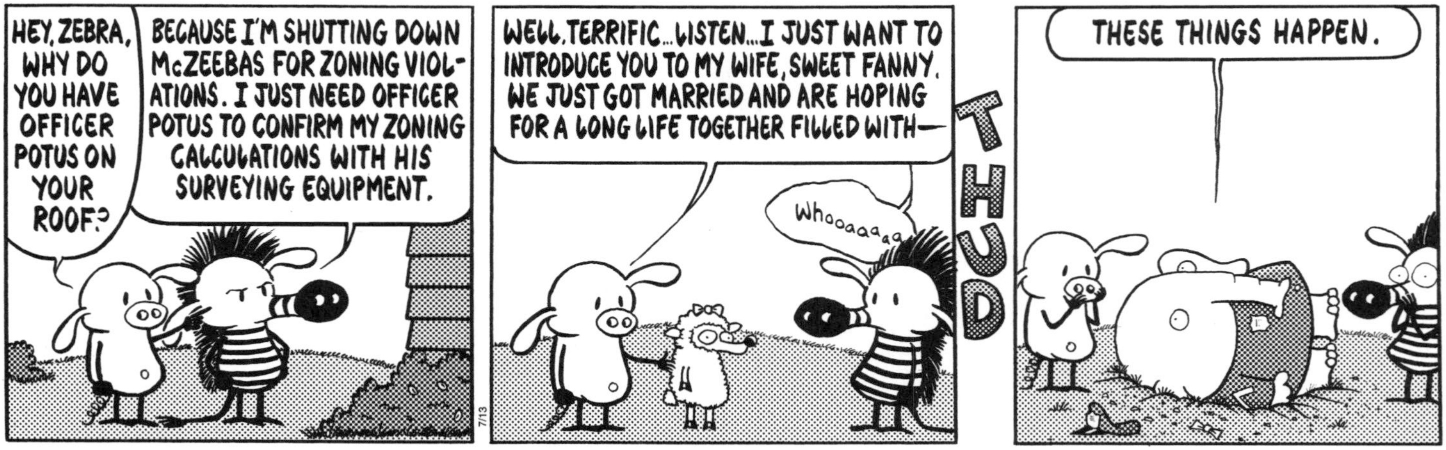
HEY, ZEBRA, WHY DO YOU HAVE OFFICER POTUS ON YOUR ROOF?
BECAUSE I'M SHUTTING DOWN McZEEBAS FOR ZONING VIOLATIONS. I JUST NEED OFFICER POTUS TO CONFIRM MY ZONING CALCULATIONS WITH HIS SURVEYING EQUIPMENT.
7/13
WELL, TERRIFIC... LISTEN... I JUST WANT TO INTRODUCE YOU TO MY WIFE, SWEET FANNY. WE JUST GOT MARRIED AND ARE HOPING FOR A LONG LIFE TOGETHER FILLED WITH—
Whooaaaaaa
THUD
THESE THINGS HAPPEN.

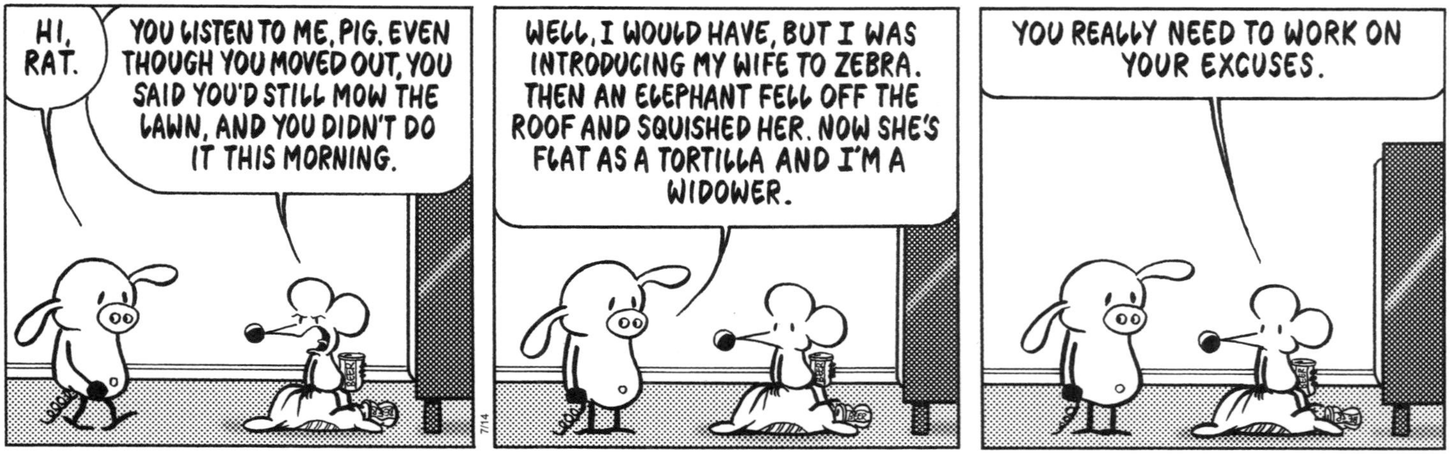
HI, RAT.
YOU LISTEN TO ME, PIG. EVEN THOUGH YOU MOVED OUT, YOU SAID YOU'D STILL MOW THE LAWN, AND YOU DIDN'T DO IT THIS MORNING.
7/14
WELL, I WOULD HAVE, BUT I WAS INTRODUCING MY WIFE TO ZEBRA. THEN AN ELEPHANT FELL OFF THE ROOF AND SQUISHED HER. NOW SHE'S FLAT AS A TORTILLA AND I'M A WIDOWER.
YOU REALLY NEED TO WORK ON YOUR EXCUSES.

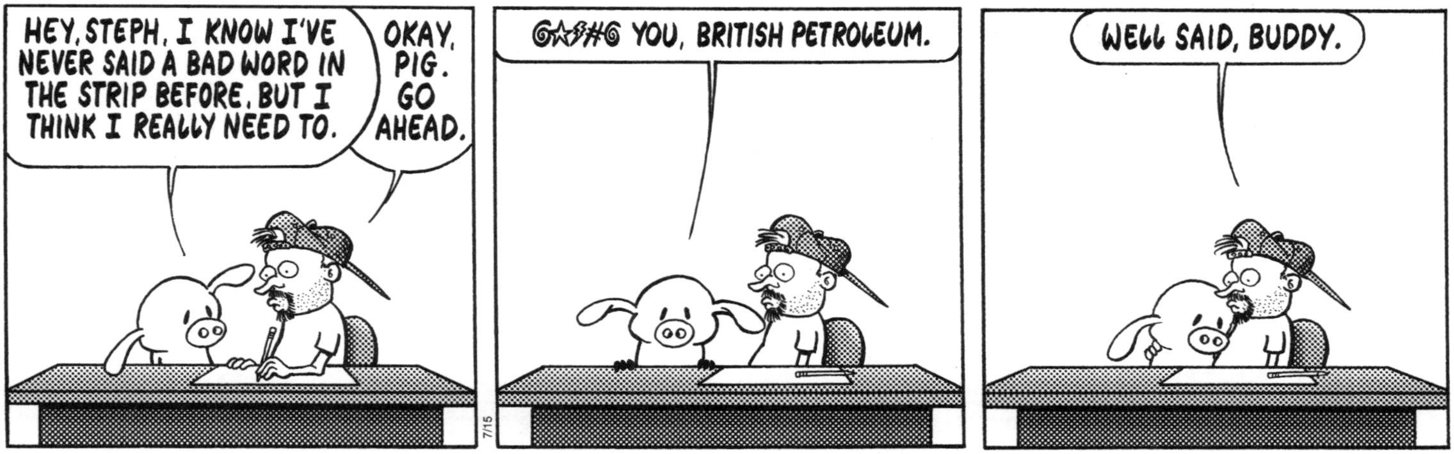
HEY, STEPH, I KNOW I'VE NEVER SAID A BAD WORD IN THE STRIP BEFORE, BUT I THINK I REALLY NEED TO.
OKAY, PIG. GO AHEAD.
7/15
G☆$#G YOU, BRITISH PETROLEUM.
WELL SAID, BUDDY.

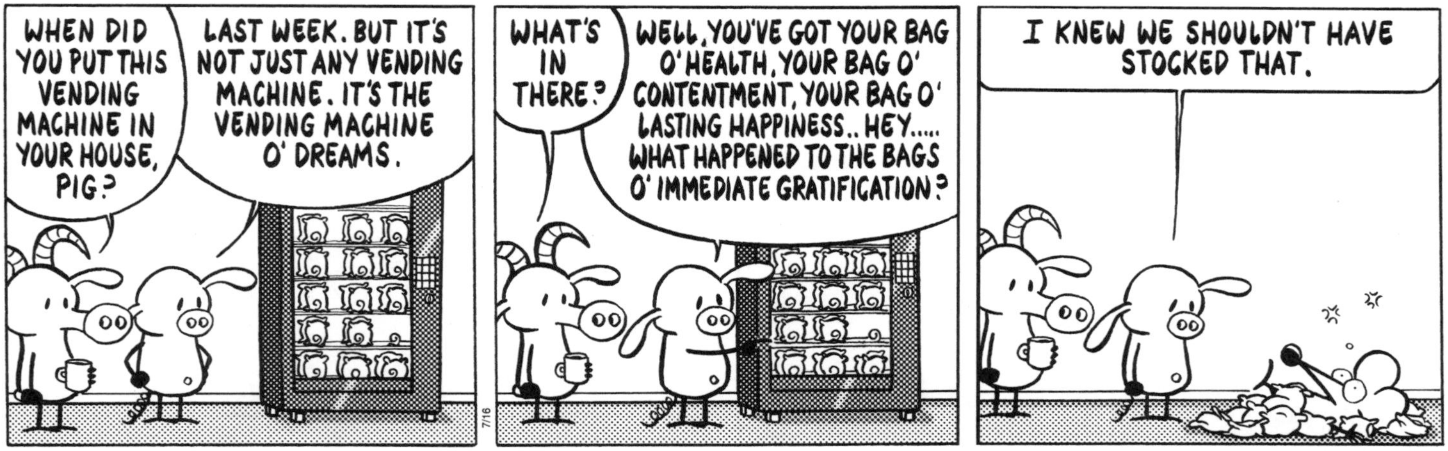
WHEN DID YOU PUT THIS VENDING MACHINE IN YOUR HOUSE, PIG?
LAST WEEK. BUT IT'S NOT JUST ANY VENDING MACHINE. IT'S THE VENDING MACHINE O' DREAMS.
7/16
WHAT'S IN THERE?
WELL, YOU'VE GOT YOUR BAG O' HEALTH, YOUR BAG O' CONTENTMENT, YOUR BAG O' LASTING HAPPINESS.. HEY..... WHAT HAPPENED TO THE BAGS O' IMMEDIATE GRATIFICATION?
I KNEW WE SHOULDN'T HAVE STOCKED THAT.

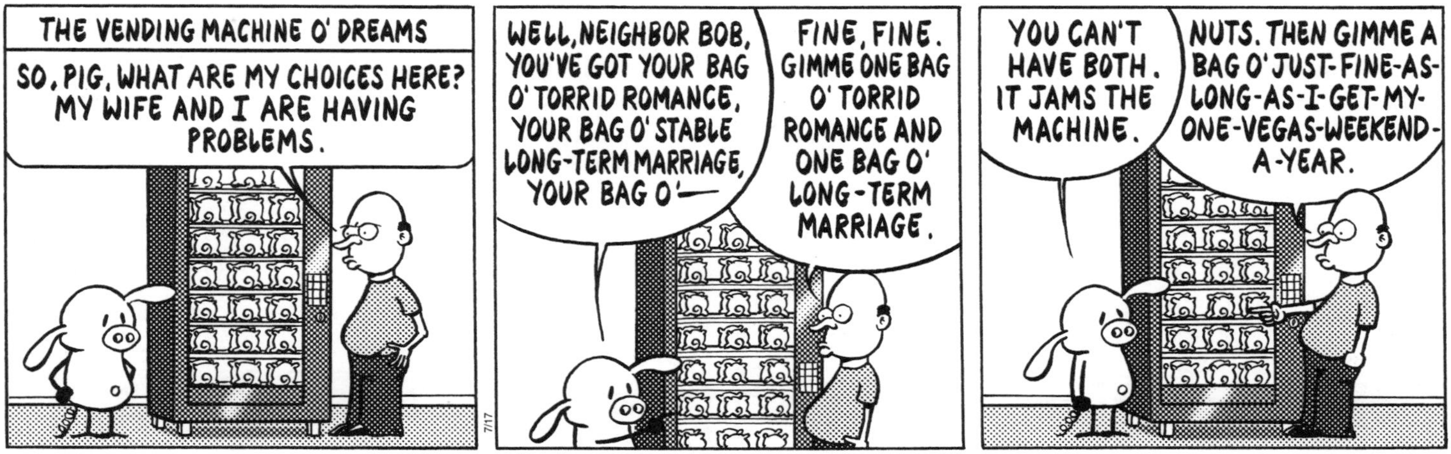
THE VENDING MACHINE O' DREAMS
SO, PIG, WHAT ARE MY CHOICES HERE? MY WIFE AND I ARE HAVING PROBLEMS.
7/17
WELL, NEIGHBOR BOB, YOU'VE GOT YOUR BAG O' TORRID ROMANCE, YOUR BAG O' STABLE LONG-TERM MARRIAGE, YOUR BAG O'—
FINE, FINE. GIMME ONE BAG O' TORRID ROMANCE AND ONE BAG O' LONG-TERM MARRIAGE.
YOU CAN'T HAVE BOTH. IT JAMS THE MACHINE.
NUTS. THEN GIMME A BAG O' JUST-FINE-AS-LONG-AS-I-GET-MY-ONE-VEGAS-WEEKEND-A-YEAR.

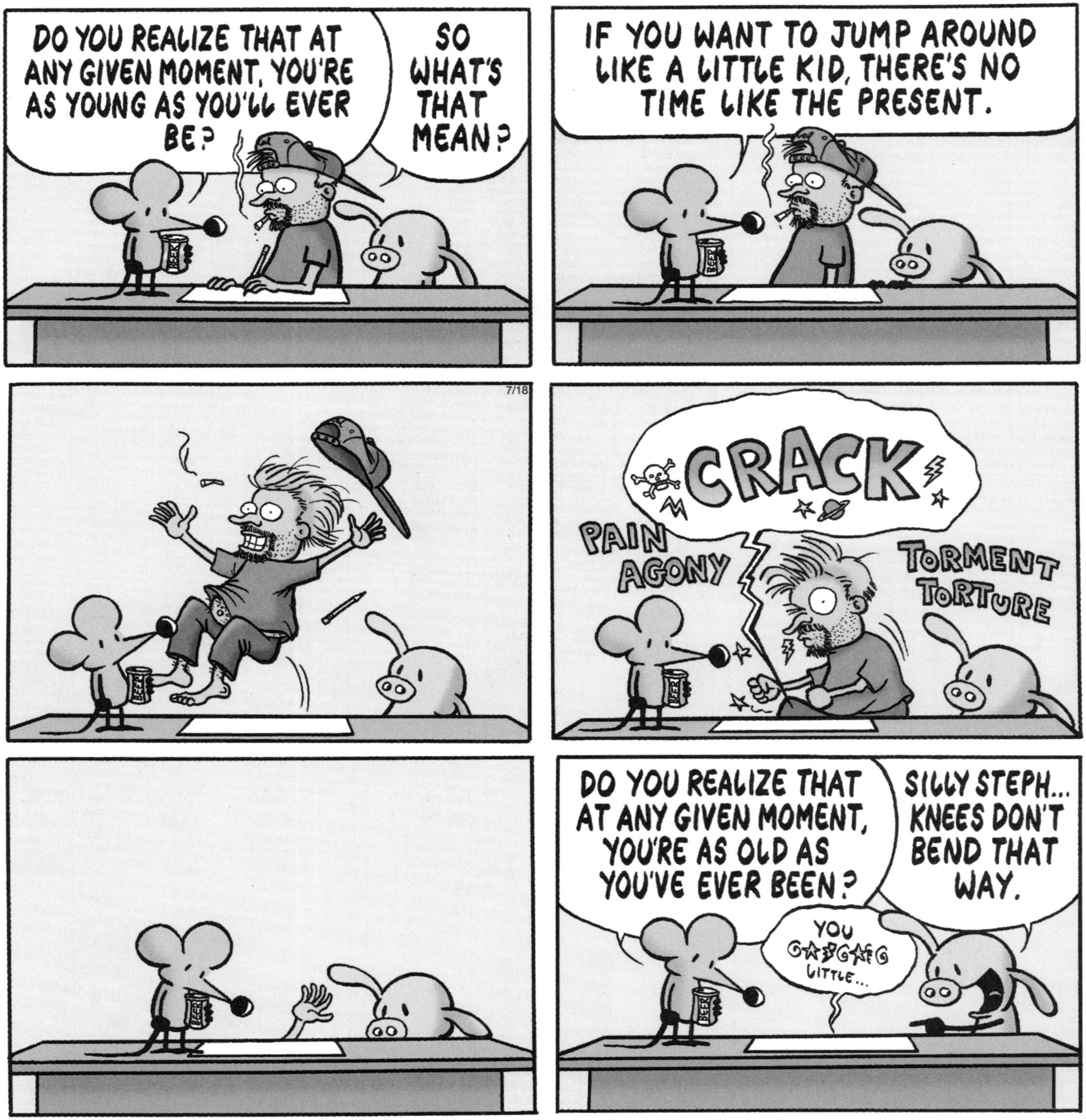

DO YOU REALIZE THAT AT ANY GIVEN MOMENT, YOU'RE AS YOUNG AS YOU'LL EVER BE?
SO WHAT'S THAT MEAN?
IF YOU WANT TO JUMP AROUND LIKE A LITTLE KID, THERE'S NO TIME LIKE THE PRESENT.
7/18
CRACK
PAIN
AGONY
TORMENT
TORTURE
DO YOU REALIZE THAT AT ANY GIVEN MOMENT, YOU'RE AS OLD AS YOU'VE EVER BEEN?
SILLY STEPH... KNEES DON'T BEND THAT WAY.
YOU
LITTLE...

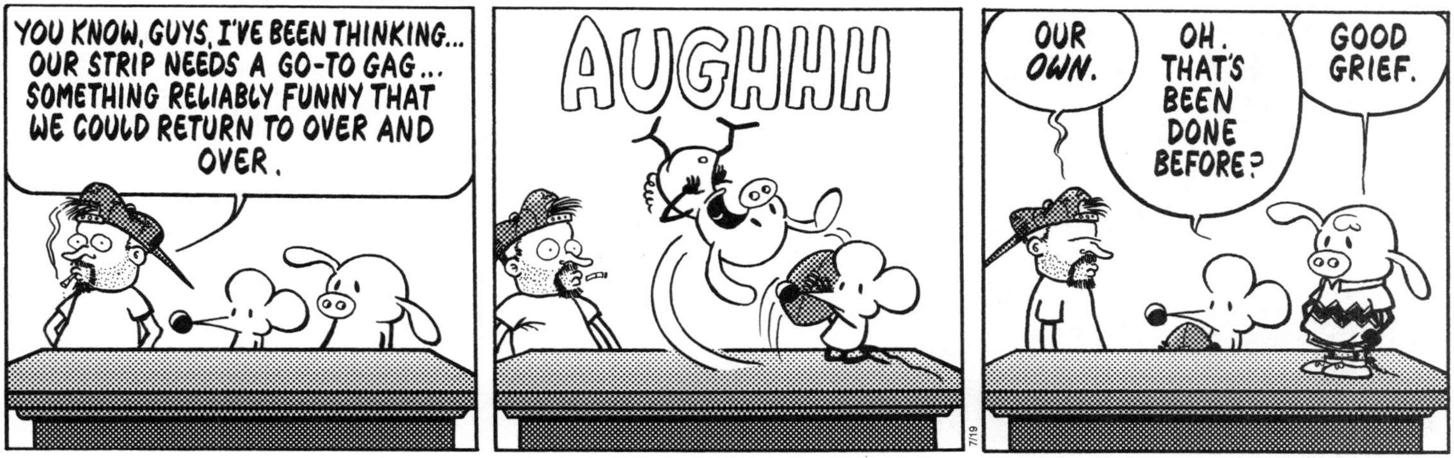
YOU KNOW, GUYS, I'VE BEEN THINKING... OUR STRIP NEEDS A GO-TO GAG... SOMETHING RELIABLY FUNNY THAT WE COULD RETURN TO OVER AND OVER.
AUGHHH
OUR OWN.
OH. THAT'S BEEN DONE BEFORE?
GOOD GRIEF.
7/19

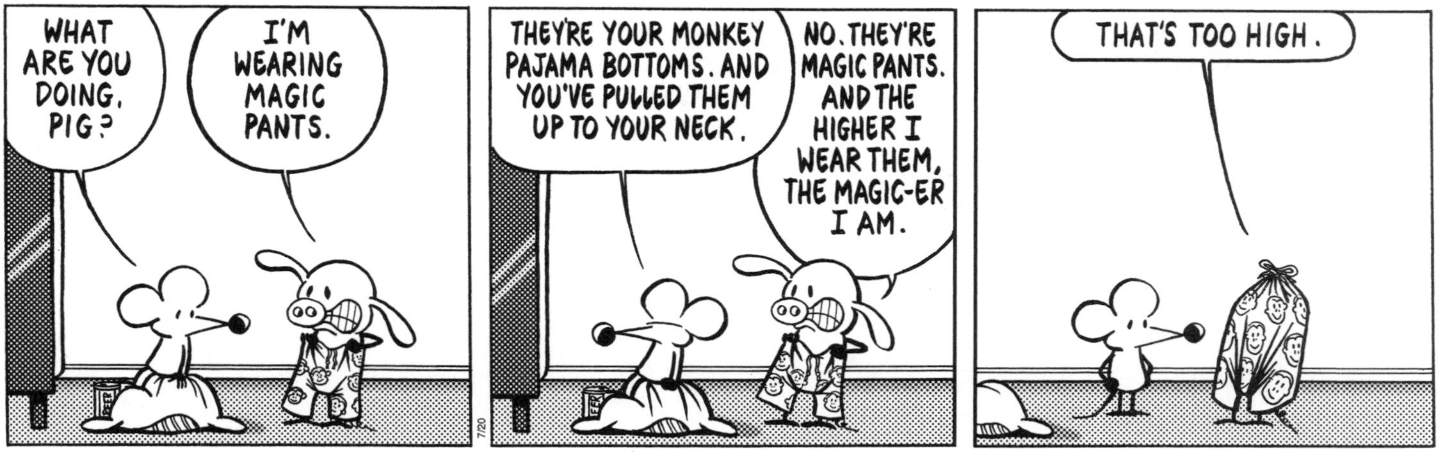
WHAT ARE YOU DOING, PIG?
I'M WEARING MAGIC PANTS.
THEY'RE YOUR MONKEY PAJAMA BOTTOMS. AND YOU'VE PULLED THEM UP TO YOUR NECK.
NO. THEY'RE MAGIC PANTS. AND THE HIGHER I WEAR THEM, THE MAGIC-ER I AM.
THAT'S TOO HIGH.
7/20

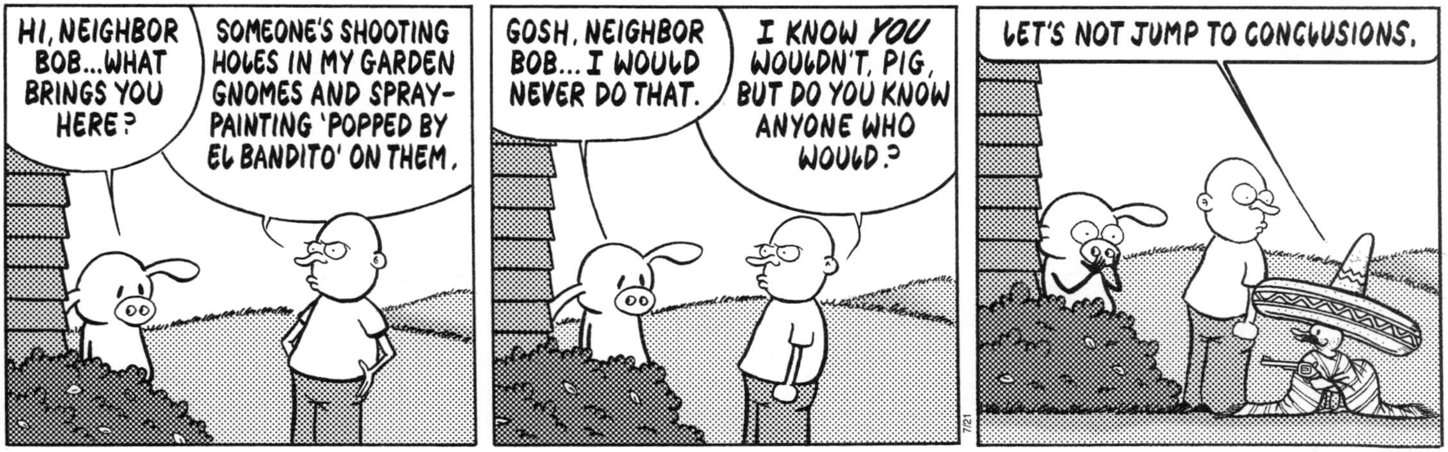
HI, NEIGHBOR BOB...WHAT BRINGS YOU HERE?
SOMEONE'S SHOOTING HOLES IN MY GARDEN GNOMES AND SPRAY-PAINTING 'POPPED BY EL BANDITO' ON THEM.
GOSH, NEIGHBOR BOB... I WOULD NEVER DO THAT.
I KNOW YOU WOULDN'T, PIG, BUT DO YOU KNOW ANYONE WHO WOULD?
LET'S NOT JUMP TO CONCLUSIONS.
7/21

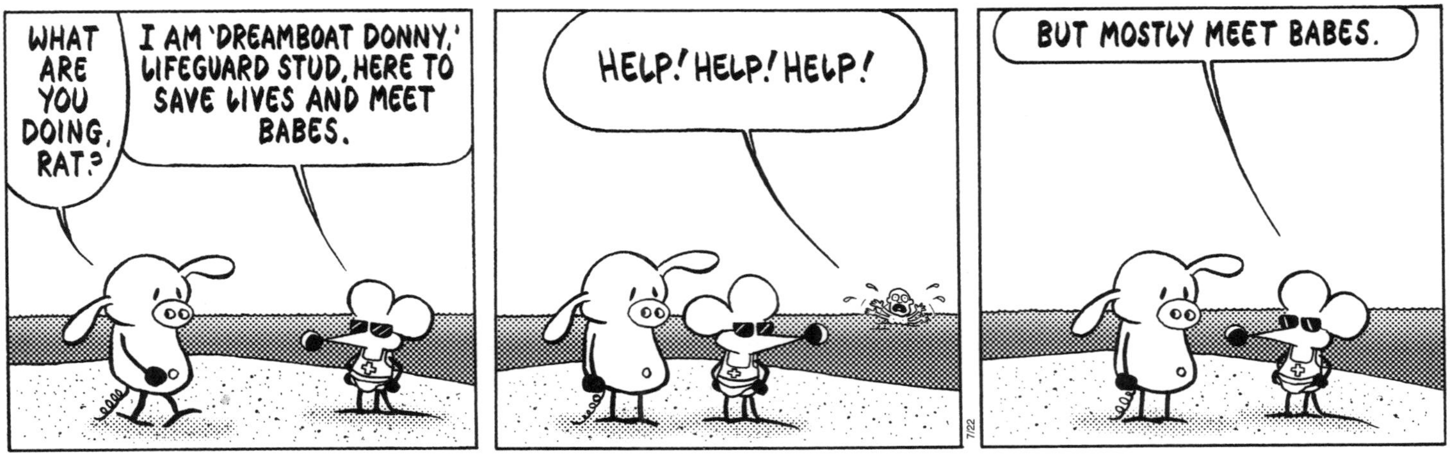
WHAT ARE YOU DOING, RAT?
I AM 'DREAMBOAT DONNY,' LIFEGUARD STUD, HERE TO SAVE LIVES AND MEET BABES.
HELP! HELP! HELP!
BUT MOSTLY MEET BABES.
7/22

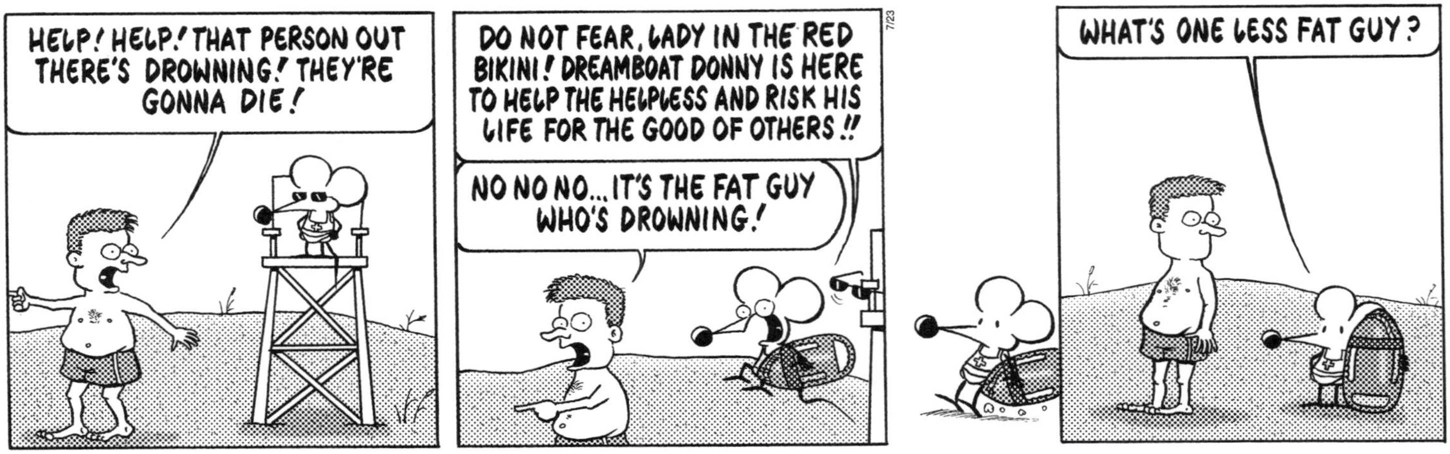
HELP! HELP! THAT PERSON OUT THERE'S DROWNING! THEY'RE GONNA DIE!
DO NOT FEAR, LADY IN THE RED BIKINI! DREAMBOAT DONNY IS HERE TO HELP THE HELPLESS AND RISK HIS LIFE FOR THE GOOD OF OTHERS!!
NO NO NO... IT'S THE FAT GUY WHO'S DROWNING!
WHAT'S ONE LESS FAT GUY?
7/23

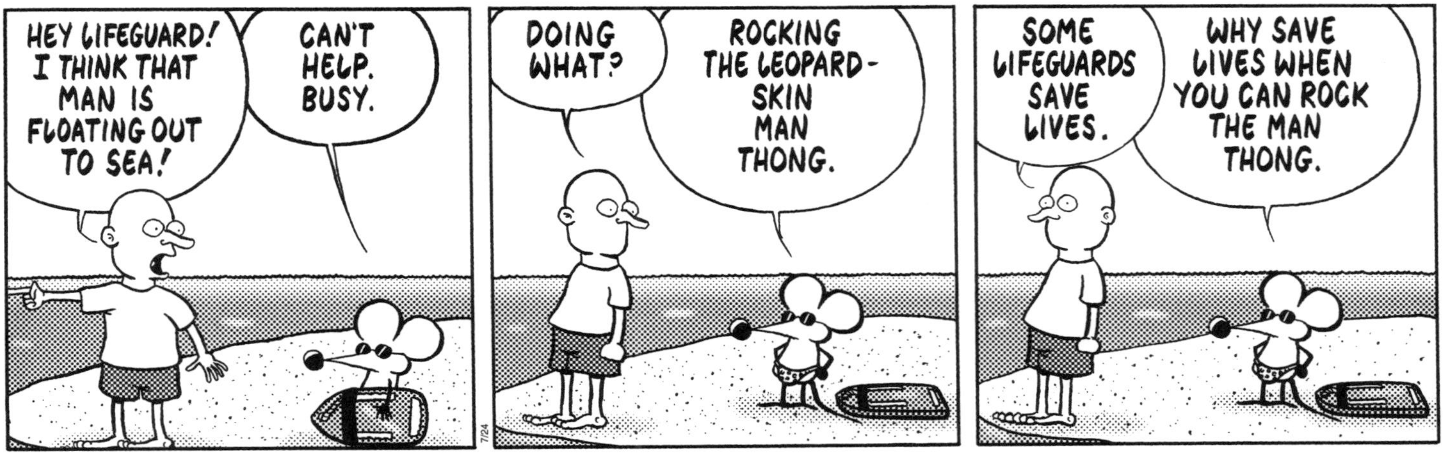
HEY LIFEGUARD! I THINK THAT MAN IS FLOATING OUT TO SEA!
CAN'T HELP. BUSY.
DOING WHAT?
ROCKING THE LEOPARD-SKIN MAN THONG.
SOME LIFEGUARDS SAVE LIVES.
WHY SAVE LIVES WHEN YOU CAN ROCK THE MAN THONG.
7/24

We are all
Gulf
residents.

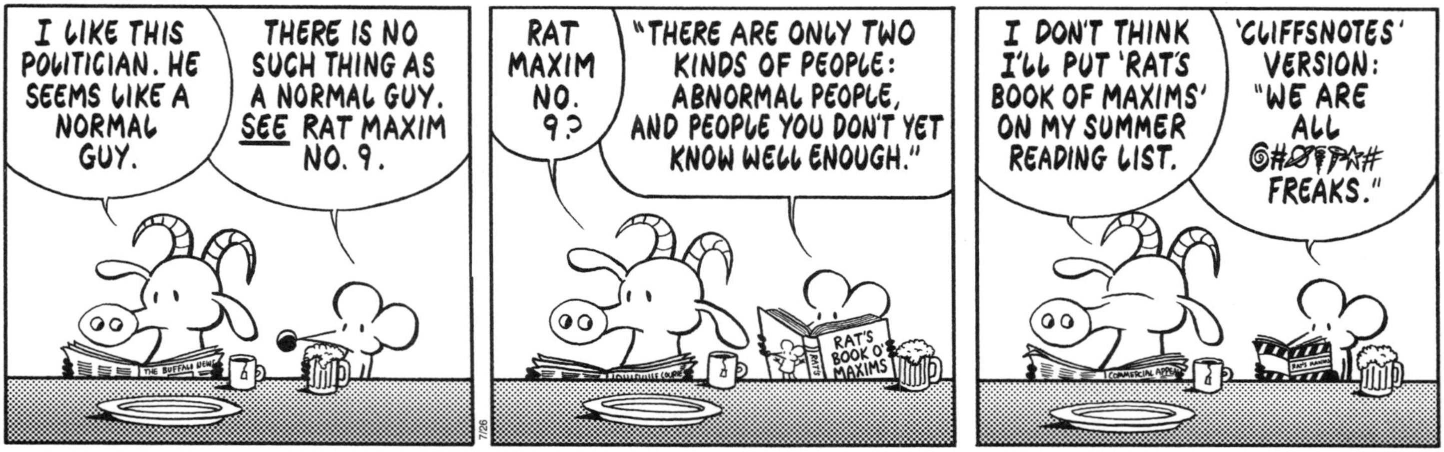
I LIKE THIS POLITICIAN. HE SEEMS LIKE A NORMAL GUY.
THERE IS NO SUCH THING AS A NORMAL GUY. SEE RAT MAXIM NO. 9.
THE BUFFALO NEWS
7/26
RAT MAXIM NO. 9?
"THERE ARE ONLY TWO KINDS OF PEOPLE: ABNORMAL PEOPLE, AND PEOPLE YOU DON'T YET KNOW WELL ENOUGH."
RAT'S BOOK O' MAXIMS
I DON'T THINK I'LL PUT 'RAT'S BOOK OF MAXIMS' ON MY SUMMER READING LIST.
'CLIFFSNOTES' VERSION: "WE ARE ALL @#Ø$%# FREAKS."
COMMERCIAL APPEAL

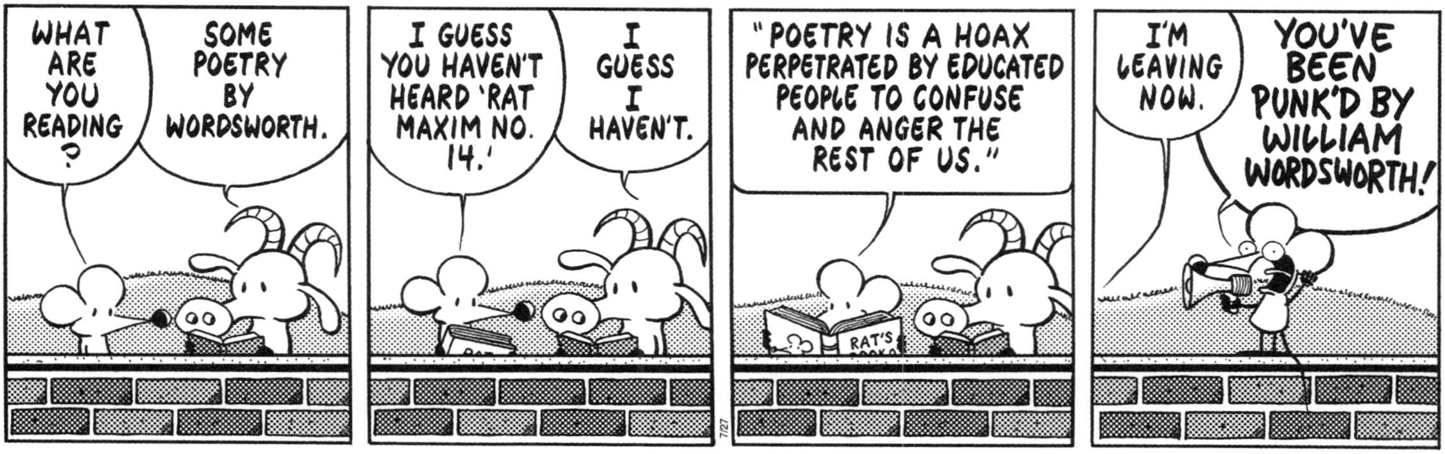
WHAT ARE YOU READING?
SOME POETRY BY WORDSWORTH.
I GUESS YOU HAVEN'T HEARD 'RAT MAXIM NO. 14.'
I GUESS I HAVEN'T.
7/27
"POETRY IS A HOAX PERPETRATED BY EDUCATED PEOPLE TO CONFUSE AND ANGER THE REST OF US."
I'M LEAVING NOW.
YOU'VE BEEN PUNK'D BY WILLIAM WORDSWORTH!

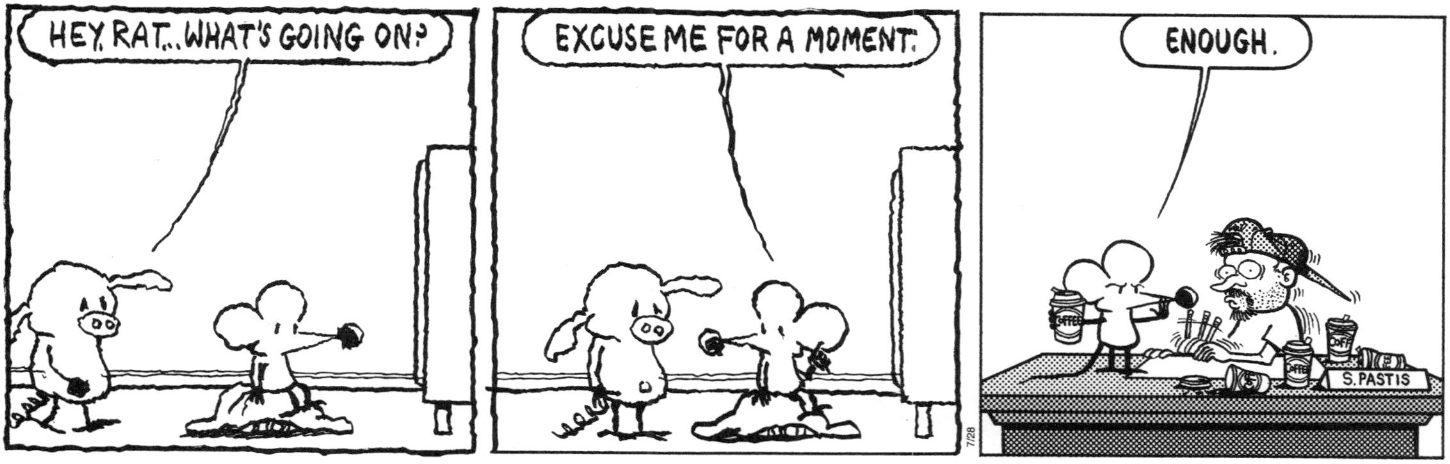
HEY, RAT... WHAT'S GOING ON?
EXCUSE ME FOR A MOMENT.
7/28
ENOUGH.
S. PASTIS

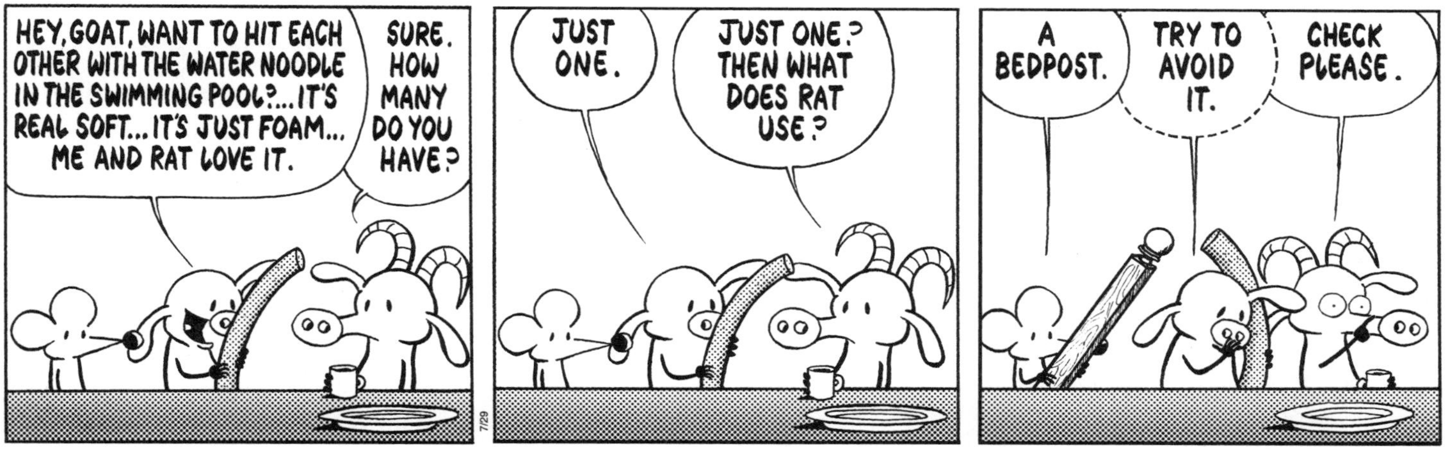
HEY, GOAT, WANT TO HIT EACH OTHER WITH THE WATER NOODLE IN THE SWIMMING POOL?... IT'S REAL SOFT... IT'S JUST FOAM... ME AND RAT LOVE IT.
SURE. HOW MANY DO YOU HAVE?
JUST ONE.
JUST ONE? THEN WHAT DOES RAT USE?
A BEDPOST.
TRY TO AVOID IT.
CHECK PLEASE.
7/29

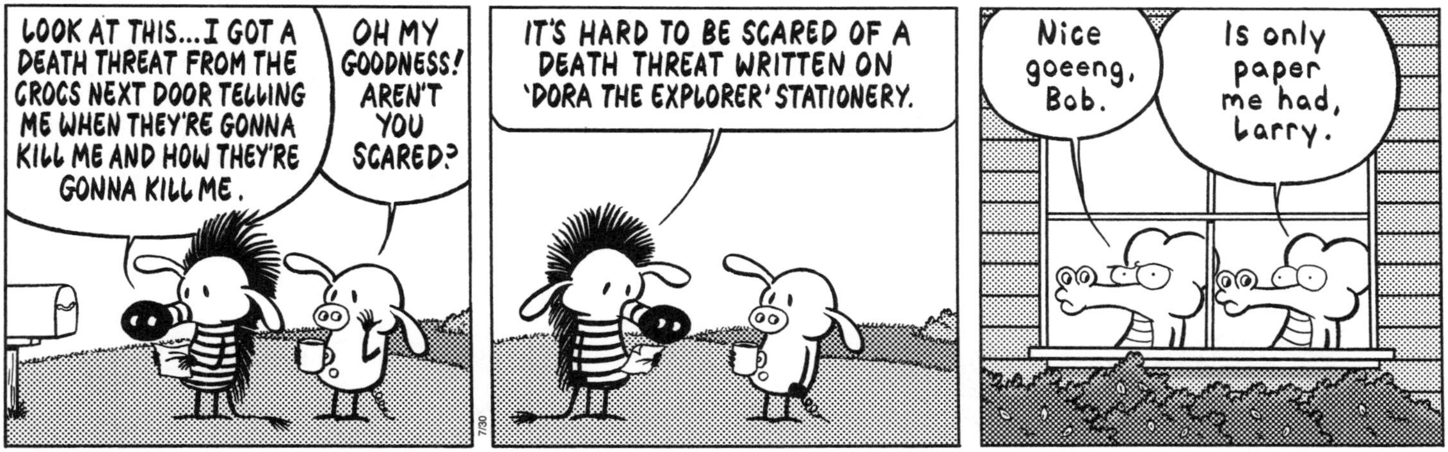
LOOK AT THIS... I GOT A DEATH THREAT FROM THE CROCS NEXT DOOR TELLING ME WHEN THEY'RE GONNA KILL ME AND HOW THEY'RE GONNA KILL ME.
OH MY GOODNESS! AREN'T YOU SCARED?
7/30
IT'S HARD TO BE SCARED OF A DEATH THREAT WRITTEN ON 'DORA THE EXPLORER' STATIONERY.
Nice goeeng, Bob.
Is only paper me had, Larry.

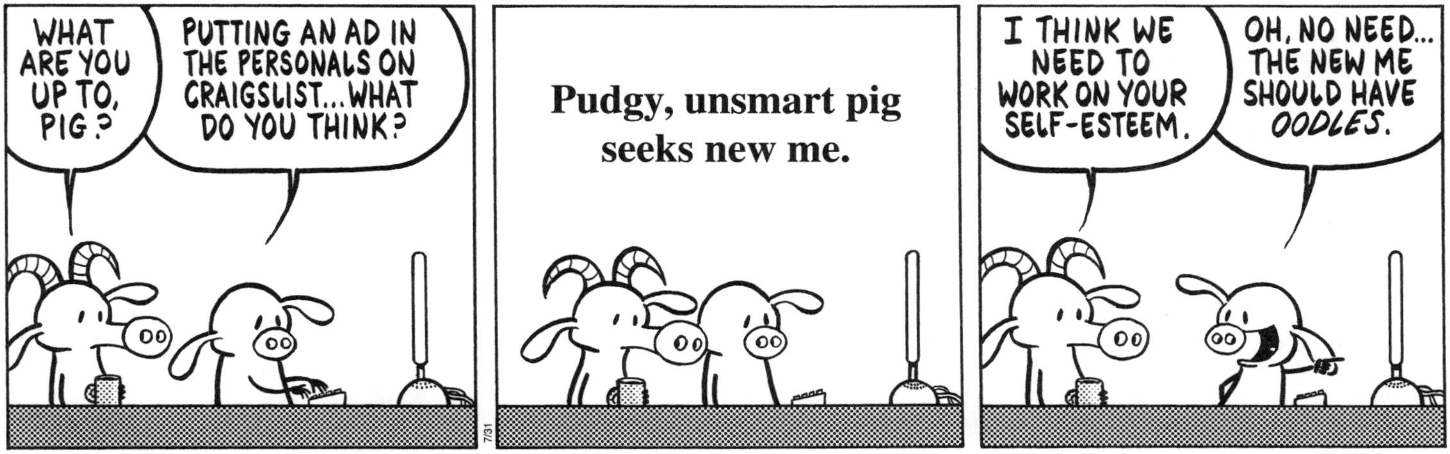
WHAT ARE YOU UP TO, PIG?
PUTTING AN AD IN THE PERSONALS ON CRAIGSLIST... WHAT DO YOU THINK?
7/31
Pudgy, unsmart pig seeks new me.
I THINK WE NEED TO WORK ON YOUR SELF-ESTEEM.
OH, NO NEED... THE NEW ME SHOULD HAVE OODLES.

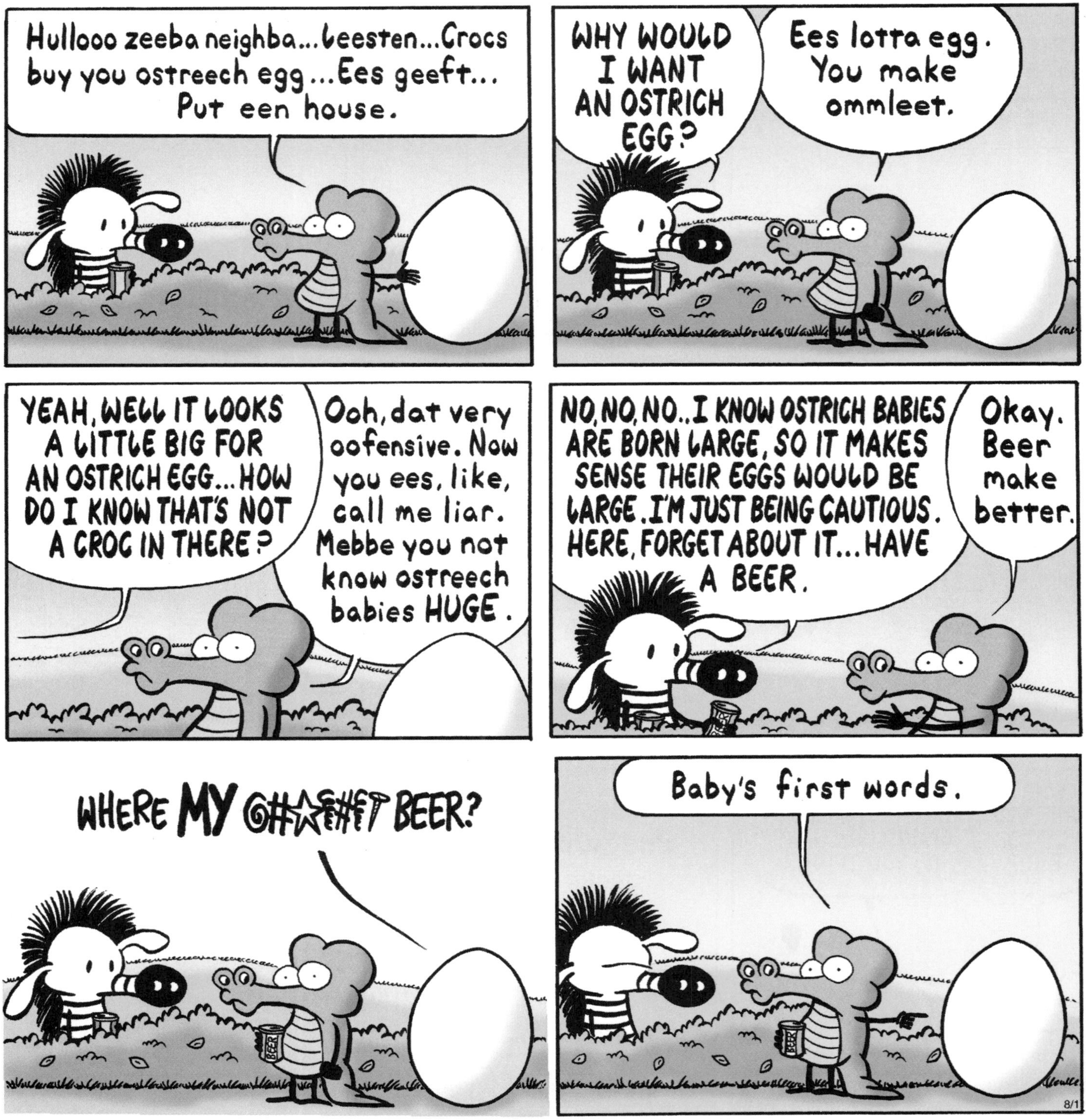
Hullooo zeeba neighba...leesten...Crocs buy you ostreech egg...Ees geeft... Put een house.
WHY WOULD I WANT AN OSTRICH EGG?
Ees lotta egg. You make ommleet.
YEAH, WELL IT LOOKS A LITTLE BIG FOR AN OSTRICH EGG...HOW DO I KNOW THAT'S NOT A CROC IN THERE?
Ooh, dat very oofensive. Now you ees, like, call me liar. Mebbe you not know ostreech babies HUGE.
NO, NO, NO..I KNOW OSTRICH BABIES ARE BORN LARGE, SO IT MAKES SENSE THEIR EGGS WOULD BE LARGE. I'M JUST BEING CAUTIOUS. HERE, FORGET ABOUT IT...HAVE A BEER.
Okay. Beer make better.
WHERE MY G#☆$#T BEER?
Baby's first words.
8/1

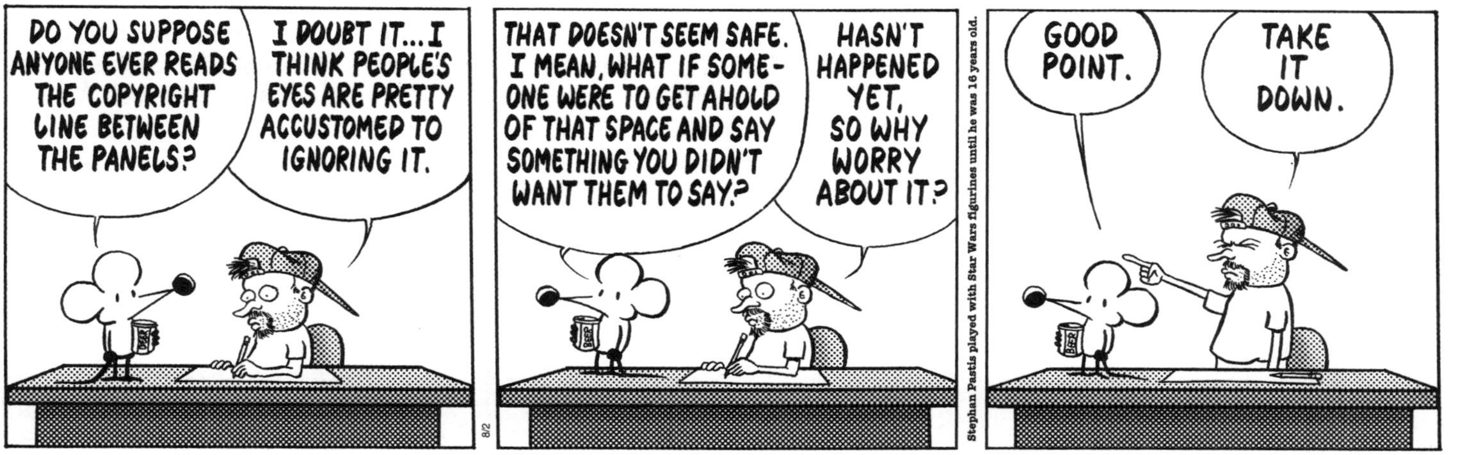
DO YOU SUPPOSE ANYONE EVER READS THE COPYRIGHT LINE BETWEEN THE PANELS?
I DOUBT IT... I THINK PEOPLE'S EYES ARE PRETTY ACCUSTOMED TO IGNORING IT.
8/2
THAT DOESN'T SEEM SAFE. I MEAN, WHAT IF SOMEONE WERE TO GET AHOLD OF THAT SPACE AND SAY SOMETHING YOU DIDN'T WANT THEM TO SAY?
HASN'T HAPPENED YET, SO WHY WORRY ABOUT IT?
Stephan Pastis played with Star Wars figurines until he was 16 years old.
GOOD POINT.
TAKE IT DOWN.

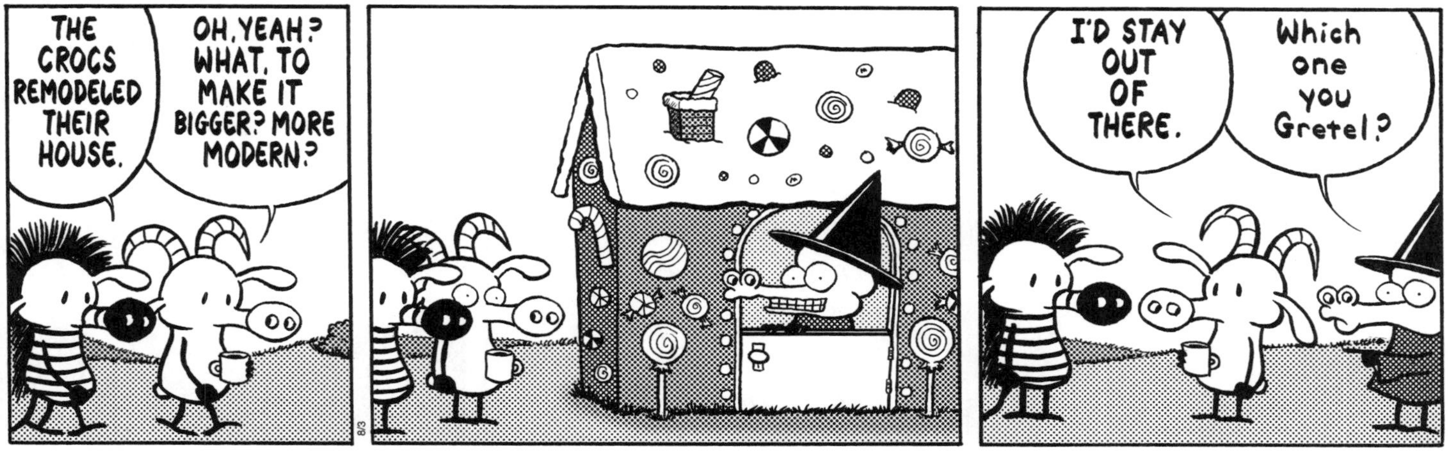
THE CROCS REMODELED THEIR HOUSE.
OH, YEAH? WHAT, TO MAKE IT BIGGER? MORE MODERN?
8/3
I'D STAY OUT OF THERE.
Which one you Gretel?

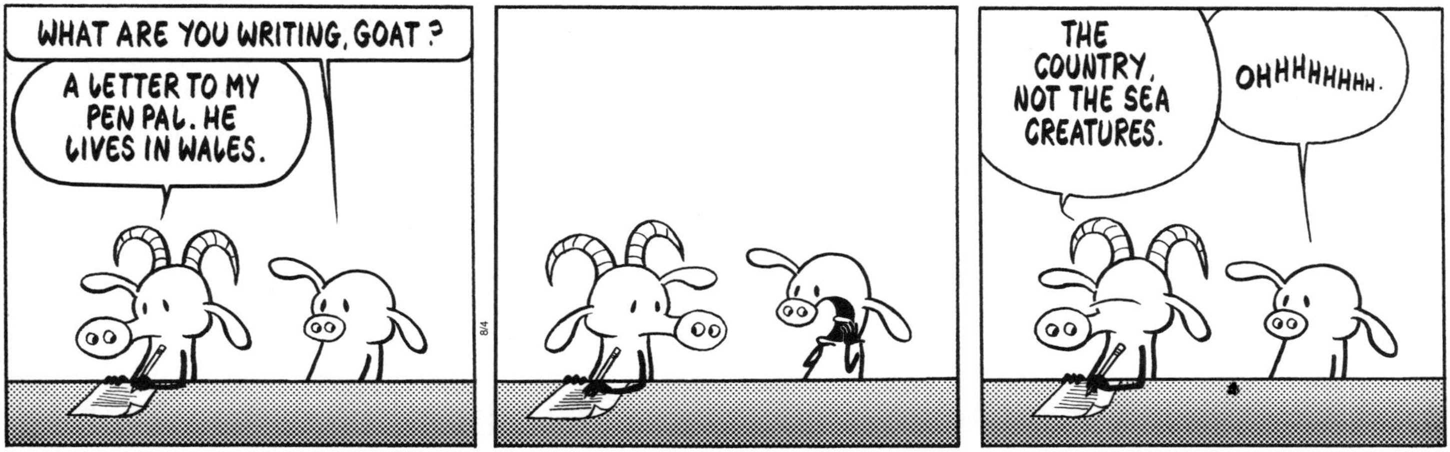
WHAT ARE YOU WRITING, GOAT?
A LETTER TO MY PEN PAL. HE LIVES IN WALES.
8/4
THE COUNTRY, NOT THE SEA CREATURES.
OHHHHHHHH.

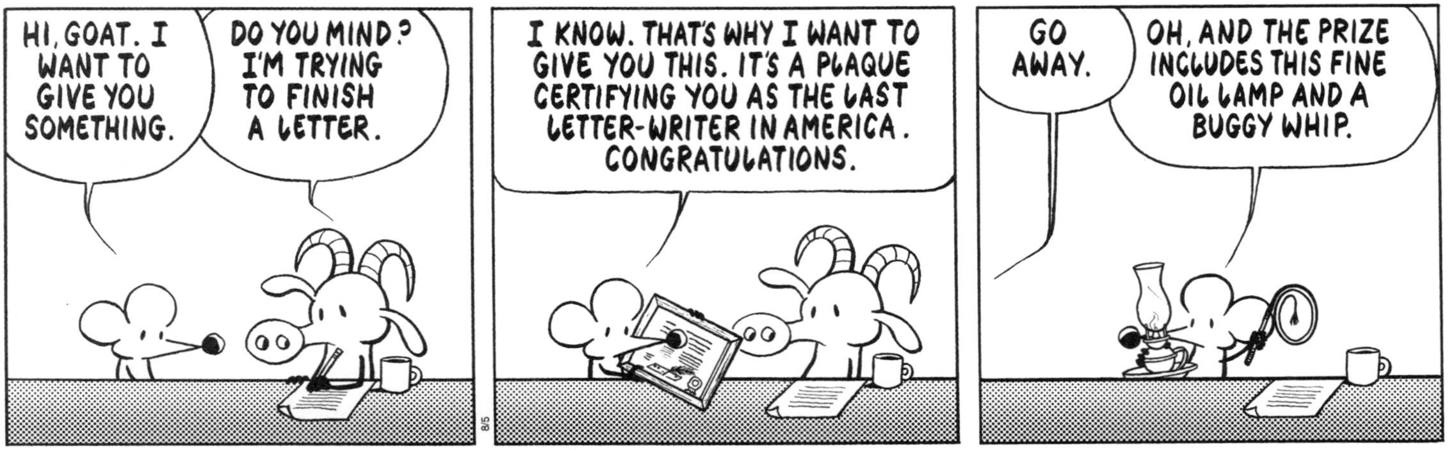
HI, GOAT. I WANT TO GIVE YOU SOMETHING.
DO YOU MIND? I'M TRYING TO FINISH A LETTER.
I KNOW. THAT'S WHY I WANT TO GIVE YOU THIS. IT'S A PLAQUE CERTIFYING YOU AS THE LAST LETTER-WRITER IN AMERICA. CONGRATULATIONS.
GO AWAY.
OH, AND THE PRIZE INCLUDES THIS FINE OIL LAMP AND A BUGGY WHIP.
8/5

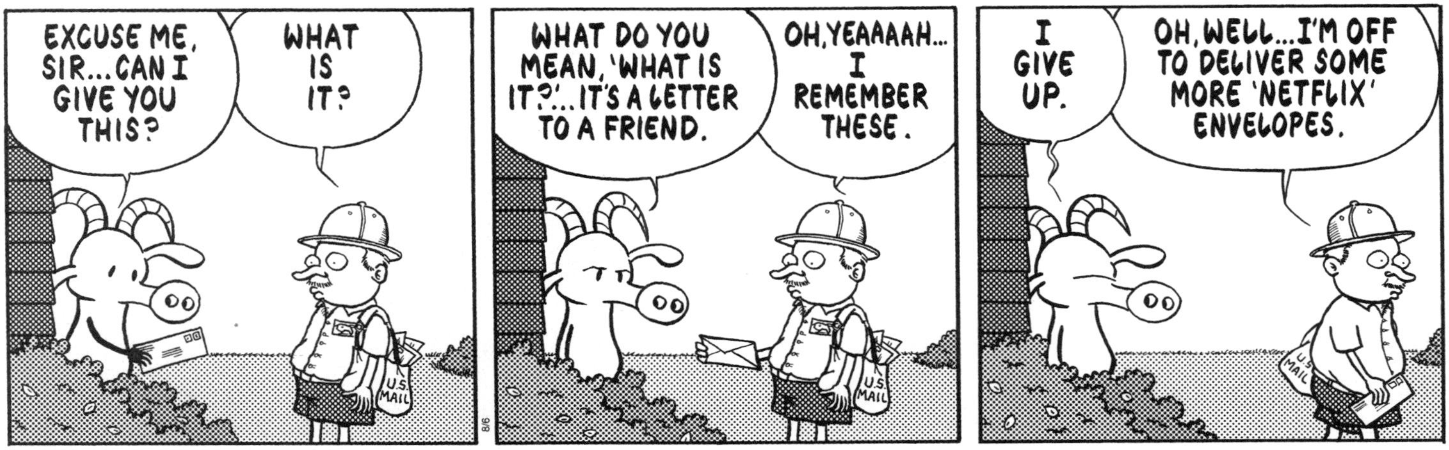
EXCUSE ME, SIR... CAN I GIVE YOU THIS?
WHAT IS IT?
U.S. MAIL
WHAT DO YOU MEAN, 'WHAT IS IT?'... IT'S A LETTER TO A FRIEND.
OH, YEAAAAH... I REMEMBER THESE.
U.S. MAIL
I GIVE UP.
OH, WELL... I'M OFF TO DELIVER SOME MORE 'NETFLIX' ENVELOPES.
U.S. MAIL
8/6

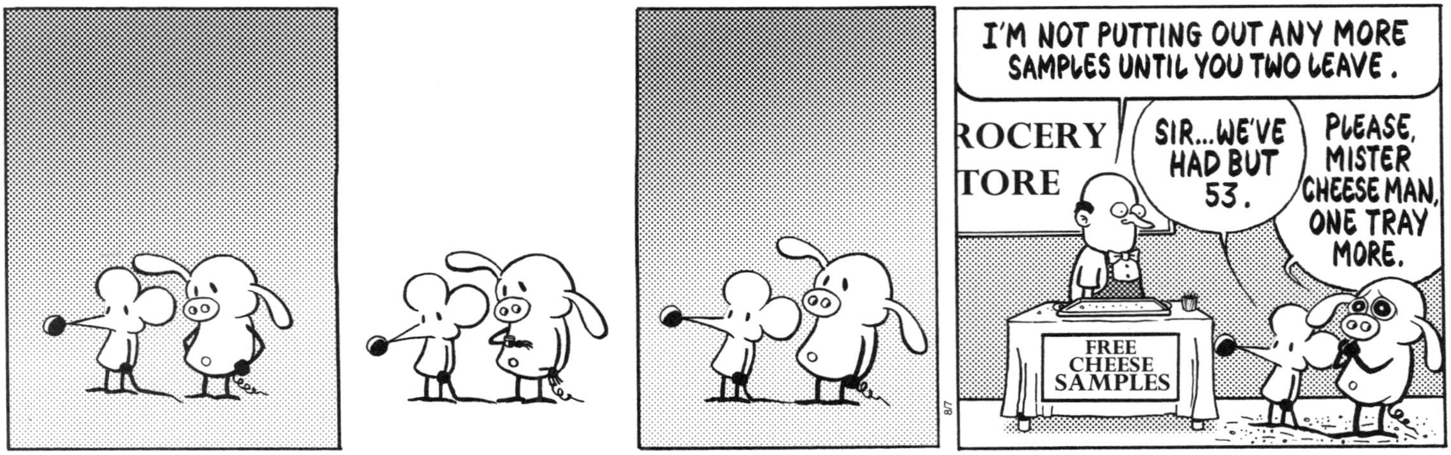
I'M NOT PUTTING OUT ANY MORE SAMPLES UNTIL YOU TWO LEAVE.
ROCERY
TORE
SIR... WE'VE HAD BUT 53.
PLEASE, MISTER CHEESE MAN, ONE TRAY MORE.
FREE CHEESE SAMPLES
8/7

HEY, RAT, WHAT ARE YOU WRITING?

AN EMAIL.

EMAIL! EMAIL! EMAIL! DOESN'T ANYONE SEND A LETTER ANYMORE?

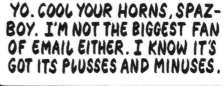

YO. COOL YOUR HORNS, SPAZ-BOY. I'M NOT THE BIGGEST FAN OF EMAIL EITHER. I KNOW IT'S GOT ITS PLUSSES AND MINUSES.

YOU DO?

YEAH... FOR EXAMPLE, EMAIL TENDS TO RUDIFY ALL COMMUNICATION.

RUDIFY?

YEAH...MAKES IT RUDER. MAKES NICE PEOPLE SOUND RUDE. MAKES RUDE PEOPLE SOUND RUDER.

8/8

YES! EXACTLY! AND THAT ALONE OUTWEIGHS ITS PLUSSES!

THOSE **ARE** ITS PLUSSES.

PLEASE MAKE YOUR EVIL LIPS STOP MOVING.

PREPARE FOR AN EMAIL!!

41

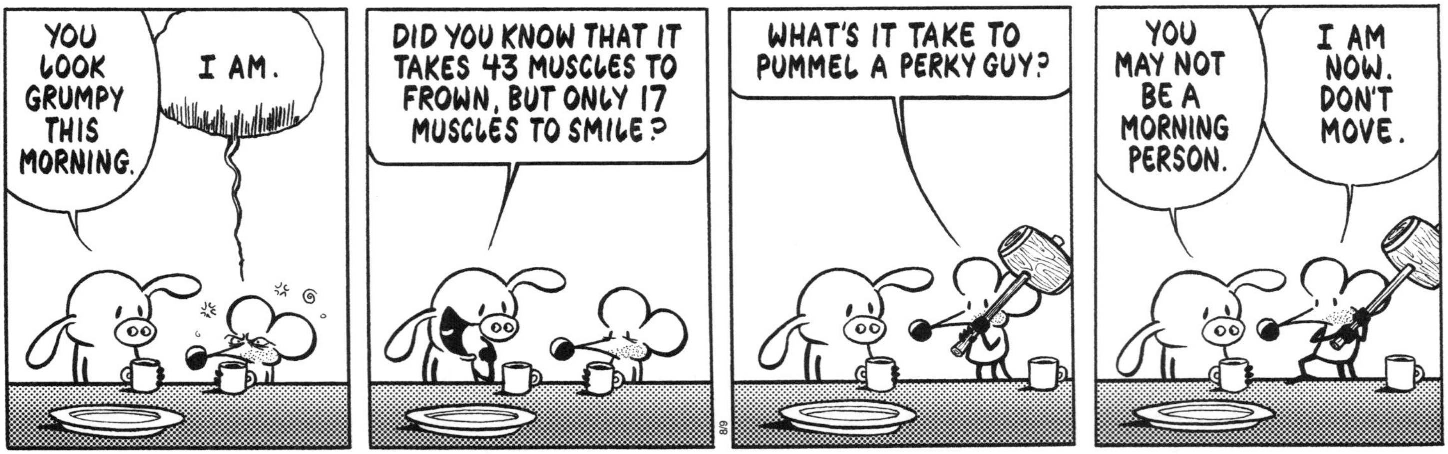
YOU LOOK GRUMPY THIS MORNING.
I AM.
DID YOU KNOW THAT IT TAKES 43 MUSCLES TO FROWN, BUT ONLY 17 MUSCLES TO SMILE?
WHAT'S IT TAKE TO PUMMEL A PERKY GUY?
YOU MAY NOT BE A MORNING PERSON.
I AM NOW. DON'T MOVE.
8/9

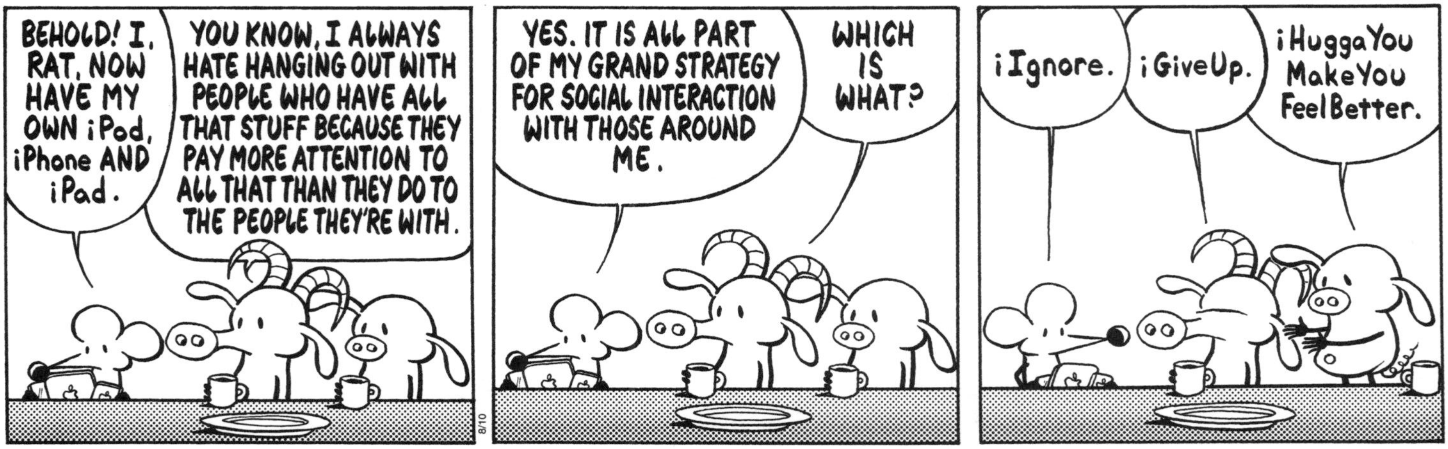
BEHOLD! I, RAT, NOW HAVE MY OWN iPod, iPhone AND iPad.
YOU KNOW, I ALWAYS HATE HANGING OUT WITH PEOPLE WHO HAVE ALL THAT STUFF BECAUSE THEY PAY MORE ATTENTION TO ALL THAT THAN THEY DO TO THE PEOPLE THEY'RE WITH.
YES. IT IS ALL PART OF MY GRAND STRATEGY FOR SOCIAL INTERACTION WITH THOSE AROUND ME.
WHICH IS WHAT?
i Ignore.
i GiveUp.
i HuggaYou MakeYou FeelBetter.
8/10

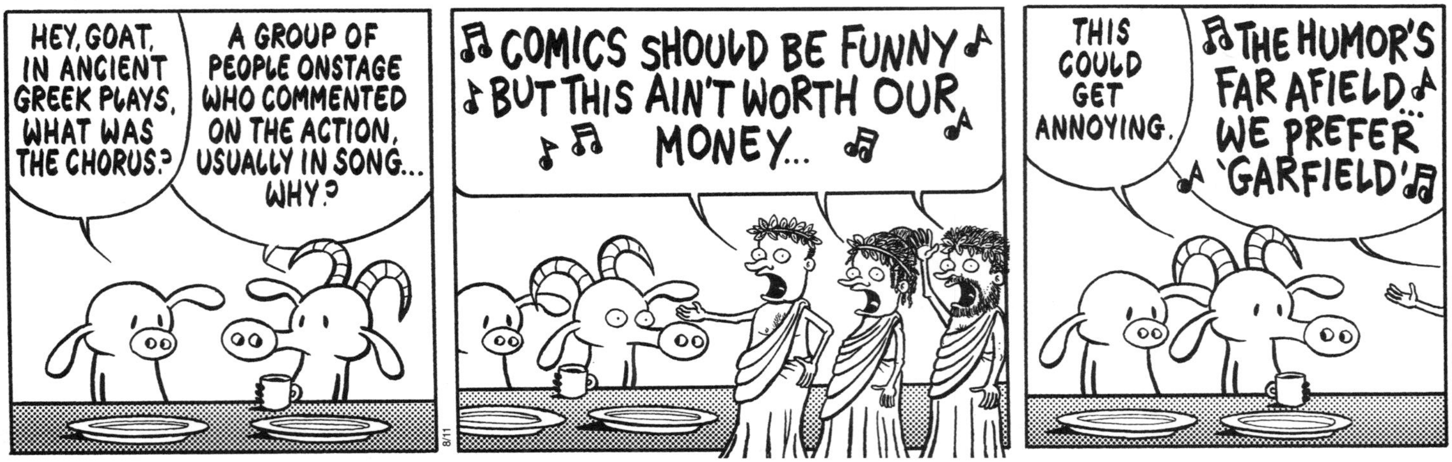
HEY, GOAT, IN ANCIENT GREEK PLAYS, WHAT WAS THE CHORUS?
A GROUP OF PEOPLE ONSTAGE WHO COMMENTED ON THE ACTION, USUALLY IN SONG... WHY?
COMICS SHOULD BE FUNNY BUT THIS AIN'T WORTH OUR MONEY...
THIS COULD GET ANNOYING.
THE HUMOR'S FAR AFIELD... WE PREFER 'GARFIELD'
8/11

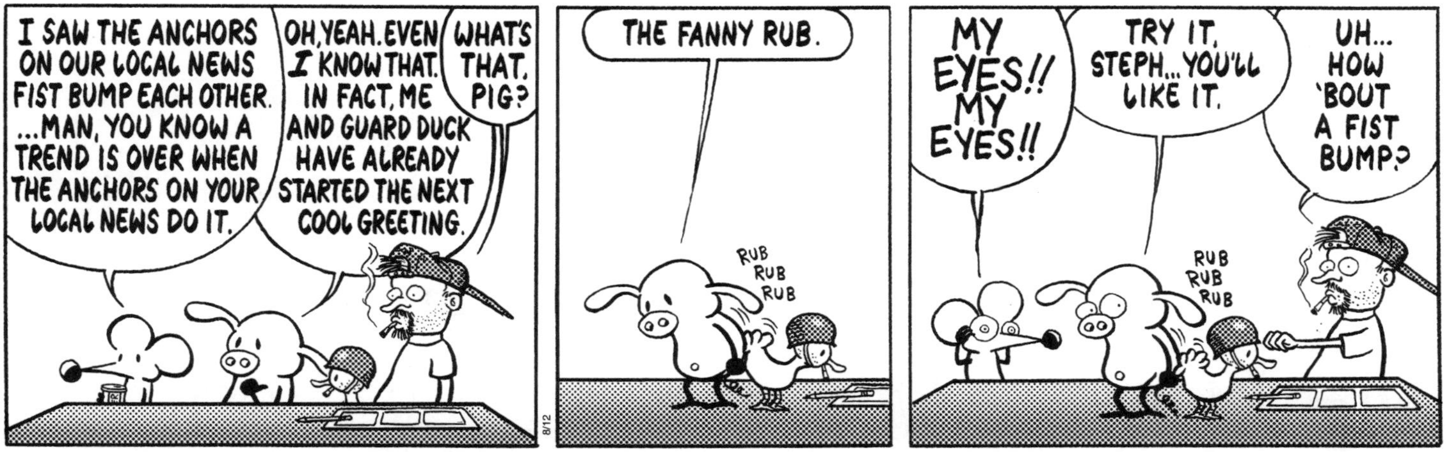
I SAW THE ANCHORS ON OUR LOCAL NEWS FIST BUMP EACH OTHER. ...MAN, YOU KNOW A TREND IS OVER WHEN THE ANCHORS ON YOUR LOCAL NEWS DO IT.
OH, YEAH. EVEN I KNOW THAT. IN FACT, ME AND GUARD DUCK HAVE ALREADY STARTED THE NEXT COOL GREETING.
WHAT'S THAT, PIG?
8/12
THE FANNY RUB.
RUB RUB RUB
MY EYES!! MY EYES!!
TRY IT, STEPH... YOU'LL LIKE IT.
UH... HOW 'BOUT A FIST BUMP?
RUB RUB RUB

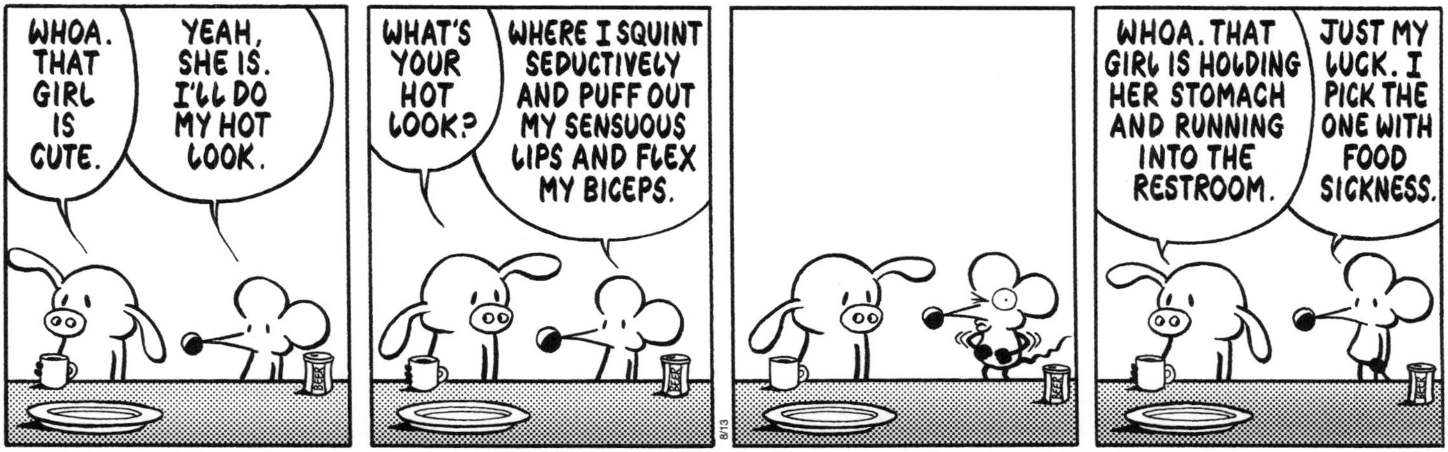
WHOA. THAT GIRL IS CUTE.
YEAH, SHE IS. I'LL DO MY HOT LOOK.
WHAT'S YOUR HOT LOOK?
WHERE I SQUINT SEDUCTIVELY AND PUFF OUT MY SENSUOUS LIPS AND FLEX MY BICEPS.
8/13
WHOA. THAT GIRL IS HOLDING HER STOMACH AND RUNNING INTO THE RESTROOM.
JUST MY LUCK. I PICK THE ONE WITH FOOD SICKNESS.

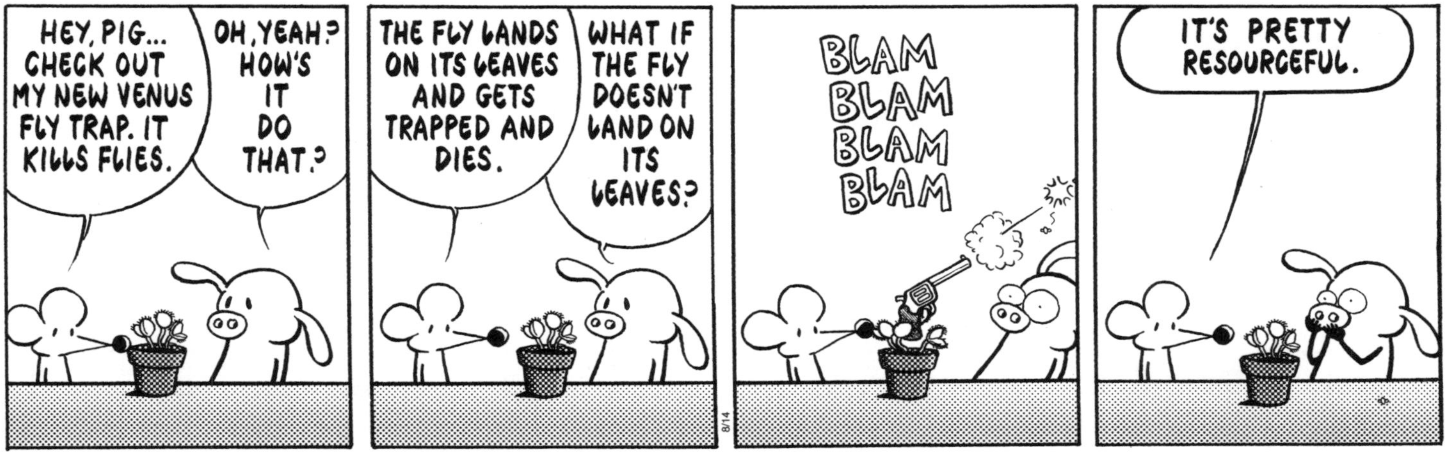
HEY, PIG... CHECK OUT MY NEW VENUS FLY TRAP. IT KILLS FLIES.
OH, YEAH? HOW'S IT DO THAT?
THE FLY LANDS ON ITS LEAVES AND GETS TRAPPED AND DIES.
WHAT IF THE FLY DOESN'T LAND ON ITS LEAVES?
8/14
BLAM BLAM BLAM BLAM
IT'S PRETTY RESOURCEFUL.

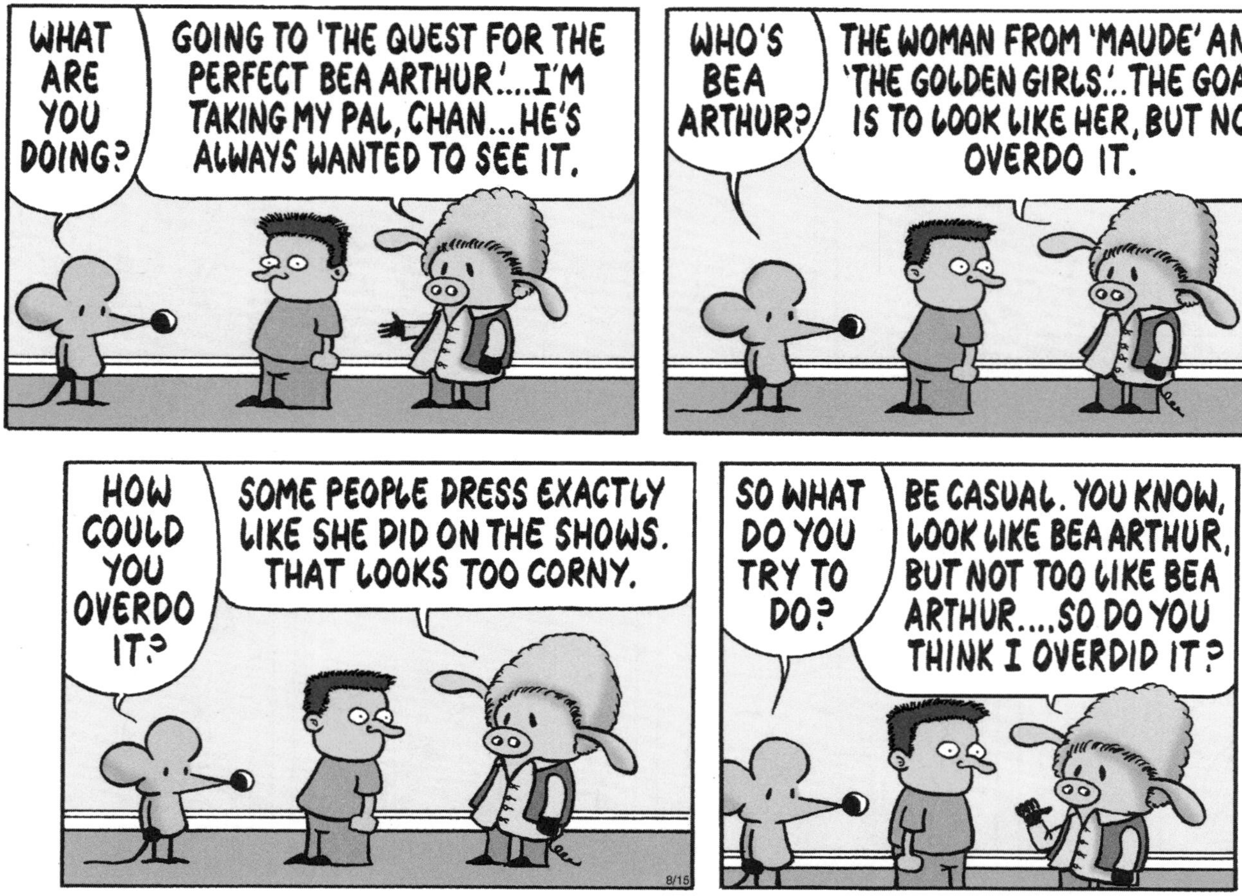
WHAT ARE YOU DOING?
GOING TO 'THE QUEST FOR THE PERFECT BEA ARTHUR.'...I'M TAKING MY PAL, CHAN...HE'S ALWAYS WANTED TO SEE IT.
WHO'S BEA ARTHUR?
THE WOMAN FROM 'MAUDE' AND 'THE GOLDEN GIRLS.'..THE GOAL IS TO LOOK LIKE HER, BUT NOT OVERDO IT.
HOW COULD YOU OVERDO IT?
SOME PEOPLE DRESS EXACTLY LIKE SHE DID ON THE SHOWS. THAT LOOKS TOO CORNY.
SO WHAT DO YOU TRY TO DO?
BE CASUAL. YOU KNOW, LOOK LIKE BEA ARTHUR, BUT NOT TOO LIKE BEA ARTHUR....SO DO YOU THINK I OVERDID IT?
8/15

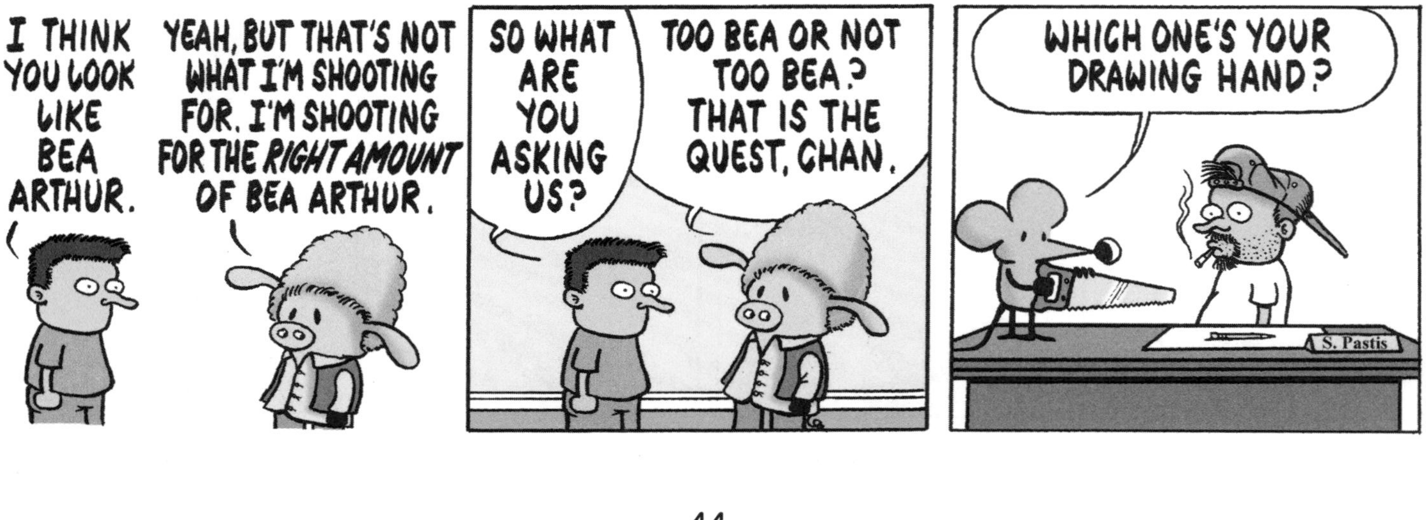
I THINK YOU LOOK LIKE BEA ARTHUR.
YEAH, BUT THAT'S NOT WHAT I'M SHOOTING FOR. I'M SHOOTING FOR THE *RIGHT AMOUNT* OF BEA ARTHUR.
SO WHAT ARE YOU ASKING US?
TOO BEA OR NOT TOO BEA? THAT IS THE QUEST, CHAN.
WHICH ONE'S YOUR DRAWING HAND?
S. Pastis

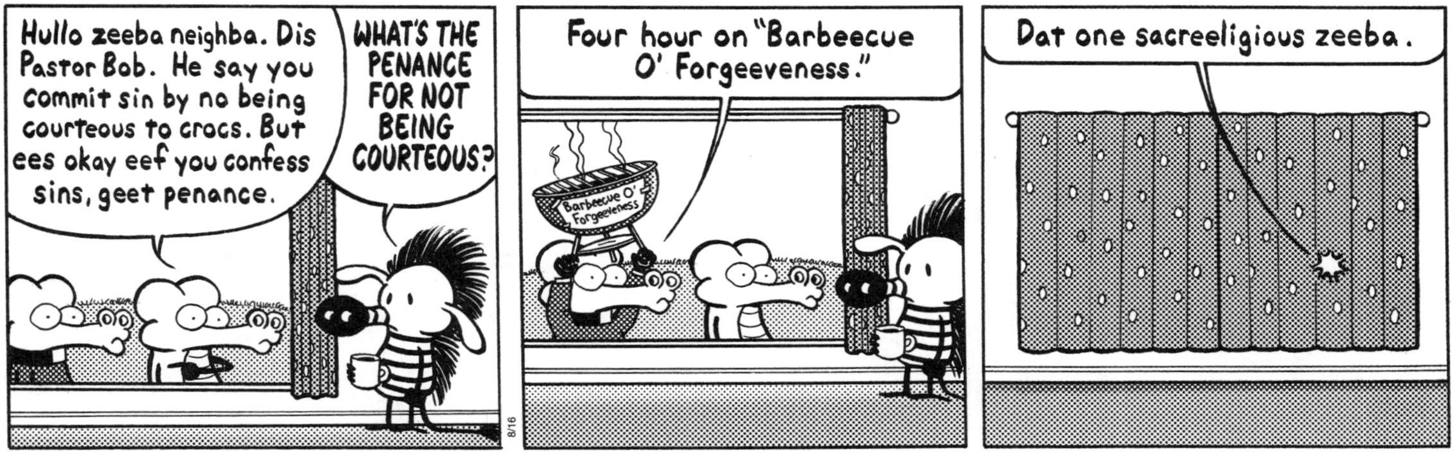
Hullo zeeba neighba. Dis Pastor Bob. He say you commit sin by no being courteous to crocs. But ees okay eef you confess sins, geet penance.
WHAT'S THE PENANCE FOR NOT BEING COURTEOUS?
8/16
Four hour on "Barbeecue O' Forgeeveness."
Barbeecue O' Forgeeveness
Dat one sacreeligious zeeba.

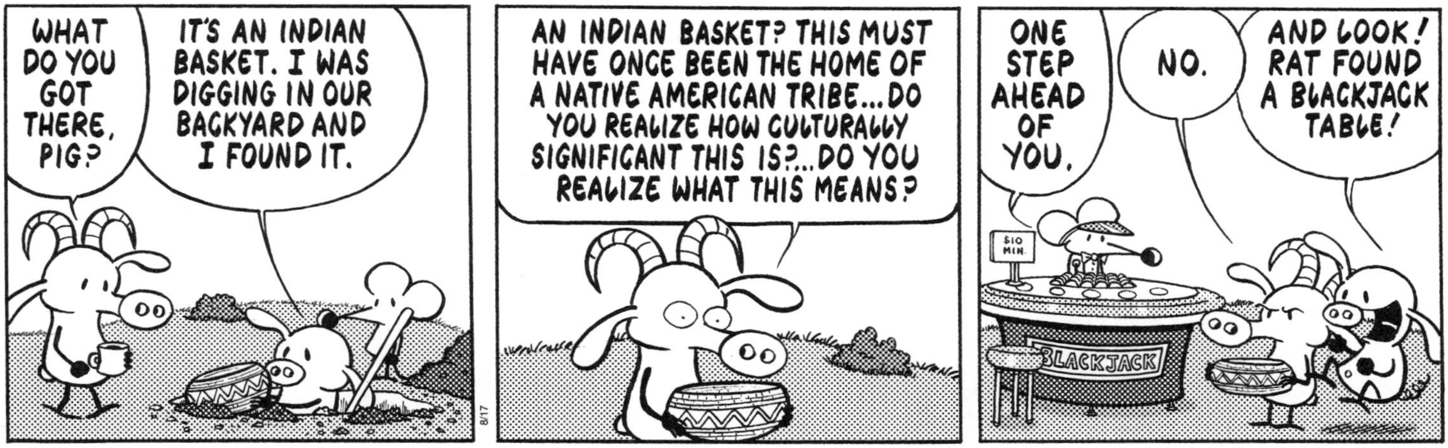
WHAT DO YOU GOT THERE, PIG?
IT'S AN INDIAN BASKET. I WAS DIGGING IN OUR BACKYARD AND I FOUND IT.
8/17
AN INDIAN BASKET? THIS MUST HAVE ONCE BEEN THE HOME OF A NATIVE AMERICAN TRIBE... DO YOU REALIZE HOW CULTURALLY SIGNIFICANT THIS IS?... DO YOU REALIZE WHAT THIS MEANS?
ONE STEP AHEAD OF YOU.
NO.
AND LOOK! RAT FOUND A BLACKJACK TABLE!
$10 MIN.
BLACKJACK

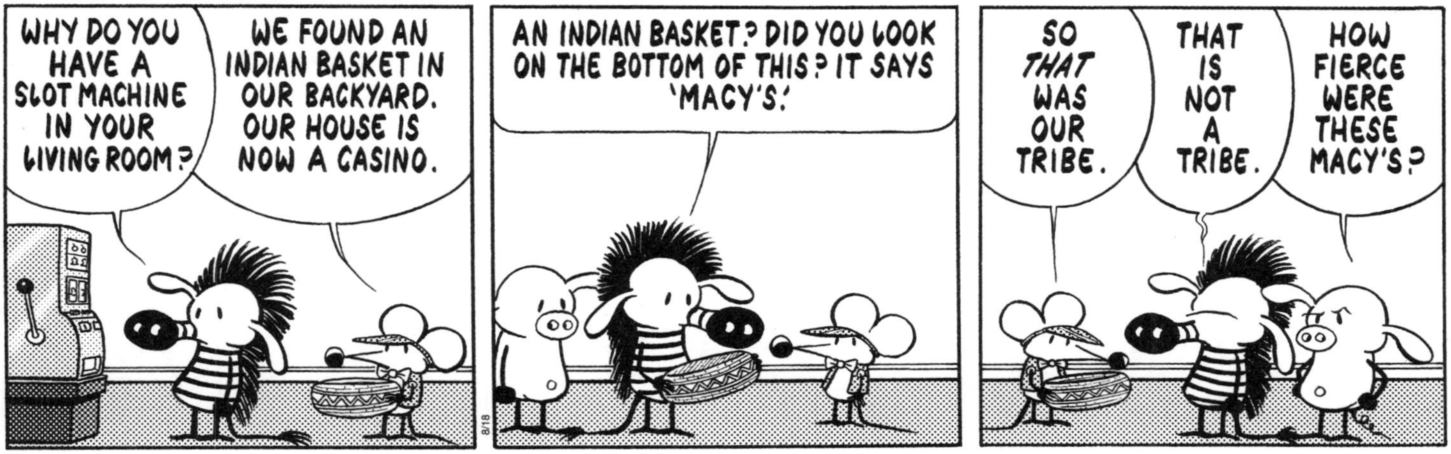
WHY DO YOU HAVE A SLOT MACHINE IN YOUR LIVING ROOM?
WE FOUND AN INDIAN BASKET IN OUR BACKYARD. OUR HOUSE IS NOW A CASINO.
8/18
AN INDIAN BASKET? DID YOU LOOK ON THE BOTTOM OF THIS? IT SAYS 'MACY'S.'
SO *THAT* WAS OUR TRIBE.
THAT IS NOT A TRIBE.
HOW FIERCE WERE THESE MACY'S?

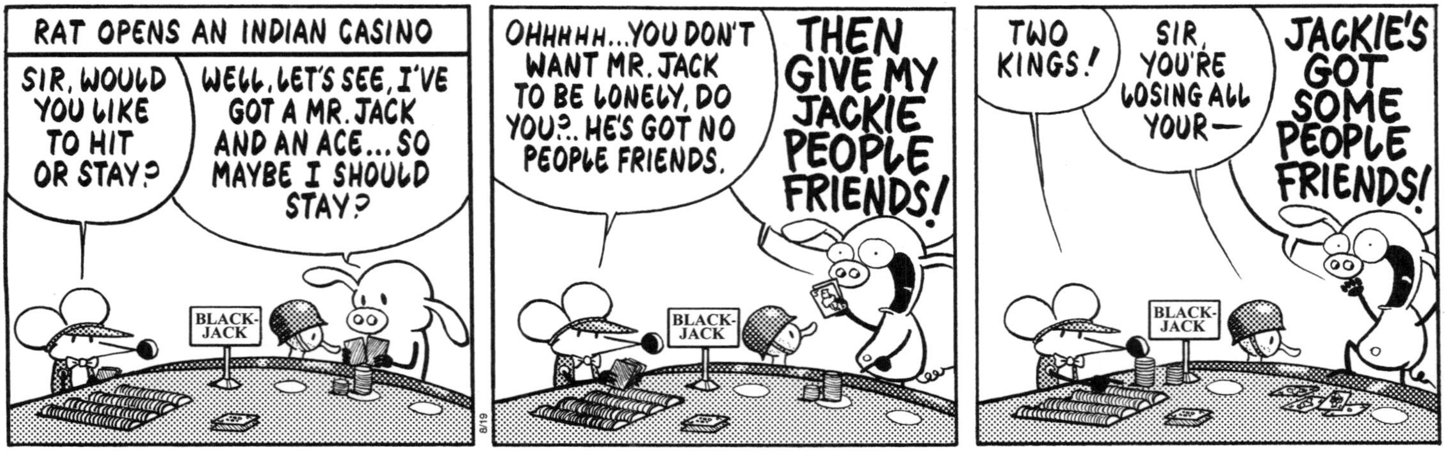
RAT OPENS AN INDIAN CASINO
SIR, WOULD YOU LIKE TO HIT OR STAY?
WELL, LET'S SEE, I'VE GOT A MR. JACK AND AN ACE... SO MAYBE I SHOULD STAY?
BLACK-JACK
8/19
OHHHHH... YOU DON'T WANT MR. JACK TO BE LONELY, DO YOU?.. HE'S GOT NO PEOPLE FRIENDS.
THEN GIVE MY JACKIE PEOPLE FRIENDS!
BLACK-JACK
TWO KINGS!
SIR, YOU'RE LOSING ALL YOUR—
JACKIE'S GOT SOME PEOPLE FRIENDS!
BLACK-JACK

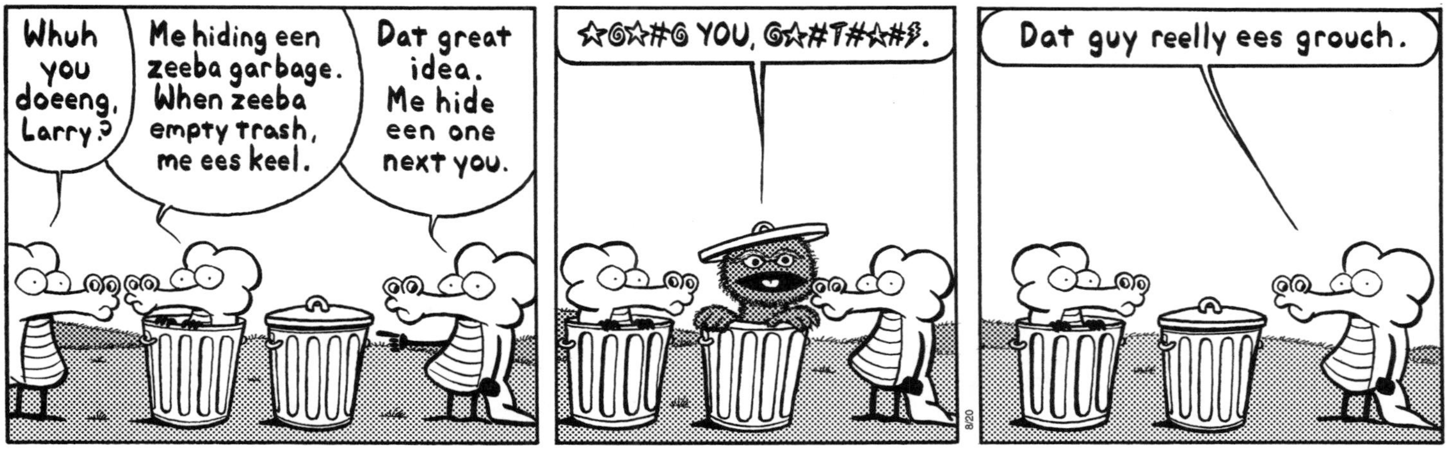
Whuh you doeeng, Larry?
Me hiding een zeeba garbage. When zeeba empty trash, me ees keel.
Dat great idea. Me hide een one next you.
☆@☆#@ YOU, @☆#T#☆#$.
8/20
Dat guy reelly ees grouch.

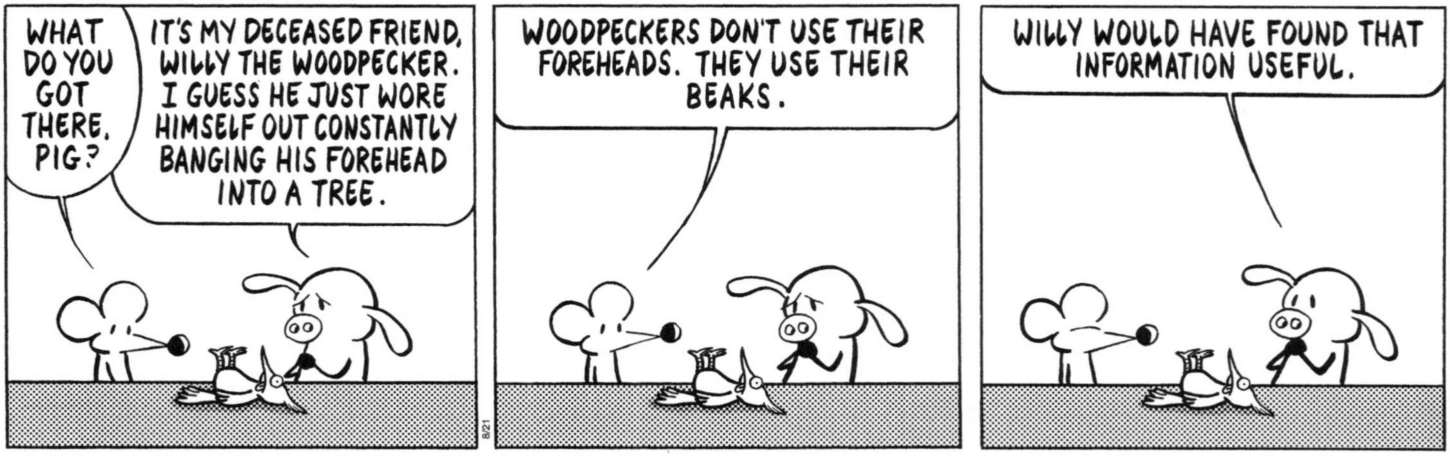
WHAT DO YOU GOT THERE, PIG?
IT'S MY DECEASED FRIEND, WILLY THE WOODPECKER. I GUESS HE JUST WORE HIMSELF OUT CONSTANTLY BANGING HIS FOREHEAD INTO A TREE.
8/21
WOODPECKERS DON'T USE THEIR FOREHEADS. THEY USE THEIR BEAKS.
WILLY WOULD HAVE FOUND THAT INFORMATION USEFUL.

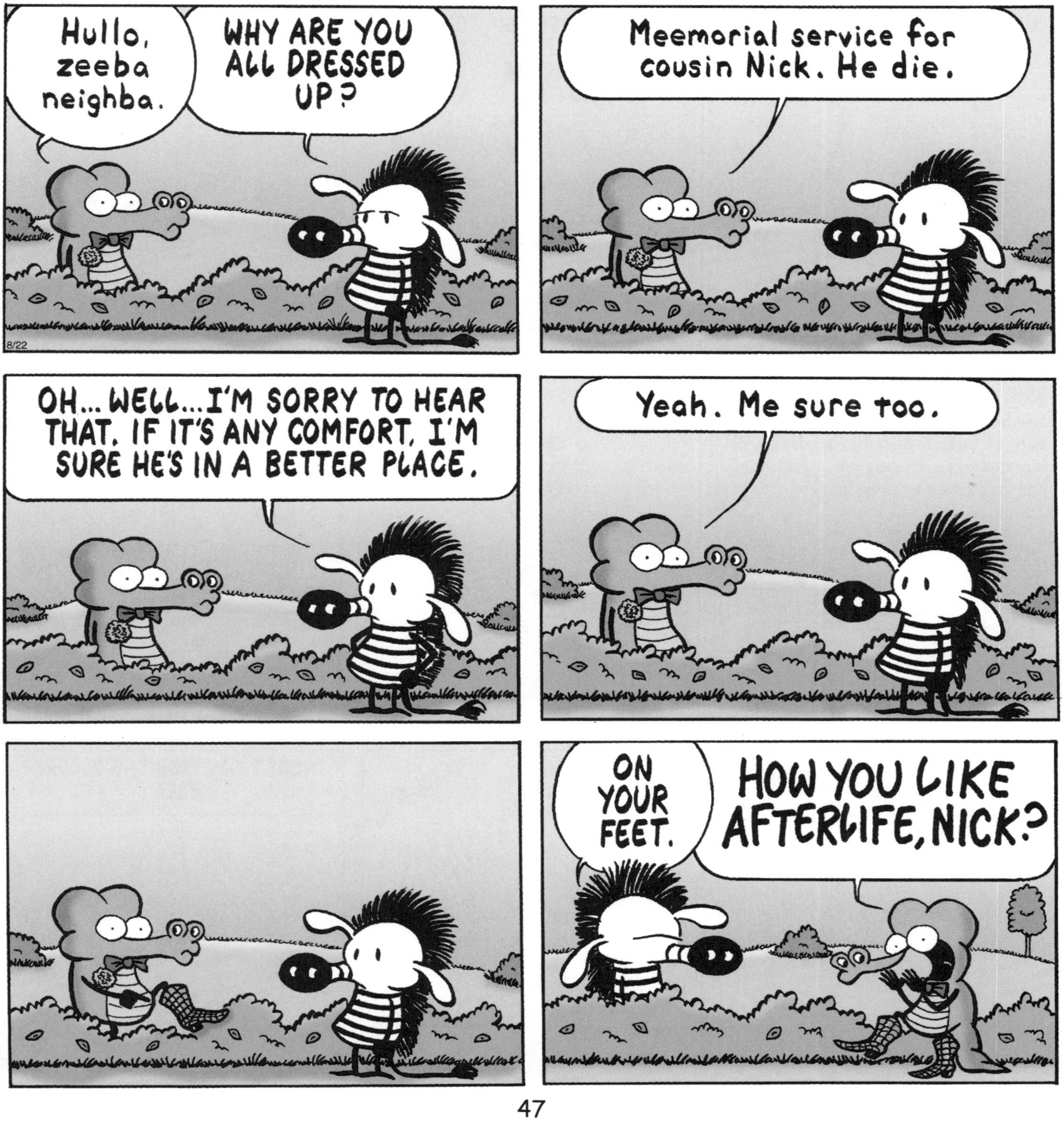
Hullo, zeeba neighba.
WHY ARE YOU ALL DRESSED UP?
8/22
Meemorial service for cousin Nick. He die.
OH... WELL... I'M SORRY TO HEAR THAT. IF IT'S ANY COMFORT, I'M SURE HE'S IN A BETTER PLACE.
Yeah. Me sure too.
ON YOUR FEET.
HOW YOU LIKE AFTERLIFE, NICK?

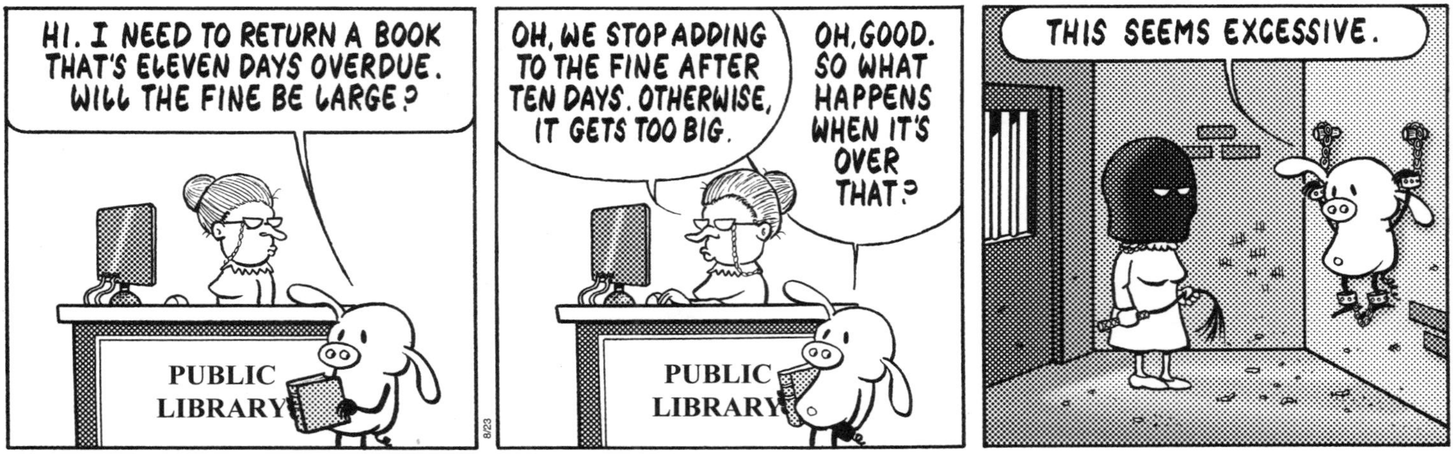
HI. I NEED TO RETURN A BOOK THAT'S ELEVEN DAYS OVERDUE. WILL THE FINE BE LARGE?
PUBLIC LIBRARY
OH, WE STOP ADDING TO THE FINE AFTER TEN DAYS. OTHERWISE, IT GETS TOO BIG.
OH, GOOD. SO WHAT HAPPENS WHEN IT'S OVER THAT?
PUBLIC LIBRARY
THIS SEEMS EXCESSIVE.

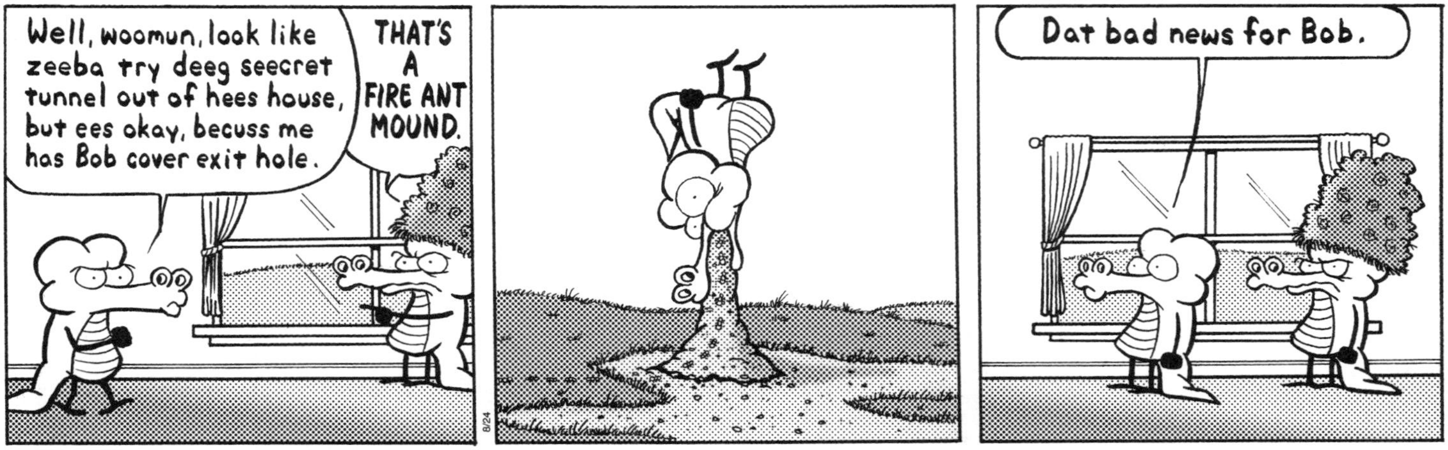
Well, woomun, look like zeeba try deeg seecret tunnel out of hees house, but ees okay, becuss me has Bob cover exit hole.
THAT'S A FIRE ANT MOUND.
Dat bad news for Bob.

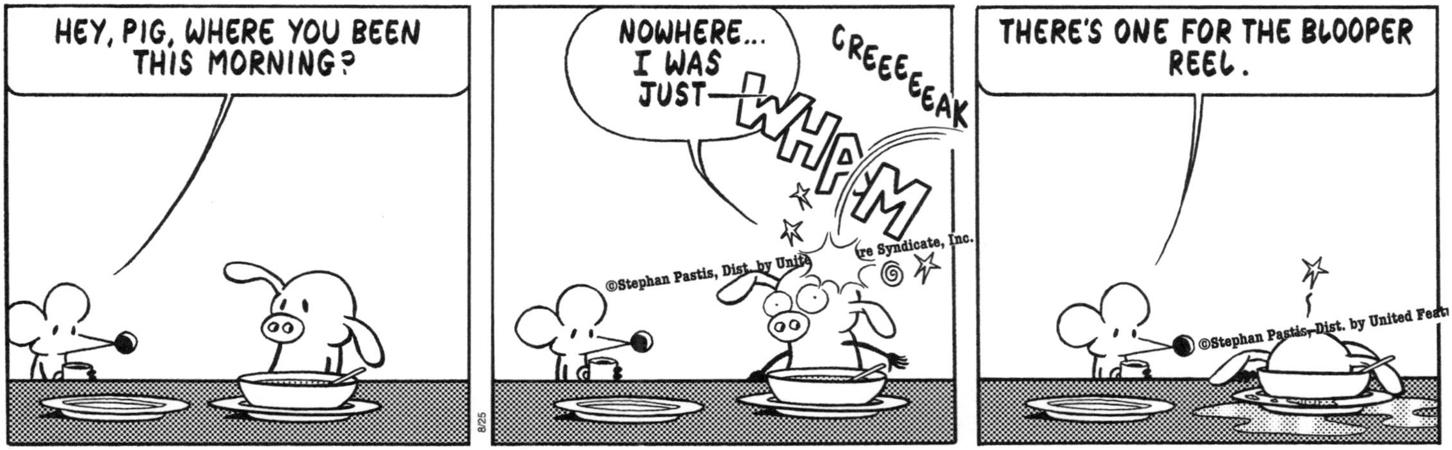
HEY, PIG, WHERE YOU BEEN THIS MORNING?
NOWHERE... I WAS JUST—
CREEEEEEAK
WHAM
THERE'S ONE FOR THE BLOOPER REEL.

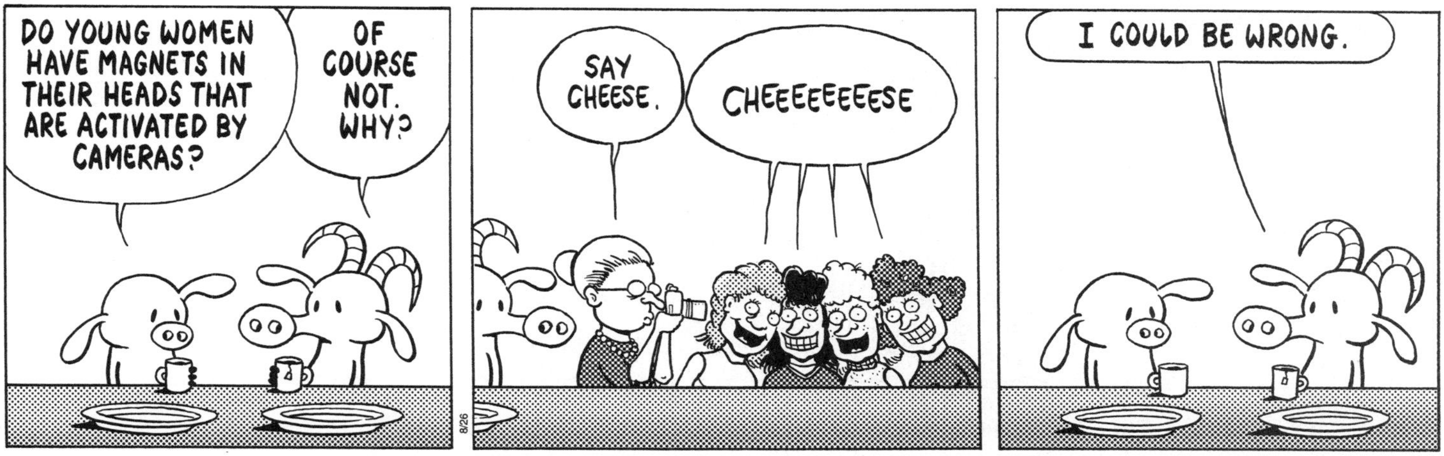
DO YOUNG WOMEN HAVE MAGNETS IN THEIR HEADS THAT ARE ACTIVATED BY CAMERAS?
OF COURSE NOT. WHY?
8/26
SAY CHEESE.
CHEEEEEEEEESE
I COULD BE WRONG.

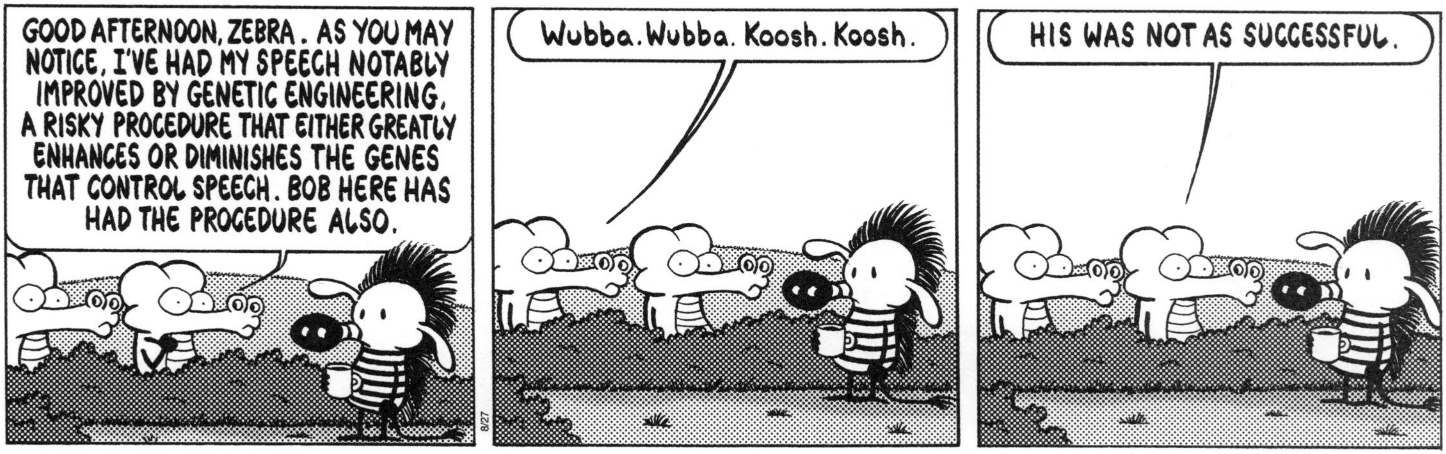
GOOD AFTERNOON, ZEBRA. AS YOU MAY NOTICE, I'VE HAD MY SPEECH NOTABLY IMPROVED BY GENETIC ENGINEERING, A RISKY PROCEDURE THAT EITHER GREATLY ENHANCES OR DIMINISHES THE GENES THAT CONTROL SPEECH. BOB HERE HAS HAD THE PROCEDURE ALSO.
8/27
Wubba. Wubba. Koosh. Koosh.
HIS WAS NOT AS SUCCESSFUL.

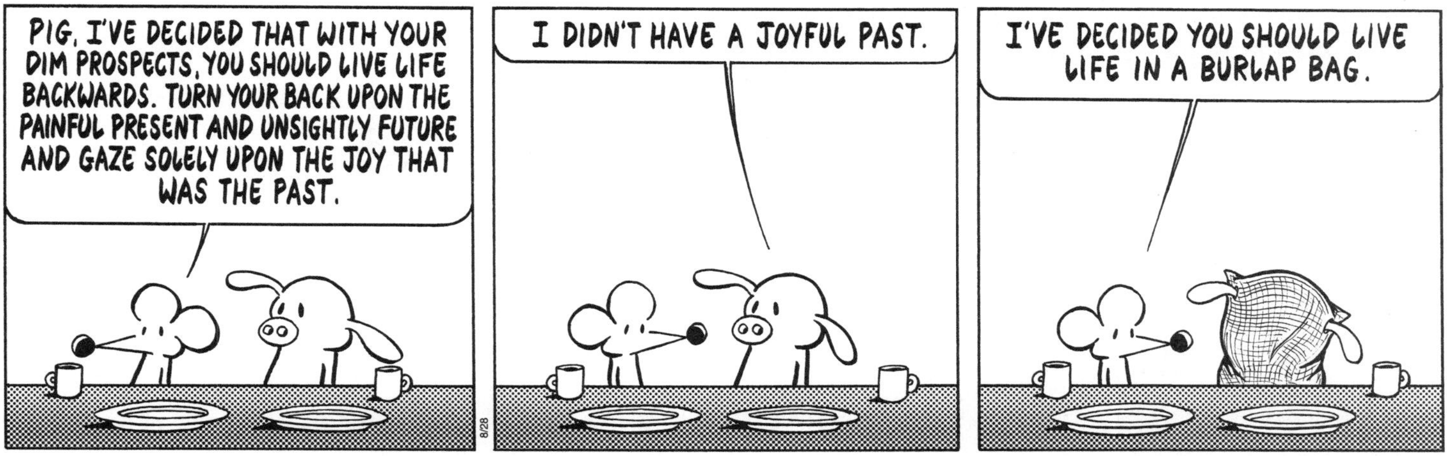
PIG, I'VE DECIDED THAT WITH YOUR DIM PROSPECTS, YOU SHOULD LIVE LIFE BACKWARDS. TURN YOUR BACK UPON THE PAINFUL PRESENT AND UNSIGHTLY FUTURE AND GAZE SOLELY UPON THE JOY THAT WAS THE PAST.
8/28
I DIDN'T HAVE A JOYFUL PAST.
I'VE DECIDED YOU SHOULD LIVE LIFE IN A BURLAP BAG.

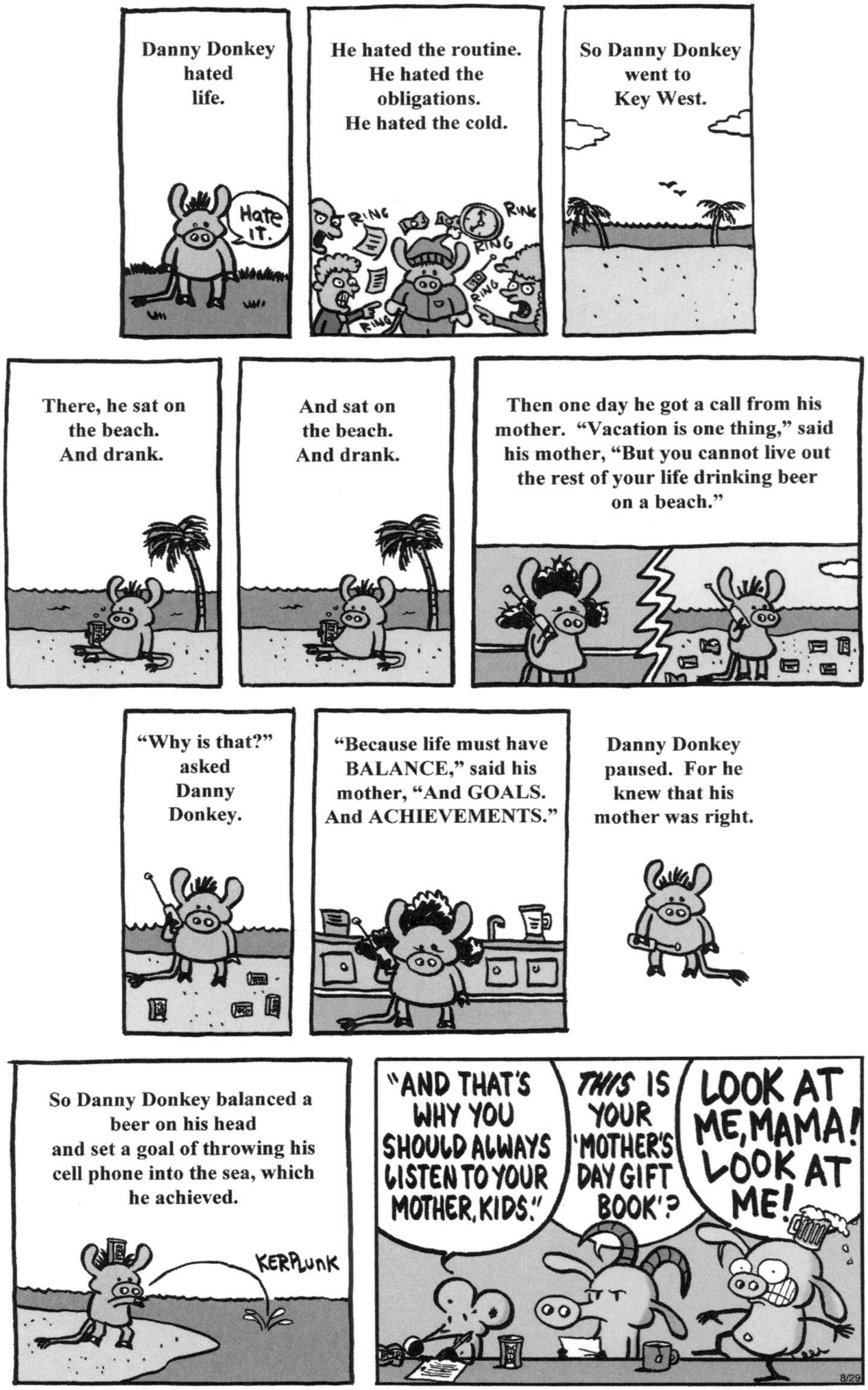
Danny Donkey hated life.
Hate it.
He hated the routine. He hated the obligations. He hated the cold.
So Danny Donkey went to Key West.
There, he sat on the beach. And drank.
And sat on the beach. And drank.
Then one day he got a call from his mother. "Vacation is one thing," said his mother, "But you cannot live out the rest of your life drinking beer on a beach."
"Why is that?" asked Danny Donkey.
"Because life must have BALANCE," said his mother, "And GOALS. And ACHIEVEMENTS."
Danny Donkey paused. For he knew that his mother was right.
So Danny Donkey balanced a beer on his head and set a goal of throwing his cell phone into the sea, which he achieved.
KERPLUNK
"AND THAT'S WHY YOU SHOULD ALWAYS LISTEN TO YOUR MOTHER, KIDS."
THIS IS YOUR 'MOTHER'S DAY GIFT BOOK'?
LOOK AT ME, MAMA! LOOK AT ME!

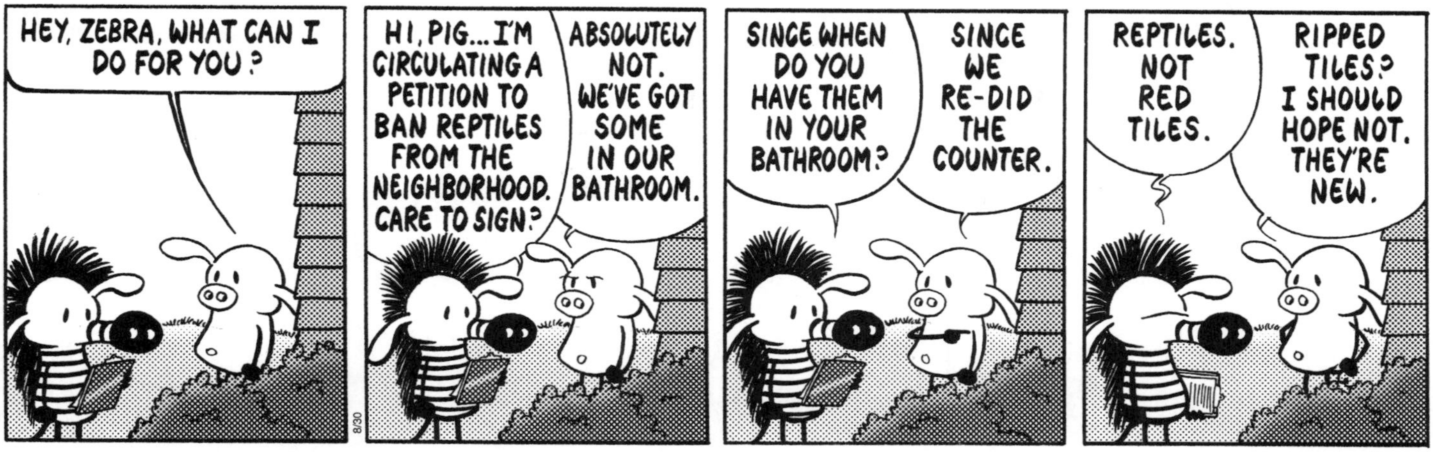
HEY, ZEBRA, WHAT CAN I DO FOR YOU?
HI, PIG... I'M CIRCULATING A PETITION TO BAN REPTILES FROM THE NEIGHBORHOOD. CARE TO SIGN?
ABSOLUTELY NOT. WE'VE GOT SOME IN OUR BATHROOM.
SINCE WHEN DO YOU HAVE THEM IN YOUR BATHROOM?
SINCE WE RE-DID THE COUNTER.
REPTILES. NOT RED TILES.
RIPPED TILES? I SHOULD HOPE NOT. THEY'RE NEW.
8/30

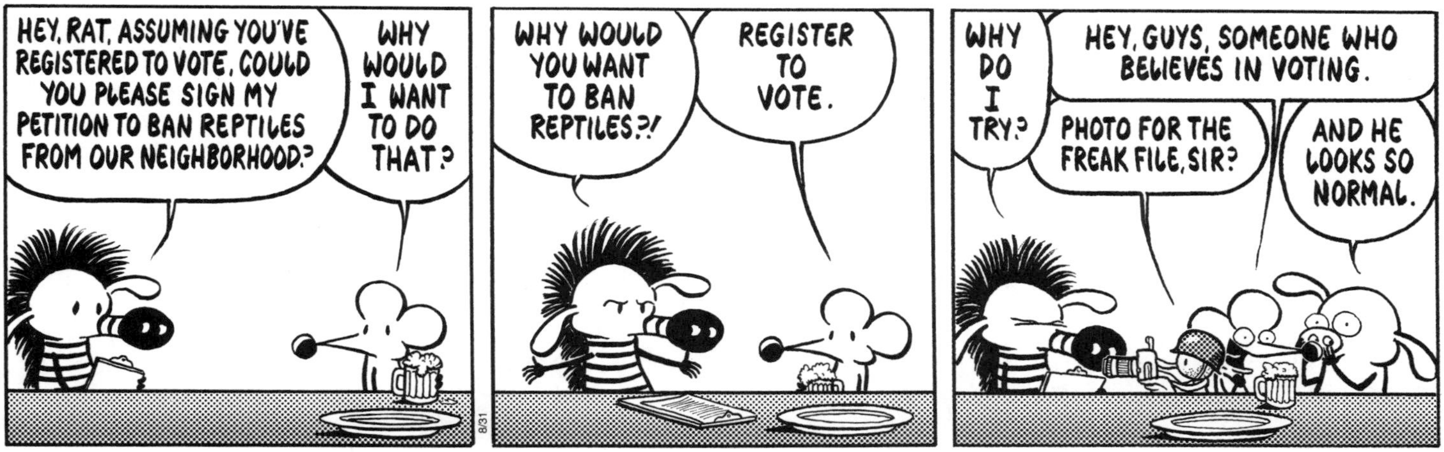
HEY, RAT, ASSUMING YOU'VE REGISTERED TO VOTE, COULD YOU PLEASE SIGN MY PETITION TO BAN REPTILES FROM OUR NEIGHBORHOOD?
WHY WOULD I WANT TO DO THAT?
WHY WOULD YOU WANT TO BAN REPTILES?!
REGISTER TO VOTE.
WHY DO I TRY?
HEY, GUYS, SOMEONE WHO BELIEVES IN VOTING.
PHOTO FOR THE FREAK FILE, SIR?
AND HE LOOKS SO NORMAL.
8/31

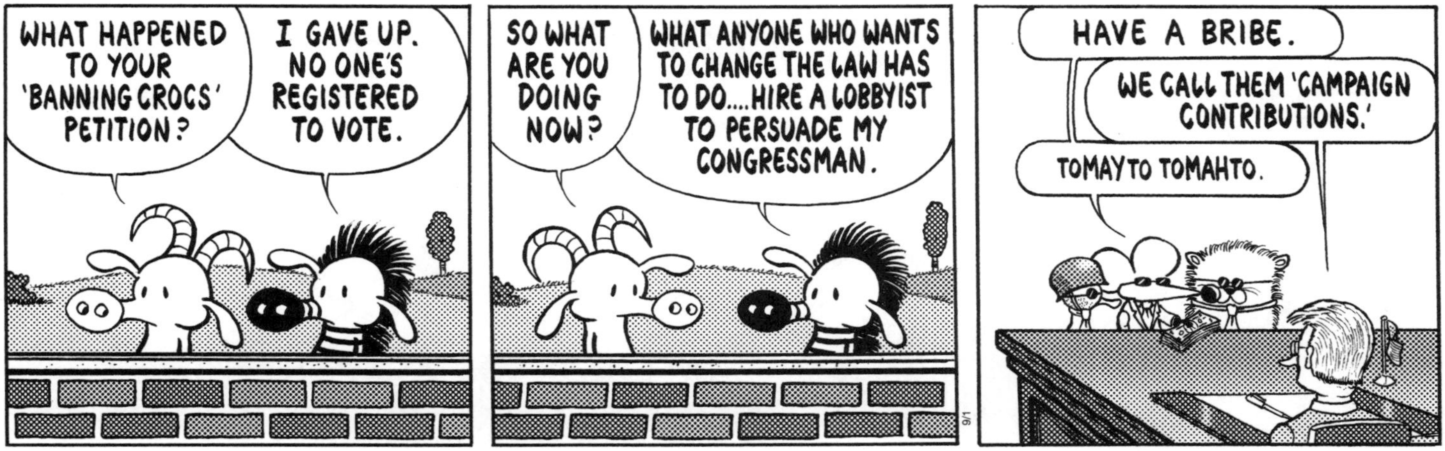
WHAT HAPPENED TO YOUR 'BANNING CROCS' PETITION?
I GAVE UP. NO ONE'S REGISTERED TO VOTE.
SO WHAT ARE YOU DOING NOW?
WHAT ANYONE WHO WANTS TO CHANGE THE LAW HAS TO DO.... HIRE A LOBBYIST TO PERSUADE MY CONGRESSMAN.
HAVE A BRIBE.
WE CALL THEM 'CAMPAIGN CONTRIBUTIONS.'
TOMAYTO TOMAHTO.
9/1

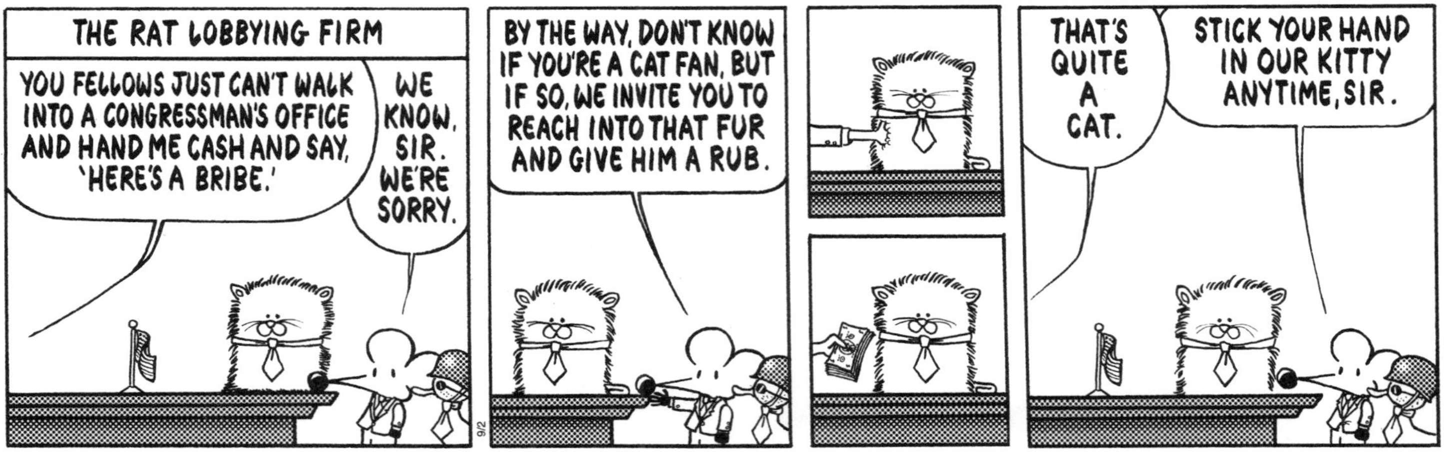
THE RAT LOBBYING FIRM
YOU FELLOWS JUST CAN'T WALK INTO A CONGRESSMAN'S OFFICE AND HAND ME CASH AND SAY, 'HERE'S A BRIBE.'
WE KNOW, SIR. WE'RE SORRY.
BY THE WAY, DON'T KNOW IF YOU'RE A CAT FAN, BUT IF SO, WE INVITE YOU TO REACH INTO THAT FUR AND GIVE HIM A RUB.
THAT'S QUITE A CAT.
STICK YOUR HAND IN OUR KITTY ANYTIME, SIR.
9/2

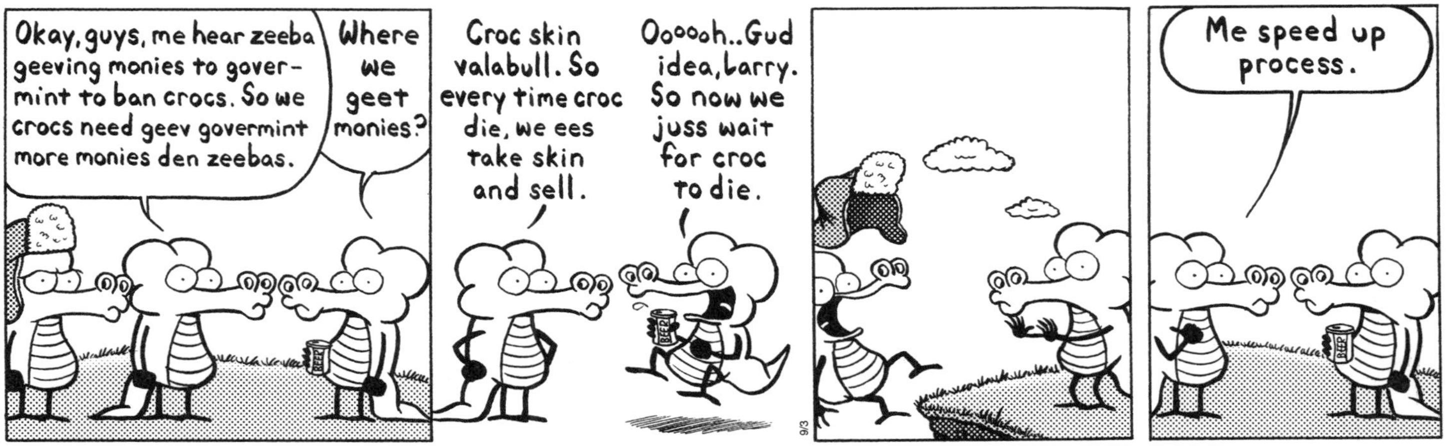
Okay, guys, me hear zeeba geeving monies to govermint to ban crocs. So we crocs need geev govermint more monies den zeebas.
Where we geet monies?
Croc skin valabull. So every time croc die, we ees take skin and sell.
Oooooh.. Gud idea, Larry. So now we juss wait for croc to die.
Me speed up process.
9/3

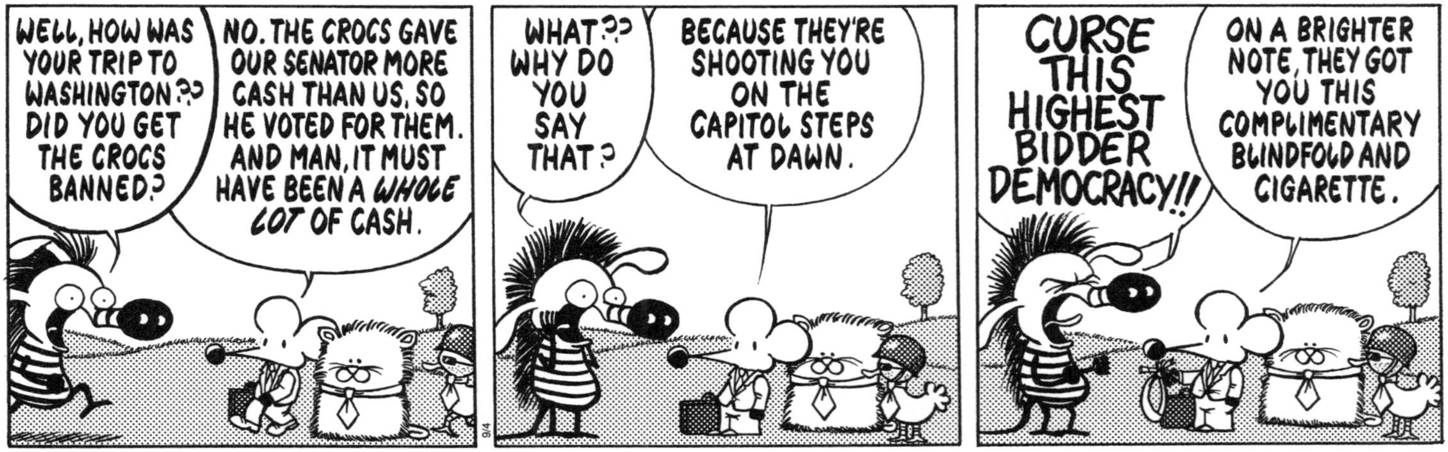
WELL, HOW WAS YOUR TRIP TO WASHINGTON?? DID YOU GET THE CROCS BANNED?
NO. THE CROCS GAVE OUR SENATOR MORE CASH THAN US, SO HE VOTED FOR THEM. AND MAN, IT MUST HAVE BEEN A WHOLE LOT OF CASH.
WHAT?? WHY DO YOU SAY THAT?
BECAUSE THEY'RE SHOOTING YOU ON THE CAPITOL STEPS AT DAWN.
CURSE THIS HIGHEST BIDDER DEMOCRACY!!
ON A BRIGHTER NOTE, THEY GOT YOU THIS COMPLIMENTARY BLINDFOLD AND CIGARETTE.
9/4

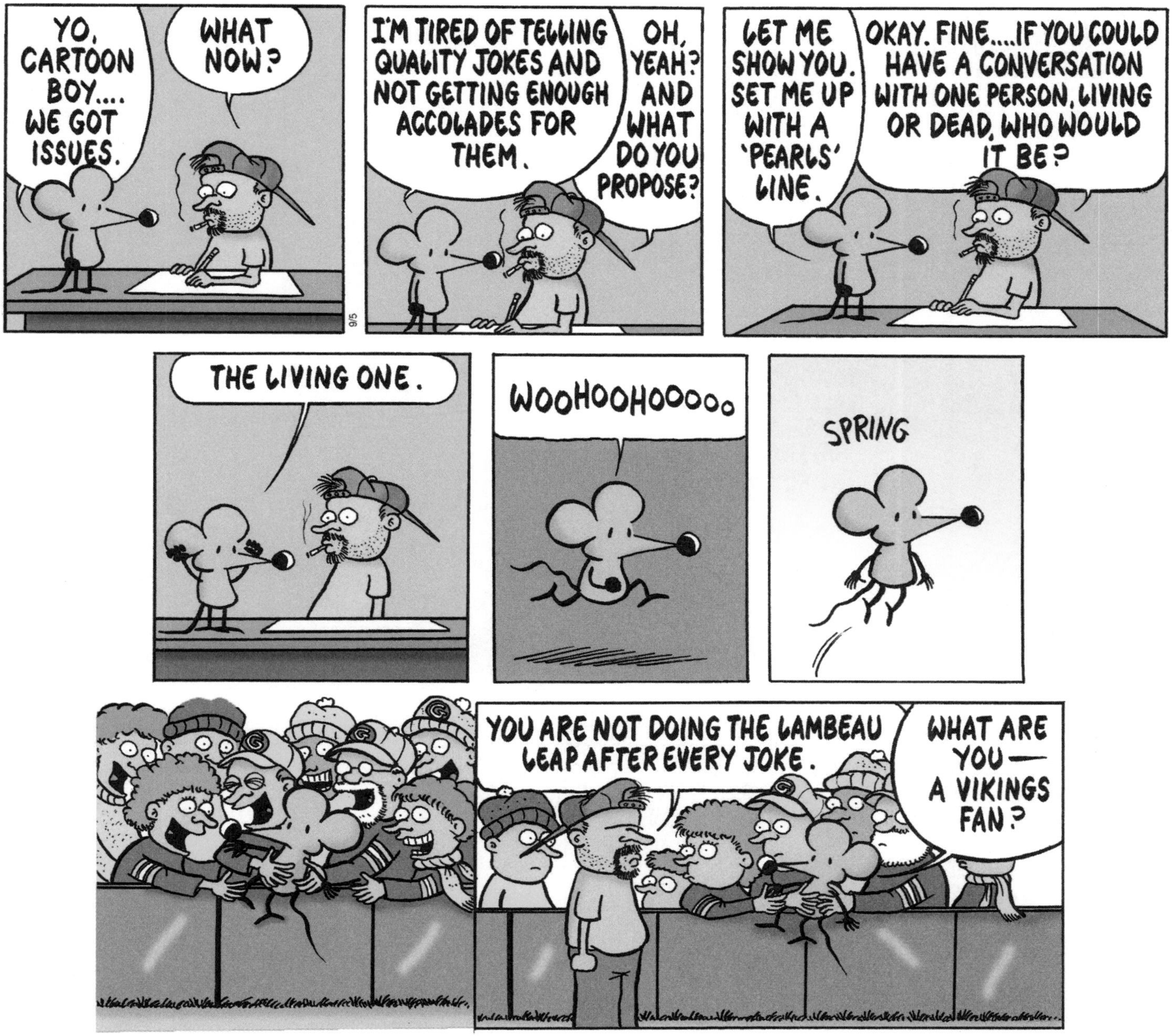
YO, CARTOON BOY.... WE GOT ISSUES.
WHAT NOW?
I'M TIRED OF TELLING QUALITY JOKES AND NOT GETTING ENOUGH ACCOLADES FOR THEM.
OH, YEAH? AND WHAT DO YOU PROPOSE?
LET ME SHOW YOU. SET ME UP WITH A 'PEARLS' LINE.
OKAY. FINE....IF YOU COULD HAVE A CONVERSATION WITH ONE PERSON, LIVING OR DEAD, WHO WOULD IT BE?
THE LIVING ONE.
WOOHOOHOOOOO
SPRING
YOU ARE NOT DOING THE LAMBEAU LEAP AFTER EVERY JOKE.
WHAT ARE YOU— A VIKINGS FAN?

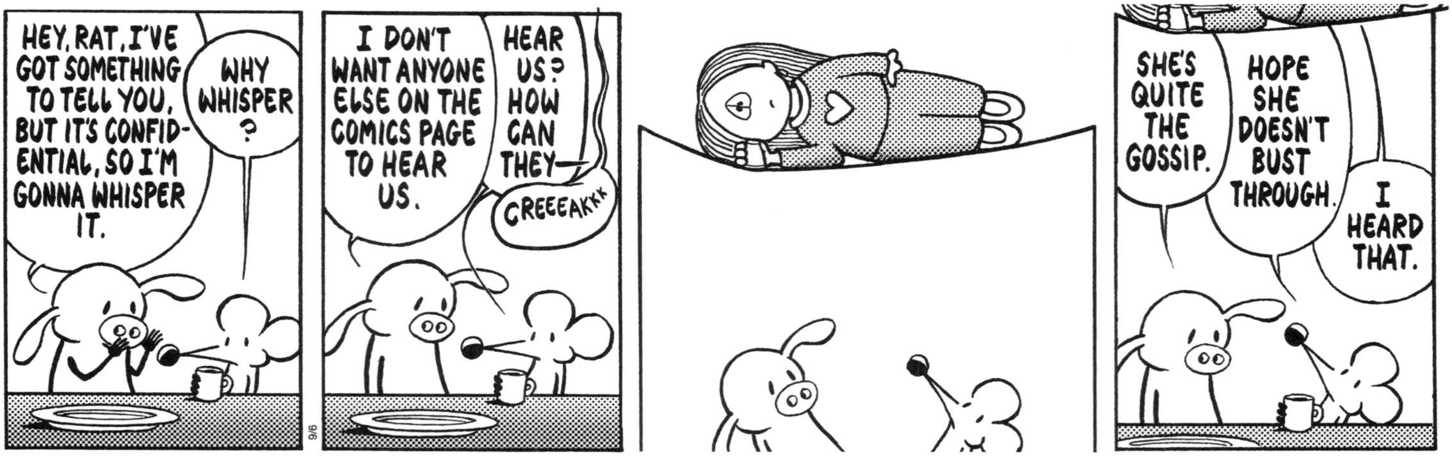
HEY, RAT, I'VE GOT SOMETHING TO TELL YOU, BUT IT'S CONFIDENTIAL, SO I'M GONNA WHISPER IT.
WHY WHISPER?
I DON'T WANT ANYONE ELSE ON THE COMICS PAGE TO HEAR US.
HEAR US? HOW CAN THEY—
CREEEAKKK
SHE'S QUITE THE GOSSIP.
HOPE SHE DOESN'T BUST THROUGH.
I HEARD THAT.

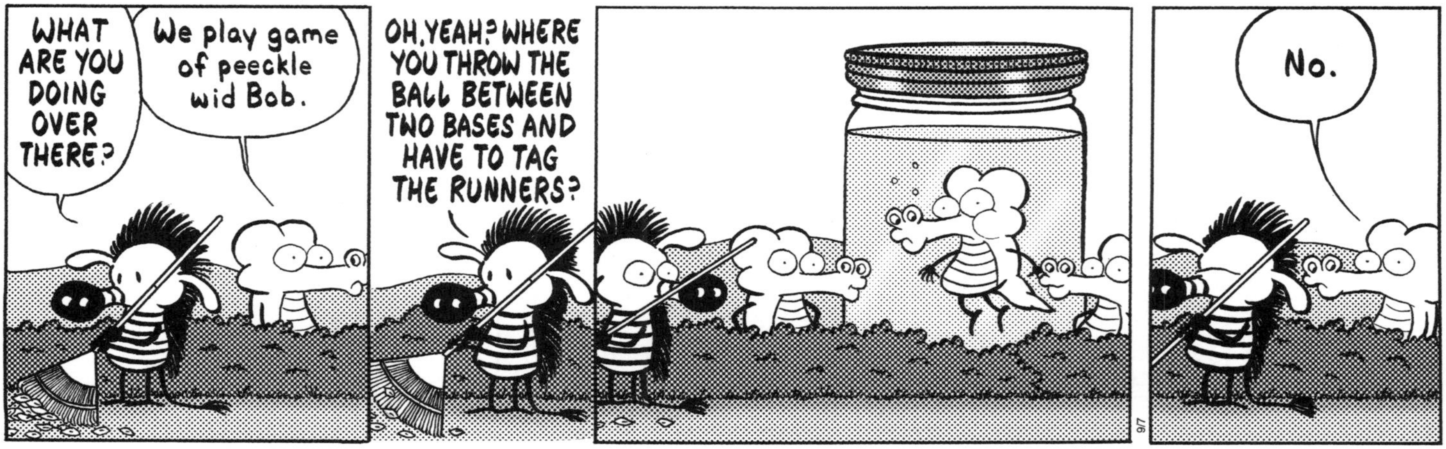
WHAT ARE YOU DOING OVER THERE?
We play game of peeckle wid Bob.
OH, YEAH? WHERE YOU THROW THE BALL BETWEEN TWO BASES AND HAVE TO TAG THE RUNNERS?
No.

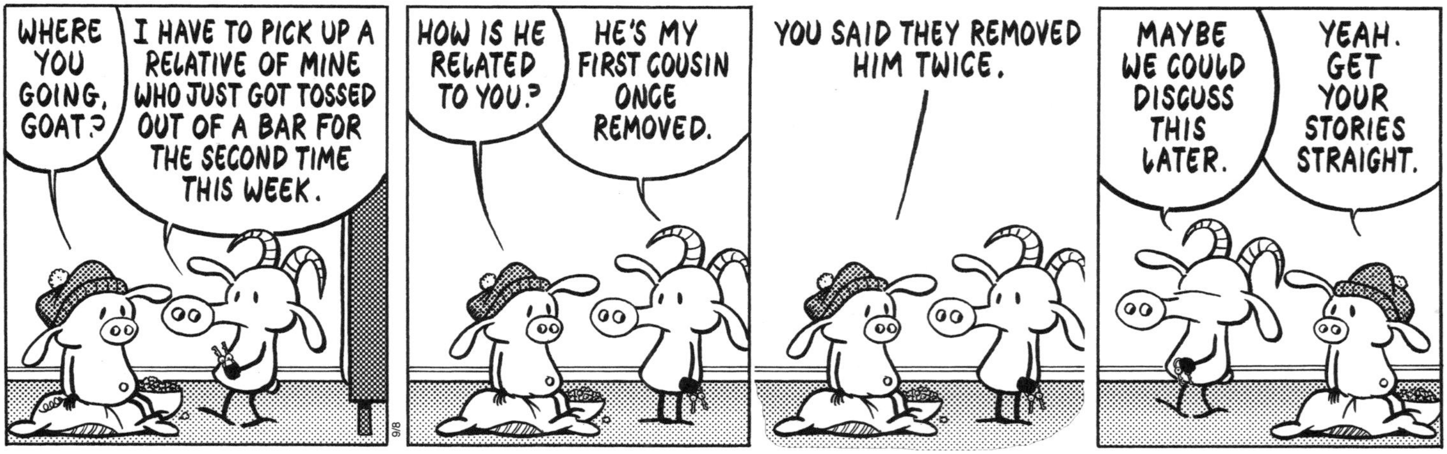
WHERE YOU GOING, GOAT?
I HAVE TO PICK UP A RELATIVE OF MINE WHO JUST GOT TOSSED OUT OF A BAR FOR THE SECOND TIME THIS WEEK.
HOW IS HE RELATED TO YOU?
HE'S MY FIRST COUSIN ONCE REMOVED.
YOU SAID THEY REMOVED HIM TWICE.
MAYBE WE COULD DISCUSS THIS LATER.
YEAH. GET YOUR STORIES STRAIGHT.

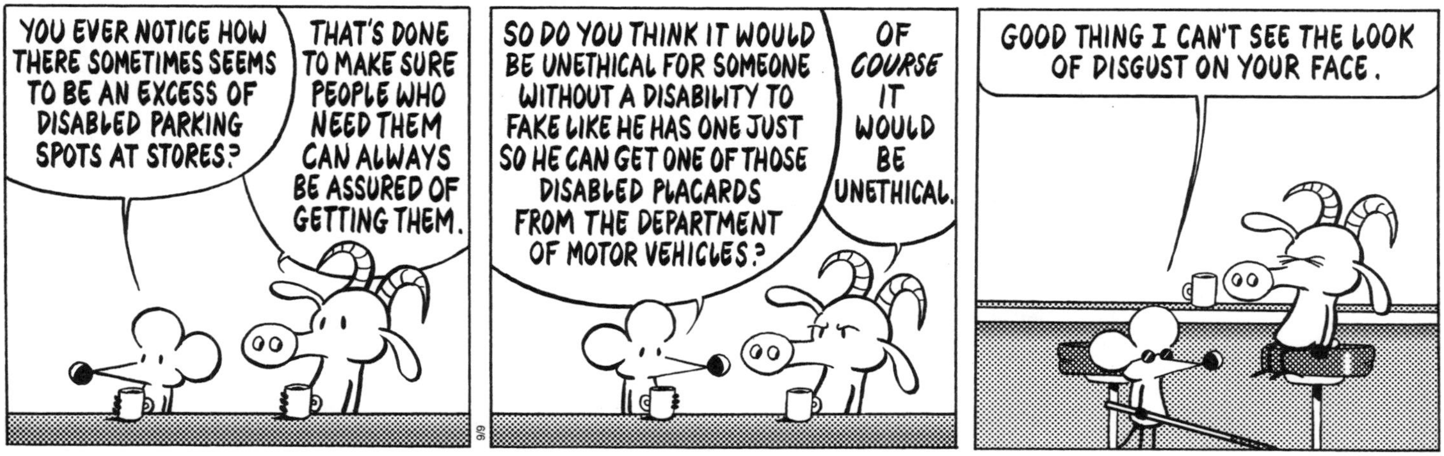
YOU EVER NOTICE HOW THERE SOMETIMES SEEMS TO BE AN EXCESS OF DISABLED PARKING SPOTS AT STORES?
THAT'S DONE TO MAKE SURE PEOPLE WHO NEED THEM CAN ALWAYS BE ASSURED OF GETTING THEM.
SO DO YOU THINK IT WOULD BE UNETHICAL FOR SOMEONE WITHOUT A DISABILITY TO FAKE LIKE HE HAS ONE JUST SO HE CAN GET ONE OF THOSE DISABLED PLACARDS FROM THE DEPARTMENT OF MOTOR VEHICLES?
OF *COURSE* IT WOULD BE UNETHICAL.
GOOD THING I CAN'T SEE THE LOOK OF DISGUST ON YOUR FACE.
9/9

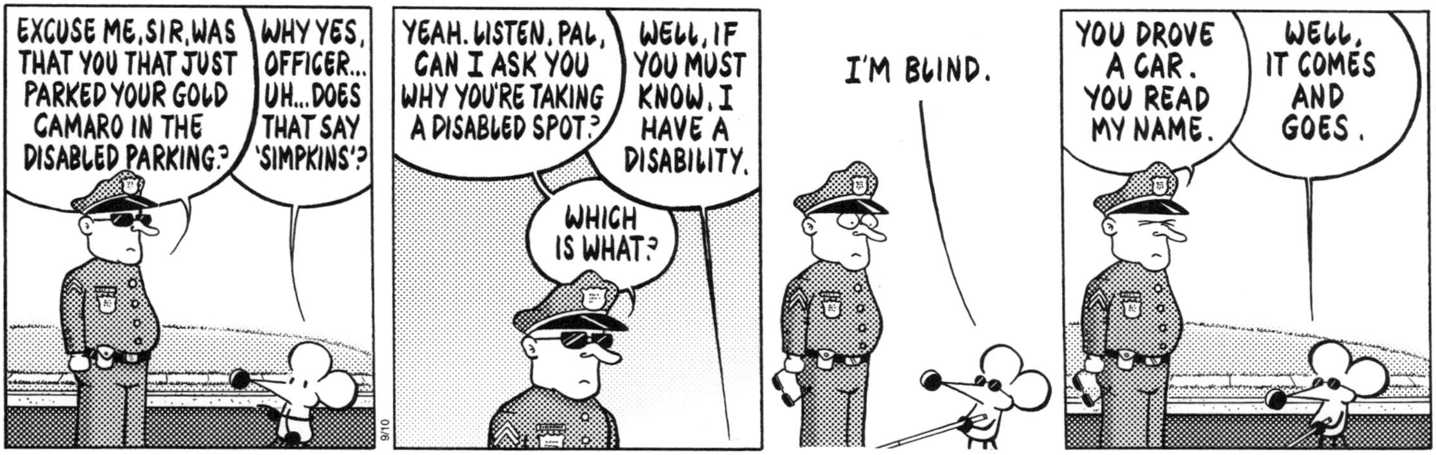
EXCUSE ME, SIR, WAS THAT YOU THAT JUST PARKED YOUR GOLD CAMARO IN THE DISABLED PARKING?
WHY YES, OFFICER... UH... DOES THAT SAY 'SIMPKINS'?
YEAH. LISTEN, PAL, CAN I ASK YOU WHY YOU'RE TAKING A DISABLED SPOT?
WELL, IF YOU MUST KNOW, I HAVE A DISABILITY.
WHICH IS WHAT?
I'M BLIND.
YOU DROVE A CAR. YOU READ MY NAME.
WELL, IT COMES AND GOES.
9/10

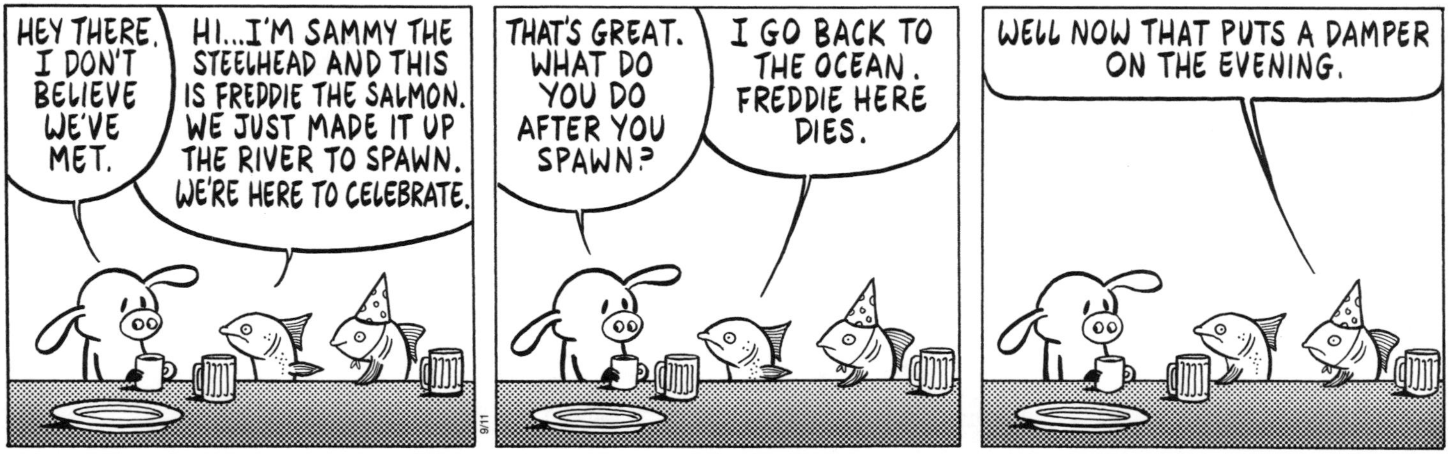
HEY THERE. I DON'T BELIEVE WE'VE MET.
HI...I'M SAMMY THE STEELHEAD AND THIS IS FREDDIE THE SALMON. WE JUST MADE IT UP THE RIVER TO SPAWN. WE'RE HERE TO CELEBRATE.
THAT'S GREAT. WHAT DO YOU DO AFTER YOU SPAWN?
I GO BACK TO THE OCEAN. FREDDIE HERE DIES.
WELL NOW THAT PUTS A DAMPER ON THE EVENING.
9/11

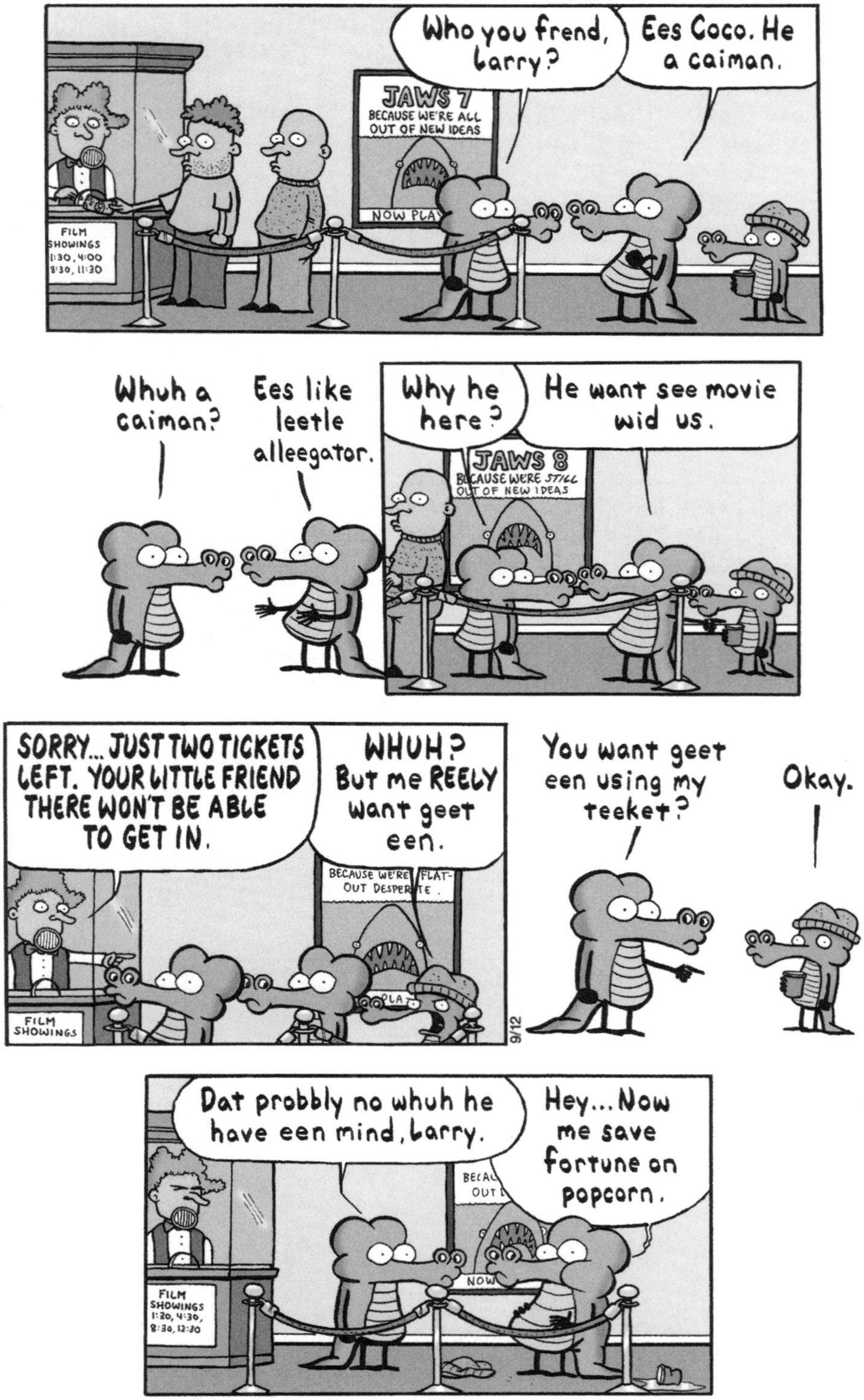

FILM SHOWINGS 1:30, 4:00 8:30, 11:30
JAWS 7 BECAUSE WE'RE ALL OUT OF NEW IDEAS
Who you frend, Larry?
Ees Coco. He a caiman.
Whuh a caiman?
Ees like leetle alleegator.
JAWS 8 BECAUSE WERE STILL OUT OF NEW IDEAS
Why he here?
He want see movie wid us.
SORRY... JUST TWO TICKETS LEFT. YOUR LITTLE FRIEND THERE WON'T BE ABLE TO GET IN.
WHUH? But me REELY want geet een.
FILM SHOWINGS
9/12
You want geet een using my teeket?
Okay.
FILM SHOWINGS 1:30, 4:30, 8:30, 12:30
Dat probbly no whuh he have een mind, Larry.
Hey... Now me save fortune on popcorn.

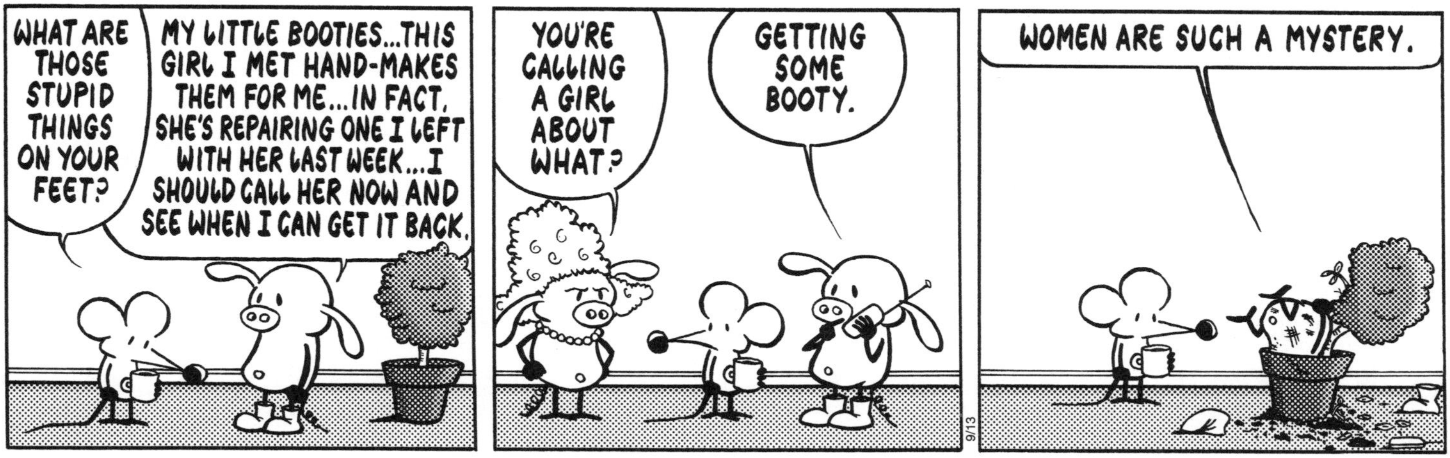
WHAT ARE THOSE STUPID THINGS ON YOUR FEET?
MY LITTLE BOOTIES...THIS GIRL I MET HAND-MAKES THEM FOR ME...IN FACT, SHE'S REPAIRING ONE I LEFT WITH HER LAST WEEK...I SHOULD CALL HER NOW AND SEE WHEN I CAN GET IT BACK.
YOU'RE CALLING A GIRL ABOUT WHAT?
GETTING SOME BOOTY.
9/13
WOMEN ARE SUCH A MYSTERY.

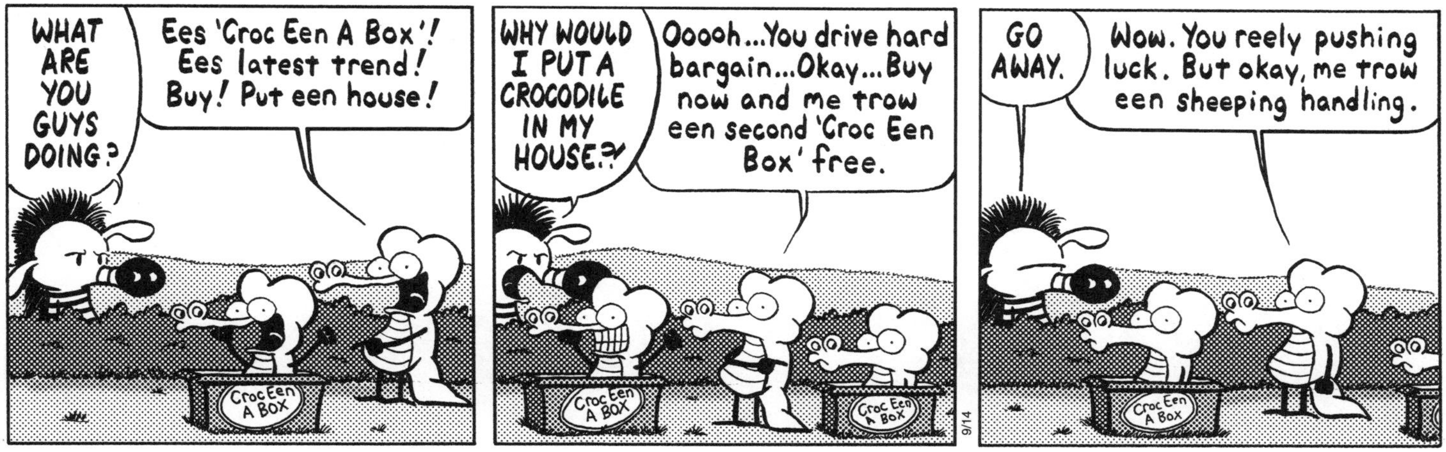
WHAT ARE YOU GUYS DOING?
Ees 'Croc Een A Box'! Ees latest trend! Buy! Put een house!
Croc Een A Box
WHY WOULD I PUT A CROCODILE IN MY HOUSE?!
Ooooh...You drive hard bargain...Okay...Buy now and me trow een second 'Croc Een Box' free.
Croc Een A BOX
Croc Een A Box
9/14
GO AWAY.
Wow. You reely pushing luck. But okay, me trow een sheeping handling.
Croc Een A Box

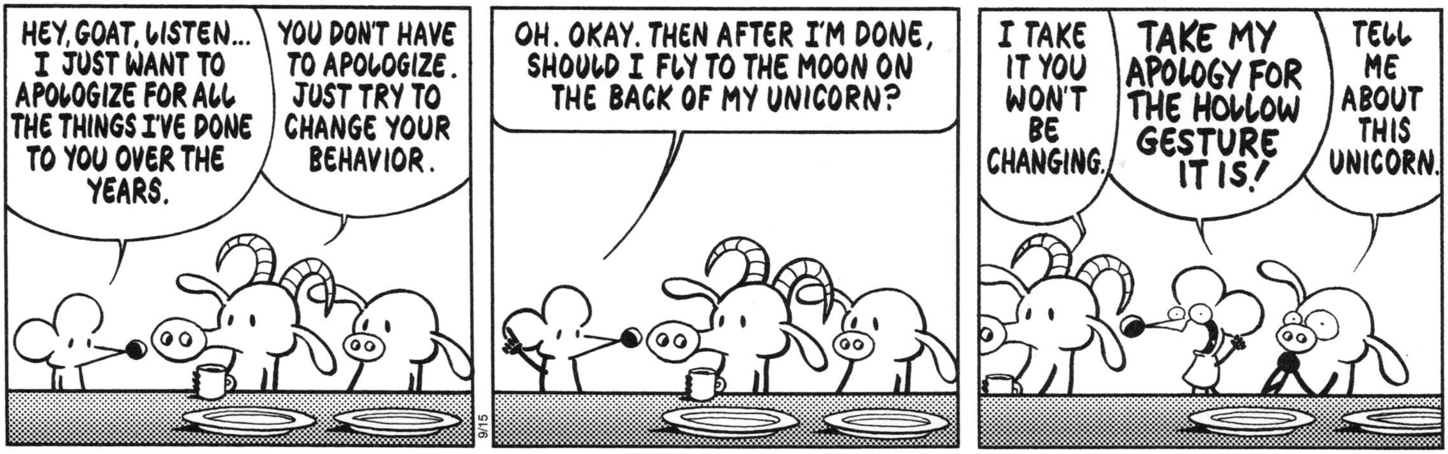
HEY, GOAT, LISTEN... I JUST WANT TO APOLOGIZE FOR ALL THE THINGS I'VE DONE TO YOU OVER THE YEARS.
YOU DON'T HAVE TO APOLOGIZE. JUST TRY TO CHANGE YOUR BEHAVIOR.
9/15
OH. OKAY. THEN AFTER I'M DONE, SHOULD I FLY TO THE MOON ON THE BACK OF MY UNICORN?
I TAKE IT YOU WON'T BE CHANGING.
TAKE MY APOLOGY FOR THE HOLLOW GESTURE IT IS!
TELL ME ABOUT THIS UNICORN.

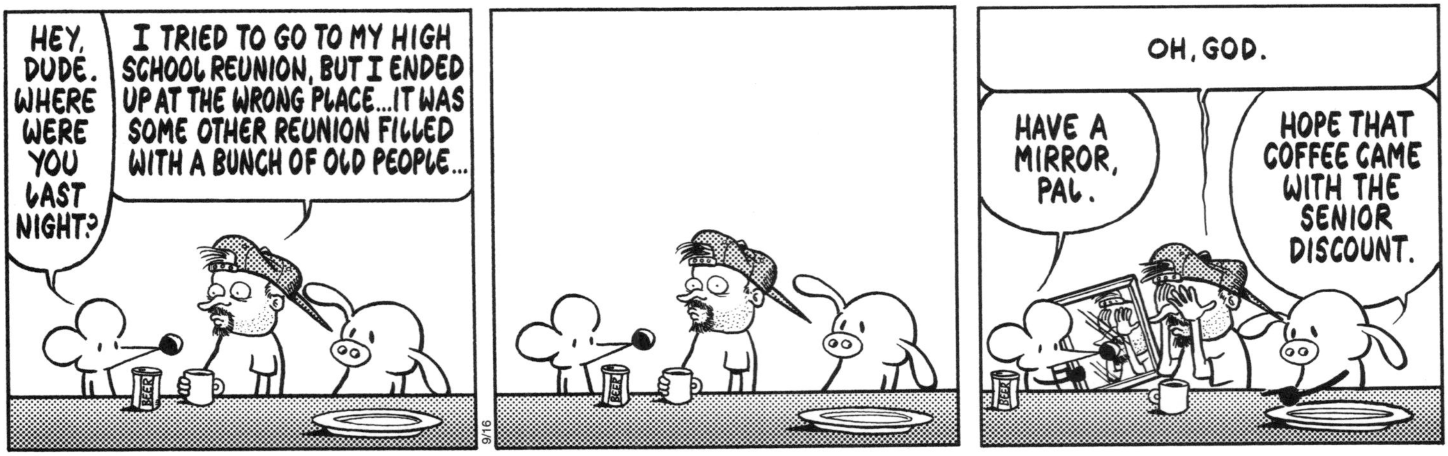
HEY, DUDE. WHERE WERE YOU LAST NIGHT?
I TRIED TO GO TO MY HIGH SCHOOL REUNION, BUT I ENDED UP AT THE WRONG PLACE...IT WAS SOME OTHER REUNION FILLED WITH A BUNCH OF OLD PEOPLE...
BEER
9/16
OH, GOD.
HAVE A MIRROR, PAL.
HOPE THAT COFFEE CAME WITH THE SENIOR DISCOUNT.

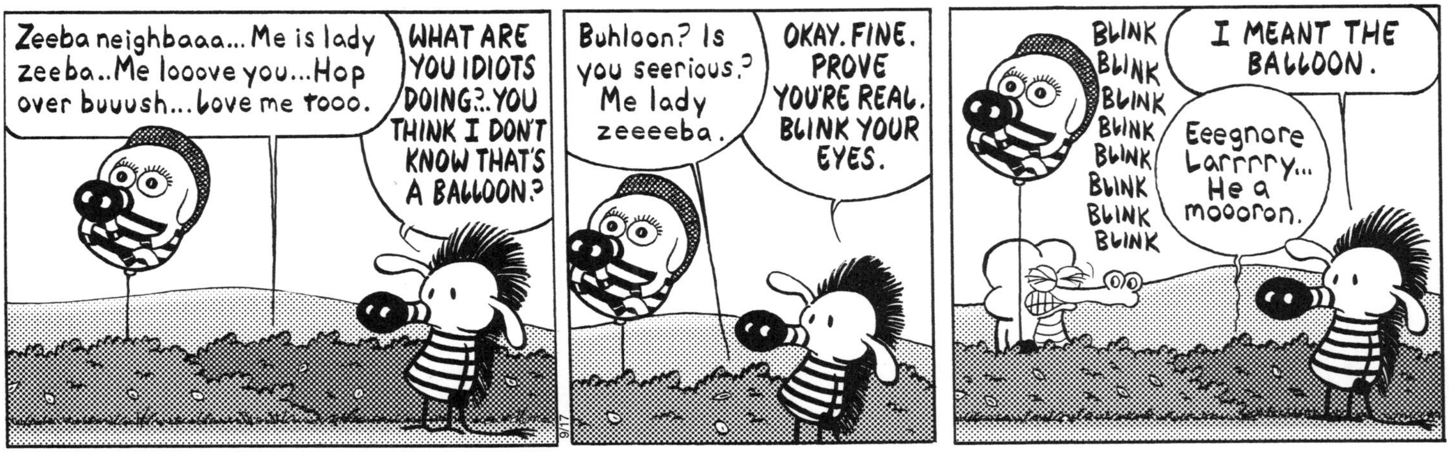
Zeeba neighbaaa... Me is lady zeeba..Me looove you...Hop over buuush...love me tooo.
WHAT ARE YOU IDIOTS DOING?..YOU THINK I DON'T KNOW THAT'S A BALLOON?
9/17
Buhloon? Is you seerious? Me lady zeeeeba.
OKAY. FINE. PROVE YOU'RE REAL. BLINK YOUR EYES.
BLINK BLINK BLINK BLINK BLINK BLINK BLINK BLINK
I MEANT THE BALLOON.
Eeegnore Larrrry... He a mooron.

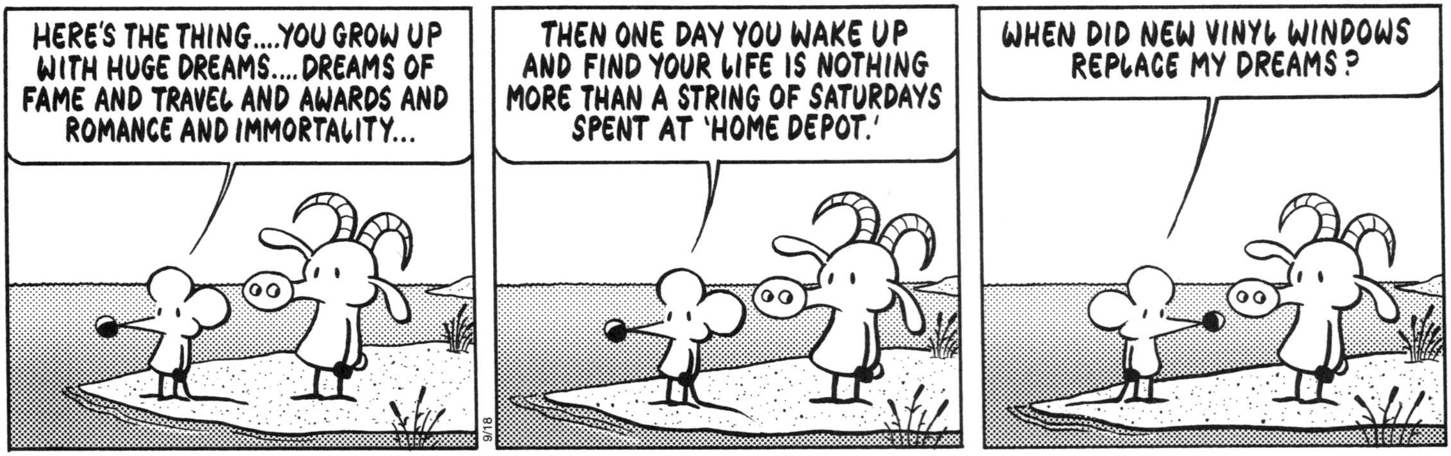
HERE'S THE THING....YOU GROW UP WITH HUGE DREAMS....DREAMS OF FAME AND TRAVEL AND AWARDS AND ROMANCE AND IMMORTALITY...
9/18
THEN ONE DAY YOU WAKE UP AND FIND YOUR LIFE IS NOTHING MORE THAN A STRING OF SATURDAYS SPENT AT 'HOME DEPOT.'
WHEN DID NEW VINYL WINDOWS REPLACE MY DREAMS?

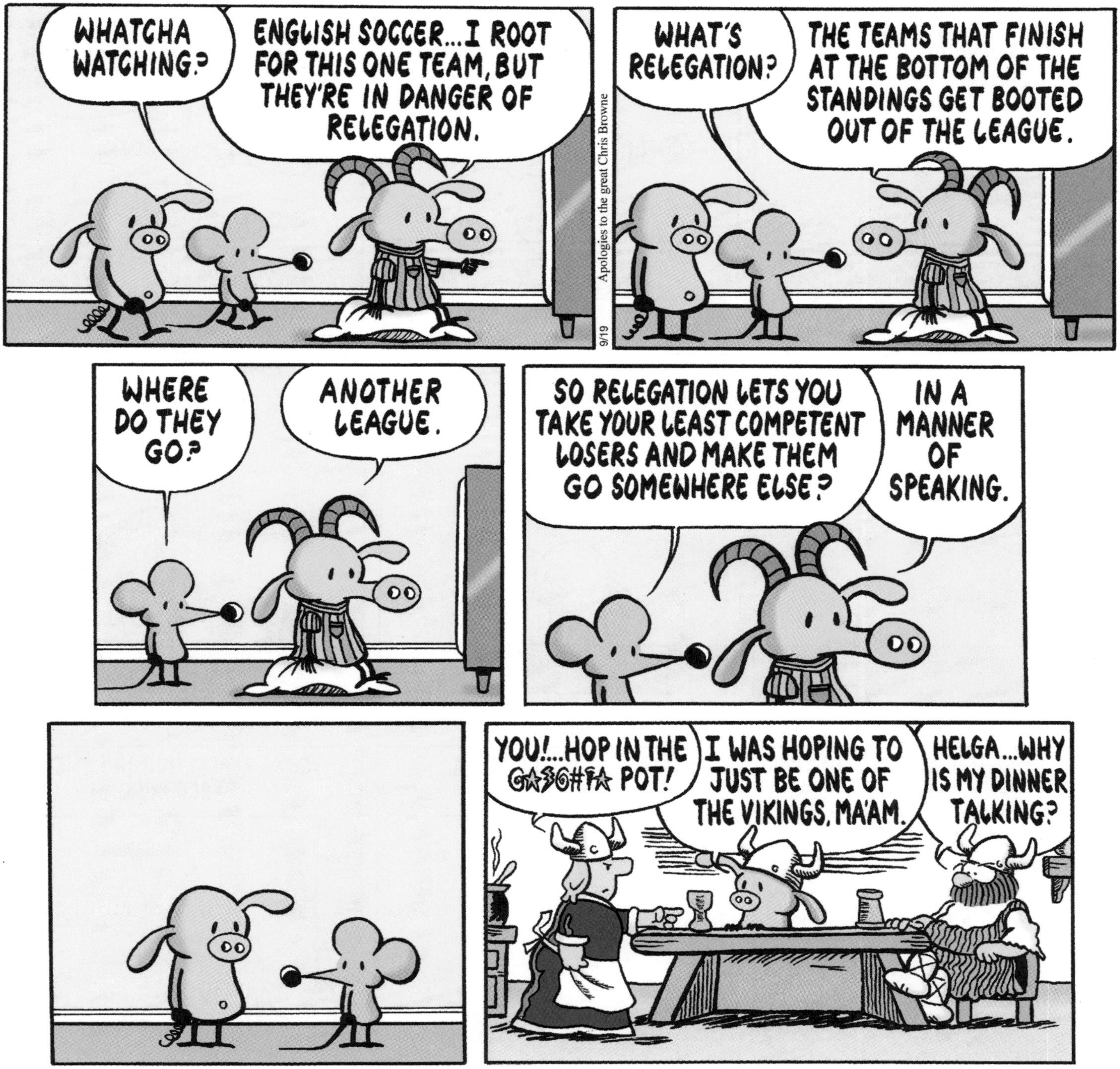
WHATCHA WATCHING?
ENGLISH SOCCER...I ROOT FOR THIS ONE TEAM, BUT THEY'RE IN DANGER OF RELEGATION.
Apologies to the great Chris Browne
9/19
WHAT'S RELEGATION?
THE TEAMS THAT FINISH AT THE BOTTOM OF THE STANDINGS GET BOOTED OUT OF THE LEAGUE.
WHERE DO THEY GO?
ANOTHER LEAGUE.
SO RELEGATION LETS YOU TAKE YOUR LEAST COMPETENT LOSERS AND MAKE THEM GO SOMEWHERE ELSE?
IN A MANNER OF SPEAKING.
YOU!...HOP IN THE G*$@#!* POT!
I WAS HOPING TO JUST BE ONE OF THE VIKINGS, MA'AM.
HELGA...WHY IS MY DINNER TALKING?

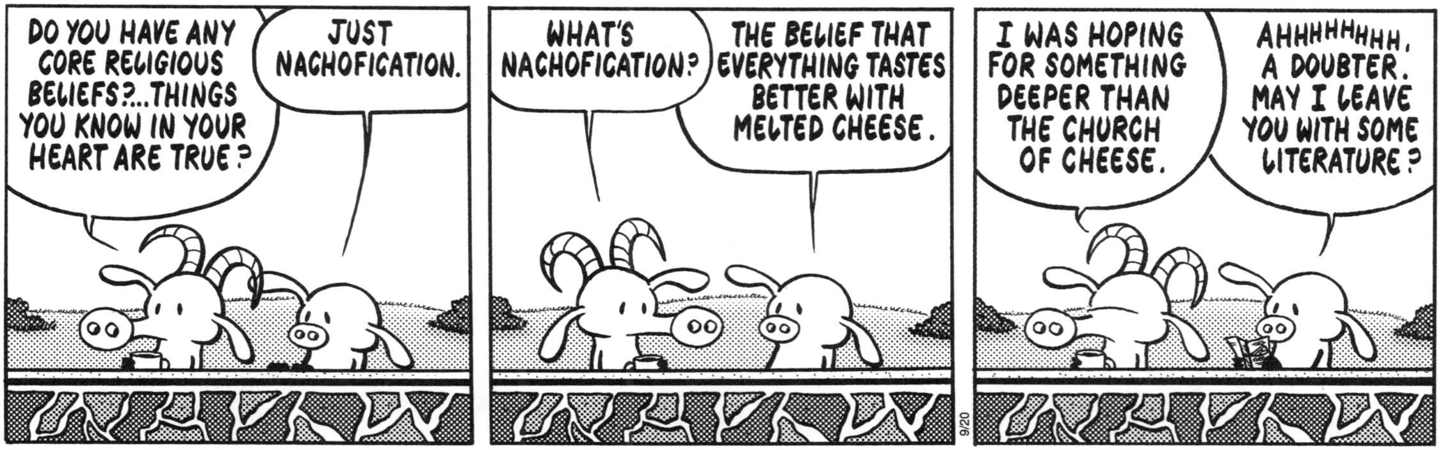
DO YOU HAVE ANY CORE RELIGIOUS BELIEFS?...THINGS YOU KNOW IN YOUR HEART ARE TRUE?
JUST NACHOFICATION.
WHAT'S NACHOFICATION?
THE BELIEF THAT EVERYTHING TASTES BETTER WITH MELTED CHEESE.
I WAS HOPING FOR SOMETHING DEEPER THAN THE CHURCH OF CHEESE.
AHHHHHHHH, A DOUBTER. MAY I LEAVE YOU WITH SOME LITERATURE?
9/20

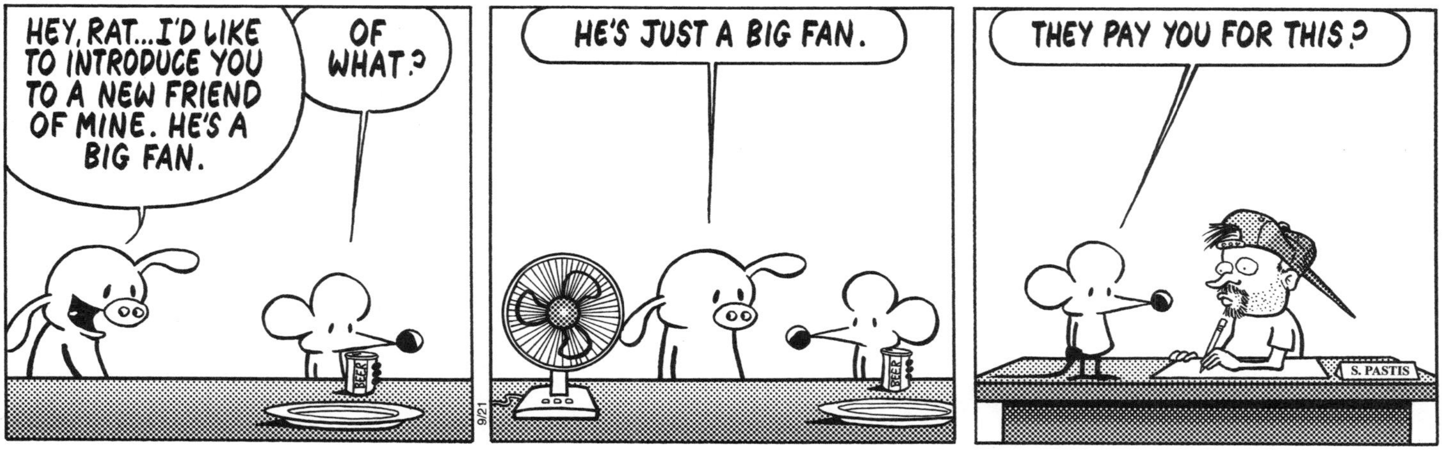
HEY, RAT...I'D LIKE TO INTRODUCE YOU TO A NEW FRIEND OF MINE. HE'S A BIG FAN.
OF WHAT?
BEER
9/21
HE'S JUST A BIG FAN.
BEER
THEY PAY YOU FOR THIS?
S. PASTIS

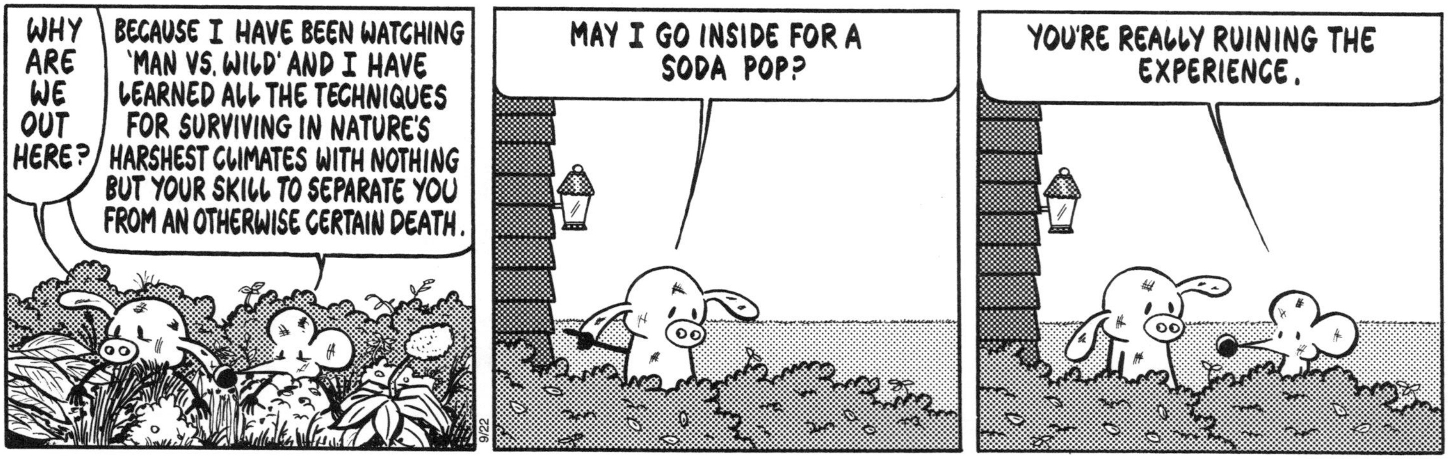
WHY ARE WE OUT HERE?
BECAUSE I HAVE BEEN WATCHING 'MAN VS. WILD' AND I HAVE LEARNED ALL THE TECHNIQUES FOR SURVIVING IN NATURE'S HARSHEST CLIMATES WITH NOTHING BUT YOUR SKILL TO SEPARATE YOU FROM AN OTHERWISE CERTAIN DEATH.
9/22
MAY I GO INSIDE FOR A SODA POP?
YOU'RE REALLY RUINING THE EXPERIENCE.

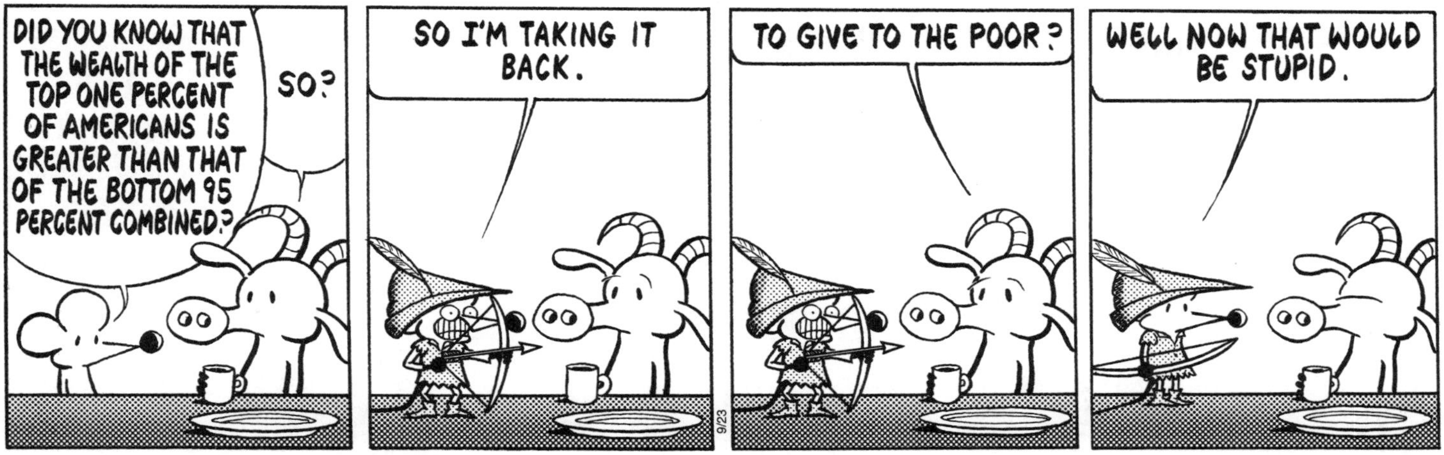
DID YOU KNOW THAT THE WEALTH OF THE TOP ONE PERCENT OF AMERICANS IS GREATER THAN THAT OF THE BOTTOM 95 PERCENT COMBINED?
SO?
SO I'M TAKING IT BACK.
9/23
TO GIVE TO THE POOR?
WELL NOW THAT WOULD BE STUPID.

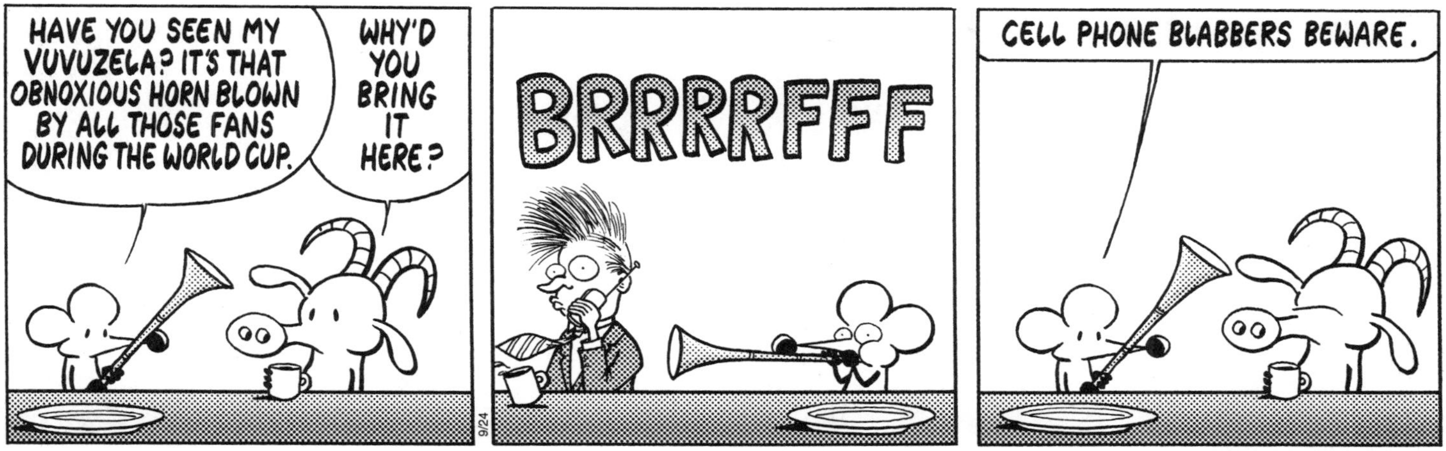
HAVE YOU SEEN MY VUVUZELA? IT'S THAT OBNOXIOUS HORN BLOWN BY ALL THOSE FANS DURING THE WORLD CUP.
WHY'D YOU BRING IT HERE?
9/24
BRRRRRFFF
CELL PHONE BLABBERS BEWARE.

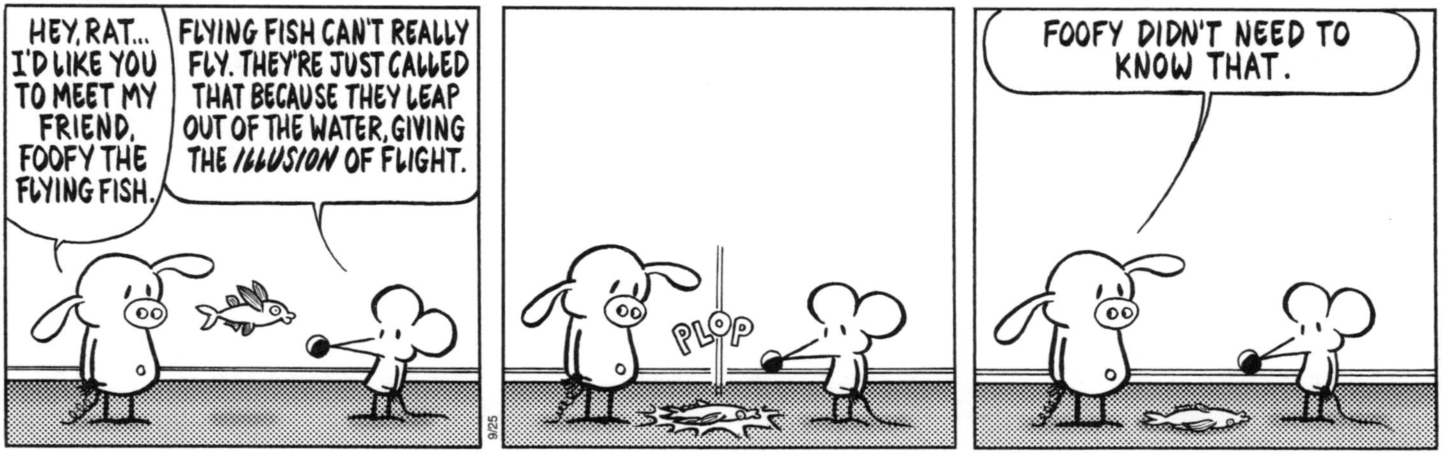
HEY, RAT... I'D LIKE YOU TO MEET MY FRIEND, FOOFY THE FLYING FISH.
FLYING FISH CAN'T REALLY FLY. THEY'RE JUST CALLED THAT BECAUSE THEY LEAP OUT OF THE WATER, GIVING THE *ILLUSION* OF FLIGHT.
9/25
PLOP
FOOFY DIDN'T NEED TO KNOW THAT.

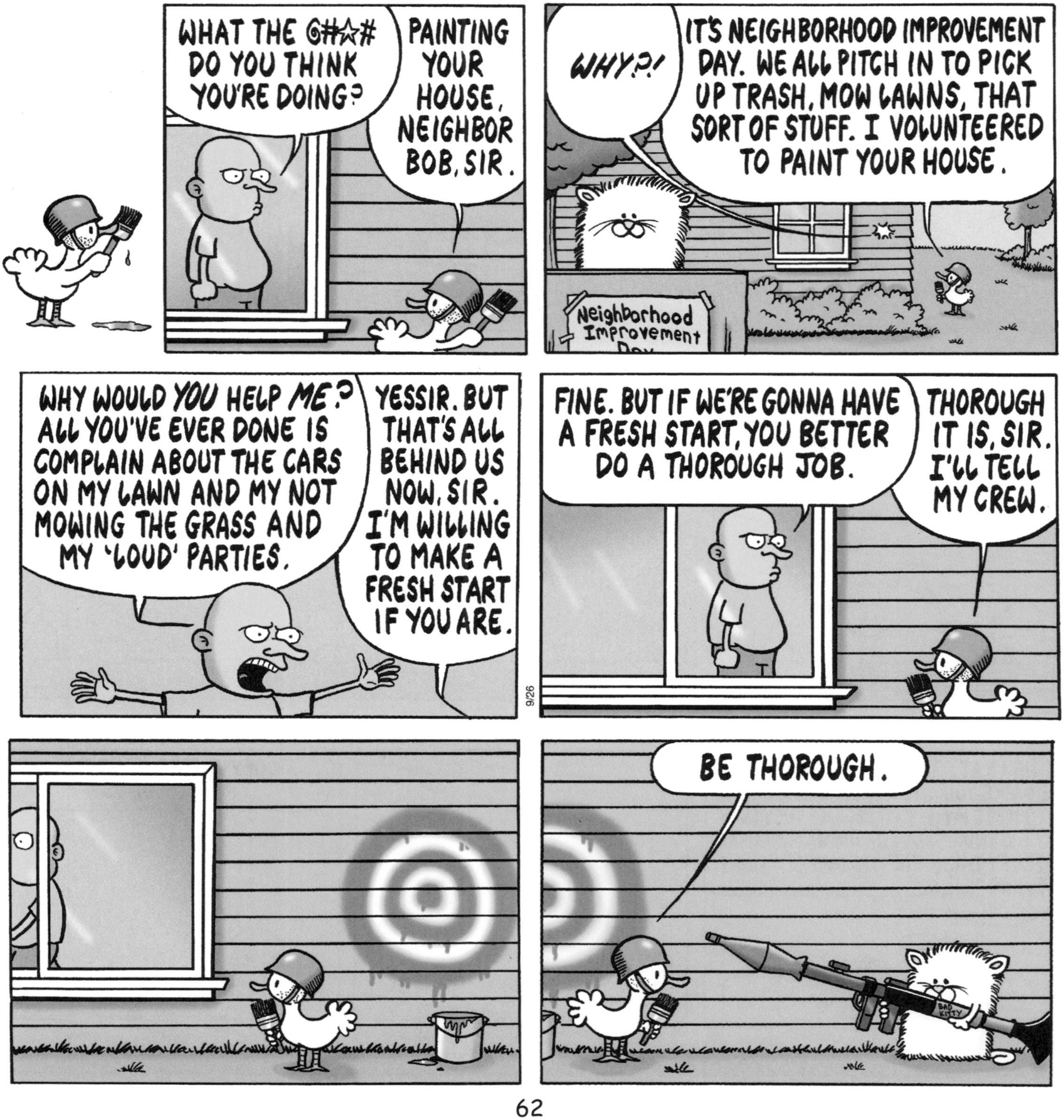
WHAT THE @#☆# DO YOU THINK YOU'RE DOING?
PAINTING YOUR HOUSE, NEIGHBOR BOB, SIR.
WHY?!
IT'S NEIGHBORHOOD IMPROVEMENT DAY. WE ALL PITCH IN TO PICK UP TRASH, MOW LAWNS, THAT SORT OF STUFF. I VOLUNTEERED TO PAINT YOUR HOUSE.
Neighborhood Improvement
WHY WOULD *YOU* HELP *ME*? ALL YOU'VE EVER DONE IS COMPLAIN ABOUT THE CARS ON MY LAWN AND MY NOT MOWING THE GRASS AND MY 'LOUD' PARTIES.
YESSIR. BUT THAT'S ALL BEHIND US NOW, SIR. I'M WILLING TO MAKE A FRESH START IF YOU ARE.
FINE. BUT IF WE'RE GONNA HAVE A FRESH START, YOU BETTER DO A THOROUGH JOB.
THOROUGH IT IS, SIR. I'LL TELL MY CREW.
BE THOROUGH.

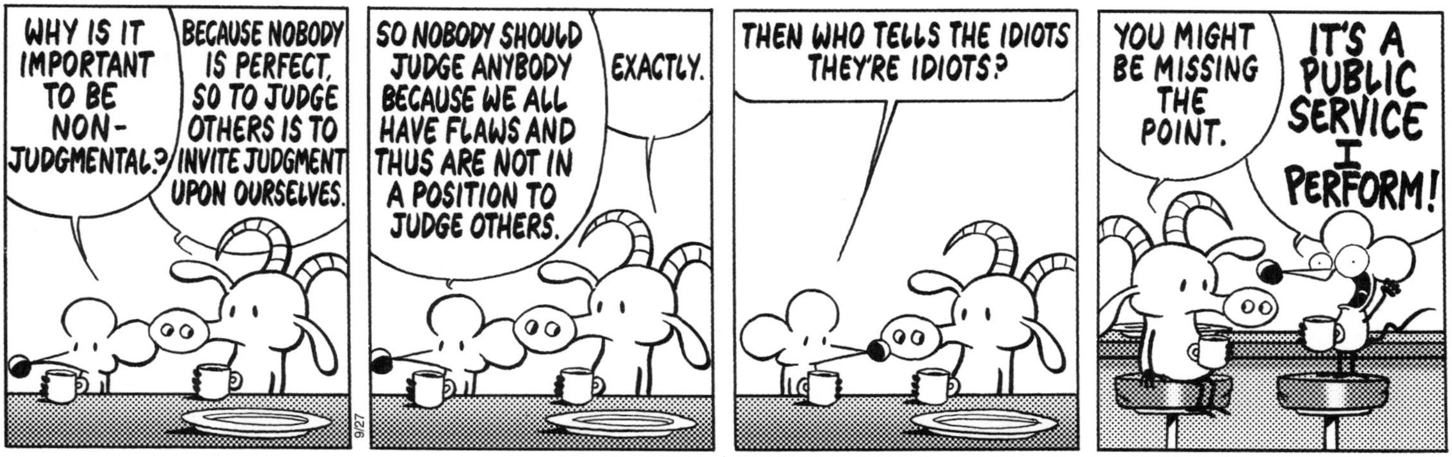
WHY IS IT IMPORTANT TO BE NON-JUDGMENTAL?
BECAUSE NOBODY IS PERFECT, SO TO JUDGE OTHERS IS TO INVITE JUDGMENT UPON OURSELVES.
9/27
SO NOBODY SHOULD JUDGE ANYBODY BECAUSE WE ALL HAVE FLAWS AND THUS ARE NOT IN A POSITION TO JUDGE OTHERS.
EXACTLY.
THEN WHO TELLS THE IDIOTS THEY'RE IDIOTS?
YOU MIGHT BE MISSING THE POINT.
IT'S A PUBLIC SERVICE I PERFORM!

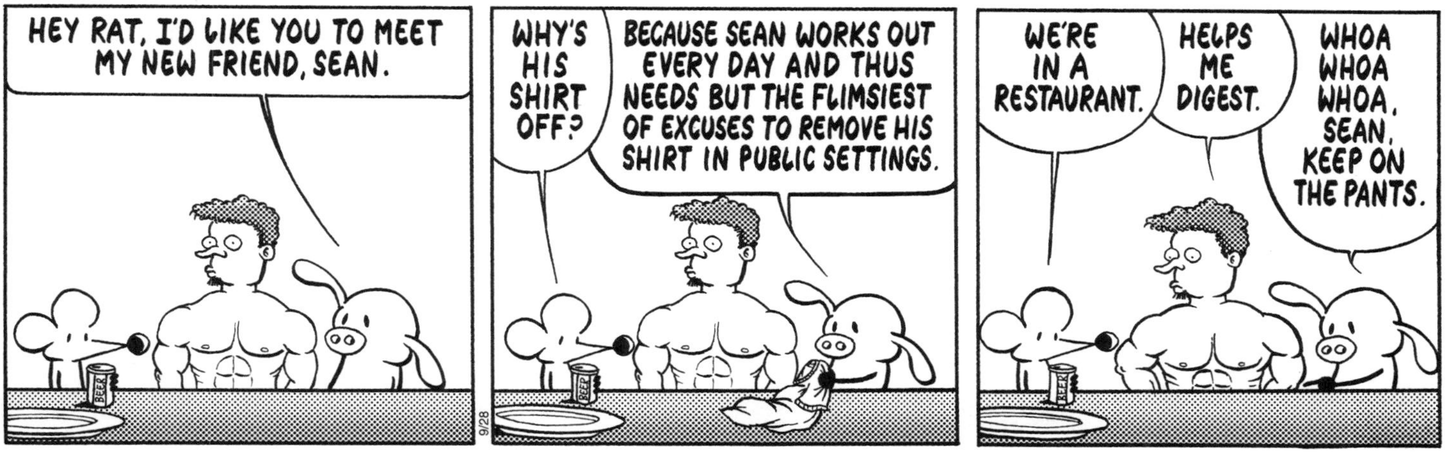
HEY RAT, I'D LIKE YOU TO MEET MY NEW FRIEND, SEAN.
BEER
9/28
WHY'S HIS SHIRT OFF?
BECAUSE SEAN WORKS OUT EVERY DAY AND THUS NEEDS BUT THE FLIMSIEST OF EXCUSES TO REMOVE HIS SHIRT IN PUBLIC SETTINGS.
WE'RE IN A RESTAURANT.
HELPS ME DIGEST.
WHOA WHOA WHOA, SEAN, KEEP ON THE PANTS.

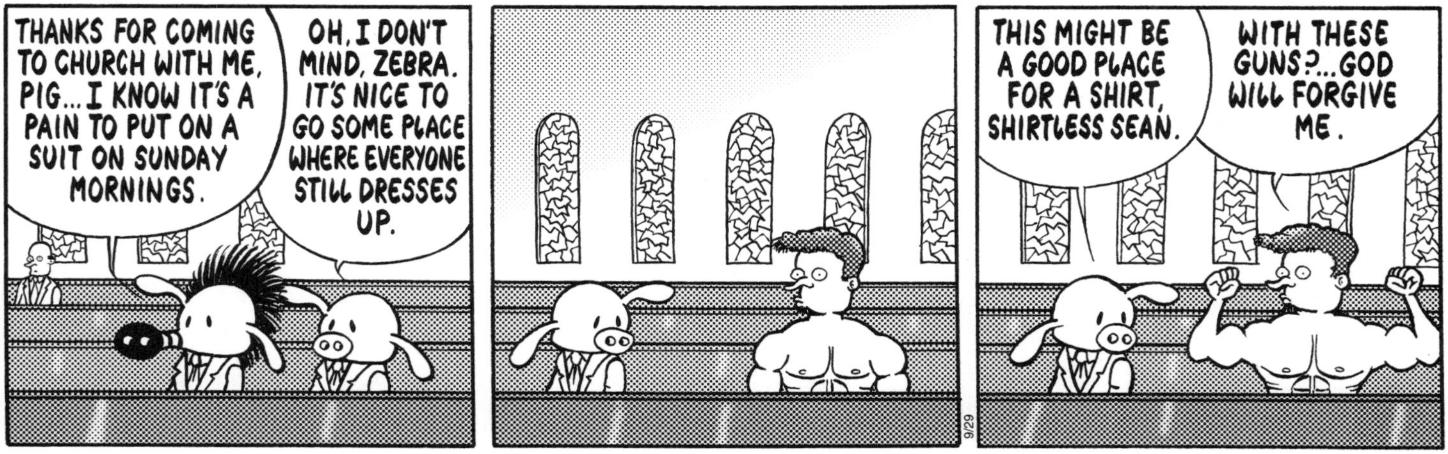
THANKS FOR COMING TO CHURCH WITH ME, PIG... I KNOW IT'S A PAIN TO PUT ON A SUIT ON SUNDAY MORNINGS.
OH, I DON'T MIND, ZEBRA. IT'S NICE TO GO SOME PLACE WHERE EVERYONE STILL DRESSES UP.
9/29
THIS MIGHT BE A GOOD PLACE FOR A SHIRT, SHIRTLESS SEAN.
WITH THESE GUNS?...GOD WILL FORGIVE ME.

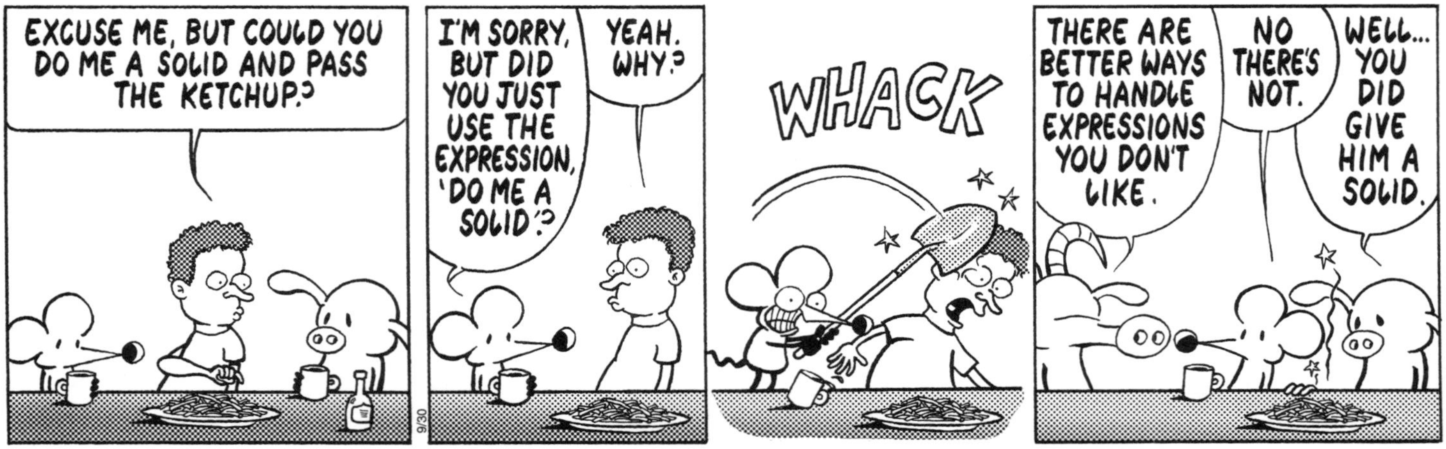
EXCUSE ME, BUT COULD YOU DO ME A SOLID AND PASS THE KETCHUP?
9/30
I'M SORRY, BUT DID YOU JUST USE THE EXPRESSION, 'DO ME A SOLID'?
YEAH. WHY?
WHACK
THERE ARE BETTER WAYS TO HANDLE EXPRESSIONS YOU DON'T LIKE.
NO THERE'S NOT.
WELL... YOU DID GIVE HIM A SOLID.

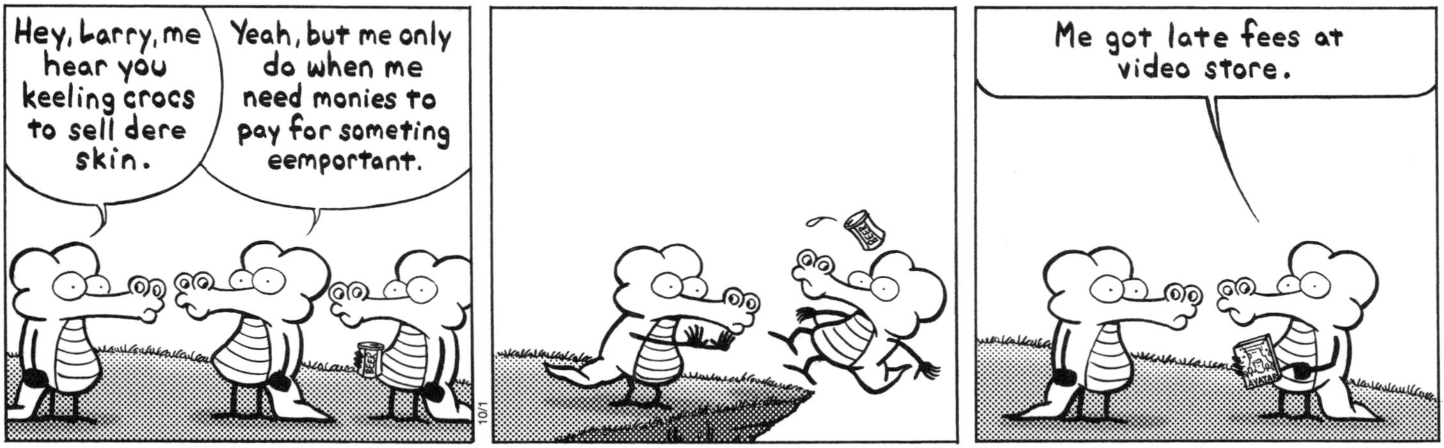
Hey, Larry, me hear you keeling crocs to sell dere skin.
Yeah, but me only do when me need monies to pay for someting eemportant.
BEER
10/1
Me got late fees at video store.
AVATAR

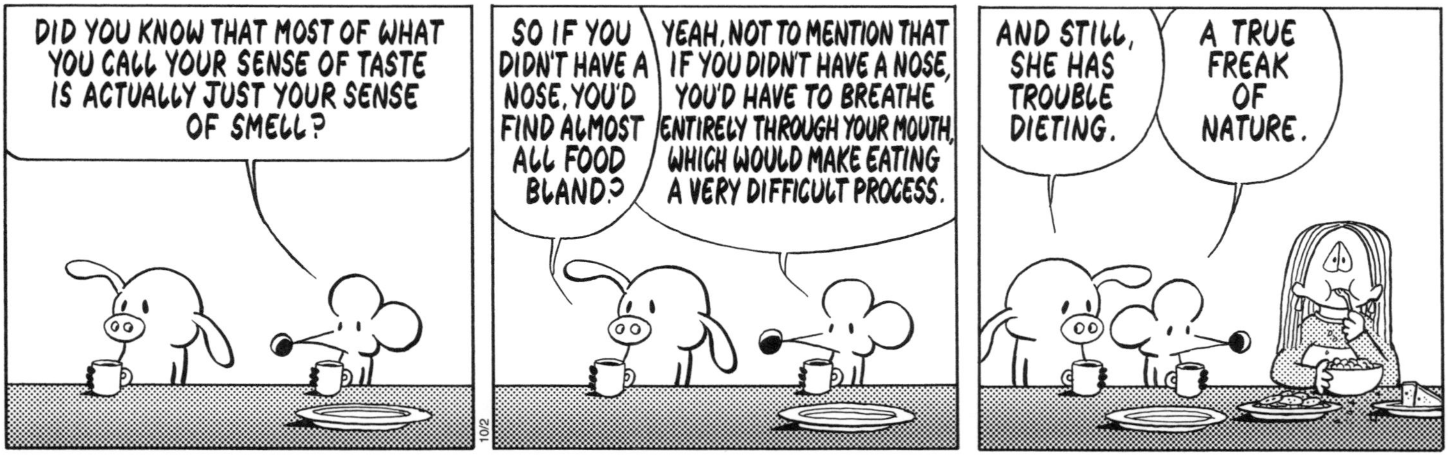
DID YOU KNOW THAT MOST OF WHAT YOU CALL YOUR SENSE OF TASTE IS ACTUALLY JUST YOUR SENSE OF SMELL?
10/2
SO IF YOU DIDN'T HAVE A NOSE, YOU'D FIND ALMOST ALL FOOD BLAND?
YEAH, NOT TO MENTION THAT IF YOU DIDN'T HAVE A NOSE, YOU'D HAVE TO BREATHE ENTIRELY THROUGH YOUR MOUTH, WHICH WOULD MAKE EATING A VERY DIFFICULT PROCESS.
AND STILL, SHE HAS TROUBLE DIETING.
A TRUE FREAK OF NATURE.

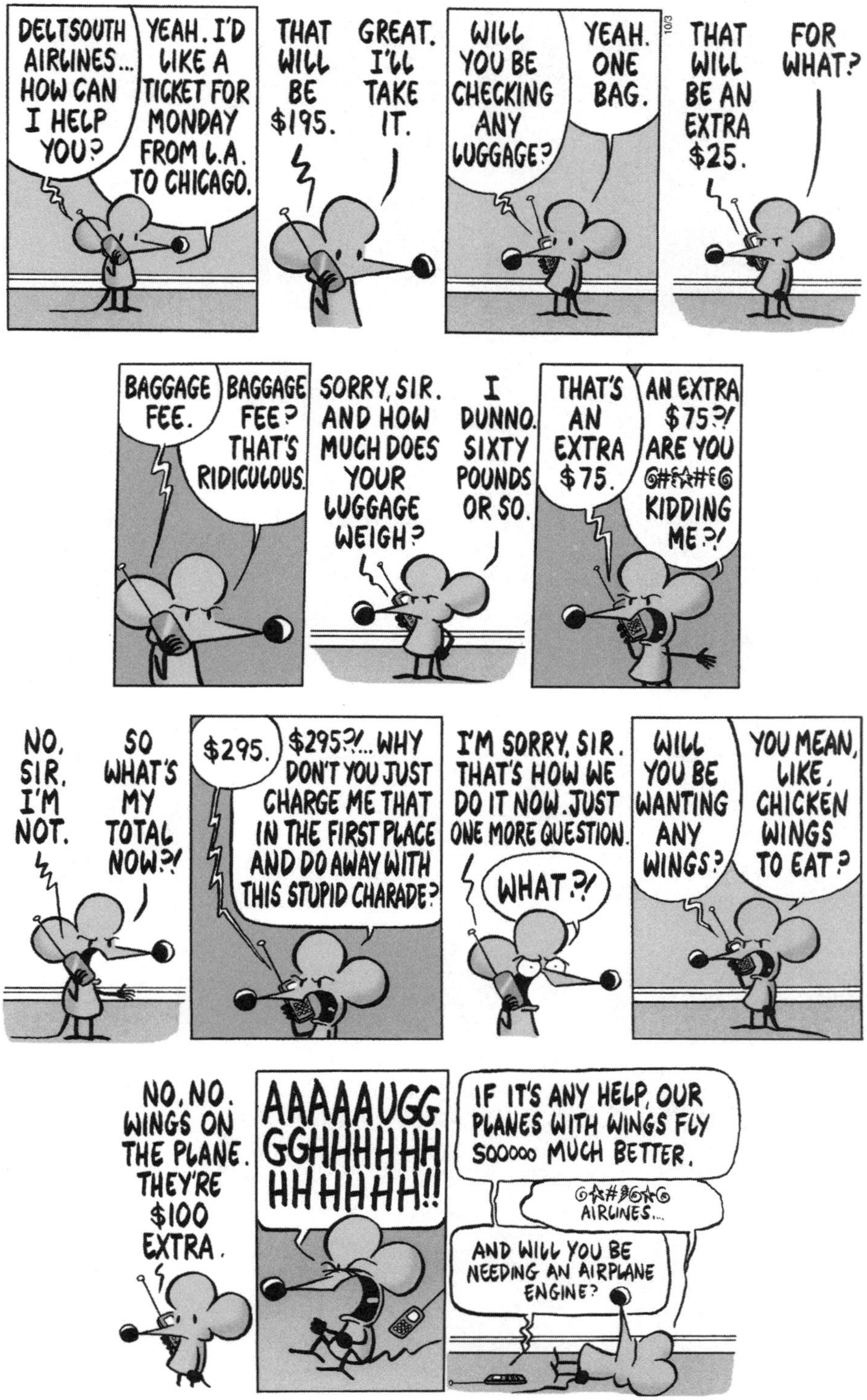
DELTSOUTH AIRLINES... HOW CAN I HELP YOU?
YEAH. I'D LIKE A TICKET FOR MONDAY FROM L.A. TO CHICAGO.
THAT WILL BE $195.
GREAT. I'LL TAKE IT.
WILL YOU BE CHECKING ANY LUGGAGE?
YEAH. ONE BAG.
10/3
THAT WILL BE AN EXTRA $25.
FOR WHAT?
BAGGAGE FEE.
BAGGAGE FEE? THAT'S RIDICULOUS.
SORRY, SIR. AND HOW MUCH DOES YOUR LUGGAGE WEIGH?
I DUNNO. SIXTY POUNDS OR SO.
THAT'S AN EXTRA $75.
AN EXTRA $75?! ARE YOU KIDDING ME?!
NO, SIR, I'M NOT.
SO WHAT'S MY TOTAL NOW?!
$295.
$295?!... WHY DON'T YOU JUST CHARGE ME THAT IN THE FIRST PLACE AND DO AWAY WITH THIS STUPID CHARADE?
I'M SORRY, SIR. THAT'S HOW WE DO IT NOW. JUST ONE MORE QUESTION.
WHAT?!
WILL YOU BE WANTING ANY WINGS?
YOU MEAN, LIKE, CHICKEN WINGS TO EAT?
NO, NO. WINGS ON THE PLANE. THEY'RE $100 EXTRA.
AAAAAUGGGGHHHHHHHHHHHH!!
IF IT'S ANY HELP, OUR PLANES WITH WINGS FLY SOOOOO MUCH BETTER.
AIRLINES...
AND WILL YOU BE NEEDING AN AIRPLANE ENGINE?

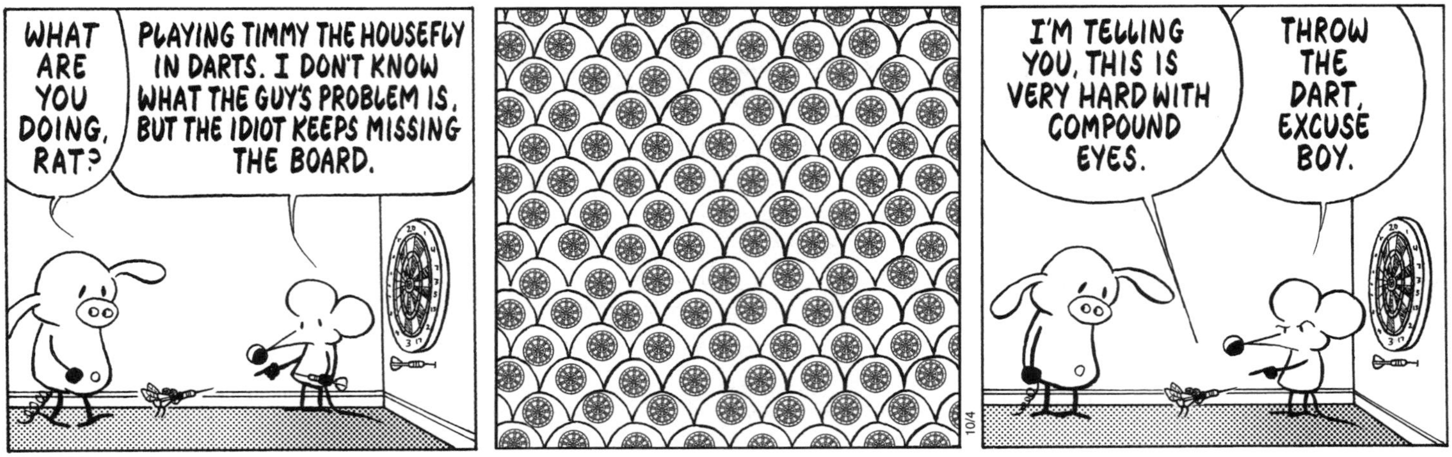
WHAT ARE YOU DOING, RAT?
PLAYING TIMMY THE HOUSEFLY IN DARTS. I DON'T KNOW WHAT THE GUY'S PROBLEM IS, BUT THE IDIOT KEEPS MISSING THE BOARD.
I'M TELLING YOU, THIS IS VERY HARD WITH COMPOUND EYES.
THROW THE DART, EXCUSE BOY.
10/4

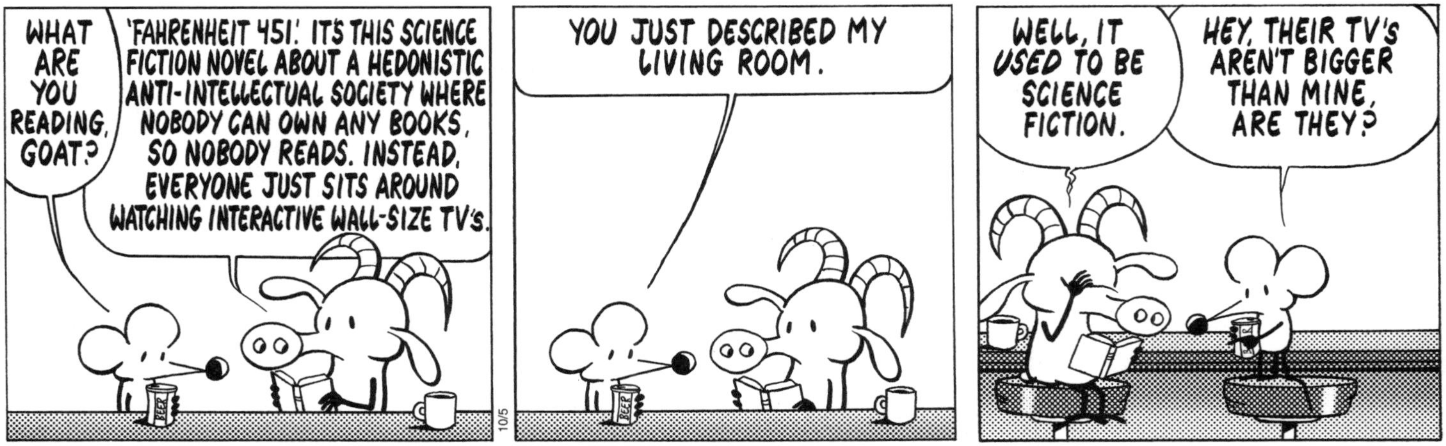
WHAT ARE YOU READING, GOAT?
'FAHRENHEIT 451.' IT'S THIS SCIENCE FICTION NOVEL ABOUT A HEDONISTIC ANTI-INTELLECTUAL SOCIETY WHERE NOBODY CAN OWN ANY BOOKS, SO NOBODY READS. INSTEAD, EVERYONE JUST SITS AROUND WATCHING INTERACTIVE WALL-SIZE TV's.
BEER
10/5
YOU JUST DESCRIBED MY LIVING ROOM.
WELL, IT *USED* TO BE SCIENCE FICTION.
HEY, THEIR TV's AREN'T BIGGER THAN MINE, ARE THEY?

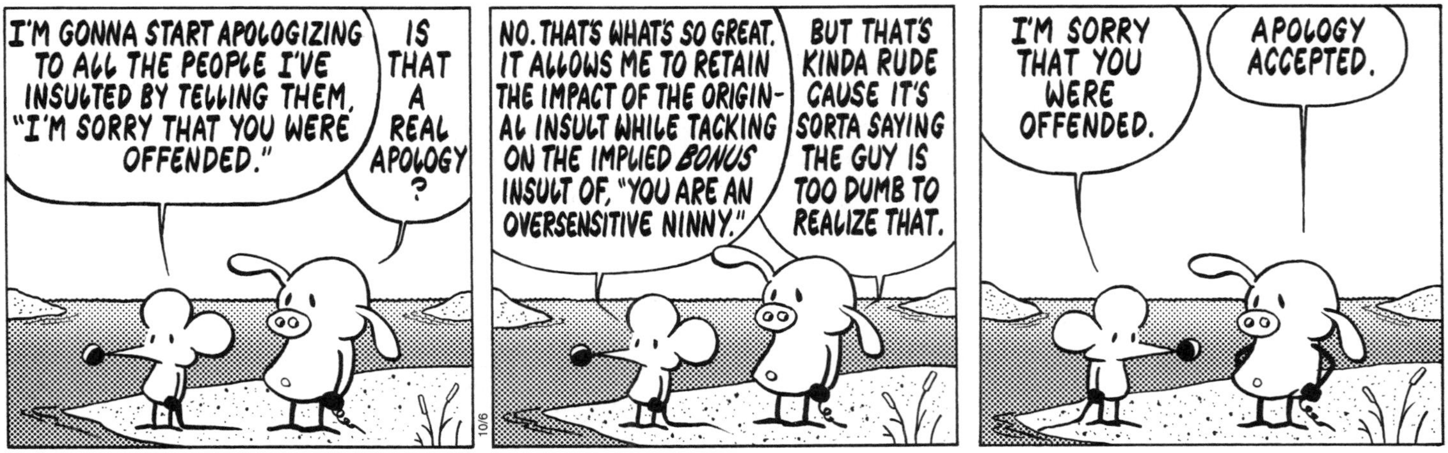
I'M GONNA START APOLOGIZING TO ALL THE PEOPLE I'VE INSULTED BY TELLING THEM, "I'M SORRY THAT YOU WERE OFFENDED."
IS THAT A REAL APOLOGY?
10/6
NO. THAT'S WHAT'S SO GREAT. IT ALLOWS ME TO RETAIN THE IMPACT OF THE ORIGINAL INSULT WHILE TACKING ON THE IMPLIED *BONUS* INSULT OF, "YOU ARE AN OVERSENSITIVE NINNY."
BUT THAT'S KINDA RUDE CAUSE IT'S SORTA SAYING THE GUY IS TOO DUMB TO REALIZE THAT.
I'M SORRY THAT YOU WERE OFFENDED.
APOLOGY ACCEPTED.

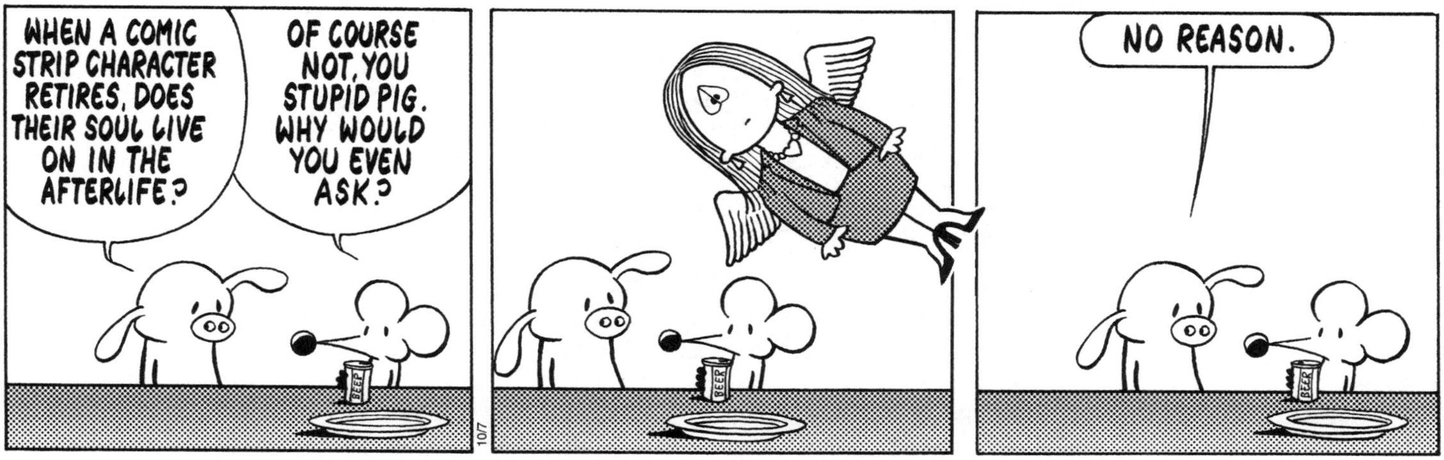
WHEN A COMIC STRIP CHARACTER RETIRES, DOES THEIR SOUL LIVE ON IN THE AFTERLIFE?
OF COURSE NOT, YOU STUPID PIG. WHY WOULD YOU EVEN ASK?
BEER
10/7
NO REASON.

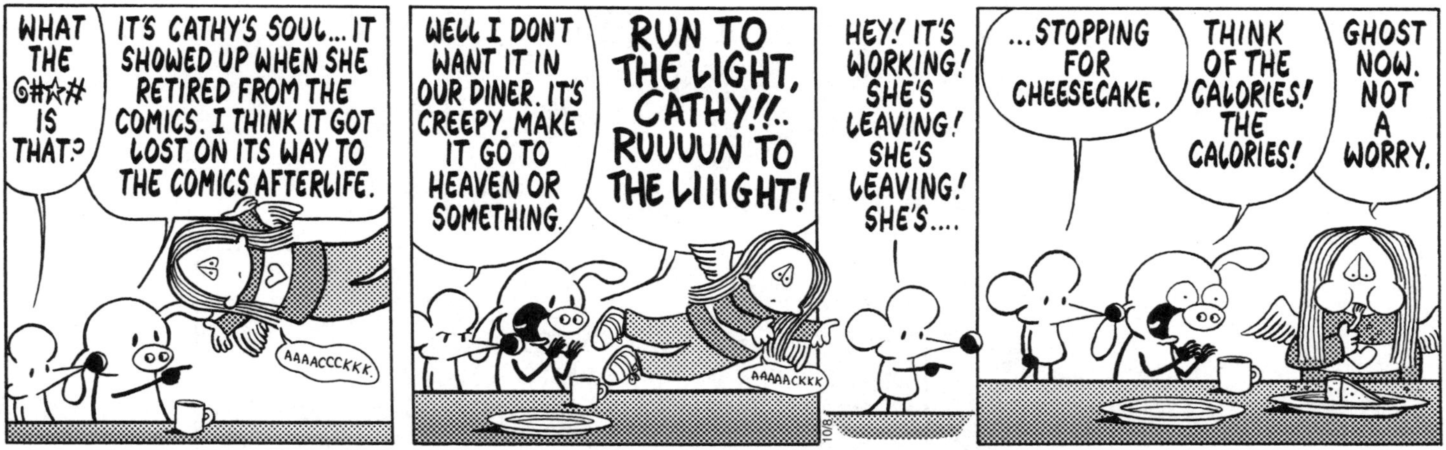
WHAT THE @#☆# IS THAT?
IT'S CATHY'S SOUL... IT SHOWED UP WHEN SHE RETIRED FROM THE COMICS. I THINK IT GOT LOST ON ITS WAY TO THE COMICS AFTERLIFE.
AAAACCCKKK.
WELL I DON'T WANT IT IN OUR DINER. IT'S CREEPY. MAKE IT GO TO HEAVEN OR SOMETHING.
RUN TO THE LIGHT, CATHY!!.. RUUUUN TO THE LIIIGHT!
AAAAACKKK
10/8
HEY! IT'S WORKING! SHE'S LEAVING! SHE'S LEAVING! SHE'S....
...STOPPING FOR CHEESECAKE.
THINK OF THE CALORIES! THE CALORIES!
GHOST NOW. NOT A WORRY.

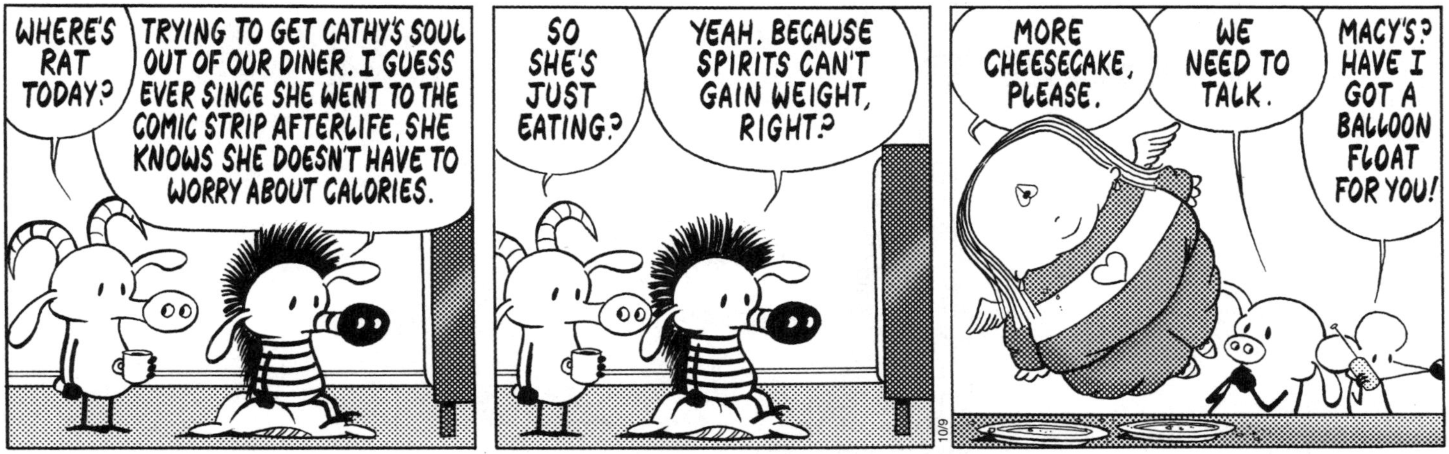
WHERE'S RAT TODAY?
TRYING TO GET CATHY'S SOUL OUT OF OUR DINER. I GUESS EVER SINCE SHE WENT TO THE COMIC STRIP AFTERLIFE, SHE KNOWS SHE DOESN'T HAVE TO WORRY ABOUT CALORIES.
SO SHE'S JUST EATING?
YEAH. BECAUSE SPIRITS CAN'T GAIN WEIGHT, RIGHT?
10/9
MORE CHEESECAKE, PLEASE.
WE NEED TO TALK.
MACY'S? HAVE I GOT A BALLOON FLOAT FOR YOU!

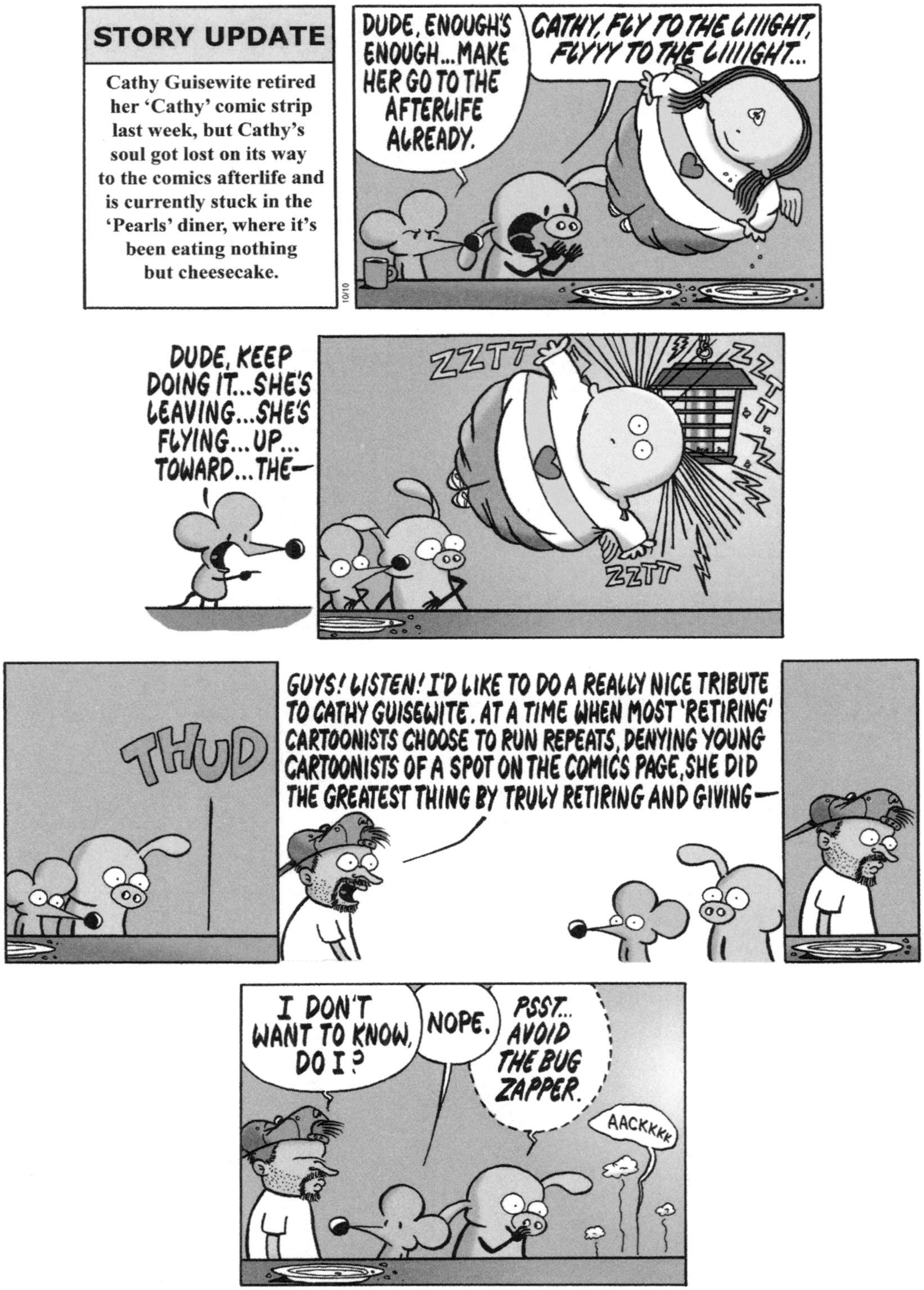
STORY UPDATE
Cathy Guisewite retired her 'Cathy' comic strip last week, but Cathy's soul got lost on its way to the comics afterlife and is currently stuck in the 'Pearls' diner, where it's been eating nothing but cheesecake.
10/10
DUDE, ENOUGH'S ENOUGH...MAKE HER GO TO THE AFTERLIFE ALREADY.
CATHY, FLY TO THE LIIIGHT, FLYYY TO THE LIIIGHT...
DUDE, KEEP DOING IT...SHE'S LEAVING...SHE'S FLYING... UP... TOWARD...THE—
ZZTT
ZZT
T
ZZTT
THUD
GUYS! LISTEN! I'D LIKE TO DO A REALLY NICE TRIBUTE TO CATHY GUISEWITE. AT A TIME WHEN MOST 'RETIRING' CARTOONISTS CHOOSE TO RUN REPEATS, DENYING YOUNG CARTOONISTS OF A SPOT ON THE COMICS PAGE, SHE DID THE GREATEST THING BY TRULY RETIRING AND GIVING—
I DON'T WANT TO KNOW, DO I?
NOPE.
PSST... AVOID THE BUG ZAPPER.
AACKKKK

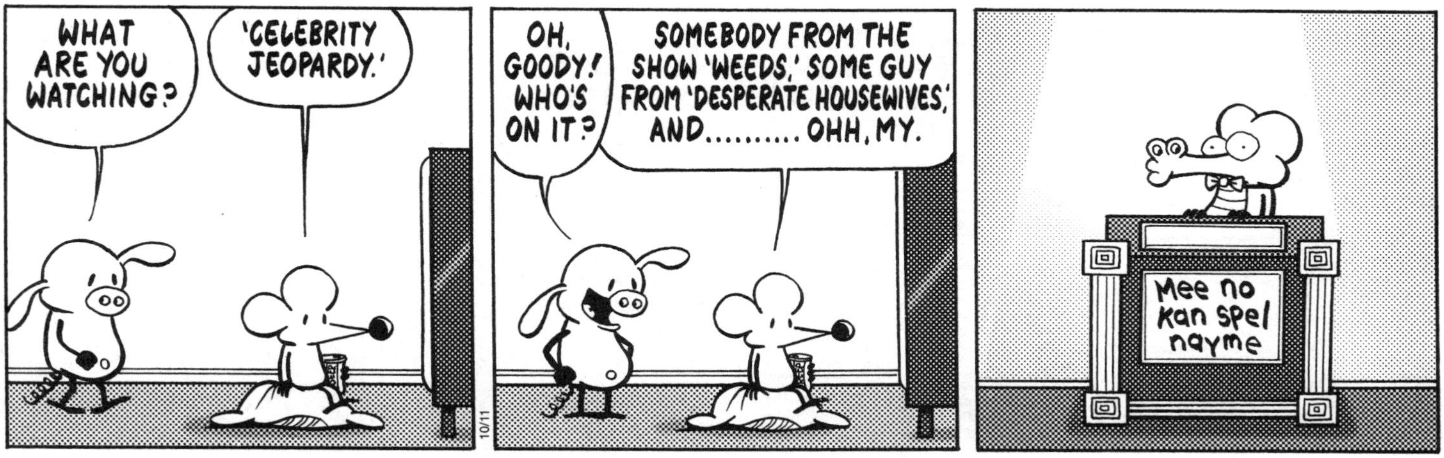
WHAT ARE YOU WATCHING?
'CELEBRITY JEOPARDY.'
OH, GOODY! WHO'S ON IT?
SOMEBODY FROM THE SHOW 'WEEDS,' SOME GUY FROM 'DESPERATE HOUSEWIVES,' AND.......... OHH, MY.
Mee no kan spel nayme
10/11

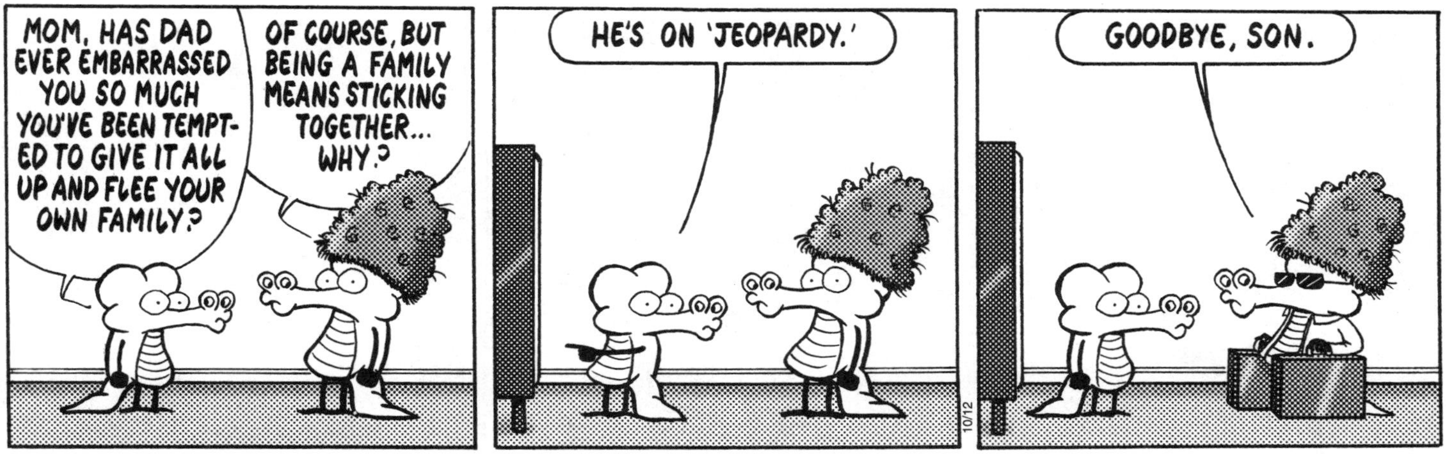
MOM, HAS DAD EVER EMBARRASSED YOU SO MUCH YOU'VE BEEN TEMPTED TO GIVE IT ALL UP AND FLEE YOUR OWN FAMILY?
OF COURSE, BUT BEING A FAMILY MEANS STICKING TOGETHER... WHY?
HE'S ON 'JEOPARDY.'
GOODBYE, SON.
10/12

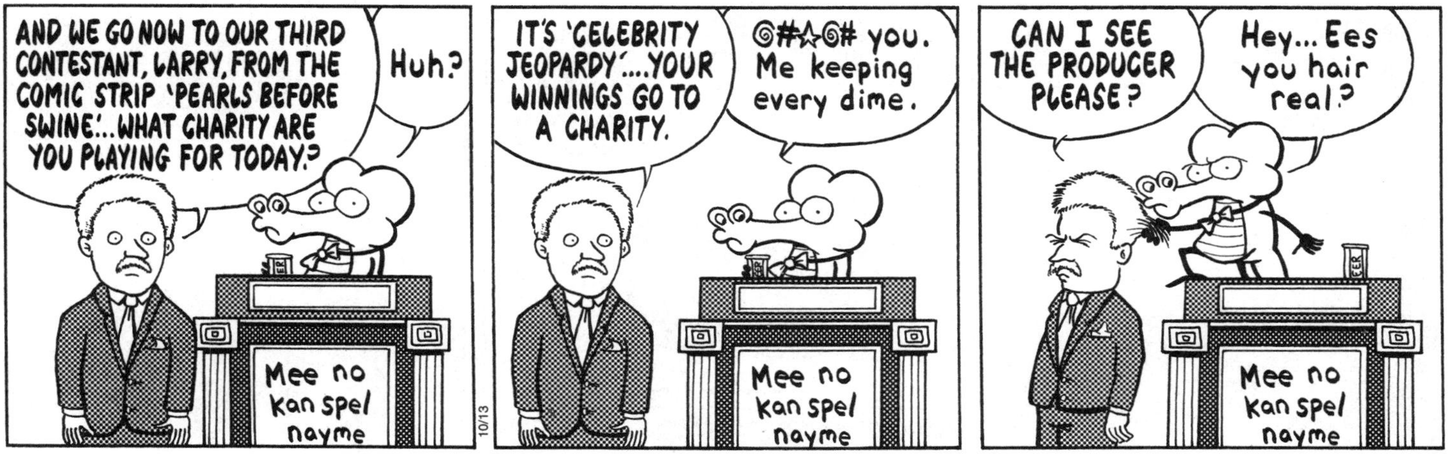
AND WE GO NOW TO OUR THIRD CONTESTANT, LARRY, FROM THE COMIC STRIP 'PEARLS BEFORE SWINE.'...WHAT CHARITY ARE YOU PLAYING FOR TODAY?
Huh?
Mee no kan spel nayme
IT'S 'CELEBRITY JEOPARDY'....YOUR WINNINGS GO TO A CHARITY.
@#☆@# you. Me keeping every dime.
Mee no kan spel nayme
CAN I SEE THE PRODUCER PLEASE?
Hey... Ees you hair real?
Mee no kan spel nayme
10/13

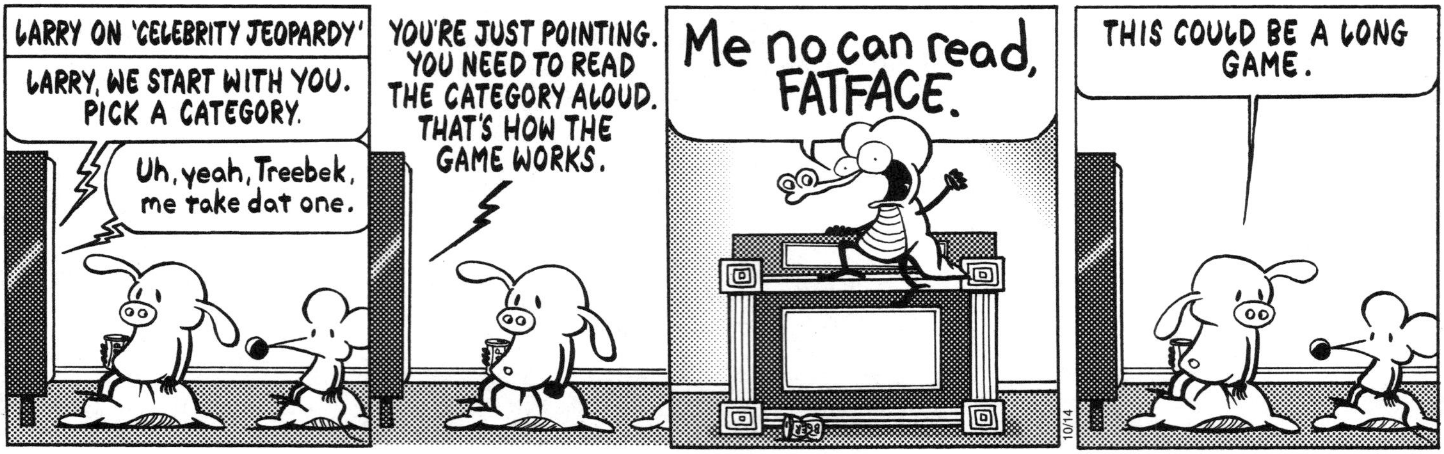
LARRY ON 'CELEBRITY JEOPARDY'
LARRY, WE START WITH YOU. PICK A CATEGORY.
Uh, yeah, Treebek, me take dat one.
YOU'RE JUST POINTING. YOU NEED TO READ THE CATEGORY ALOUD. THAT'S HOW THE GAME WORKS.
Me no can read, FATFACE.
THIS COULD BE A LONG GAME.
10/14

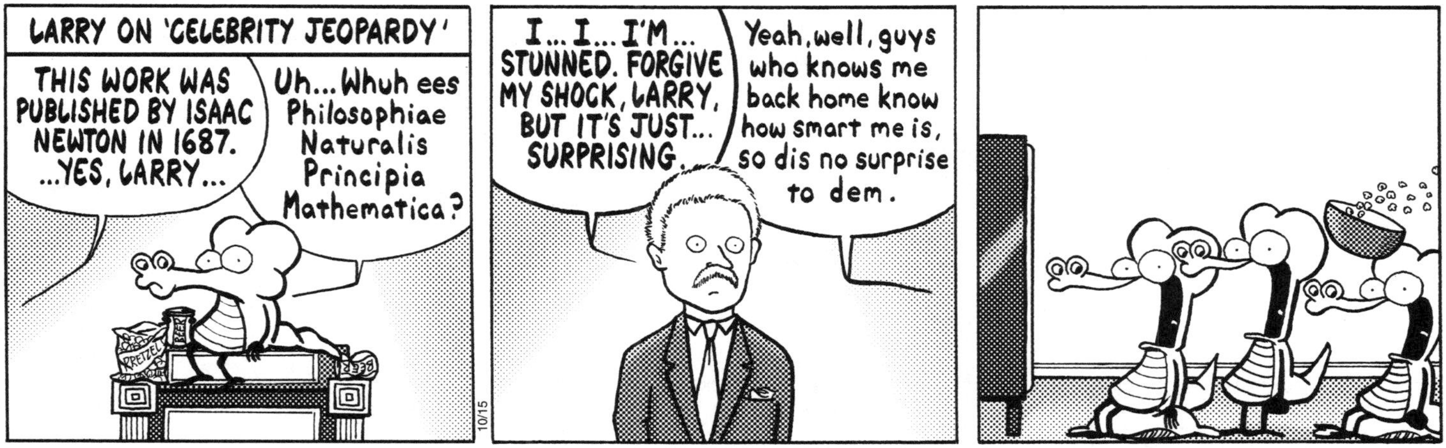
LARRY ON 'CELEBRITY JEOPARDY'
THIS WORK WAS PUBLISHED BY ISAAC NEWTON IN 1687. ...YES, LARRY...
Uh... Whuh ees Philosophiae Naturalis Principia Mathematica?
10/15
I... I... I'M... STUNNED. FORGIVE MY SHOCK, LARRY, BUT IT'S JUST... SURPRISING.
Yeah, well, guys who knows me back home know how smart me is, so dis no surprise to dem.

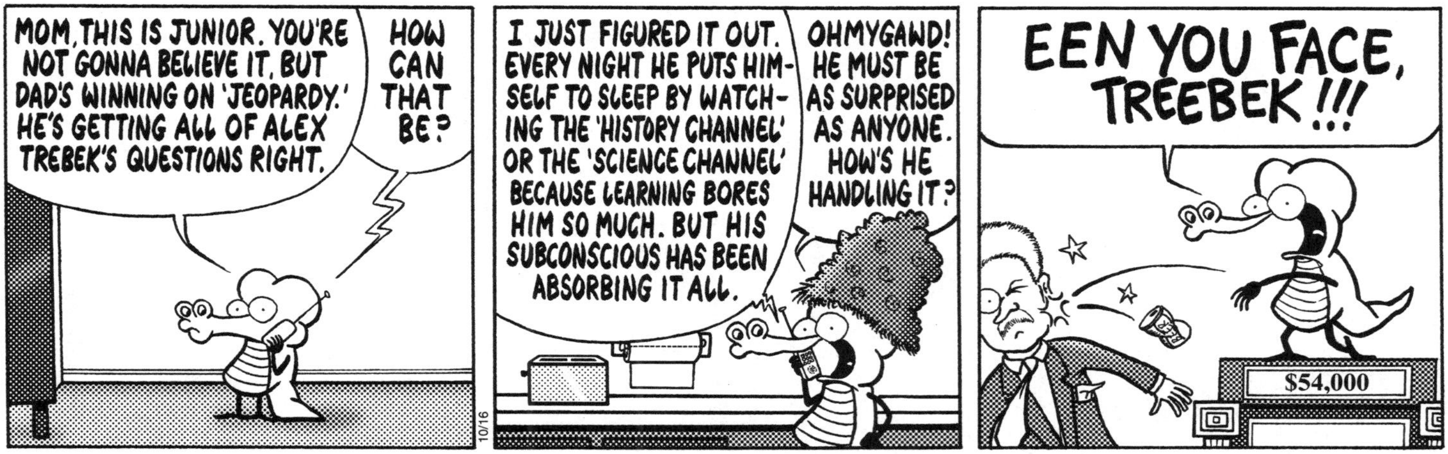
MOM, THIS IS JUNIOR. YOU'RE NOT GONNA BELIEVE IT, BUT DAD'S WINNING ON 'JEOPARDY.' HE'S GETTING ALL OF ALEX TREBEK'S QUESTIONS RIGHT.
HOW CAN THAT BE?
10/16
I JUST FIGURED IT OUT. EVERY NIGHT HE PUTS HIMSELF TO SLEEP BY WATCHING THE 'HISTORY CHANNEL' OR THE 'SCIENCE CHANNEL' BECAUSE LEARNING BORES HIM SO MUCH. BUT HIS SUBCONSCIOUS HAS BEEN ABSORBING IT ALL.
OHMYGAWD! HE MUST BE AS SURPRISED AS ANYONE. HOW'S HE HANDLING IT?
EEN YOU FACE, TREEBEK!!!
$54,000

STORY UPDATE:

Larry the Croc has been on "Celebrity Jeopardy." Because of his ability to absorb the "History Channel" while asleep on the couch, he has been more knowledgeable than expected and is winning the game.

TODAY'S FINAL JEOPARDY CLUE IS THE FOLLOWING...'THIS BLACK AND WHITE STRIPED, HORSE-LIKE MAMMAL IS OFTEN THE PREY OF CROCODILES AND OTHER PREDATORS.'
THIS BLACK AND WHITE STRIPED HORSE-LIKE MAMMAL IS OFTEN THE PREY OF CROCODILES AND OTHER PREDATORS.
$64,000

OHMYGAWD, THAT IDIOT CROC IS GONNA WIN.
Stoopid Larry gonna be weener!
MY FATHER... A 'JEOPARDY' CHAMP.
MY HUSBAND, A WINNER... AT LAST.
JEOPARDY THEME MUSIC JEOPARDY THEME JEOPARDY THEME JEOPARDY THEME MU
10/17

LARRY, YOU WERE IN THE LEAD WITH $64,000, OF WHICH YOU'VE BET EVERYTHING. AND YOU SAID...
$64,000
Whuh is zeeba?
OH, I'M SORRY. THE ANSWER IS 'ZEBRA,' NOT 'ZEEBA'... YOU'VE LOST EVERYTHING.

AHHHHHH HHHHHHHHH
AHHHHHHHHHHHH
ME HAS SPEECH IMPEEDIMINT!!!
SORRY, PAL. A 'ZEEBA' IS NOT A 'ZEBRA.'
G#*☆!
PLEASE RELEASE MR. TREBEK'S HEAD.
G#*☆!

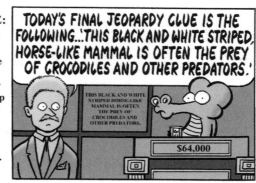

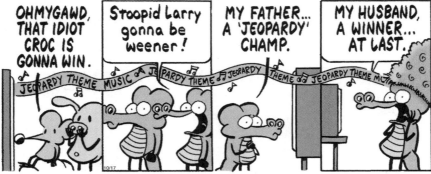

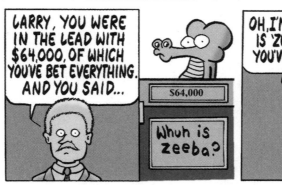

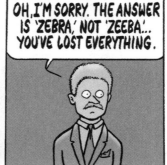

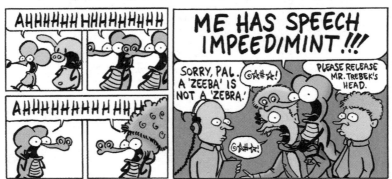

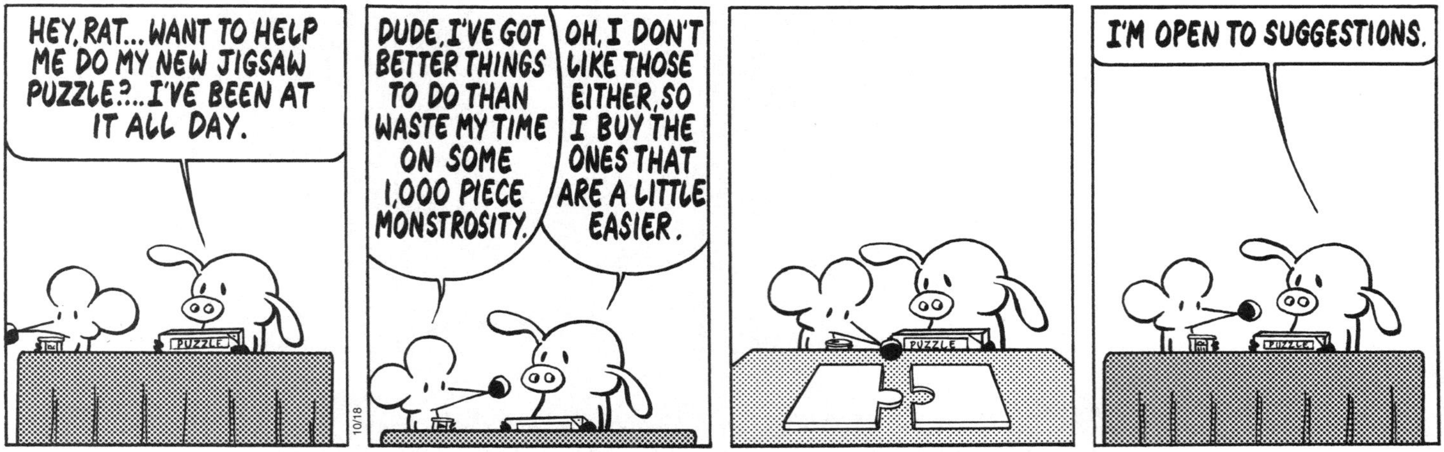
HEY, RAT... WANT TO HELP ME DO MY NEW JIGSAW PUZZLE?... I'VE BEEN AT IT ALL DAY.
PUZZLE
10/18
DUDE, I'VE GOT BETTER THINGS TO DO THAN WASTE MY TIME ON SOME 1,000 PIECE MONSTROSITY.
OH, I DON'T LIKE THOSE EITHER, SO I BUY THE ONES THAT ARE A LITTLE EASIER.
PUZZLE
I'M OPEN TO SUGGESTIONS.
PUZZLE

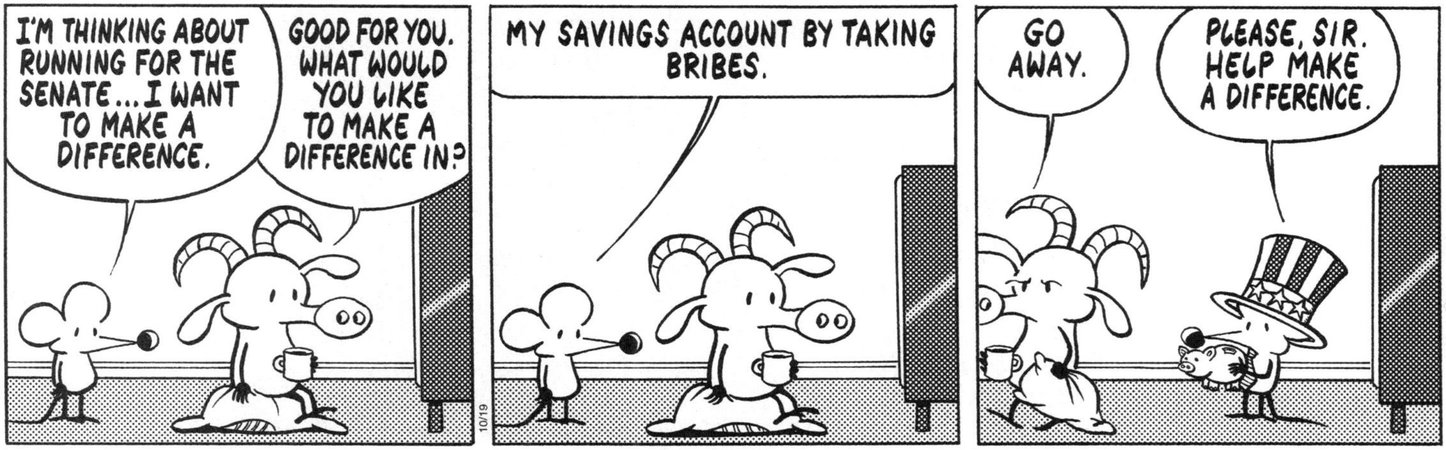
I'M THINKING ABOUT RUNNING FOR THE SENATE... I WANT TO MAKE A DIFFERENCE.
GOOD FOR YOU. WHAT WOULD YOU LIKE TO MAKE A DIFFERENCE IN?
10/19
MY SAVINGS ACCOUNT BY TAKING BRIBES.
GO AWAY.
PLEASE, SIR. HELP MAKE A DIFFERENCE.

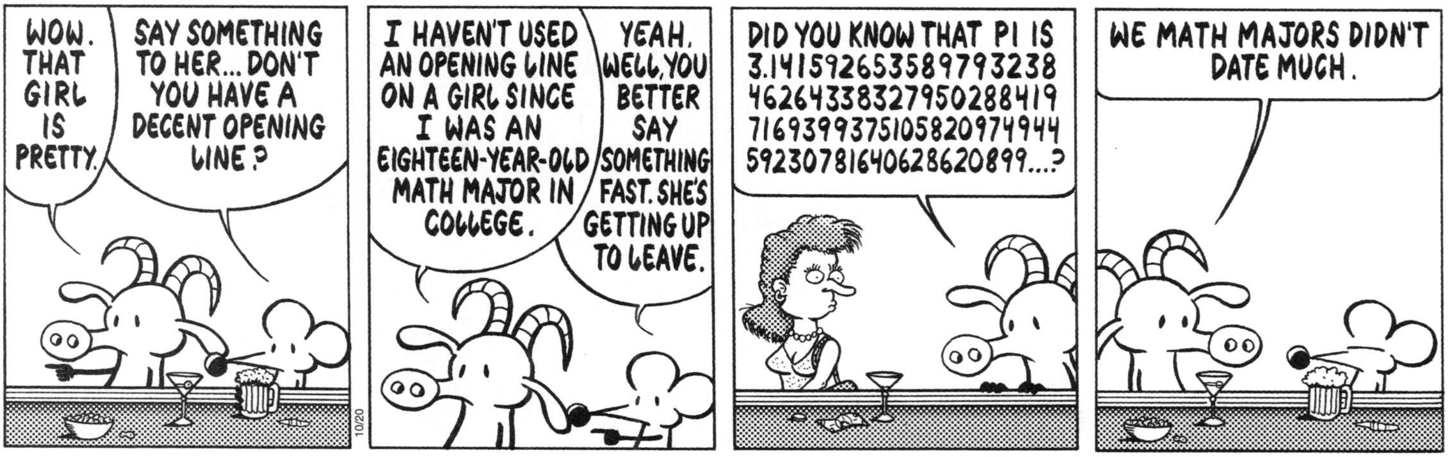
WOW. THAT GIRL IS PRETTY.
SAY SOMETHING TO HER... DON'T YOU HAVE A DECENT OPENING LINE?
10/20
I HAVEN'T USED AN OPENING LINE ON A GIRL SINCE I WAS AN EIGHTEEN-YEAR-OLD MATH MAJOR IN COLLEGE.
YEAH. WELL, YOU BETTER SAY SOMETHING FAST. SHE'S GETTING UP TO LEAVE.
DID YOU KNOW THAT PI IS 3.14159265358979323846264338327950288419716939937510582097494459230781640628620899...?
WE MATH MAJORS DIDN'T DATE MUCH.

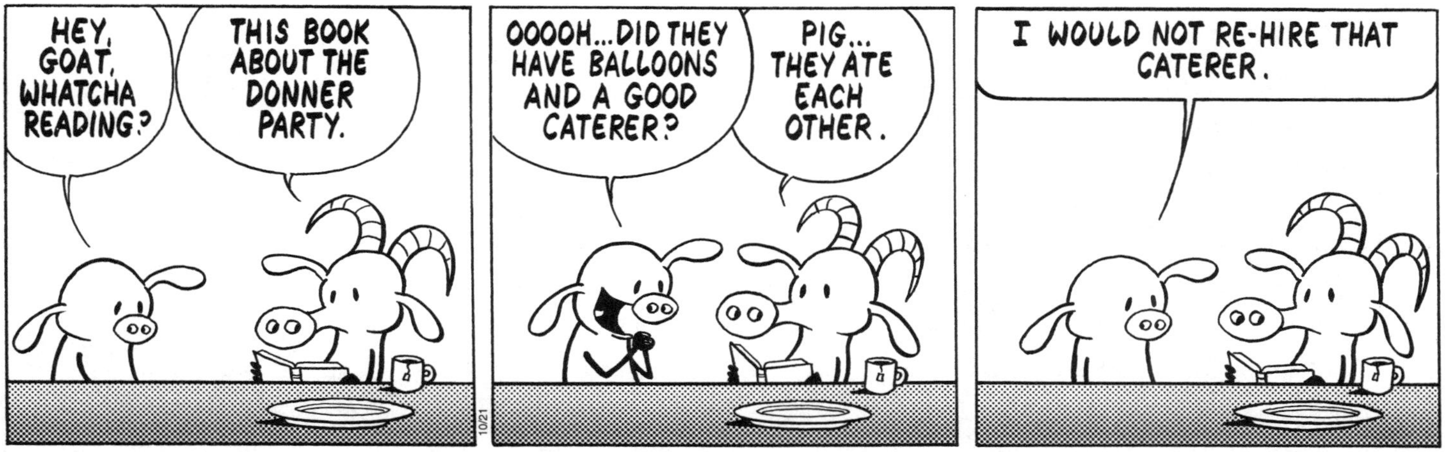
HEY, GOAT, WHATCHA READING?
THIS BOOK ABOUT THE DONNER PARTY.
OOOOH...DID THEY HAVE BALLOONS AND A GOOD CATERER?
PIG... THEY ATE EACH OTHER.
I WOULD NOT RE-HIRE THAT CATERER.
10/21

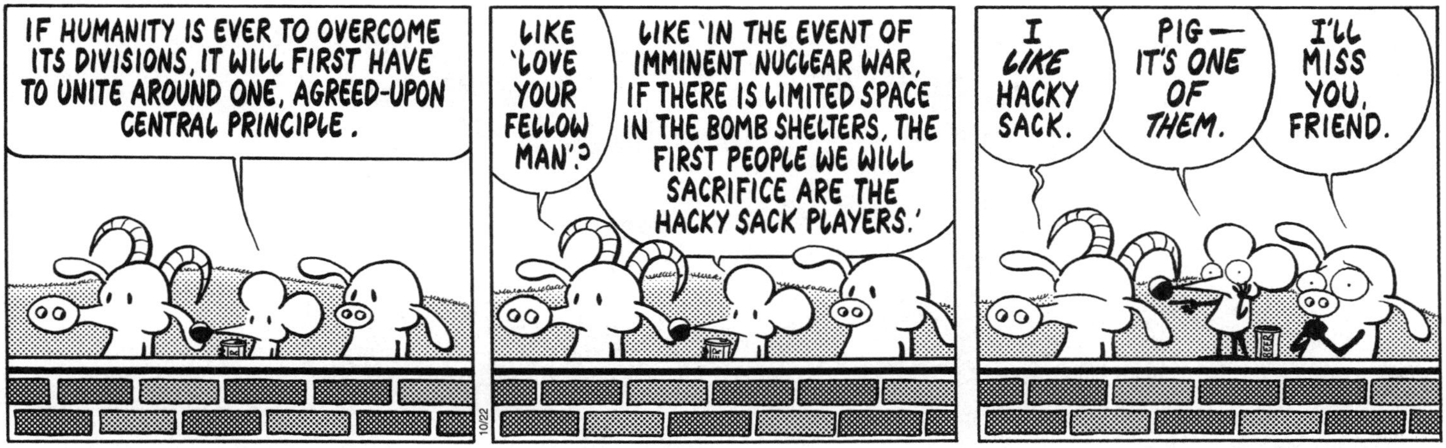
IF HUMANITY IS EVER TO OVERCOME ITS DIVISIONS, IT WILL FIRST HAVE TO UNITE AROUND ONE, AGREED-UPON CENTRAL PRINCIPLE.
LIKE 'LOVE YOUR FELLOW MAN'?
LIKE 'IN THE EVENT OF IMMINENT NUCLEAR WAR, IF THERE IS LIMITED SPACE IN THE BOMB SHELTERS, THE FIRST PEOPLE WE WILL SACRIFICE ARE THE HACKY SACK PLAYERS.'
I *LIKE* HACKY SACK.
PIG— IT'S *ONE OF THEM*.
I'LL MISS YOU, FRIEND.
10/22

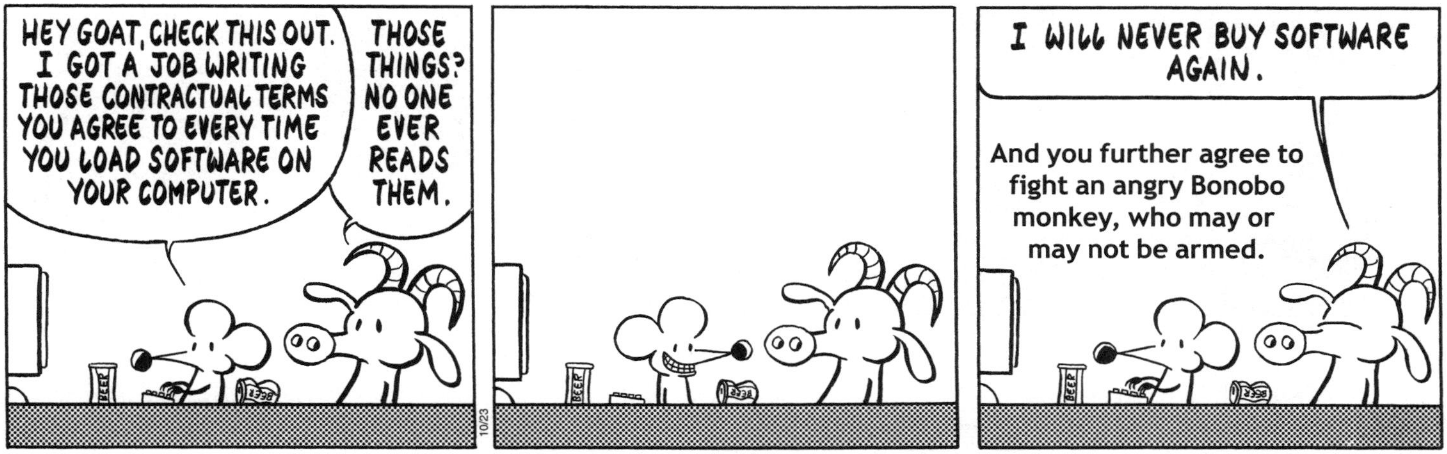
HEY GOAT, CHECK THIS OUT. I GOT A JOB WRITING THOSE CONTRACTUAL TERMS YOU AGREE TO EVERY TIME YOU LOAD SOFTWARE ON YOUR COMPUTER.
THOSE THINGS? NO ONE EVER READS THEM.
I WILL NEVER BUY SOFTWARE AGAIN.
And you further agree to fight an angry Bonobo monkey, who may or may not be armed.
10/23

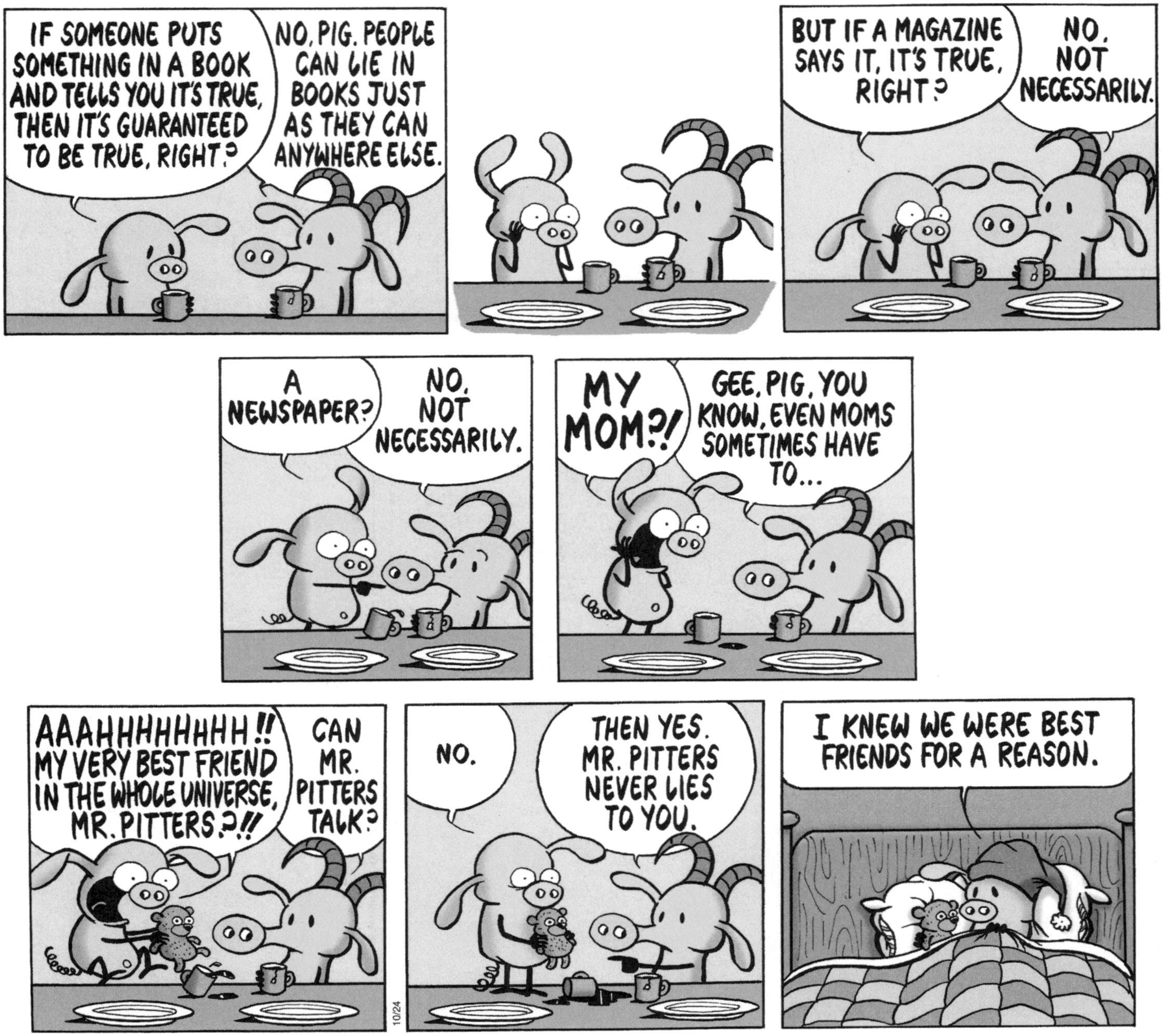
IF SOMEONE PUTS SOMETHING IN A BOOK AND TELLS YOU IT'S TRUE, THEN IT'S GUARANTEED TO BE TRUE, RIGHT?
NO, PIG. PEOPLE CAN LIE IN BOOKS JUST AS THEY CAN ANYWHERE ELSE.
BUT IF A MAGAZINE SAYS IT, IT'S TRUE, RIGHT?
NO. NOT NECESSARILY.
A NEWSPAPER?
NO. NOT NECESSARILY.
MY MOM?!
GEE, PIG, YOU KNOW, EVEN MOMS SOMETIMES HAVE TO...
AAAHHHHHHHH!! MY VERY BEST FRIEND IN THE WHOLE UNIVERSE, MR. PITTERS?!!
CAN MR. PITTERS TALK?
NO.
THEN YES. MR. PITTERS NEVER LIES TO YOU.
I KNEW WE WERE BEST FRIENDS FOR A REASON.
10/24

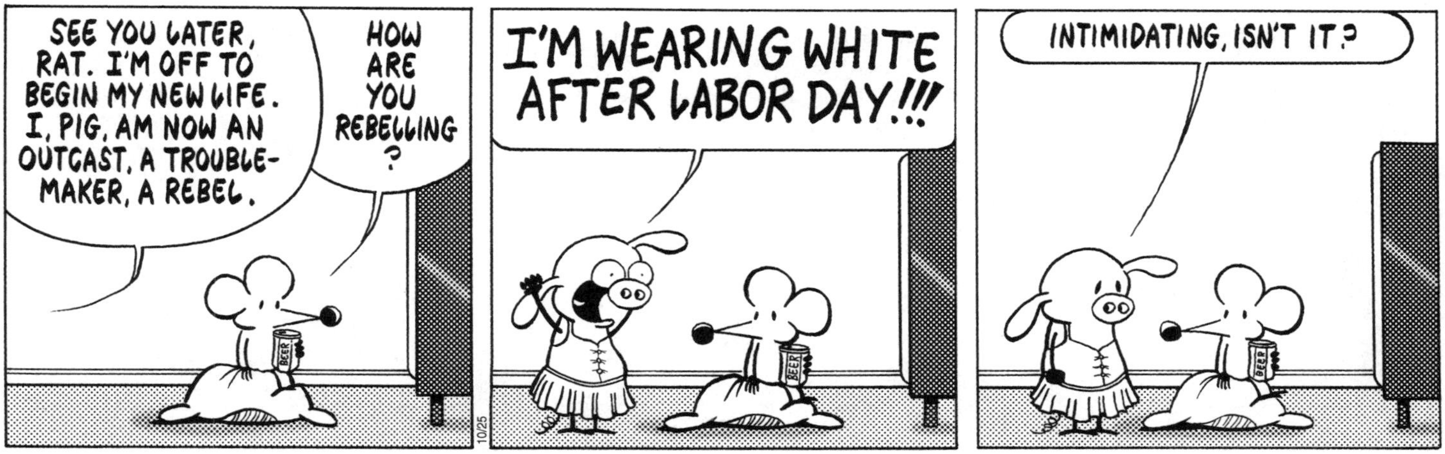
SEE YOU LATER, RAT. I'M OFF TO BEGIN MY NEW LIFE. I, PIG, AM NOW AN OUTCAST, A TROUBLE-MAKER, A REBEL.
HOW ARE YOU REBELLING?
I'M WEARING WHITE AFTER LABOR DAY!!!
INTIMIDATING, ISN'T IT?
10/25

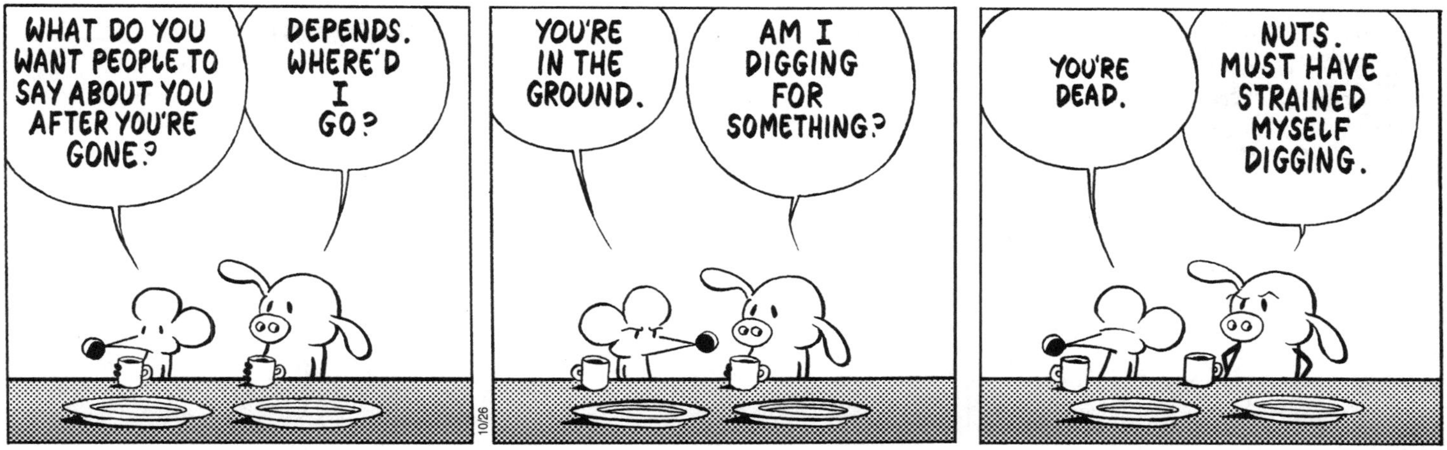
WHAT DO YOU WANT PEOPLE TO SAY ABOUT YOU AFTER YOU'RE GONE?
DEPENDS. WHERE'D I GO?
YOU'RE IN THE GROUND.
AM I DIGGING FOR SOMETHING?
YOU'RE DEAD.
NUTS. MUST HAVE STRAINED MYSELF DIGGING.
10/26

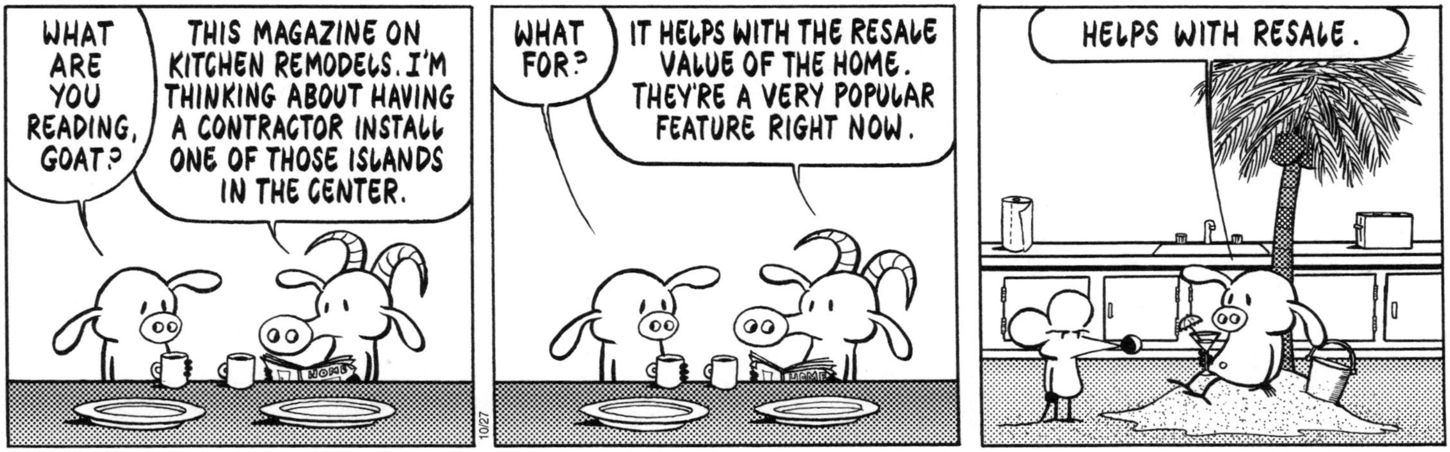
WHAT ARE YOU READING, GOAT?
THIS MAGAZINE ON KITCHEN REMODELS. I'M THINKING ABOUT HAVING A CONTRACTOR INSTALL ONE OF THOSE ISLANDS IN THE CENTER.
WHAT FOR?
IT HELPS WITH THE RESALE VALUE OF THE HOME. THEY'RE A VERY POPULAR FEATURE RIGHT NOW.
HELPS WITH RESALE.
10/27

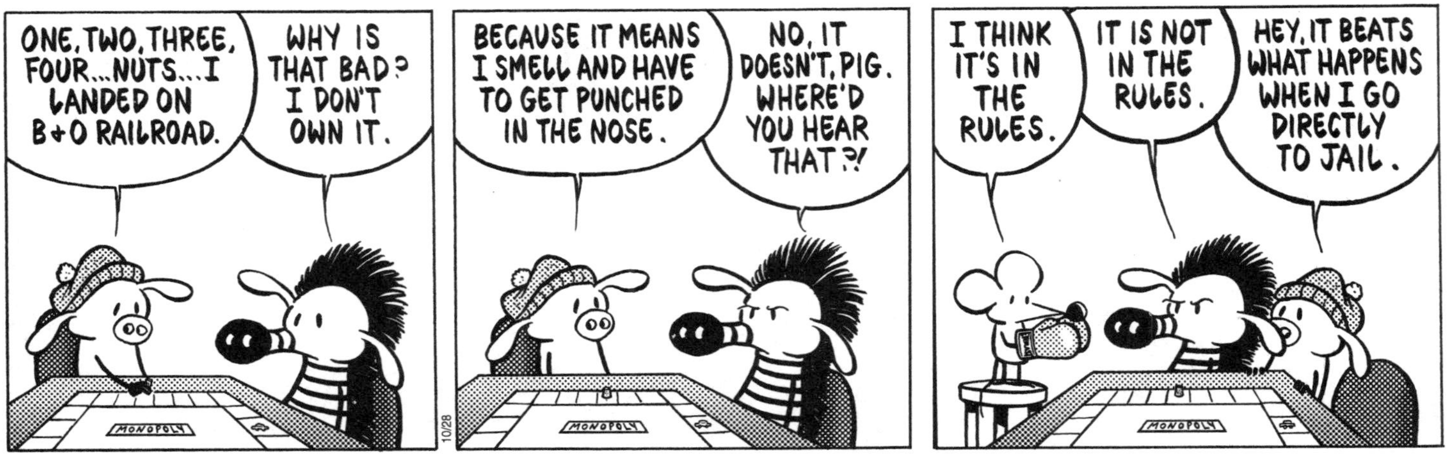
ONE, TWO, THREE, FOUR...NUTS...I LANDED ON B+O RAILROAD.
WHY IS THAT BAD? I DON'T OWN IT.
BECAUSE IT MEANS I SMELL AND HAVE TO GET PUNCHED IN THE NOSE.
NO, IT DOESN'T, PIG. WHERE'D YOU HEAR THAT?!
MONOPOLY
I THINK IT'S IN THE RULES.
IT IS NOT IN THE RULES.
HEY, IT BEATS WHAT HAPPENS WHEN I GO DIRECTLY TO JAIL.

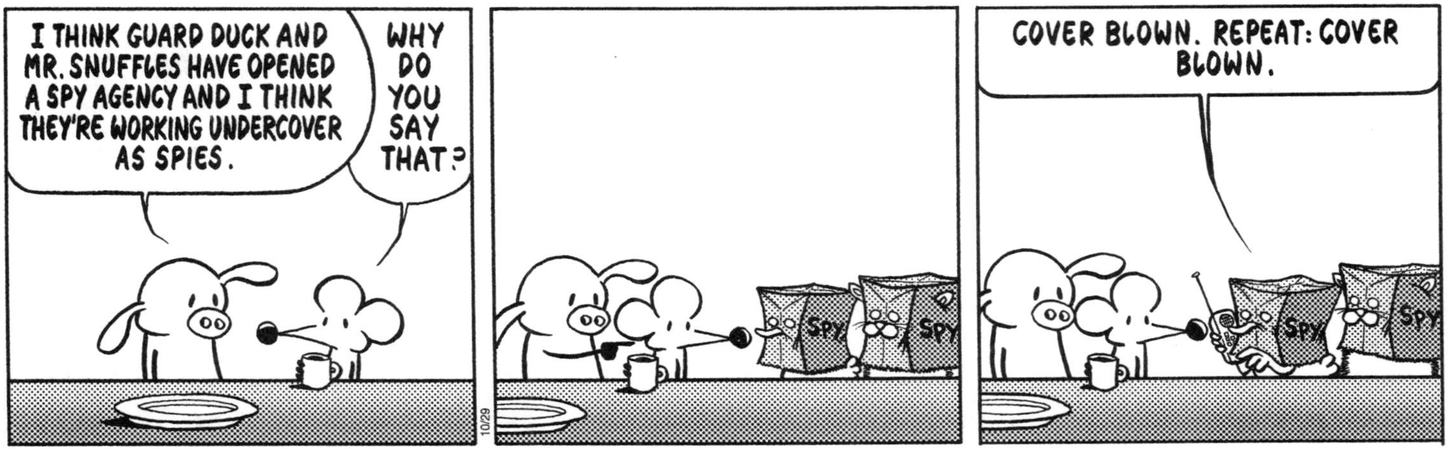
I THINK GUARD DUCK AND MR. SNUFFLES HAVE OPENED A SPY AGENCY AND I THINK THEY'RE WORKING UNDERCOVER AS SPIES.
WHY DO YOU SAY THAT?
SPY
SPY
COVER BLOWN. REPEAT: COVER BLOWN.

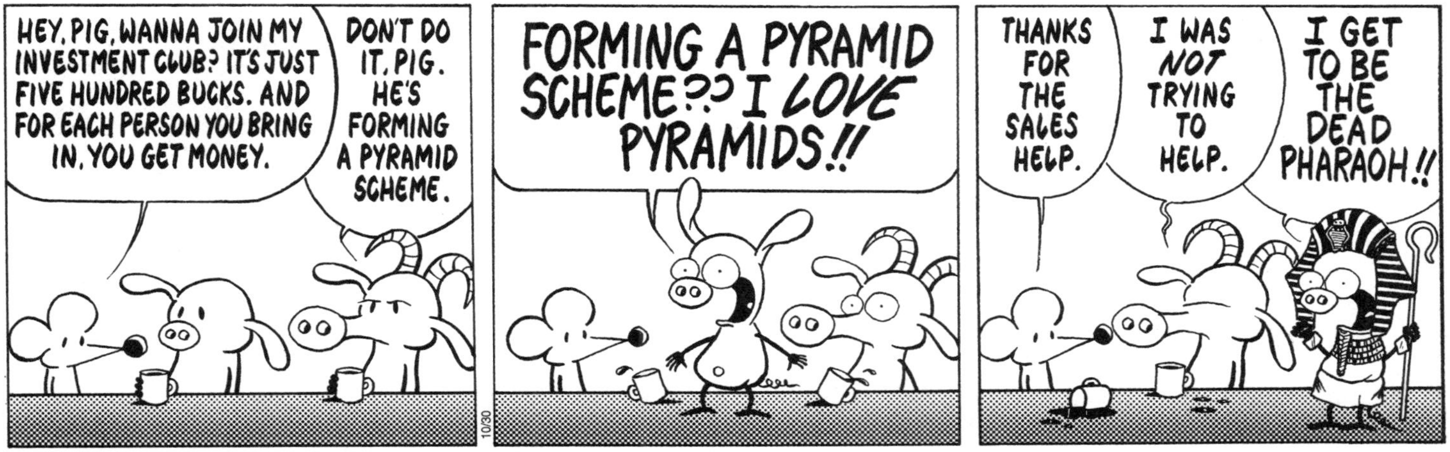
HEY, PIG, WANNA JOIN MY INVESTMENT CLUB? IT'S JUST FIVE HUNDRED BUCKS. AND FOR EACH PERSON YOU BRING IN, YOU GET MONEY.
DON'T DO IT, PIG. HE'S FORMING A PYRAMID SCHEME.
FORMING A PYRAMID SCHEME?? I LOVE PYRAMIDS!!
THANKS FOR THE SALES HELP.
I WAS NOT TRYING TO HELP.
I GET TO BE THE DEAD PHARAOH!!

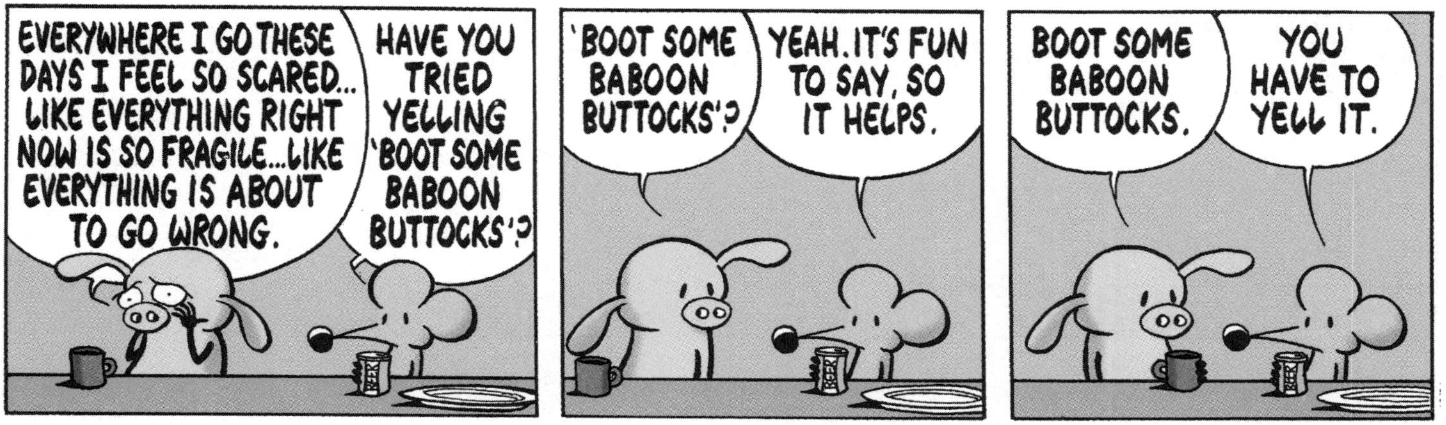
EVERYWHERE I GO THESE DAYS I FEEL SO SCARED... LIKE EVERYTHING RIGHT NOW IS SO FRAGILE...LIKE EVERYTHING IS ABOUT TO GO WRONG.
HAVE YOU TRIED YELLING 'BOOT SOME BABOON BUTTOCKS'?
'BOOT SOME BABOON BUTTOCKS'?
YEAH. IT'S FUN TO SAY, SO IT HELPS.
BOOT SOME BABOON BUTTOCKS.
YOU HAVE TO YELL IT.

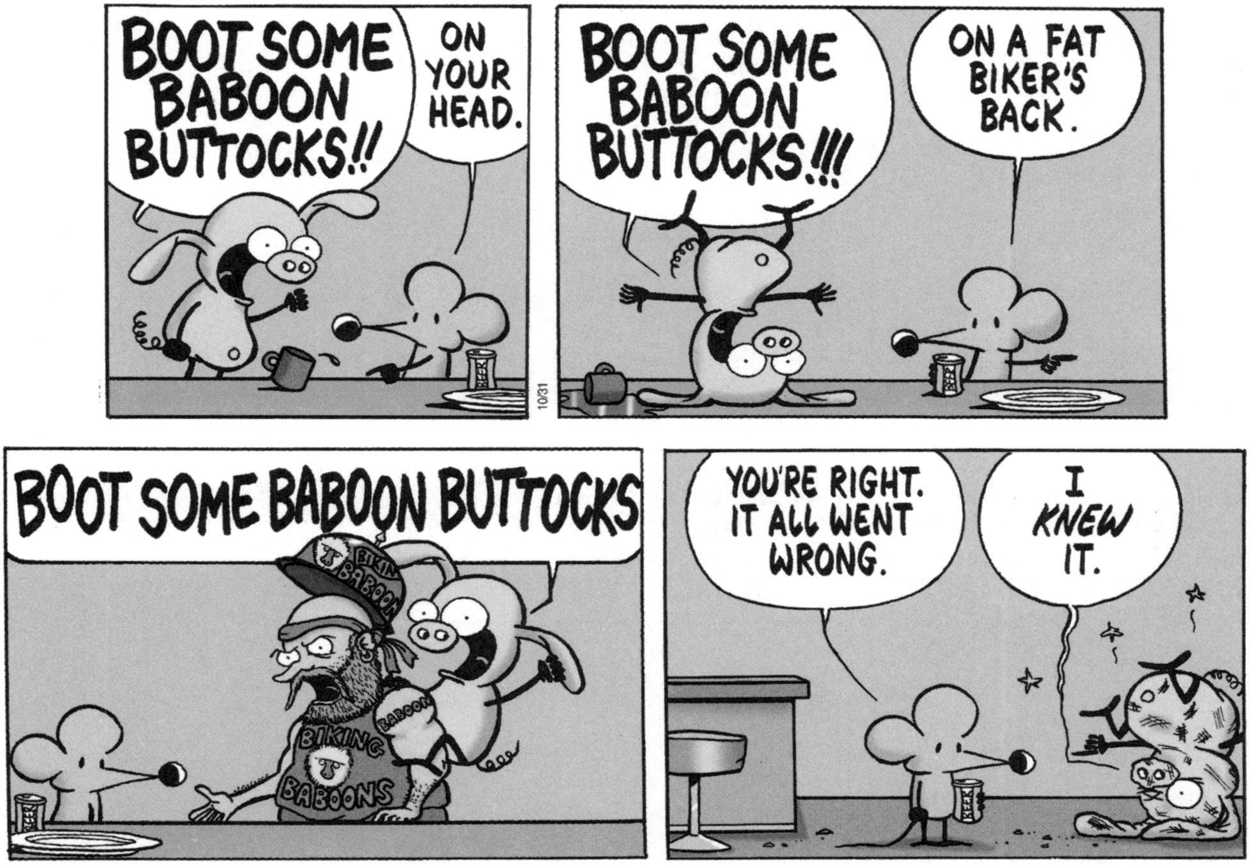
BOOT SOME BABOON BUTTOCKS!!
ON YOUR HEAD.
10/31
BOOT SOME BABOON BUTTOCKS!!!
ON A FAT BIKER'S BACK.
BOOT SOME BABOON BUTTOCKS
BIKING BABOONS
YOU'RE RIGHT. IT ALL WENT WRONG.
I *KNEW* IT.

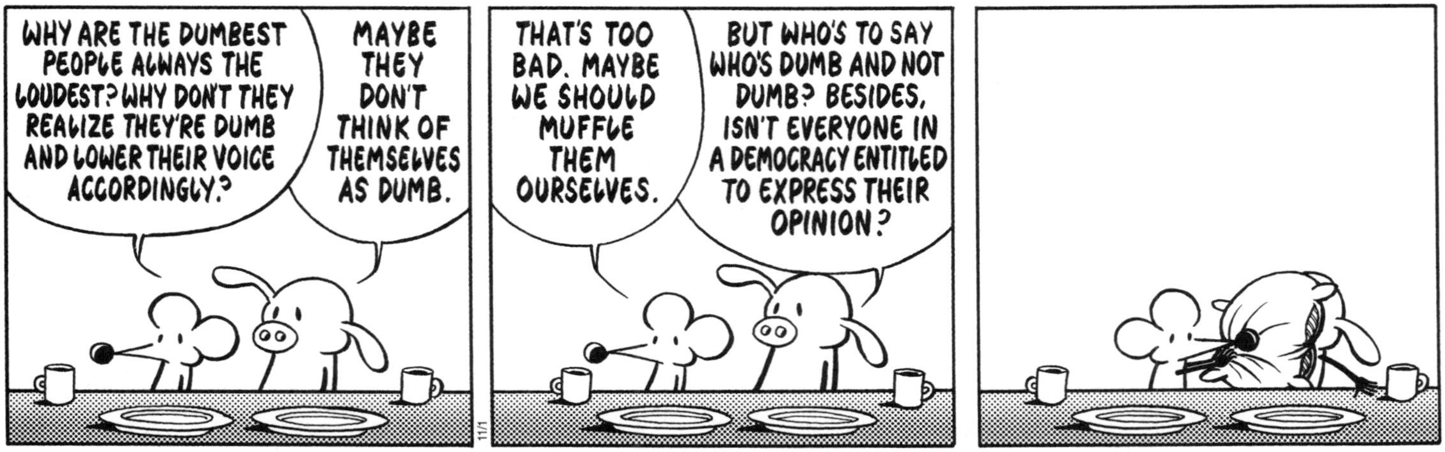
WHY ARE THE DUMBEST PEOPLE ALWAYS THE LOUDEST? WHY DON'T THEY REALIZE THEY'RE DUMB AND LOWER THEIR VOICE ACCORDINGLY?
MAYBE THEY DON'T THINK OF THEMSELVES AS DUMB.
THAT'S TOO BAD. MAYBE WE SHOULD MUFFLE THEM OURSELVES.
BUT WHO'S TO SAY WHO'S DUMB AND NOT DUMB? BESIDES, ISN'T EVERYONE IN A DEMOCRACY ENTITLED TO EXPRESS THEIR OPINION?
11/1

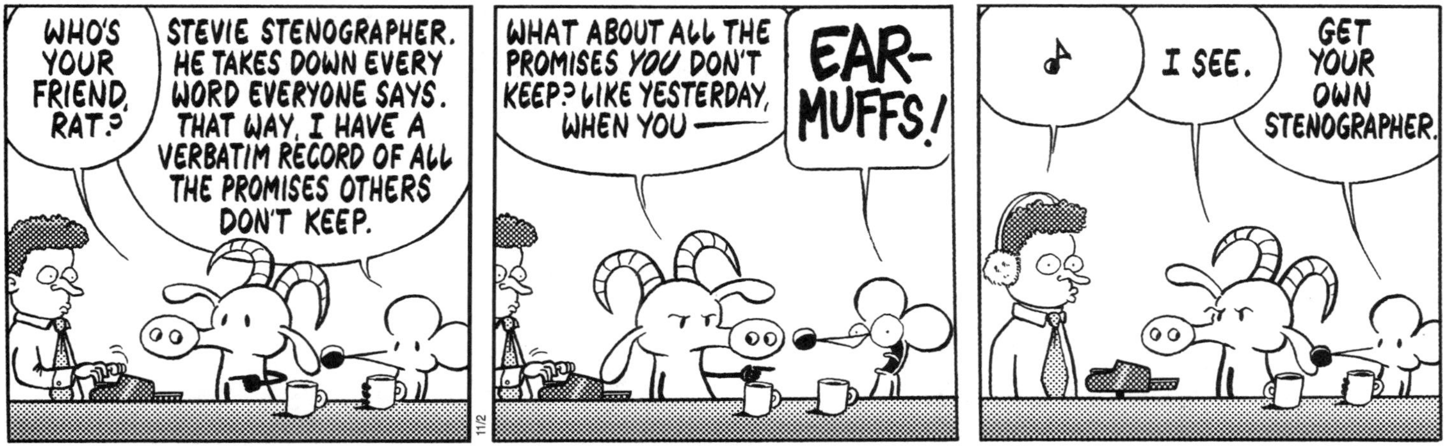
WHO'S YOUR FRIEND, RAT?
STEVIE STENOGRAPHER. HE TAKES DOWN EVERY WORD EVERYONE SAYS. THAT WAY, I HAVE A VERBATIM RECORD OF ALL THE PROMISES OTHERS DON'T KEEP.
WHAT ABOUT ALL THE PROMISES YOU DON'T KEEP? LIKE YESTERDAY, WHEN YOU —
EAR-MUFFS!
♪
I SEE.
GET YOUR OWN STENOGRAPHER.
11/2

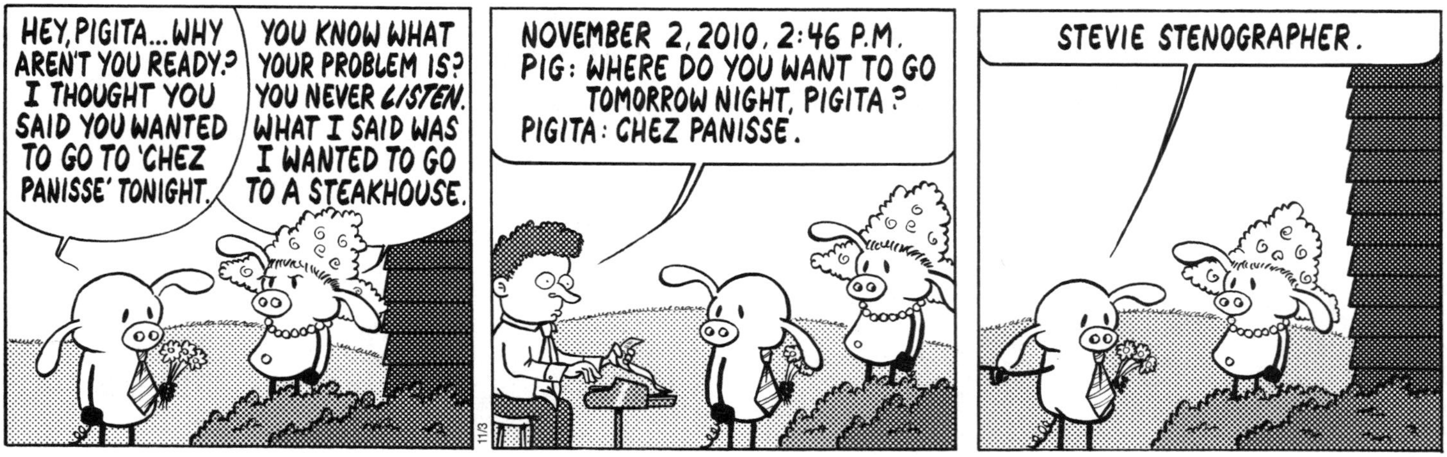
HEY, PIGITA... WHY AREN'T YOU READY? I THOUGHT YOU SAID YOU WANTED TO GO TO 'CHEZ PANISSE' TONIGHT.
YOU KNOW WHAT YOUR PROBLEM IS? YOU NEVER LISTEN. WHAT I SAID WAS I WANTED TO GO TO A STEAKHOUSE.
NOVEMBER 2, 2010, 2:46 P.M.
PIG: WHERE DO YOU WANT TO GO TOMORROW NIGHT, PIGITA?
PIGITA: CHEZ PANISSE.
STEVIE STENOGRAPHER.
11/3

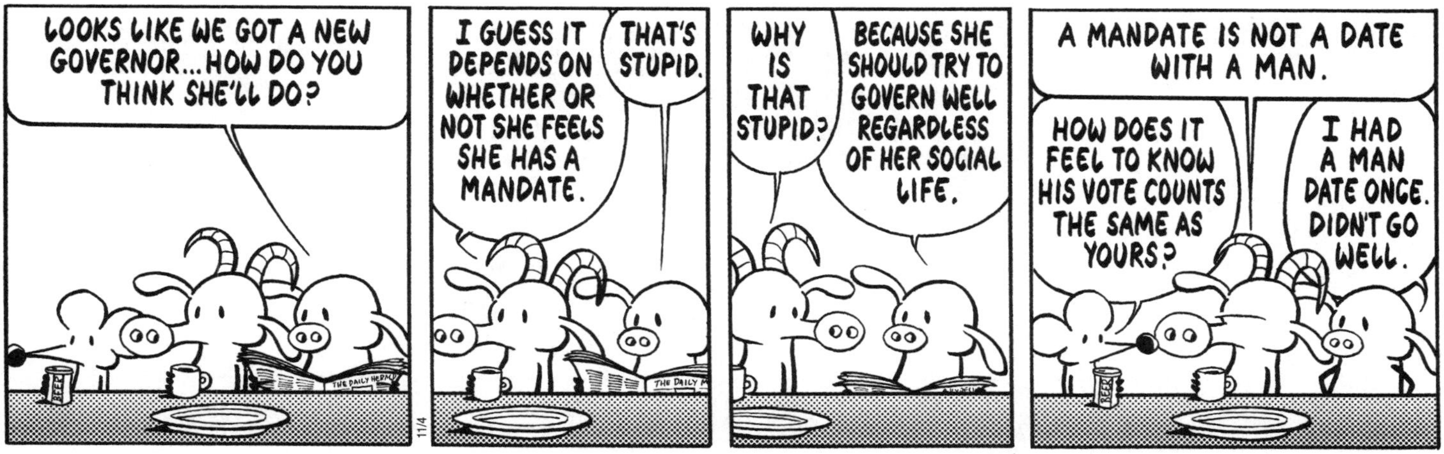
LOOKS LIKE WE GOT A NEW GOVERNOR... HOW DO YOU THINK SHE'LL DO?
I GUESS IT DEPENDS ON WHETHER OR NOT SHE FEELS SHE HAS A MANDATE.
THAT'S STUPID.
WHY IS THAT STUPID?
BECAUSE SHE SHOULD TRY TO GOVERN WELL REGARDLESS OF HER SOCIAL LIFE.
A MANDATE IS NOT A DATE WITH A MAN.
HOW DOES IT FEEL TO KNOW HIS VOTE COUNTS THE SAME AS YOURS?
I HAD A MAN DATE ONCE. DIDN'T GO WELL.

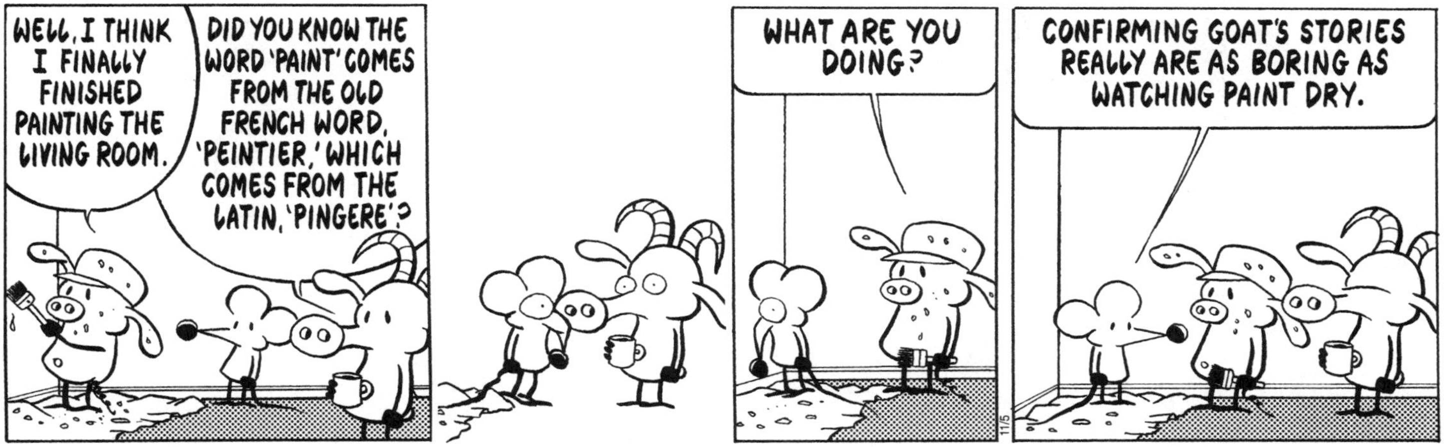
WELL, I THINK I FINALLY FINISHED PAINTING THE LIVING ROOM.
DID YOU KNOW THE WORD 'PAINT' COMES FROM THE OLD FRENCH WORD, 'PEINTIER,' WHICH COMES FROM THE LATIN, 'PINGERE'?
WHAT ARE YOU DOING?
CONFIRMING GOAT'S STORIES REALLY ARE AS BORING AS WATCHING PAINT DRY.

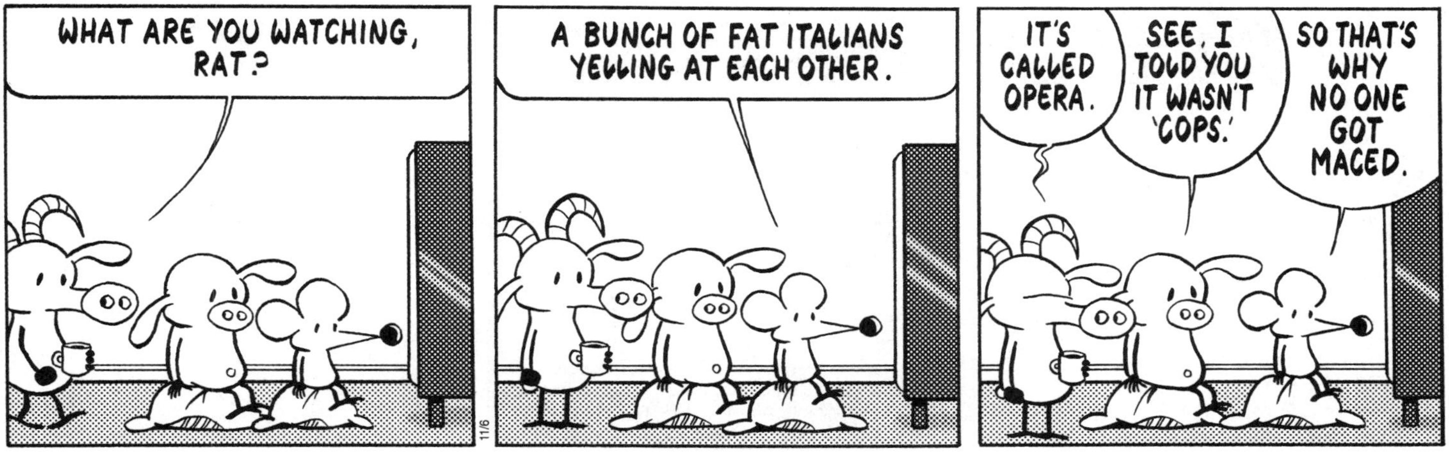
WHAT ARE YOU WATCHING, RAT?
A BUNCH OF FAT ITALIANS YELLING AT EACH OTHER.
IT'S CALLED OPERA.
SEE, I TOLD YOU IT WASN'T 'COPS.'
SO THAT'S WHY NO ONE GOT MACED.

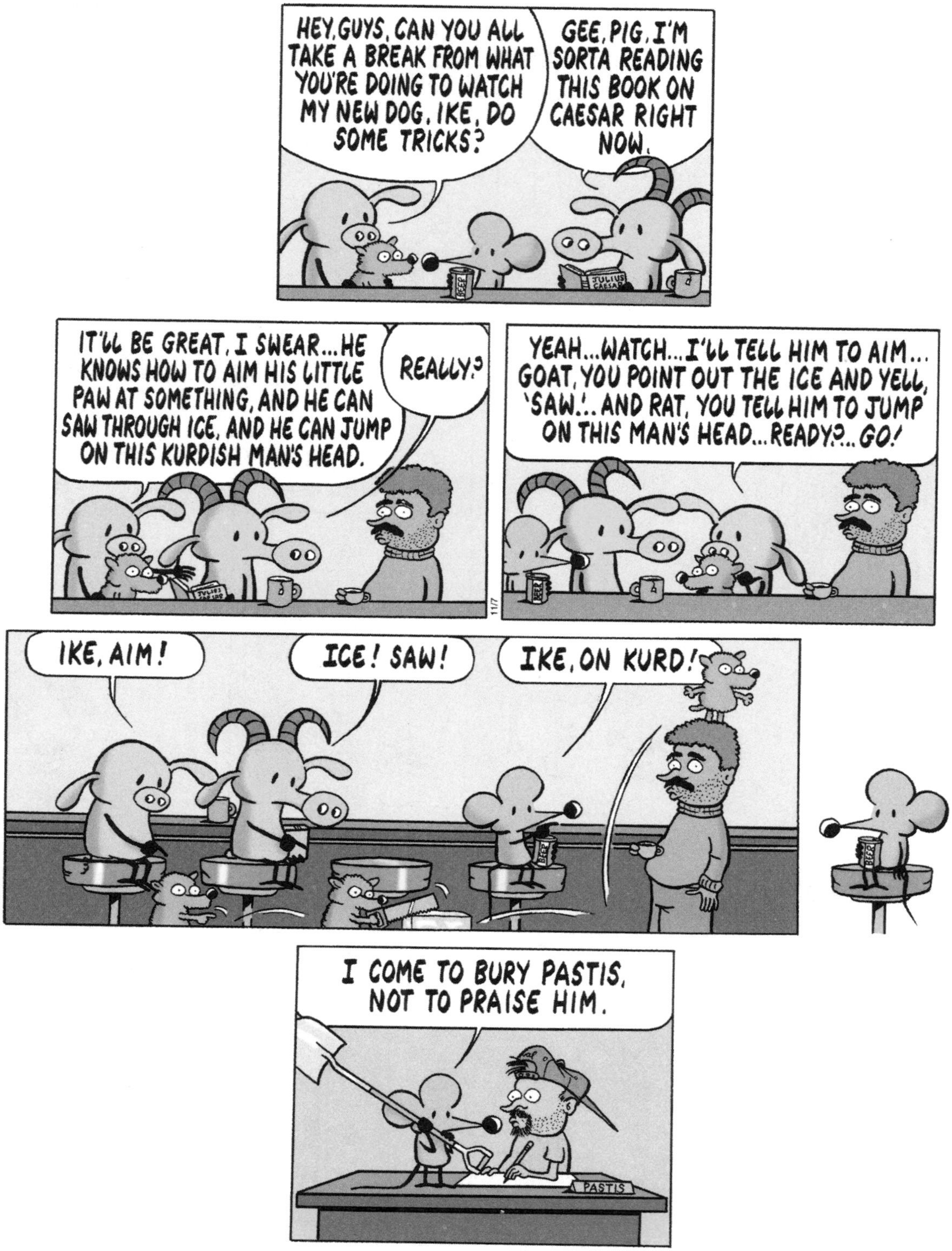
HEY, GUYS, CAN YOU ALL TAKE A BREAK FROM WHAT YOU'RE DOING TO WATCH MY NEW DOG, IKE, DO SOME TRICKS?
GEE, PIG, I'M SORTA READING THIS BOOK ON CAESAR RIGHT NOW.
JULIUS CAESAR
BEER
IT'LL BE GREAT, I SWEAR... HE KNOWS HOW TO AIM HIS LITTLE PAW AT SOMETHING, AND HE CAN SAW THROUGH ICE, AND HE CAN JUMP ON THIS KURDISH MAN'S HEAD.
REALLY?
YEAH... WATCH... I'LL TELL HIM TO AIM... GOAT, YOU POINT OUT THE ICE AND YELL, 'SAW!'... AND RAT, YOU TELL HIM TO JUMP ON THIS MAN'S HEAD... READY?... GO!
BEER
IKE, AIM!
ICE! SAW!
IKE, ON KURD!
BEER
BEER
I COME TO BURY PASTIS, NOT TO PRAISE HIM.
PASTIS

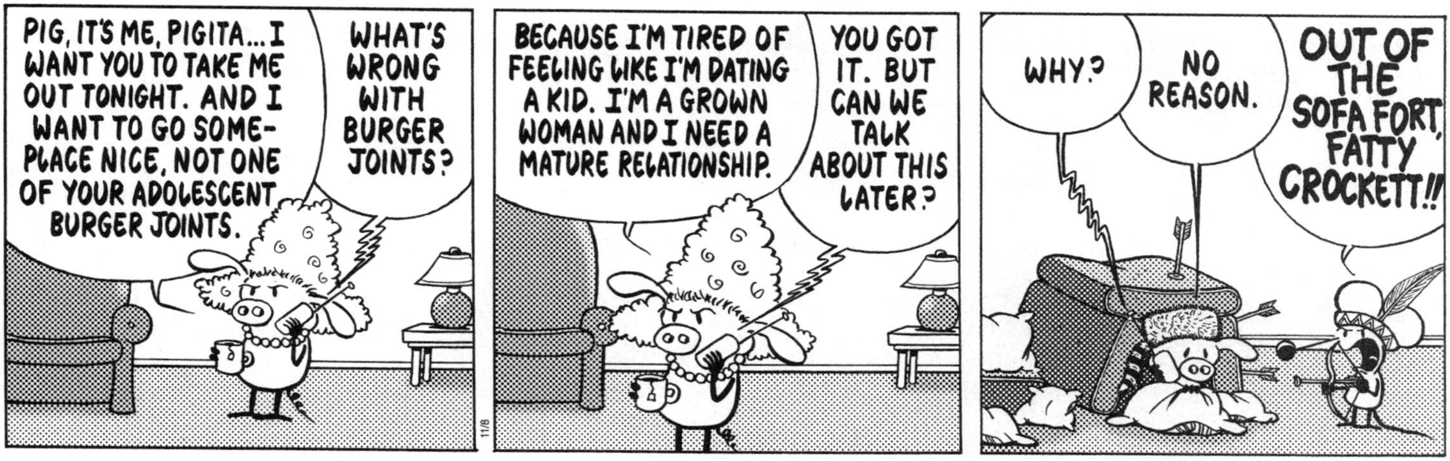
PIG, IT'S ME, PIGITA... I WANT YOU TO TAKE ME OUT TONIGHT. AND I WANT TO GO SOME-PLACE NICE, NOT ONE OF YOUR ADOLESCENT BURGER JOINTS.
WHAT'S WRONG WITH BURGER JOINTS?
BECAUSE I'M TIRED OF FEELING LIKE I'M DATING A KID. I'M A GROWN WOMAN AND I NEED A MATURE RELATIONSHIP.
YOU GOT IT. BUT CAN WE TALK ABOUT THIS LATER?
WHY?
NO REASON.
OUT OF THE SOFA FORT, FATTY CROCKETT!!

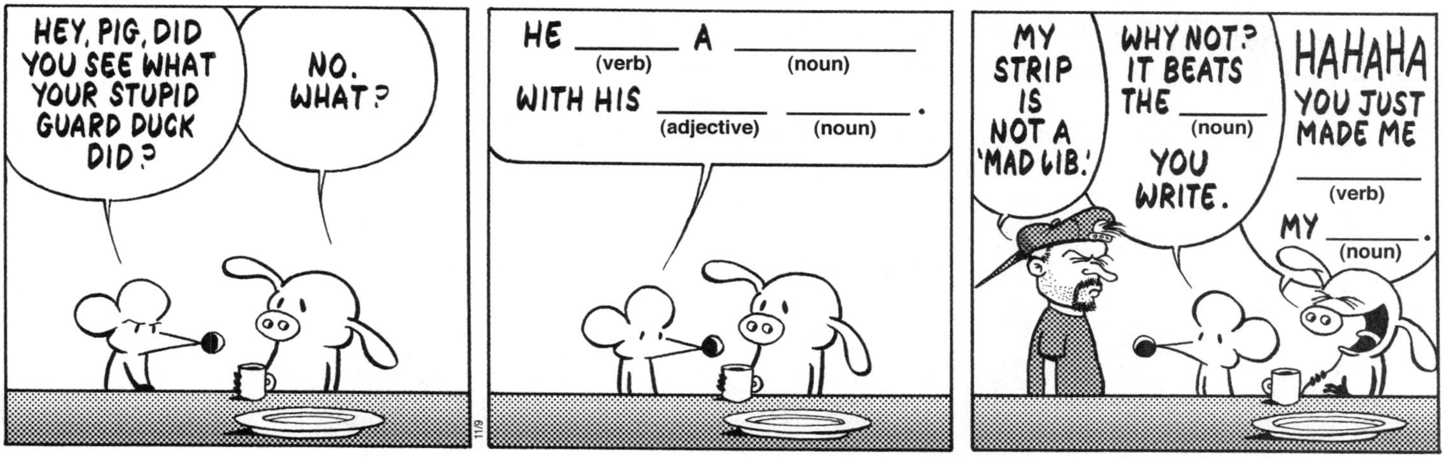
HEY, PIG, DID YOU SEE WHAT YOUR STUPID GUARD DUCK DID?
NO. WHAT?
HE ______ (verb) A ______ (noun) WITH HIS ______ (adjective) ______ (noun).
MY STRIP IS NOT A 'MAD LIB.'
WHY NOT? IT BEATS THE ______ (noun) YOU WRITE.
HAHAHA YOU JUST MADE ME ______ (verb) MY ______ (noun).

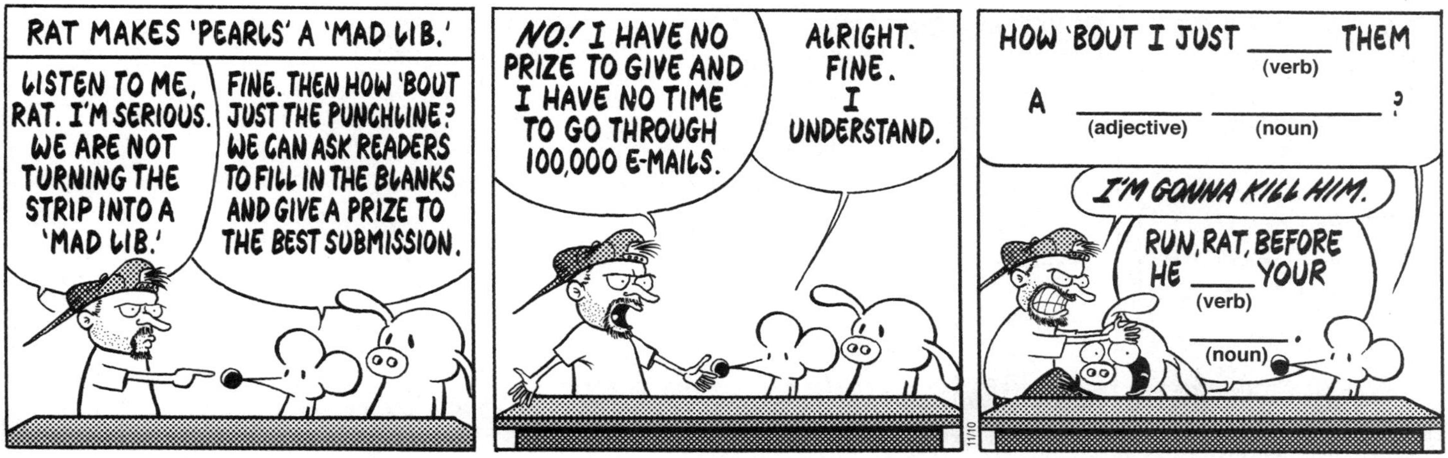
RAT MAKES 'PEARLS' A 'MAD LIB.'
LISTEN TO ME, RAT. I'M SERIOUS. WE ARE NOT TURNING THE STRIP INTO A 'MAD LIB.'
FINE. THEN HOW 'BOUT JUST THE PUNCHLINE? WE CAN ASK READERS TO FILL IN THE BLANKS AND GIVE A PRIZE TO THE BEST SUBMISSION.
NO! I HAVE NO PRIZE TO GIVE AND I HAVE NO TIME TO GO THROUGH 100,000 E-MAILS.
ALRIGHT. FINE. I UNDERSTAND.
HOW 'BOUT I JUST ____ (verb) THEM A ______ (adjective) ______ (noun)?
I'M GONNA KILL HIM.
RUN, RAT, BEFORE HE ____ (verb) YOUR ______ (noun).

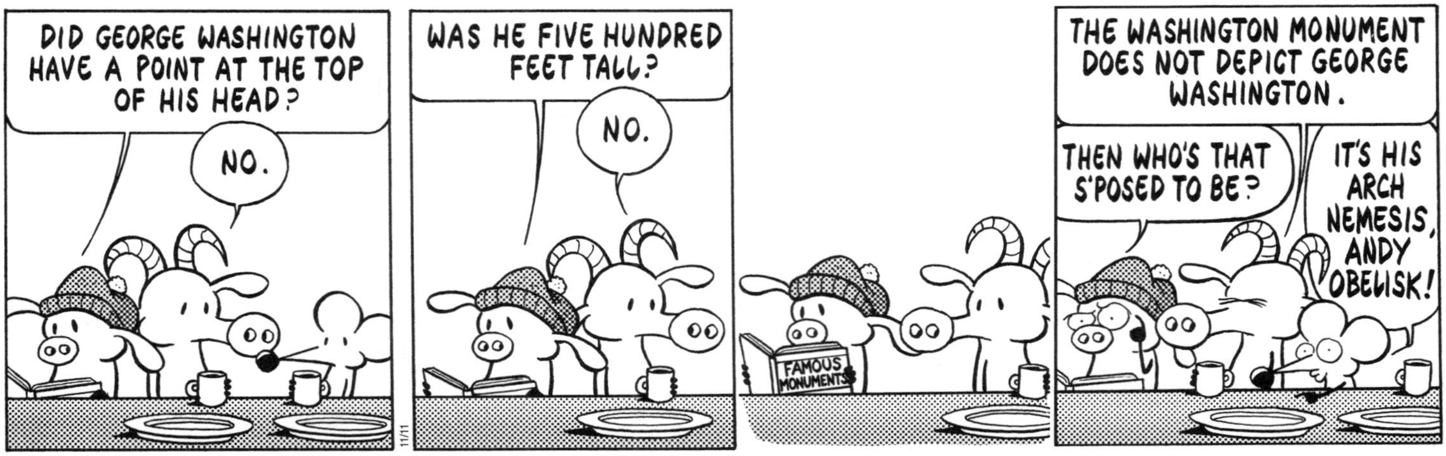
DID GEORGE WASHINGTON HAVE A POINT AT THE TOP OF HIS HEAD?
NO.
WAS HE FIVE HUNDRED FEET TALL?
NO.
11/11
FAMOUS MONUMENTS
THE WASHINGTON MONUMENT DOES NOT DEPICT GEORGE WASHINGTON.
THEN WHO'S THAT S'POSED TO BE?
IT'S HIS ARCH NEMESIS, ANDY OBELISK!

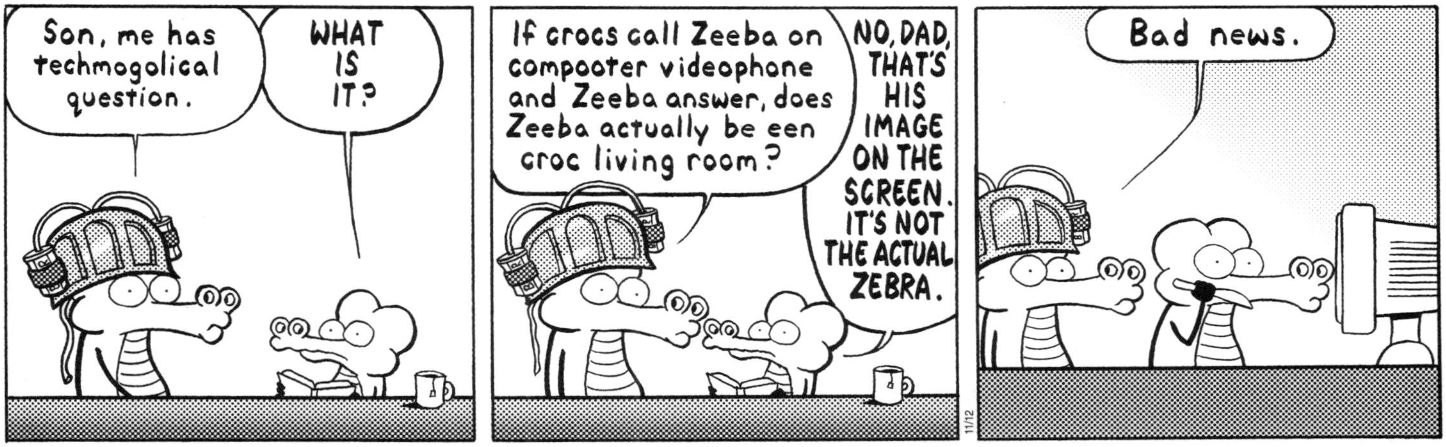
Son, me has techmogolical question.
WHAT IS IT?
If crocs call Zeeba on compooter videophone and Zeeba answer, does Zeeba actually be een croc living room?
NO, DAD, THAT'S HIS IMAGE ON THE SCREEN. IT'S NOT THE ACTUAL ZEBRA.
11/12
Bad news.

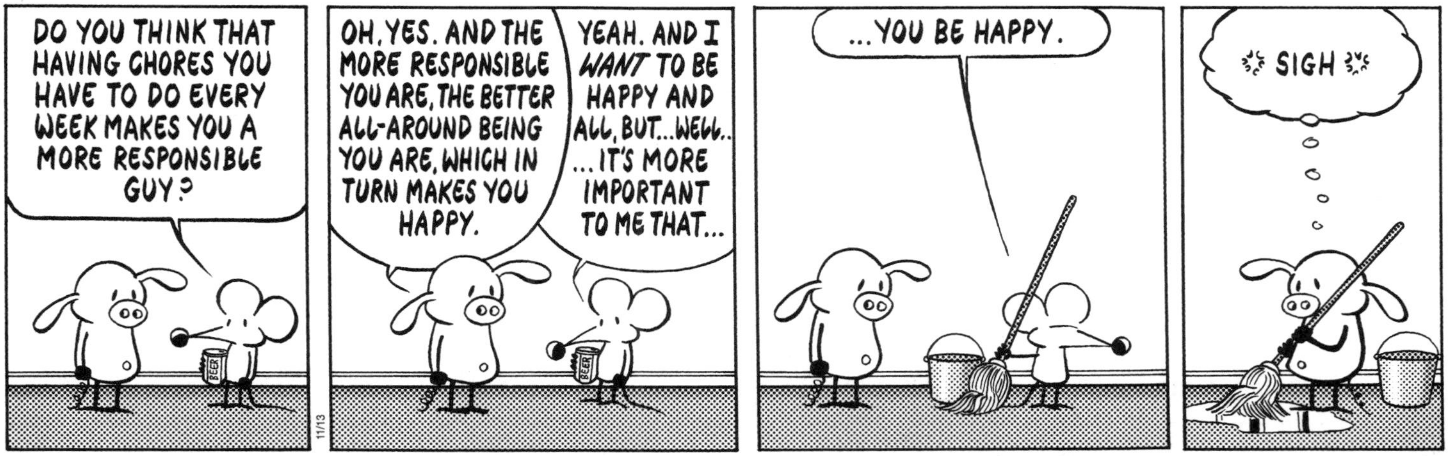
DO YOU THINK THAT HAVING CHORES YOU HAVE TO DO EVERY WEEK MAKES YOU A MORE RESPONSIBLE GUY?
BEER
11/13
OH, YES. AND THE MORE RESPONSIBLE YOU ARE, THE BETTER ALL-AROUND BEING YOU ARE, WHICH IN TURN MAKES YOU HAPPY.
YEAH. AND I *WANT* TO BE HAPPY AND ALL, BUT...WELL...
...IT'S MORE IMPORTANT TO ME THAT...
...YOU BE HAPPY.
SIGH

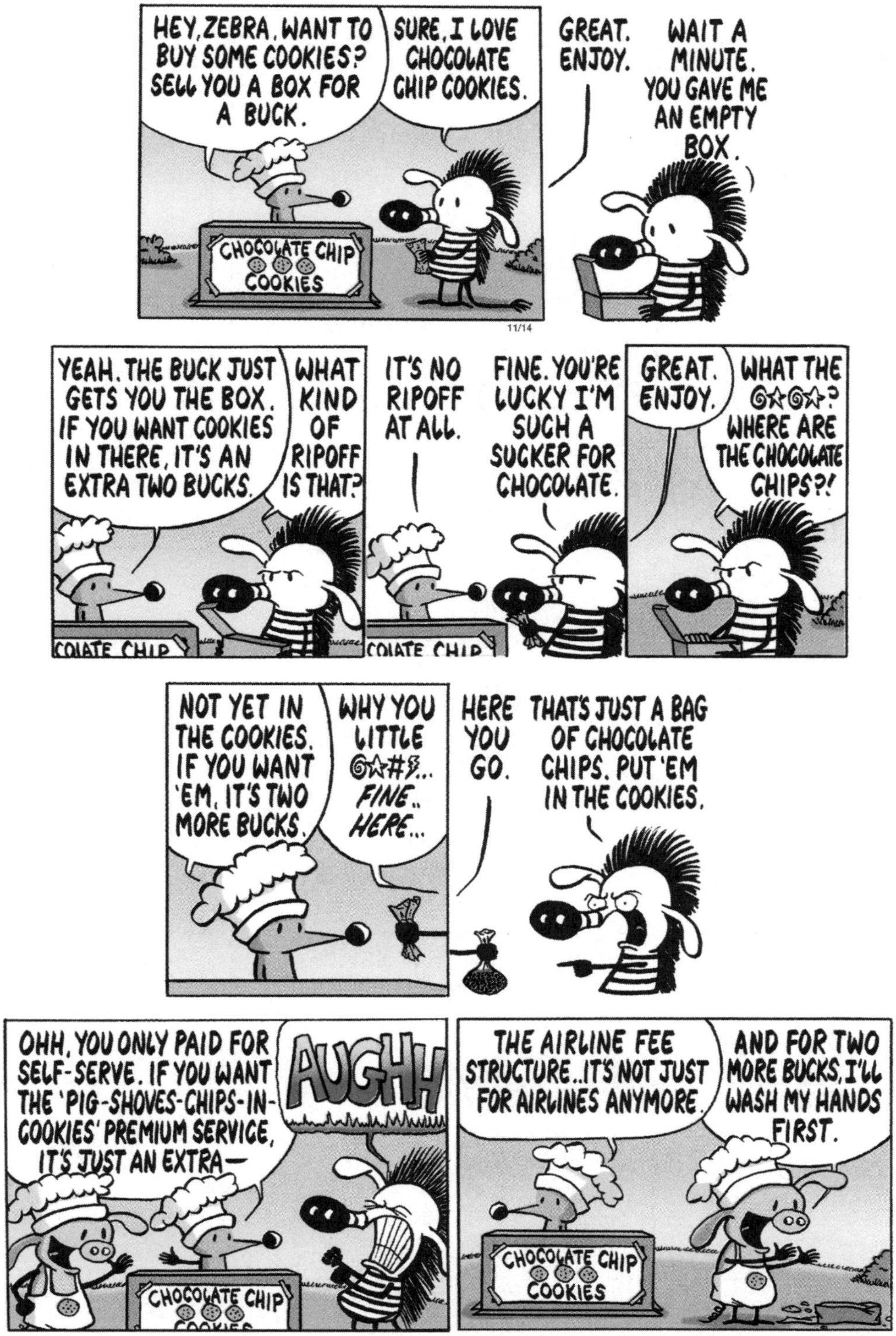
HEY, ZEBRA, WANT TO BUY SOME COOKIES? SELL YOU A BOX FOR A BUCK.
SURE, I LOVE CHOCOLATE CHIP COOKIES.
CHOCOLATE CHIP COOKIES
GREAT. ENJOY.
WAIT A MINUTE. YOU GAVE ME AN EMPTY BOX.
11/14
YEAH. THE BUCK JUST GETS YOU THE BOX. IF YOU WANT COOKIES IN THERE, IT'S AN EXTRA TWO BUCKS.
WHAT KIND OF RIPOFF IS THAT?
IT'S NO RIPOFF AT ALL.
FINE. YOU'RE LUCKY I'M SUCH A SUCKER FOR CHOCOLATE.
GREAT. ENJOY.
WHAT THE
WHERE ARE THE CHOCOLATE CHIPS?!
NOT YET IN THE COOKIES. IF YOU WANT 'EM, IT'S TWO MORE BUCKS.
WHY YOU LITTLE
FINE.. HERE...
HERE YOU GO.
THAT'S JUST A BAG OF CHOCOLATE CHIPS. PUT 'EM IN THE COOKIES.
OHH, YOU ONLY PAID FOR SELF-SERVE. IF YOU WANT THE 'PIG-SHOVES-CHIPS-IN-COOKIES' PREMIUM SERVICE, IT'S JUST AN EXTRA—
AUGHH
CHOCOLATE CHIP
THE AIRLINE FEE STRUCTURE..IT'S NOT JUST FOR AIRLINES ANYMORE.
AND FOR TWO MORE BUCKS, I'LL WASH MY HANDS FIRST.
CHOCOLATE CHIP COOKIES

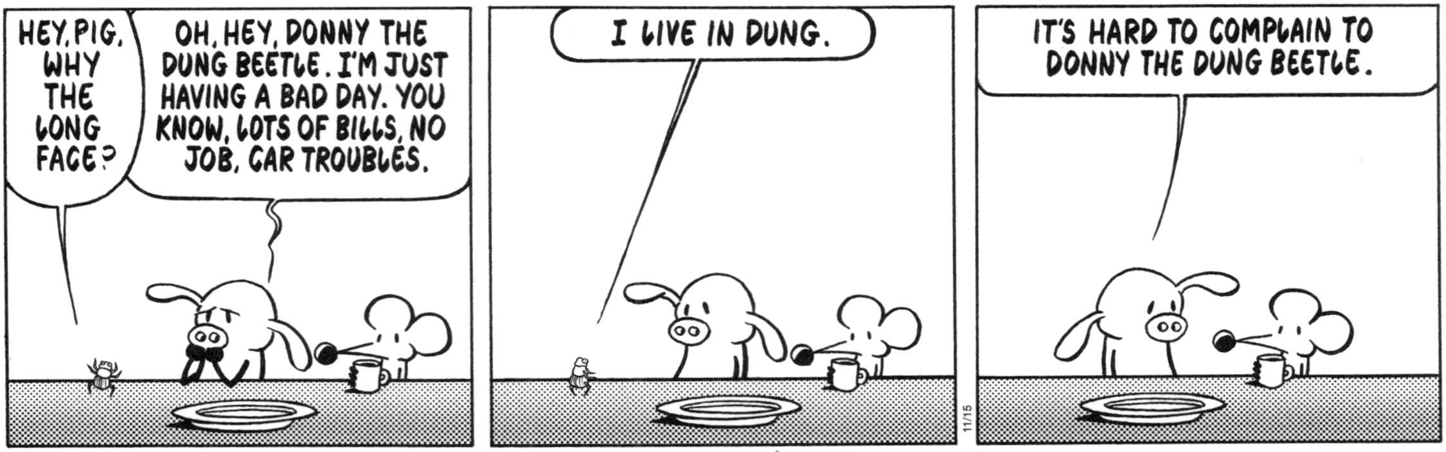
HEY, PIG, WHY THE LONG FACE?
OH, HEY, DONNY THE DUNG BEETLE. I'M JUST HAVING A BAD DAY. YOU KNOW, LOTS OF BILLS, NO JOB, CAR TROUBLES.
I LIVE IN DUNG.
IT'S HARD TO COMPLAIN TO DONNY THE DUNG BEETLE.

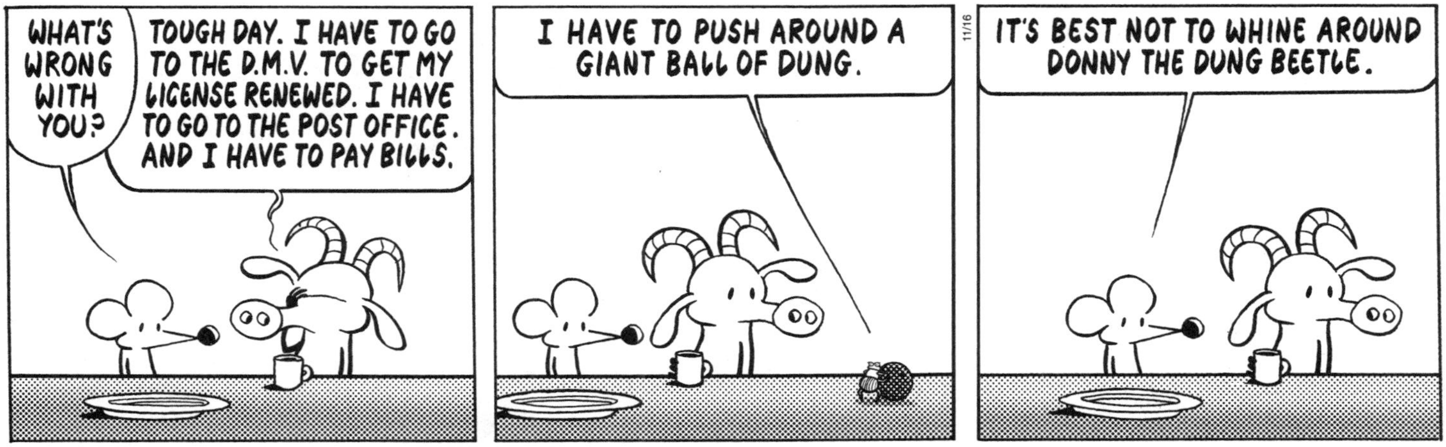
WHAT'S WRONG WITH YOU?
TOUGH DAY. I HAVE TO GO TO THE D.M.V. TO GET MY LICENSE RENEWED. I HAVE TO GO TO THE POST OFFICE. AND I HAVE TO PAY BILLS.
I HAVE TO PUSH AROUND A GIANT BALL OF DUNG.
IT'S BEST NOT TO WHINE AROUND DONNY THE DUNG BEETLE.

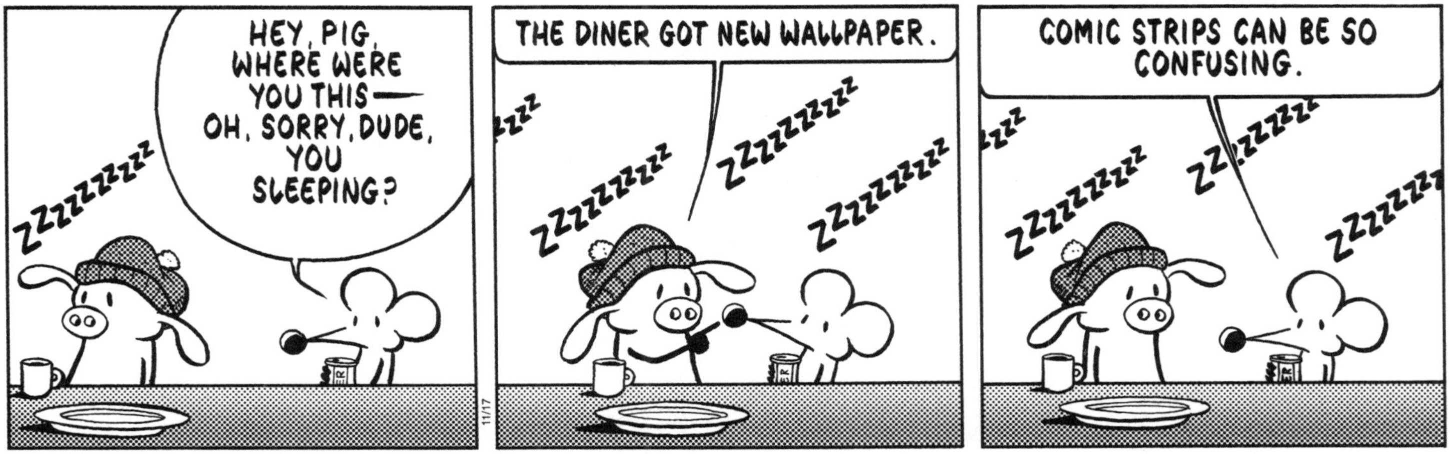
HEY, PIG, WHERE WERE YOU THIS— OH, SORRY, DUDE, YOU SLEEPING?
THE DINER GOT NEW WALLPAPER.
COMIC STRIPS CAN BE SO CONFUSING.

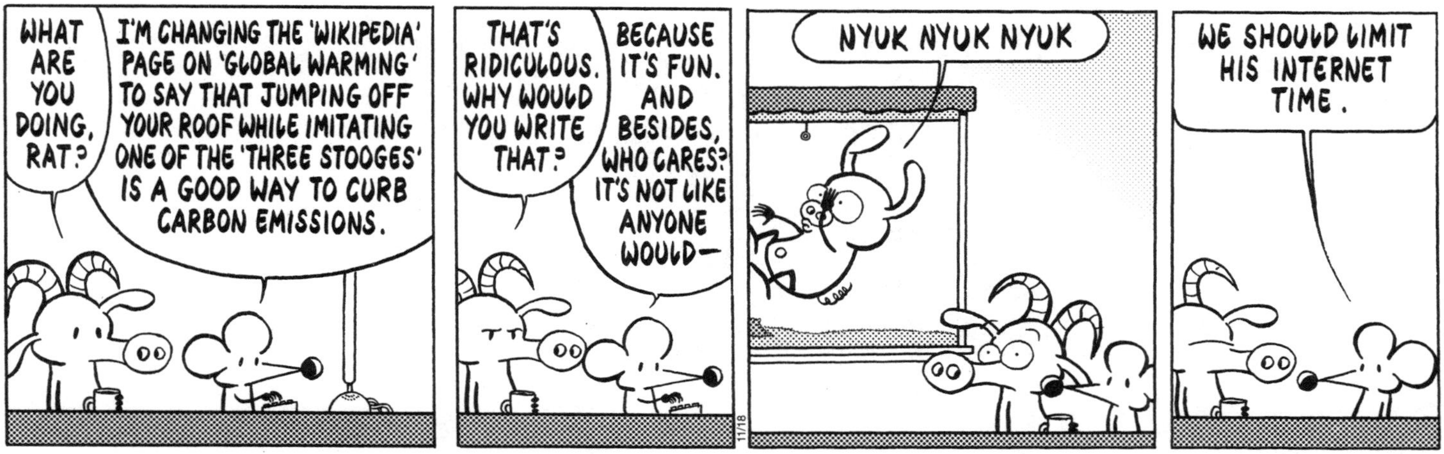
WHAT ARE YOU DOING, RAT?
I'M CHANGING THE 'WIKIPEDIA' PAGE ON 'GLOBAL WARMING' TO SAY THAT JUMPING OFF YOUR ROOF WHILE IMITATING ONE OF THE 'THREE STOOGES' IS A GOOD WAY TO CURB CARBON EMISSIONS.
THAT'S RIDICULOUS. WHY WOULD YOU WRITE THAT?
BECAUSE IT'S FUN. AND BESIDES, WHO CARES? IT'S NOT LIKE ANYONE WOULD—
11/18
NYUK NYUK NYUK
WE SHOULD LIMIT HIS INTERNET TIME.

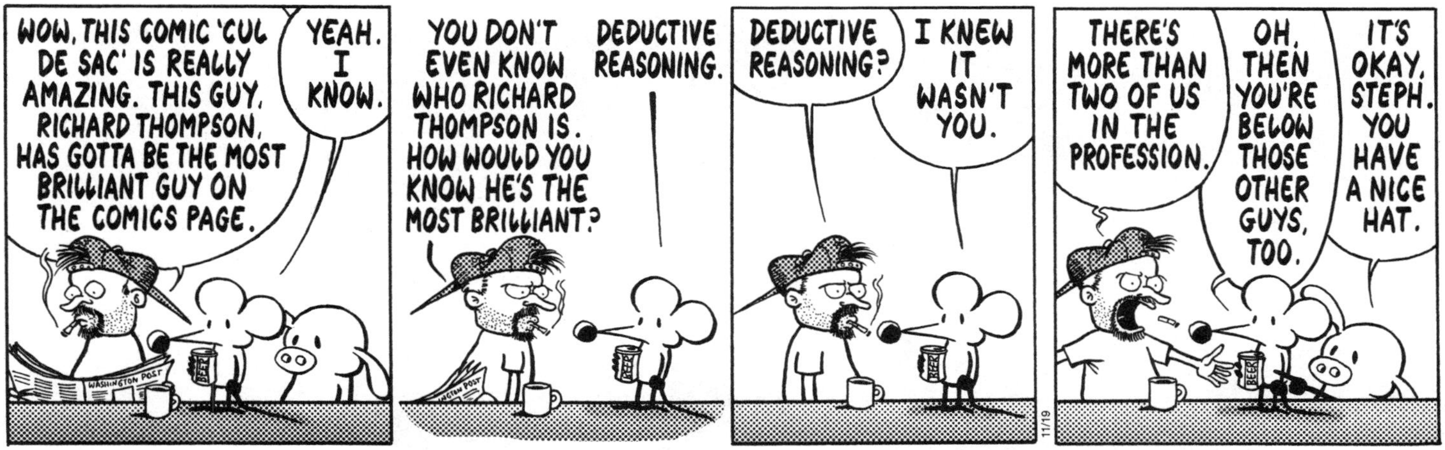
WOW, THIS COMIC 'CUL DE SAC' IS REALLY AMAZING. THIS GUY, RICHARD THOMPSON, HAS GOTTA BE THE MOST BRILLIANT GUY ON THE COMICS PAGE.
YEAH. I KNOW.
YOU DON'T EVEN KNOW WHO RICHARD THOMPSON IS. HOW WOULD YOU KNOW HE'S THE MOST BRILLIANT?
DEDUCTIVE REASONING.
DEDUCTIVE REASONING?
I KNEW IT WASN'T YOU.
11/19
THERE'S MORE THAN TWO OF US IN THE PROFESSION.
OH, THEN YOU'RE BELOW THOSE OTHER GUYS, TOO.
IT'S OKAY, STEPH. YOU HAVE A NICE HAT.

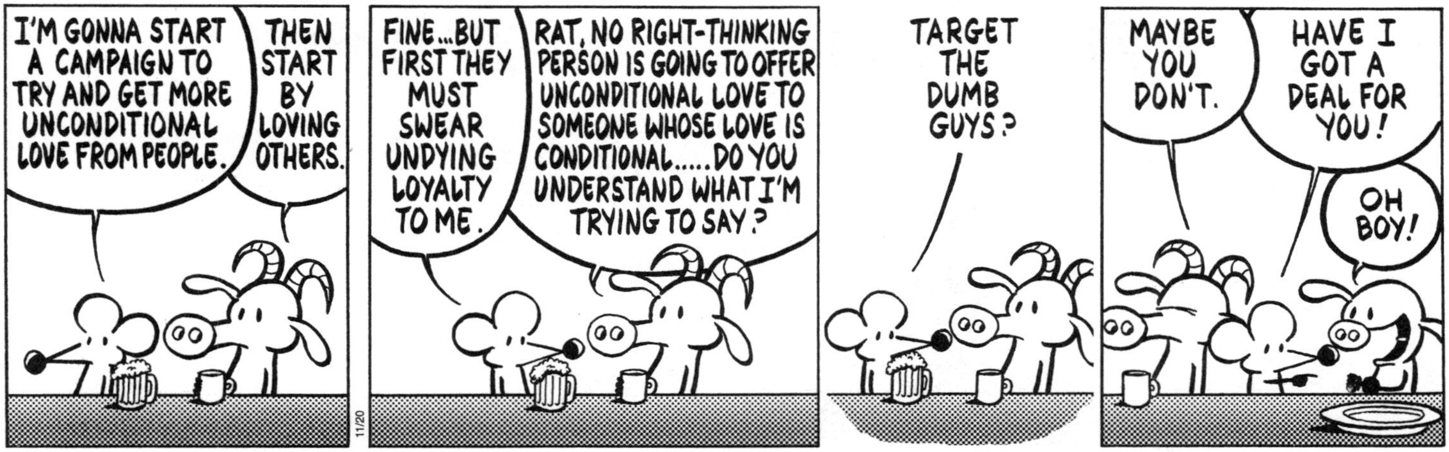
I'M GONNA START A CAMPAIGN TO TRY AND GET MORE UNCONDITIONAL LOVE FROM PEOPLE.
THEN START BY LOVING OTHERS.
11/20
FINE...BUT FIRST THEY MUST SWEAR UNDYING LOYALTY TO ME.
RAT, NO RIGHT-THINKING PERSON IS GOING TO OFFER UNCONDITIONAL LOVE TO SOMEONE WHOSE LOVE IS CONDITIONAL.....DO YOU UNDERSTAND WHAT I'M TRYING TO SAY?
TARGET THE DUMB GUYS?
MAYBE YOU DON'T.
HAVE I GOT A DEAL FOR YOU!
OH BOY!

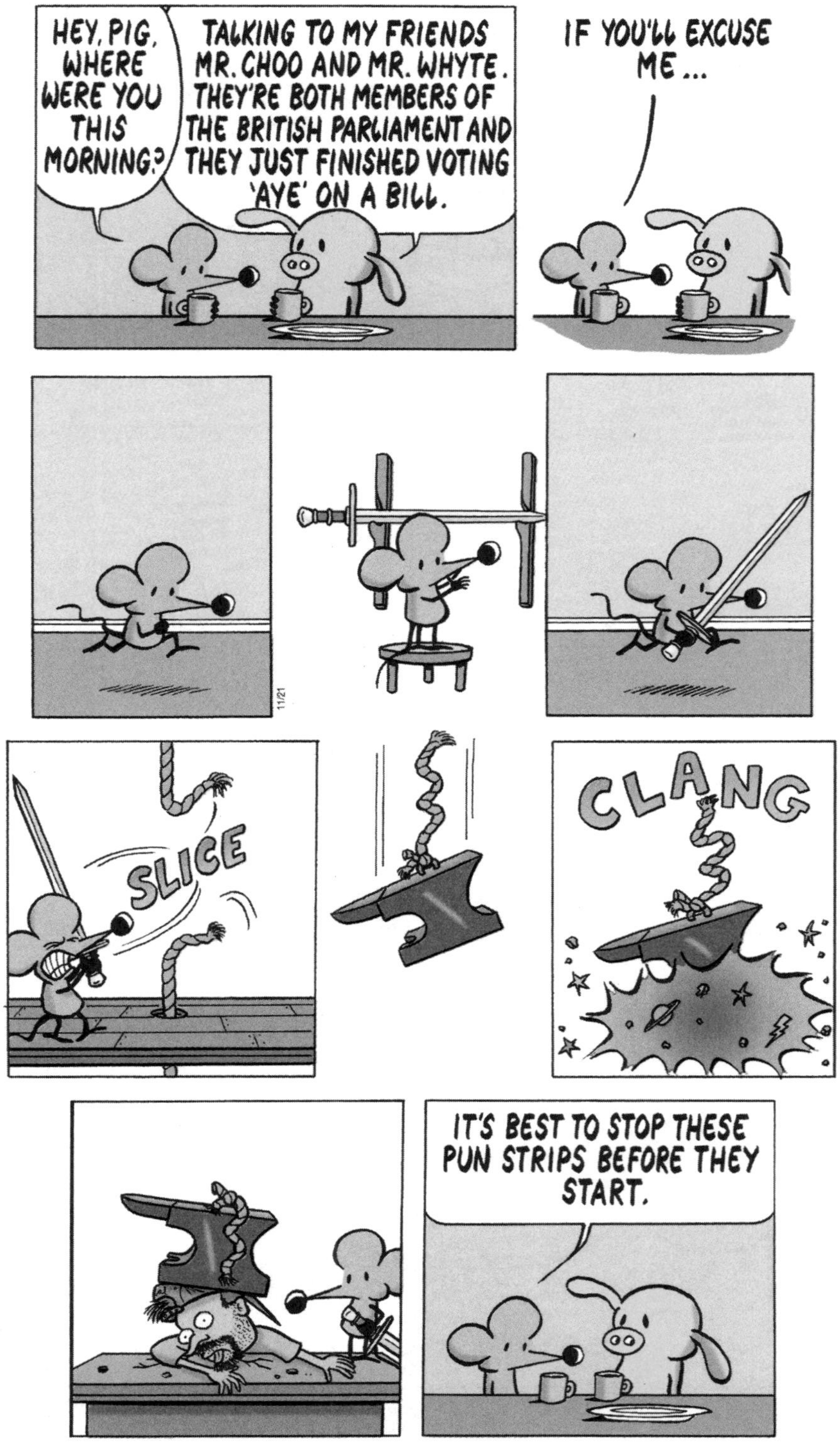
HEY, PIG, WHERE WERE YOU THIS MORNING?
TALKING TO MY FRIENDS MR. CHOO AND MR. WHYTE. THEY'RE BOTH MEMBERS OF THE BRITISH PARLIAMENT AND THEY JUST FINISHED VOTING 'AYE' ON A BILL.
IF YOU'LL EXCUSE ME...
11/21
SLICE
CLANG
IT'S BEST TO STOP THESE PUN STRIPS BEFORE THEY START.

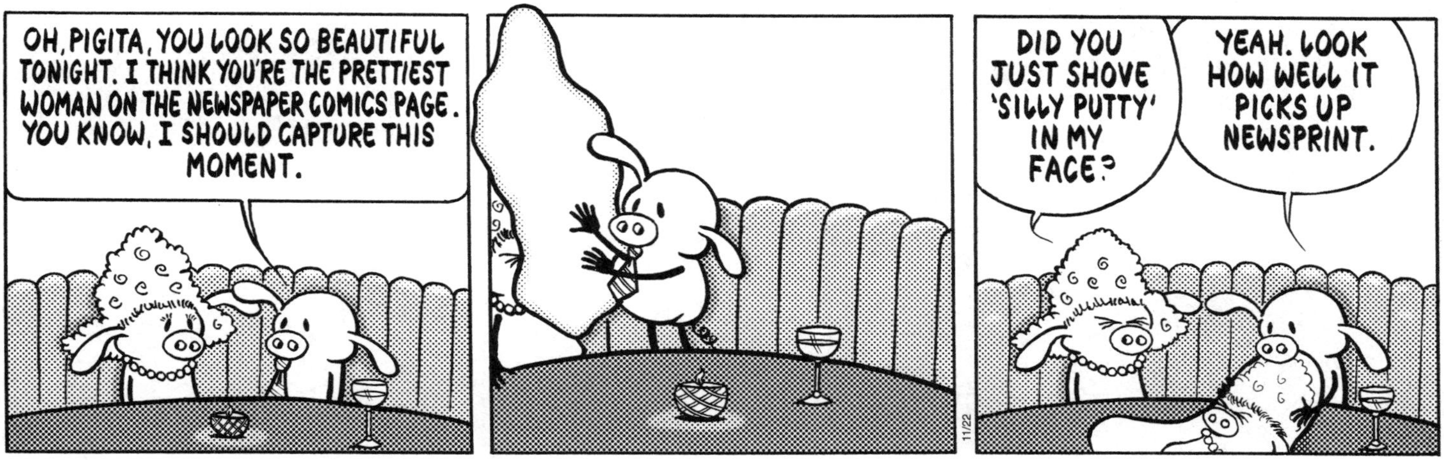
OH, PIGITA, YOU LOOK SO BEAUTIFUL TONIGHT. I THINK YOU'RE THE PRETTIEST WOMAN ON THE NEWSPAPER COMICS PAGE. YOU KNOW, I SHOULD CAPTURE THIS MOMENT.
DID YOU JUST SHOVE 'SILLY PUTTY' IN MY FACE?
YEAH. LOOK HOW WELL IT PICKS UP NEWSPRINT.
11/22

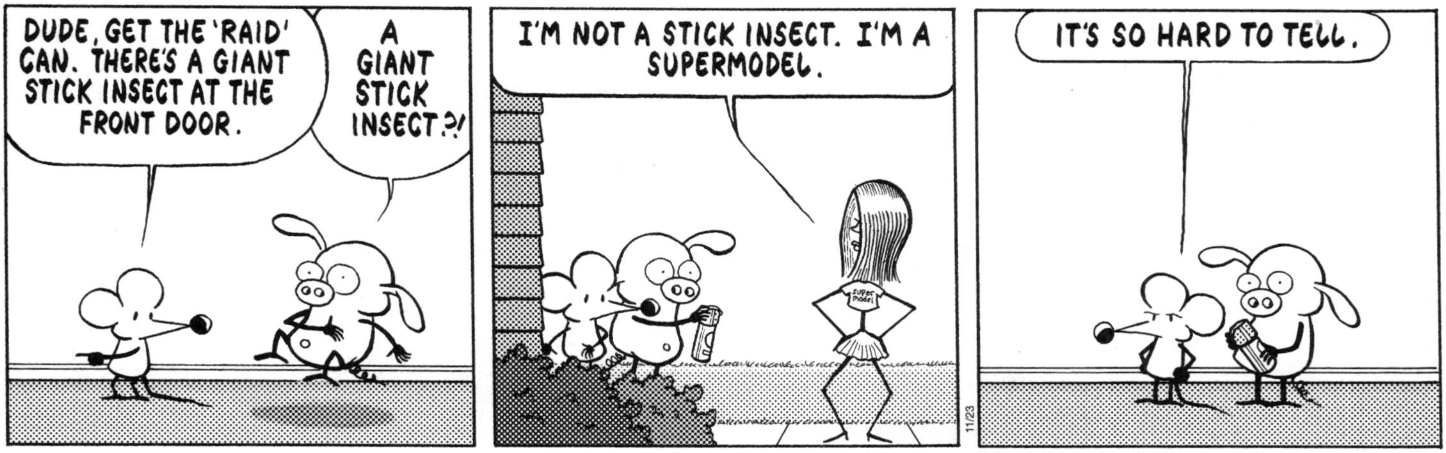
DUDE, GET THE 'RAID' CAN. THERE'S A GIANT STICK INSECT AT THE FRONT DOOR.
A GIANT STICK INSECT?!
I'M NOT A STICK INSECT. I'M A SUPERMODEL.
IT'S SO HARD TO TELL.
11/23

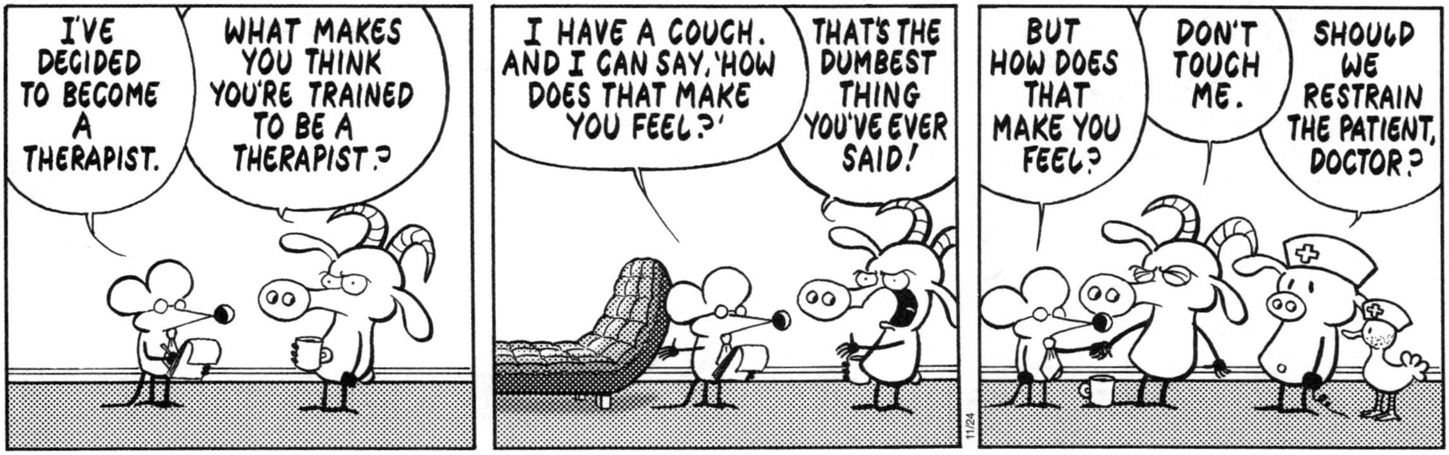
I'VE DECIDED TO BECOME A THERAPIST.
WHAT MAKES YOU THINK YOU'RE TRAINED TO BE A THERAPIST?
I HAVE A COUCH. AND I CAN SAY, 'HOW DOES THAT MAKE YOU FEEL?'
THAT'S THE DUMBEST THING YOU'VE EVER SAID!
BUT HOW DOES THAT MAKE YOU FEEL?
DON'T TOUCH ME.
SHOULD WE RESTRAIN THE PATIENT, DOCTOR?
11/24

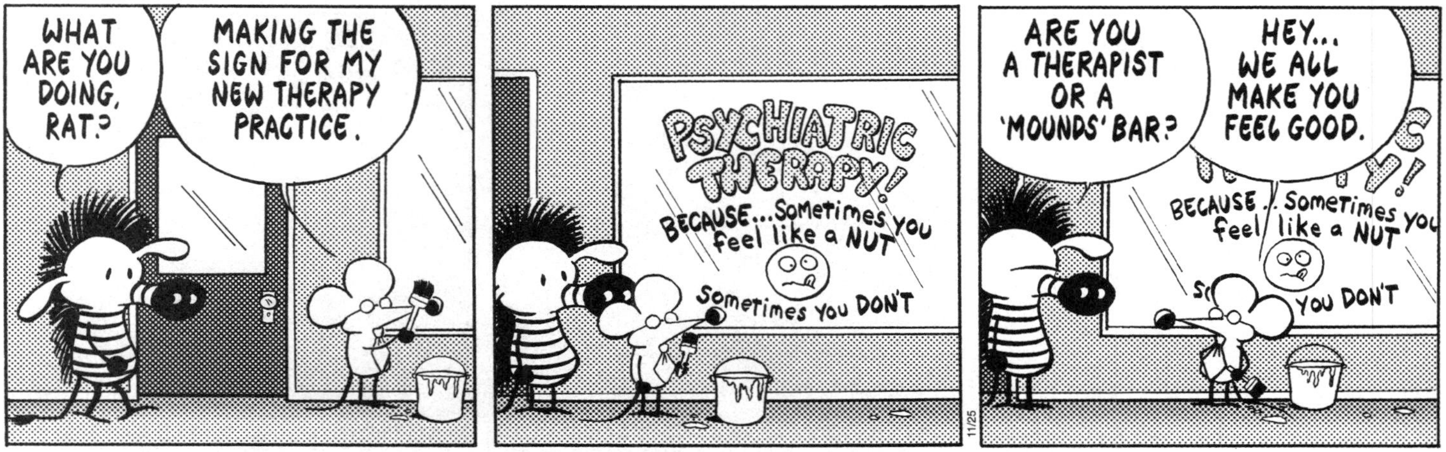
WHAT ARE YOU DOING, RAT?
MAKING THE SIGN FOR MY NEW THERAPY PRACTICE.
PSYCHIATRIC THERAPY!
BECAUSE... Sometimes you feel like a NUT
Sometimes You DON'T
ARE YOU A THERAPIST OR A 'MOUNDS' BAR?
HEY... WE ALL MAKE YOU FEEL GOOD.
11/25

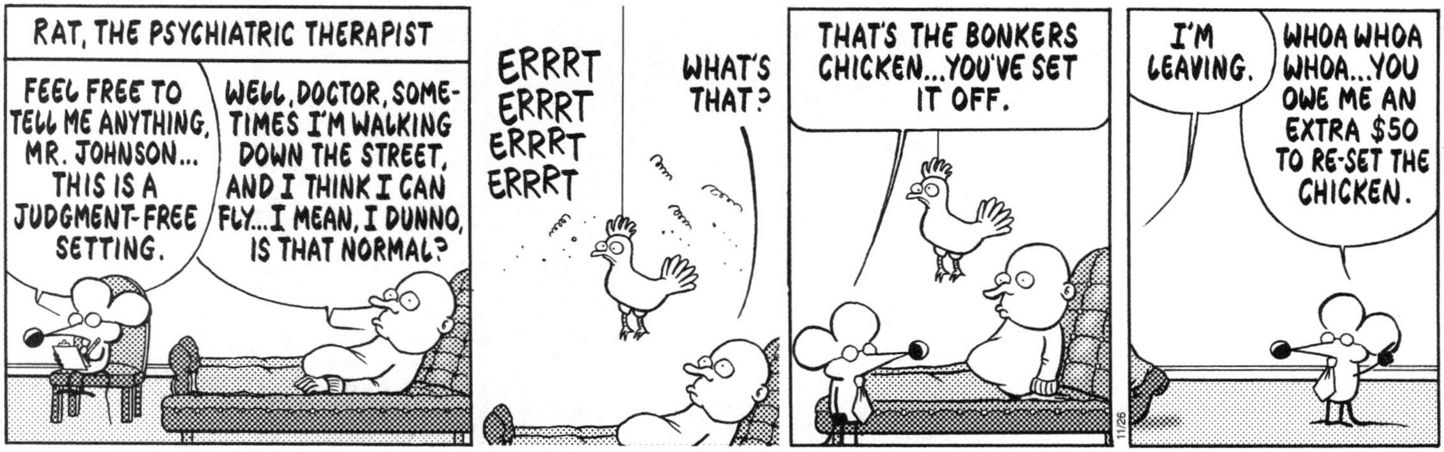
RAT, THE PSYCHIATRIC THERAPIST
FEEL FREE TO TELL ME ANYTHING, MR. JOHNSON... THIS IS A JUDGMENT-FREE SETTING.
WELL, DOCTOR, SOMETIMES I'M WALKING DOWN THE STREET, AND I THINK I CAN FLY...I MEAN, I DUNNO, IS THAT NORMAL?
ERRRT ERRRT ERRRT ERRRT
WHAT'S THAT?
THAT'S THE BONKERS CHICKEN...YOU'VE SET IT OFF.
I'M LEAVING.
WHOA WHOA WHOA...YOU OWE ME AN EXTRA $50 TO RE-SET THE CHICKEN.
11/26

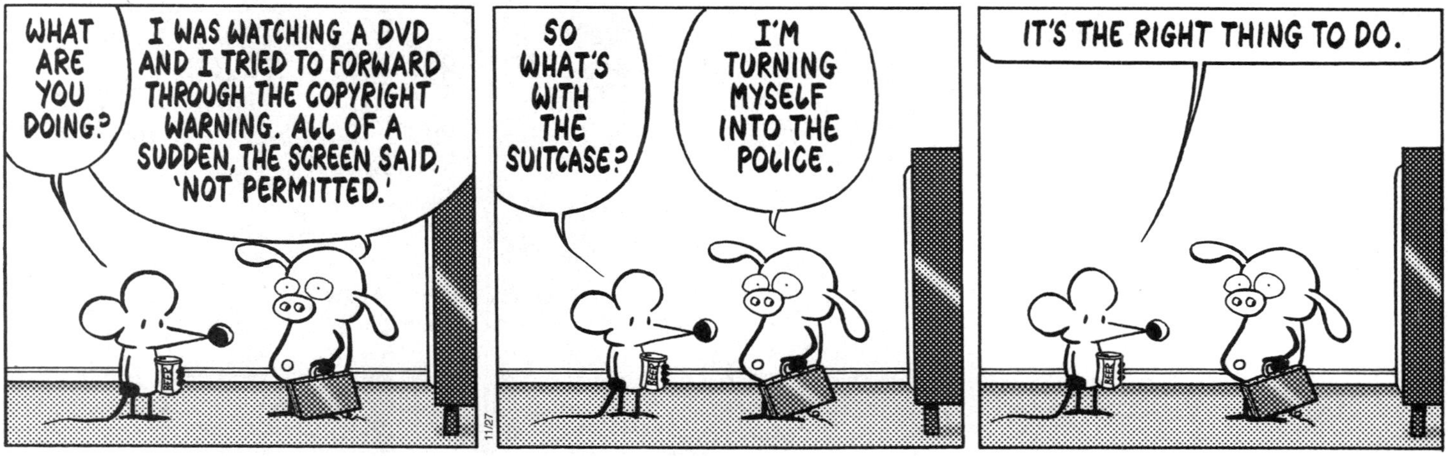
WHAT ARE YOU DOING?
I WAS WATCHING A DVD AND I TRIED TO FORWARD THROUGH THE COPYRIGHT WARNING. ALL OF A SUDDEN, THE SCREEN SAID, 'NOT PERMITTED.'
11/27
SO WHAT'S WITH THE SUITCASE?
I'M TURNING MYSELF INTO THE POLICE.
IT'S THE RIGHT THING TO DO.

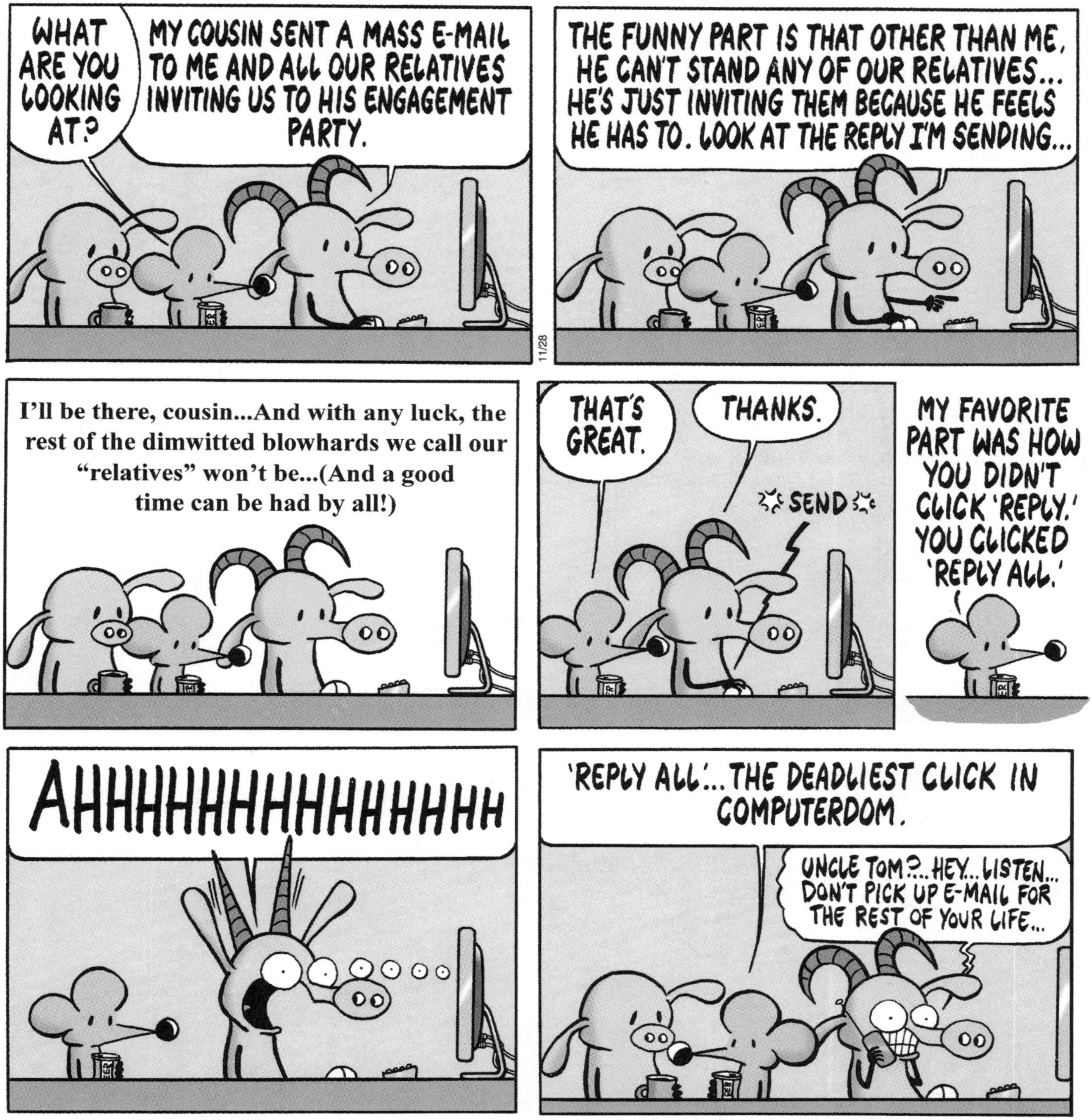
WHAT ARE YOU LOOKING AT?
MY COUSIN SENT A MASS E-MAIL TO ME AND ALL OUR RELATIVES INVITING US TO HIS ENGAGEMENT PARTY.
11/28
THE FUNNY PART IS THAT OTHER THAN ME, HE CAN'T STAND ANY OF OUR RELATIVES... HE'S JUST INVITING THEM BECAUSE HE FEELS HE HAS TO. LOOK AT THE REPLY I'M SENDING...
I'll be there, cousin...And with any luck, the rest of the dimwitted blowhards we call our "relatives" won't be...(And a good time can be had by all!)
THAT'S GREAT.
THANKS.
SEND
MY FAVORITE PART WAS HOW YOU DIDN'T CLICK 'REPLY.' YOU CLICKED 'REPLY ALL.'
AHHHHHHHHHHHHHHH
'REPLY ALL'...THE DEADLIEST CLICK IN COMPUTERDOM.
UNCLE TOM?...HEY...LISTEN... DON'T PICK UP E-MAIL FOR THE REST OF YOUR LIFE...

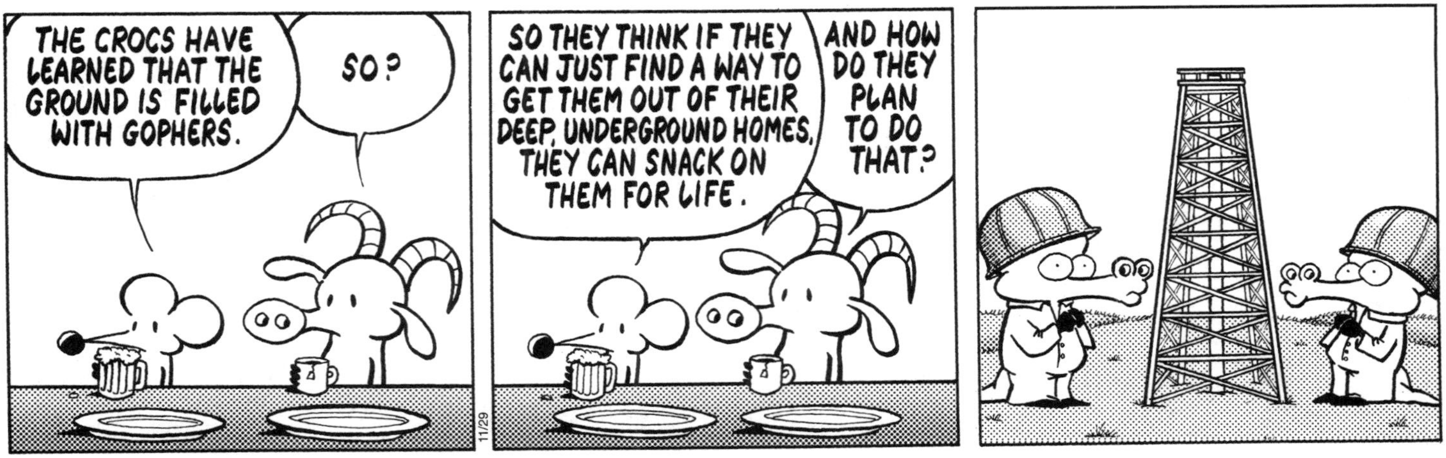
THE CROCS HAVE LEARNED THAT THE GROUND IS FILLED WITH GOPHERS.
SO?
11/29
SO THEY THINK IF THEY CAN JUST FIND A WAY TO GET THEM OUT OF THEIR DEEP, UNDERGROUND HOMES, THEY CAN SNACK ON THEM FOR LIFE.
AND HOW DO THEY PLAN TO DO THAT?

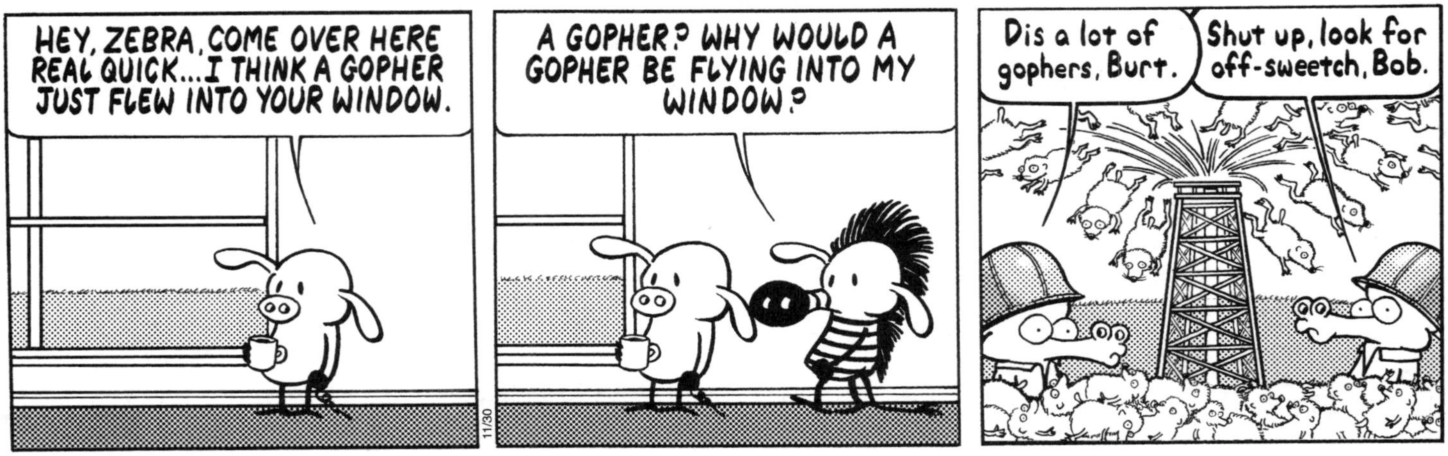
HEY, ZEBRA, COME OVER HERE REAL QUICK...I THINK A GOPHER JUST FLEW INTO YOUR WINDOW.
11/30
A GOPHER? WHY WOULD A GOPHER BE FLYING INTO MY WINDOW?
Dis a lot of gophers, Burt.
Shut up, look for off-sweetch, Bob.

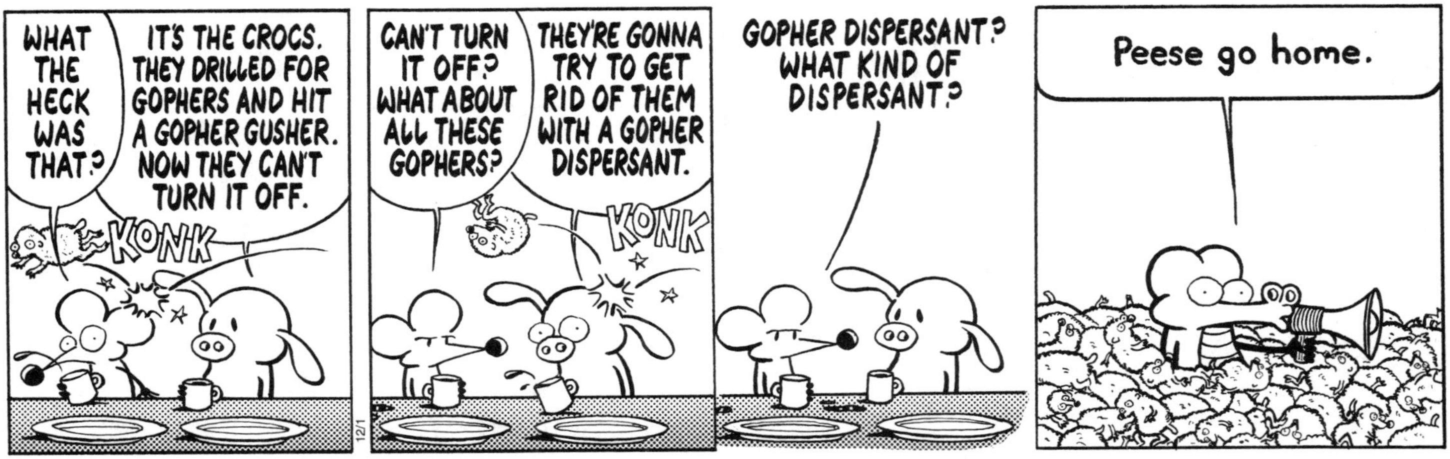
WHAT THE HECK WAS THAT?
IT'S THE CROCS. THEY DRILLED FOR GOPHERS AND HIT A GOPHER GUSHER. NOW THEY CAN'T TURN IT OFF.
KONK
12/1
CAN'T TURN IT OFF? WHAT ABOUT ALL THESE GOPHERS?
THEY'RE GONNA TRY TO GET RID OF THEM WITH A GOPHER DISPERSANT.
KONK
GOPHER DISPERSANT? WHAT KIND OF DISPERSANT?
Peese go home.

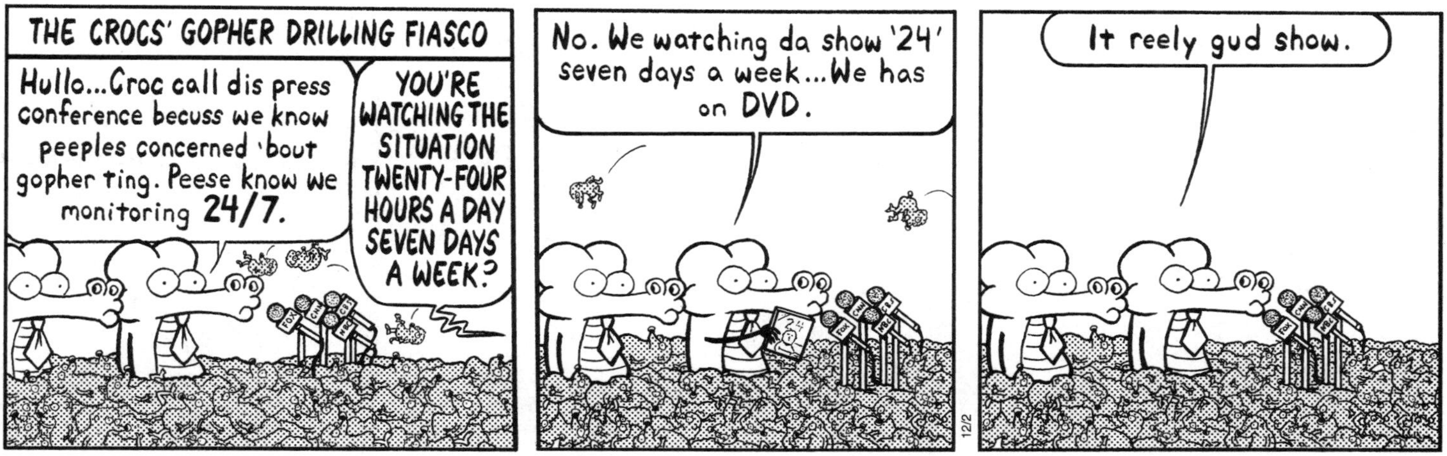
THE CROCS' GOPHER DRILLING FIASCO
Hullo...Croc call dis press conference becuss we know peeples concerned 'bout gopher ting. Peese know we monitoring 24/7.
YOU'RE WATCHING THE SITUATION TWENTY-FOUR HOURS A DAY SEVEN DAYS A WEEK?
No. We watching da show '24' seven days a week...We has on DVD.
It reely gud show.
12/2

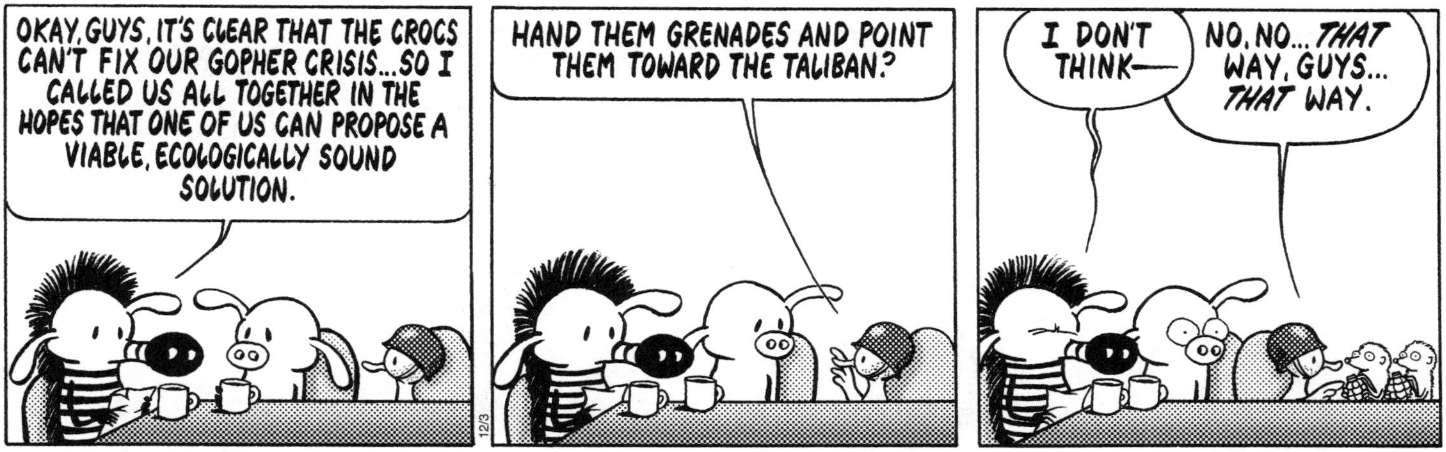
OKAY, GUYS, IT'S CLEAR THAT THE CROCS CAN'T FIX OUR GOPHER CRISIS...SO I CALLED US ALL TOGETHER IN THE HOPES THAT ONE OF US CAN PROPOSE A VIABLE, ECOLOGICALLY SOUND SOLUTION.
12/3
HAND THEM GRENADES AND POINT THEM TOWARD THE TALIBAN?
I DON'T THINK—
NO, NO...*THAT* WAY, GUYS... *THAT* WAY.

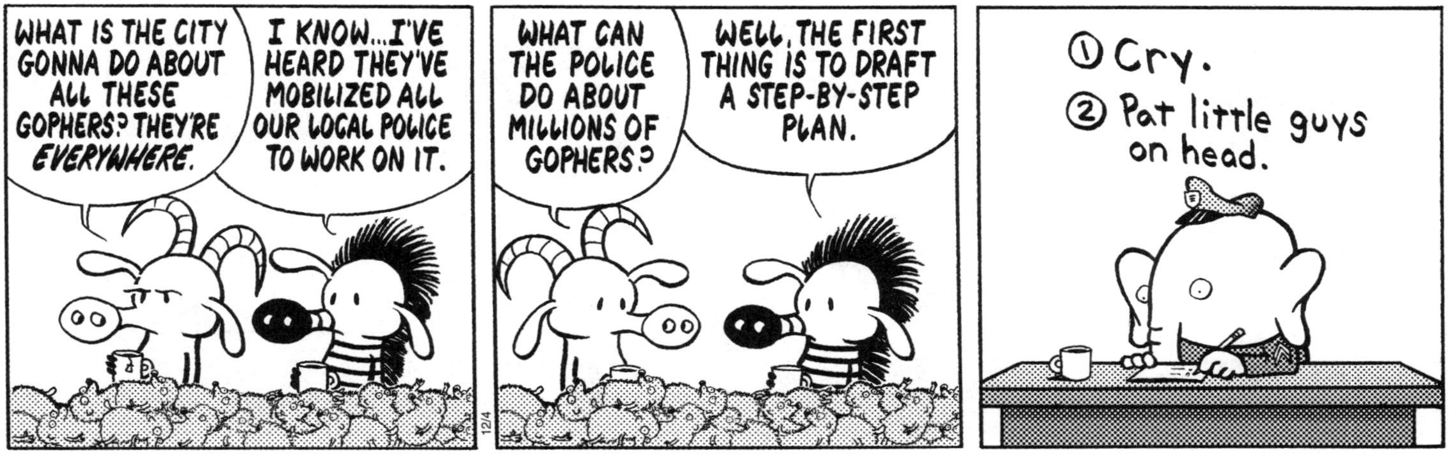
WHAT IS THE CITY GONNA DO ABOUT ALL THESE GOPHERS? THEY'RE *EVERYWHERE*.
I KNOW...I'VE HEARD THEY'VE MOBILIZED ALL OUR LOCAL POLICE TO WORK ON IT.
12/4
WHAT CAN THE POLICE DO ABOUT MILLIONS OF GOPHERS?
WELL, THE FIRST THING IS TO DRAFT A STEP-BY-STEP PLAN.
① Cry.
② Pat little guys on head.

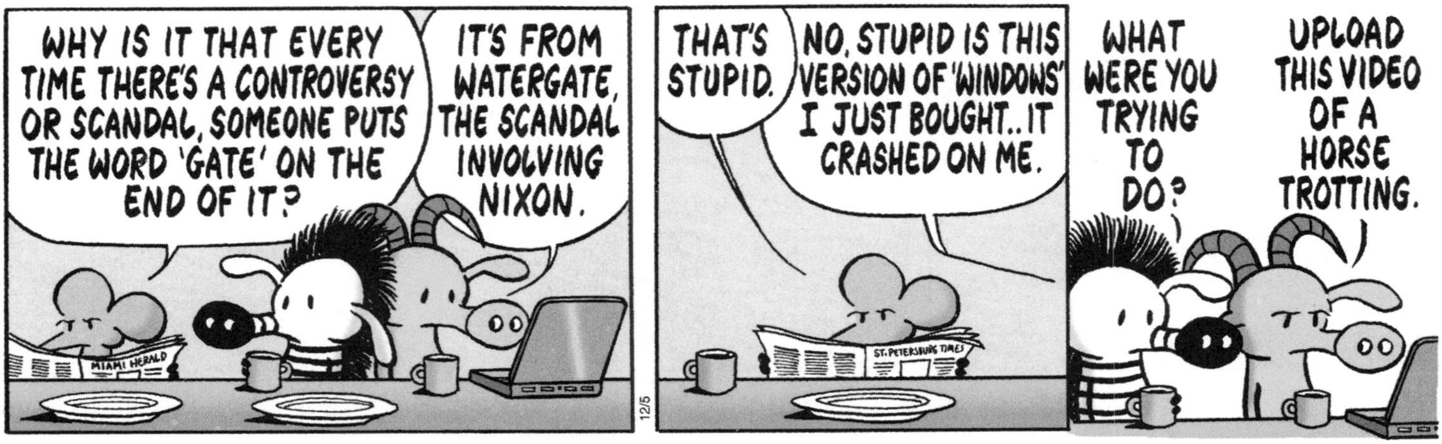
WHY IS IT THAT EVERY TIME THERE'S A CONTROVERSY OR SCANDAL, SOMEONE PUTS THE WORD 'GATE' ON THE END OF IT?
IT'S FROM WATERGATE, THE SCANDAL INVOLVING NIXON.
MIAMI HERALD
12/5
THAT'S STUPID.
NO, STUPID IS THIS VERSION OF 'WINDOWS' I JUST BOUGHT.. IT CRASHED ON ME.
ST. PETERSBURG TIMES
WHAT WERE YOU TRYING TO DO?
UPLOAD THIS VIDEO OF A HORSE TROTTING.

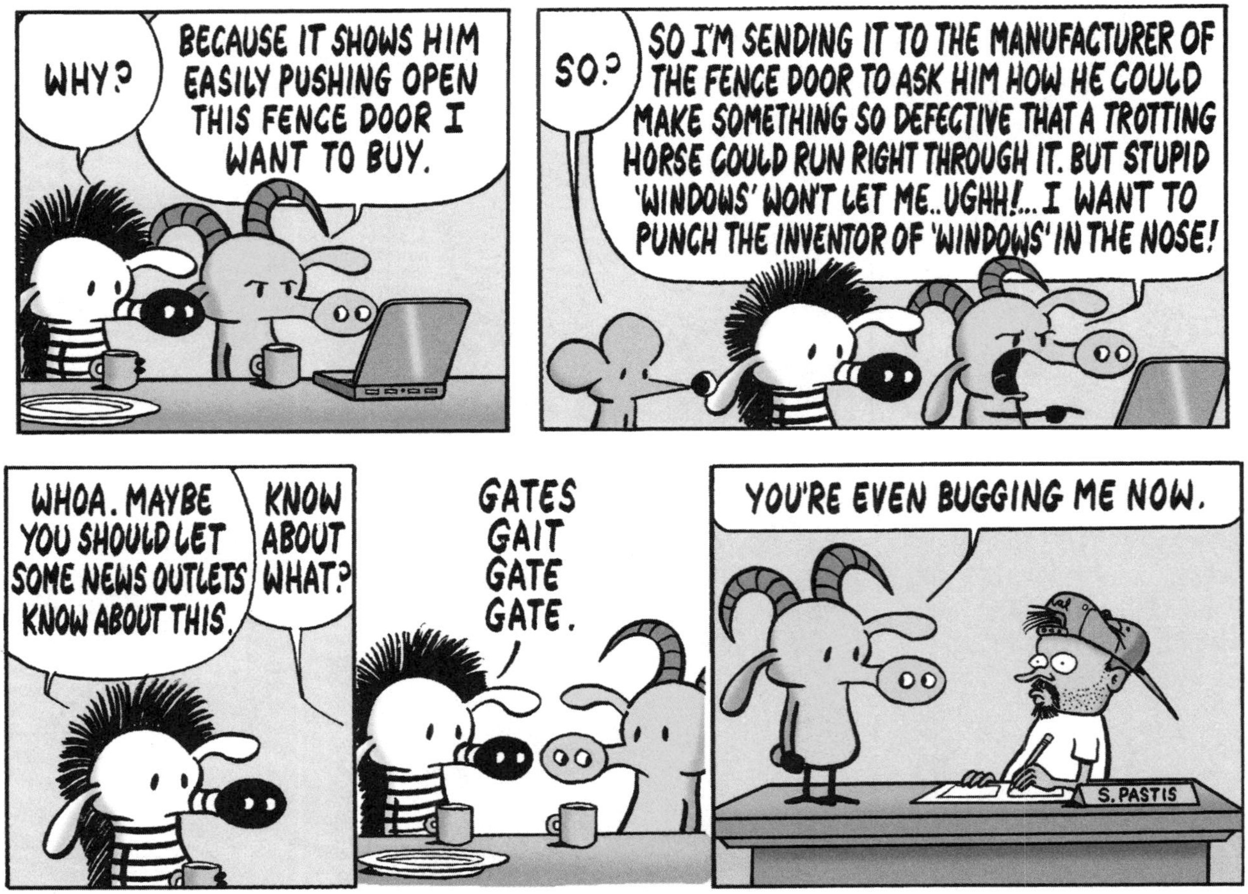
WHY?
BECAUSE IT SHOWS HIM EASILY PUSHING OPEN THIS FENCE DOOR I WANT TO BUY.
SO?
SO I'M SENDING IT TO THE MANUFACTURER OF THE FENCE DOOR TO ASK HIM HOW HE COULD MAKE SOMETHING SO DEFECTIVE THAT A TROTTING HORSE COULD RUN RIGHT THROUGH IT. BUT STUPID 'WINDOWS' WON'T LET ME.. UGHH!... I WANT TO PUNCH THE INVENTOR OF 'WINDOWS' IN THE NOSE!
WHOA. MAYBE YOU SHOULD LET SOME NEWS OUTLETS KNOW ABOUT THIS.
KNOW ABOUT WHAT?
GATES GAIT GATE GATE.
YOU'RE EVEN BUGGING ME NOW.
S. PASTIS

STORY UPDATE:

The crocs drilled deep underground for gophers and hit a gusher, which they cannot shut off.

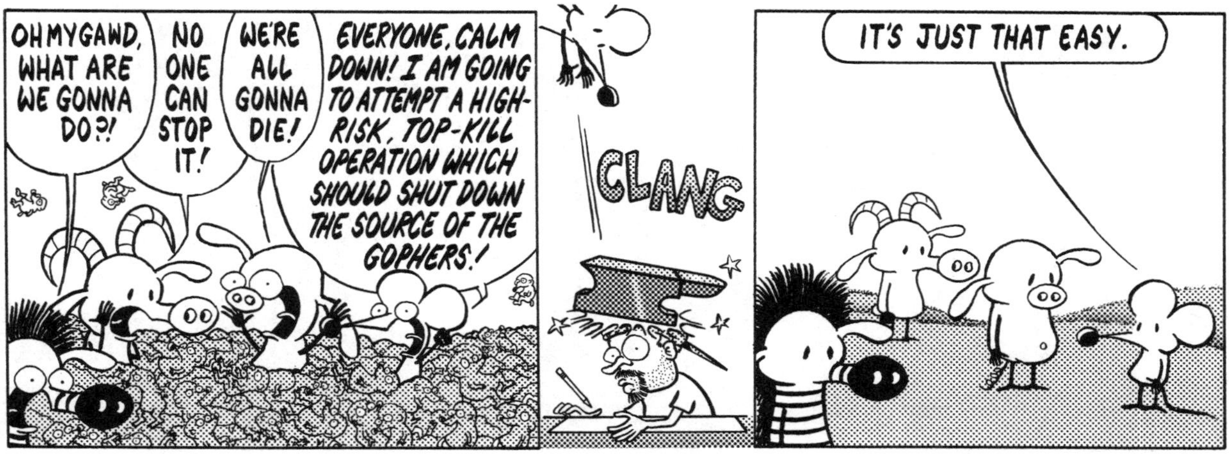
OHMYGAWD, WHAT ARE WE GONNA DO?!
NO ONE CAN STOP IT!
WE'RE ALL GONNA DIE!
EVERYONE, CALM DOWN! I AM GOING TO ATTEMPT A HIGH-RISK, TOP-KILL OPERATION WHICH SHOULD SHUT DOWN THE SOURCE OF THE GOPHERS!
CLANG
IT'S JUST THAT EASY.

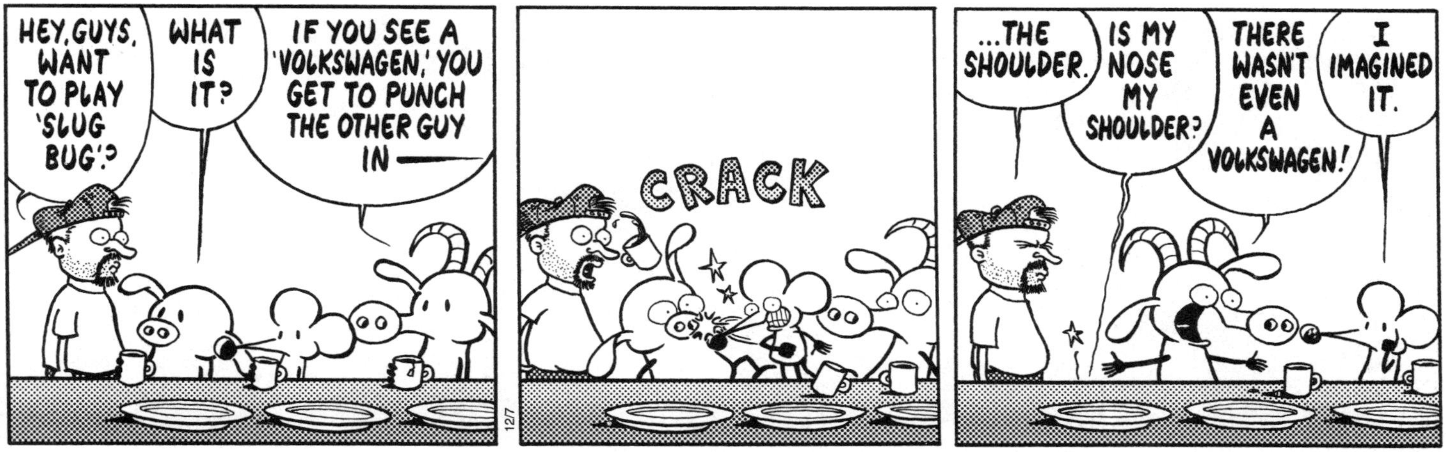
HEY, GUYS, WANT TO PLAY 'SLUG BUG'?
WHAT IS IT?
IF YOU SEE A 'VOLKSWAGEN,' YOU GET TO PUNCH THE OTHER GUY IN —
CRACK
...THE SHOULDER.
IS MY NOSE MY SHOULDER?
THERE WASN'T EVEN A VOLKSWAGEN!
I IMAGINED IT.

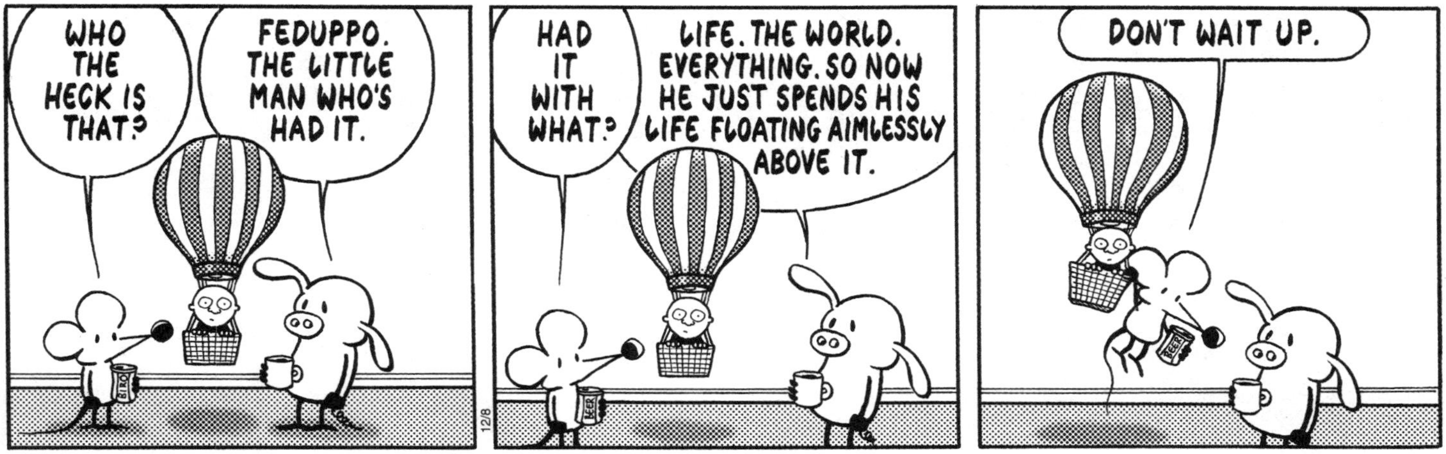
WHO THE HECK IS THAT?
FEDUPPO. THE LITTLE MAN WHO'S HAD IT.
HAD IT WITH WHAT?
LIFE. THE WORLD. EVERYTHING. SO NOW HE JUST SPENDS HIS LIFE FLOATING AIMLESSLY ABOVE IT.
DON'T WAIT UP.

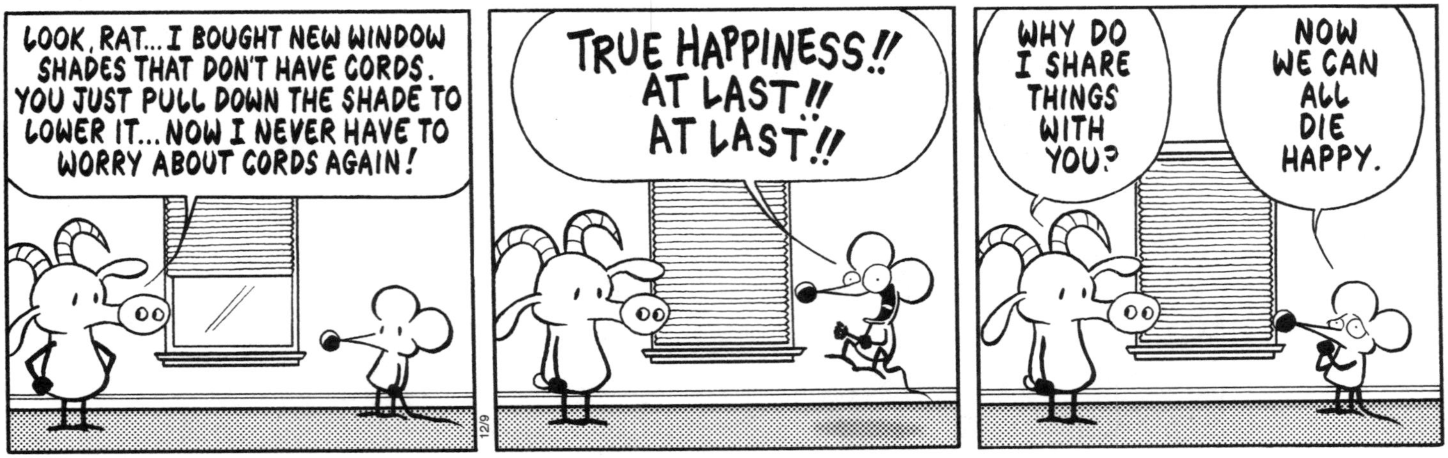
LOOK, RAT... I BOUGHT NEW WINDOW SHADES THAT DON'T HAVE CORDS. YOU JUST PULL DOWN THE SHADE TO LOWER IT... NOW I NEVER HAVE TO WORRY ABOUT CORDS AGAIN!
12/9
TRUE HAPPINESS!! AT LAST!! AT LAST!!
WHY DO I SHARE THINGS WITH YOU?
NOW WE CAN ALL DIE HAPPY.

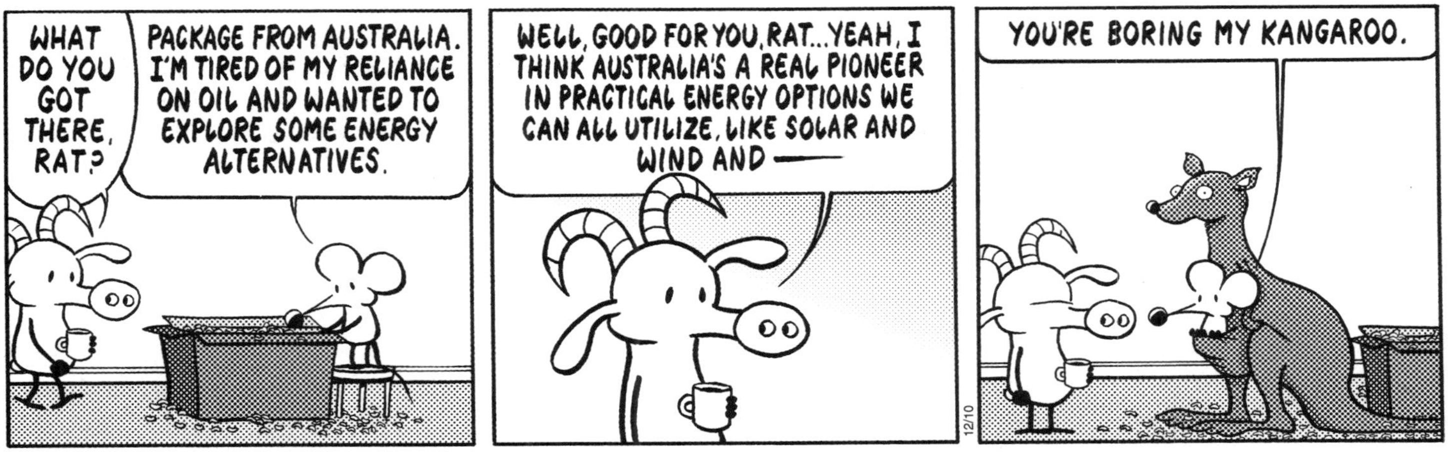
WHAT DO YOU GOT THERE, RAT?
PACKAGE FROM AUSTRALIA. I'M TIRED OF MY RELIANCE ON OIL AND WANTED TO EXPLORE SOME ENERGY ALTERNATIVES.
WELL, GOOD FOR YOU, RAT... YEAH, I THINK AUSTRALIA'S A REAL PIONEER IN PRACTICAL ENERGY OPTIONS WE CAN ALL UTILIZE, LIKE SOLAR AND WIND AND —
12/10
YOU'RE BORING MY KANGAROO.

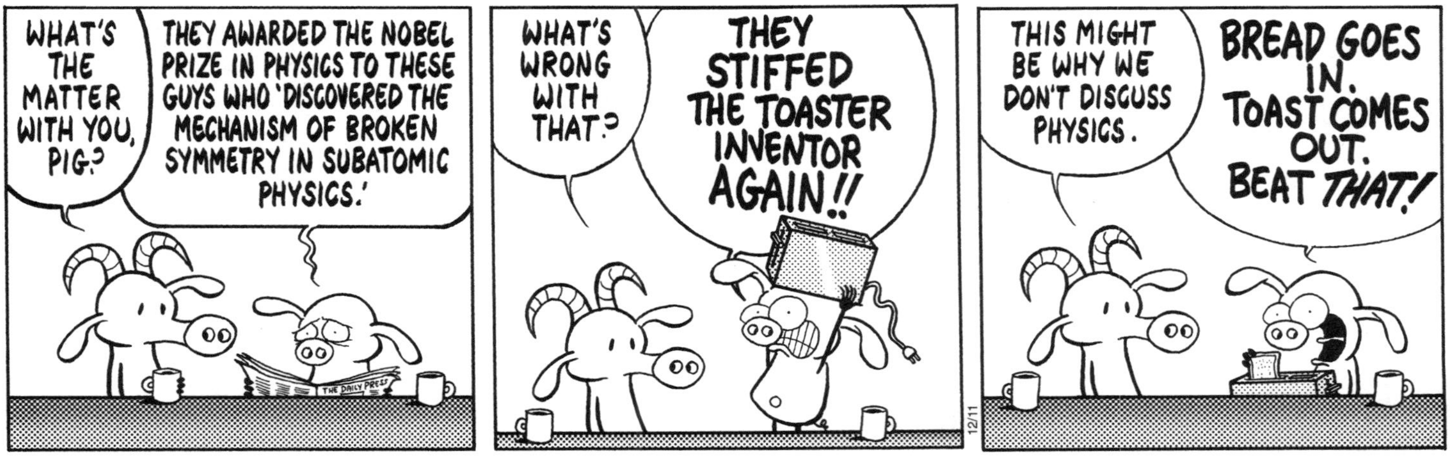
WHAT'S THE MATTER WITH YOU, PIG?
THEY AWARDED THE NOBEL PRIZE IN PHYSICS TO THESE GUYS WHO 'DISCOVERED THE MECHANISM OF BROKEN SYMMETRY IN SUBATOMIC PHYSICS.'
THE DAILY PRESS
WHAT'S WRONG WITH THAT?
THEY STIFFED THE TOASTER INVENTOR AGAIN!!
12/11
THIS MIGHT BE WHY WE DON'T DISCUSS PHYSICS.
BREAD GOES IN. TOAST COMES OUT. BEAT THAT!

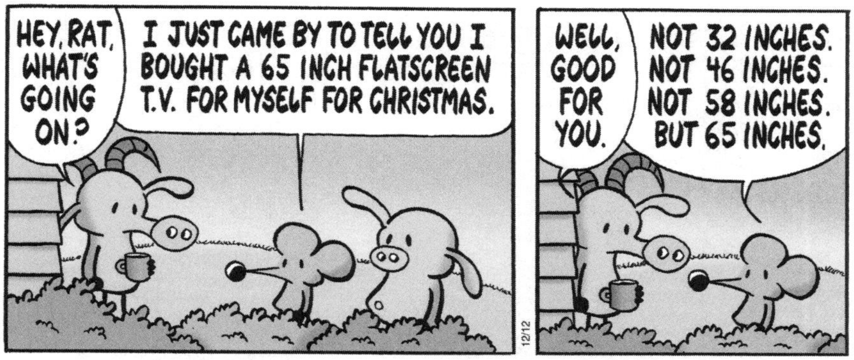
HEY, RAT, WHAT'S GOING ON?
I JUST CAME BY TO TELL YOU I BOUGHT A 65 INCH FLATSCREEN T.V. FOR MYSELF FOR CHRISTMAS.
12/12
WELL, GOOD FOR YOU.
NOT 32 INCHES. NOT 46 INCHES. NOT 58 INCHES. BUT 65 INCHES.

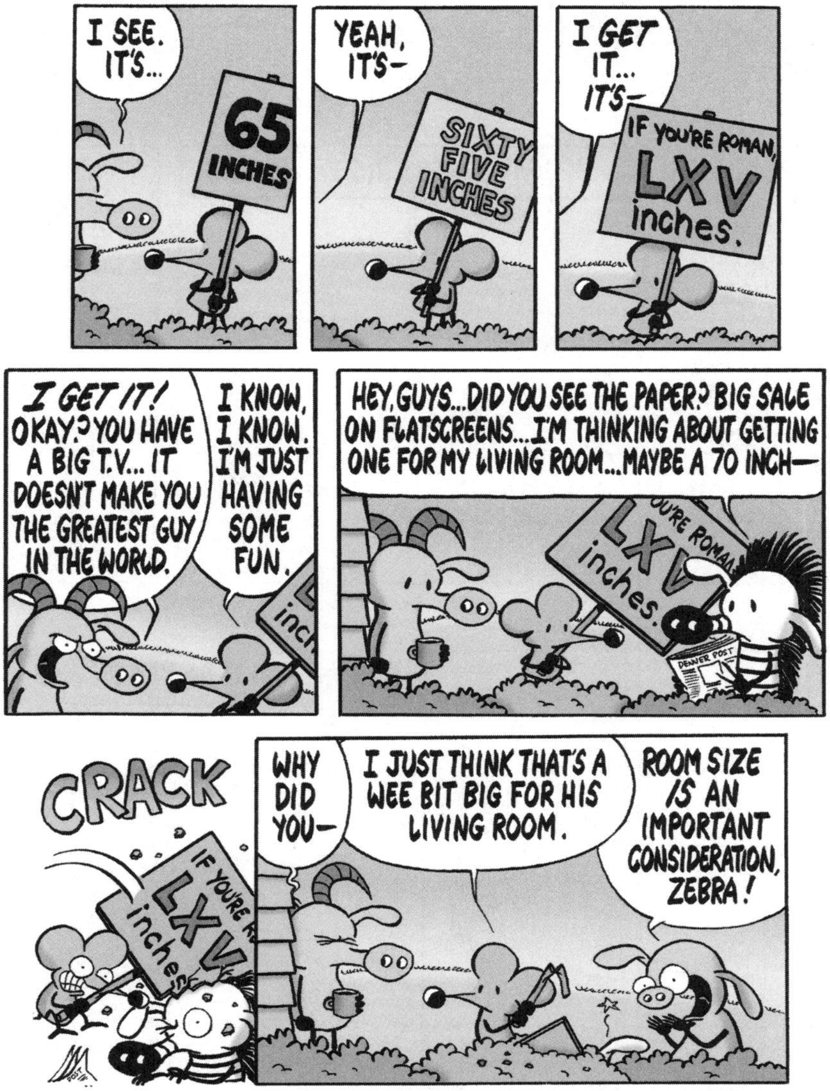
I SEE. IT'S...
65 INCHES
YEAH, IT'S—
SIXTY FIVE INCHES
I GET IT... IT'S—
IF YOU'RE ROMAN, LXV inches.
I GET IT! OKAY? YOU HAVE A BIG T.V... IT DOESN'T MAKE YOU THE GREATEST GUY IN THE WORLD.
I KNOW, I KNOW. I'M JUST HAVING SOME FUN.
HEY, GUYS...DID YOU SEE THE PAPER? BIG SALE ON FLATSCREENS...I'M THINKING ABOUT GETTING ONE FOR MY LIVING ROOM...MAYBE A 70 INCH—
DENVER POST
CRACK
WHY DID YOU—
I JUST THINK THAT'S A WEE BIT BIG FOR HIS LIVING ROOM.
ROOM SIZE IS AN IMPORTANT CONSIDERATION, ZEBRA!

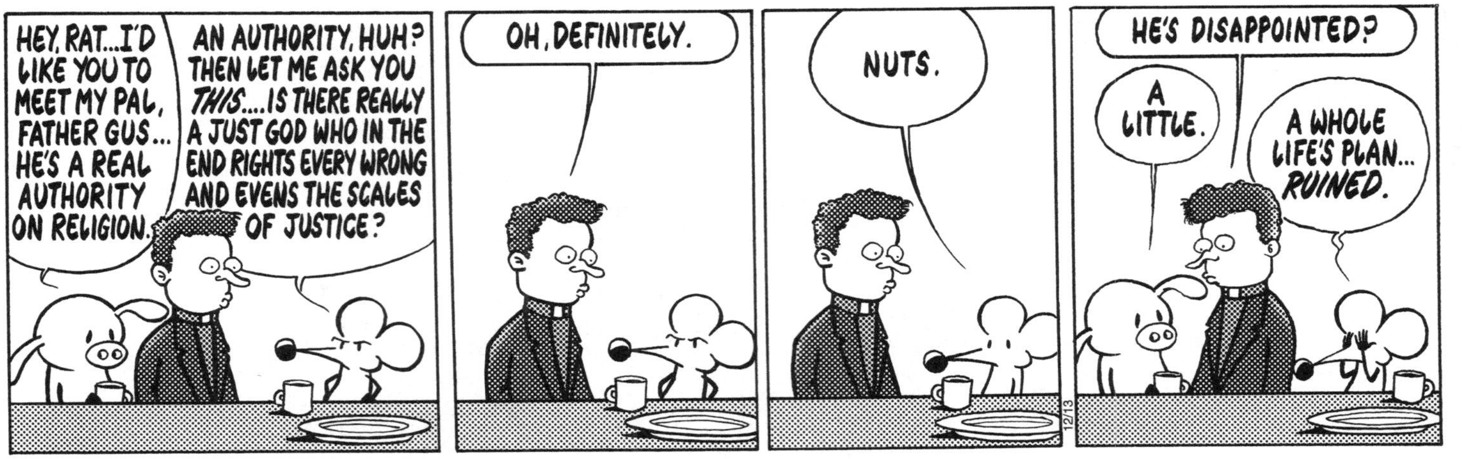
HEY, RAT...I'D LIKE YOU TO MEET MY PAL, FATHER GUS... HE'S A REAL AUTHORITY ON RELIGION.
AN AUTHORITY, HUH? THEN LET ME ASK YOU *THIS*....IS THERE REALLY A JUST GOD WHO IN THE END RIGHTS EVERY WRONG AND EVENS THE SCALES OF JUSTICE?
OH, DEFINITELY.
NUTS.
HE'S DISAPPOINTED?
A LITTLE.
A WHOLE LIFE'S PLAN... *RUINED.*
12/13

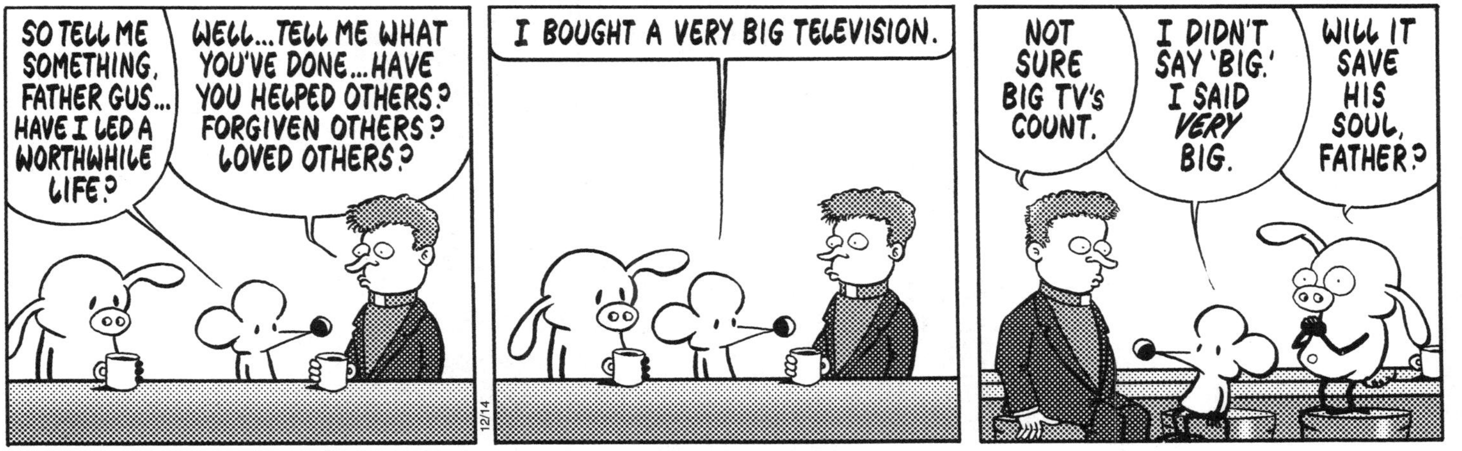
SO TELL ME SOMETHING, FATHER GUS... HAVE I LED A WORTHWHILE LIFE?
WELL...TELL ME WHAT YOU'VE DONE...HAVE YOU HELPED OTHERS? FORGIVEN OTHERS? LOVED OTHERS?
12/14
I BOUGHT A VERY BIG TELEVISION.
NOT SURE BIG TV's COUNT.
I DIDN'T SAY 'BIG.' I SAID *VERY* BIG.
WILL IT SAVE HIS SOUL, FATHER?

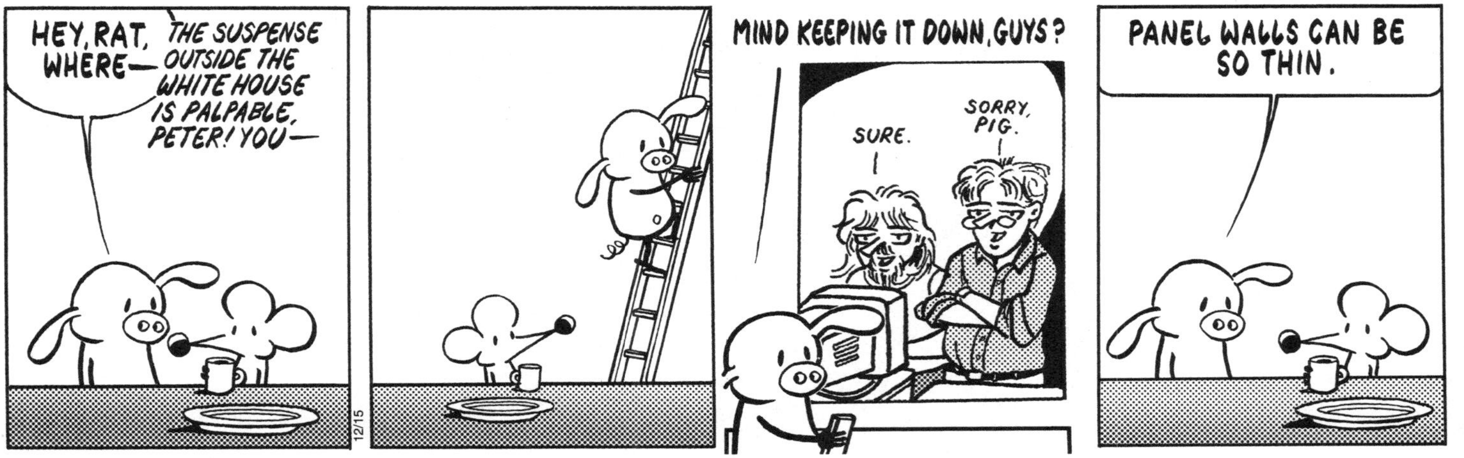
HEY, RAT, WHERE—
THE SUSPENSE OUTSIDE THE WHITE HOUSE IS PALPABLE, PETER! YOU—
12/15
MIND KEEPING IT DOWN, GUYS?
SURE.
SORRY, PIG.
PANEL WALLS CAN BE SO THIN.

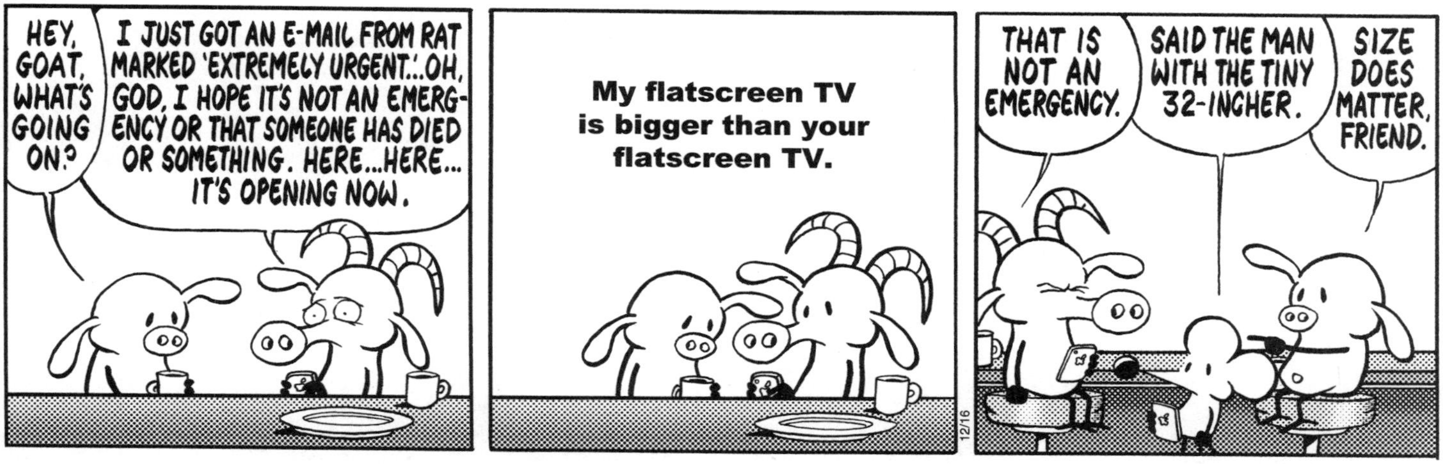
HEY, GOAT, WHAT'S GOING ON?
I JUST GOT AN E-MAIL FROM RAT MARKED 'EXTREMELY URGENT.'...OH, GOD, I HOPE IT'S NOT AN EMERGENCY OR THAT SOMEONE HAS DIED OR SOMETHING. HERE...HERE... IT'S OPENING NOW.
My flatscreen TV is bigger than your flatscreen TV.
12/16
THAT IS NOT AN EMERGENCY.
SAID THE MAN WITH THE TINY 32-INCHER.
SIZE DOES MATTER, FRIEND.

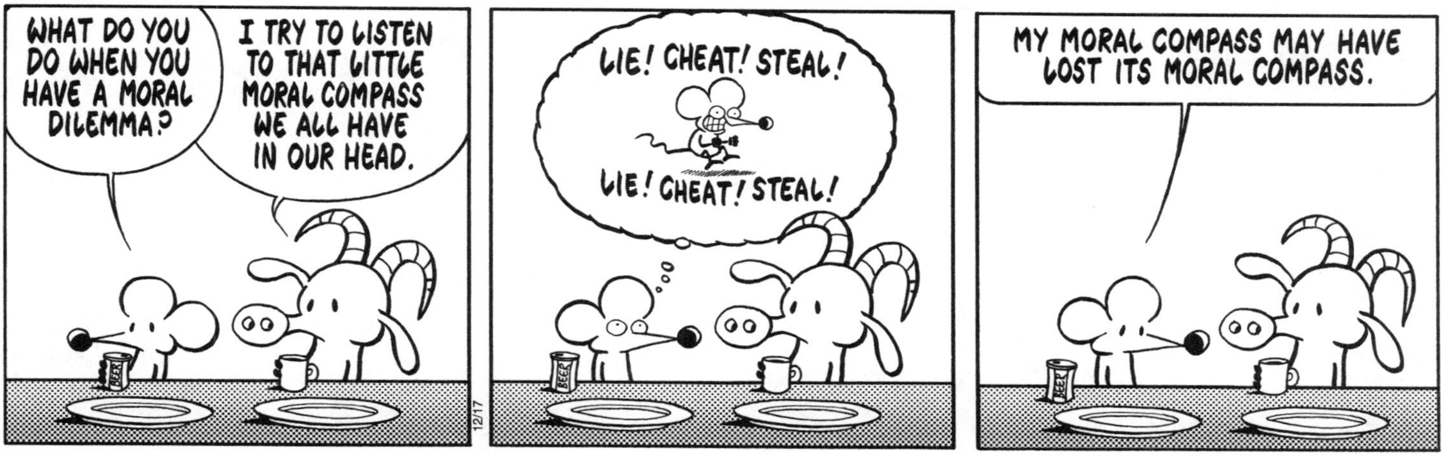
WHAT DO YOU DO WHEN YOU HAVE A MORAL DILEMMA?
I TRY TO LISTEN TO THAT LITTLE MORAL COMPASS WE ALL HAVE IN OUR HEAD.
12/17
LIE! CHEAT! STEAL!
LIE! CHEAT! STEAL!
MY MORAL COMPASS MAY HAVE LOST ITS MORAL COMPASS.

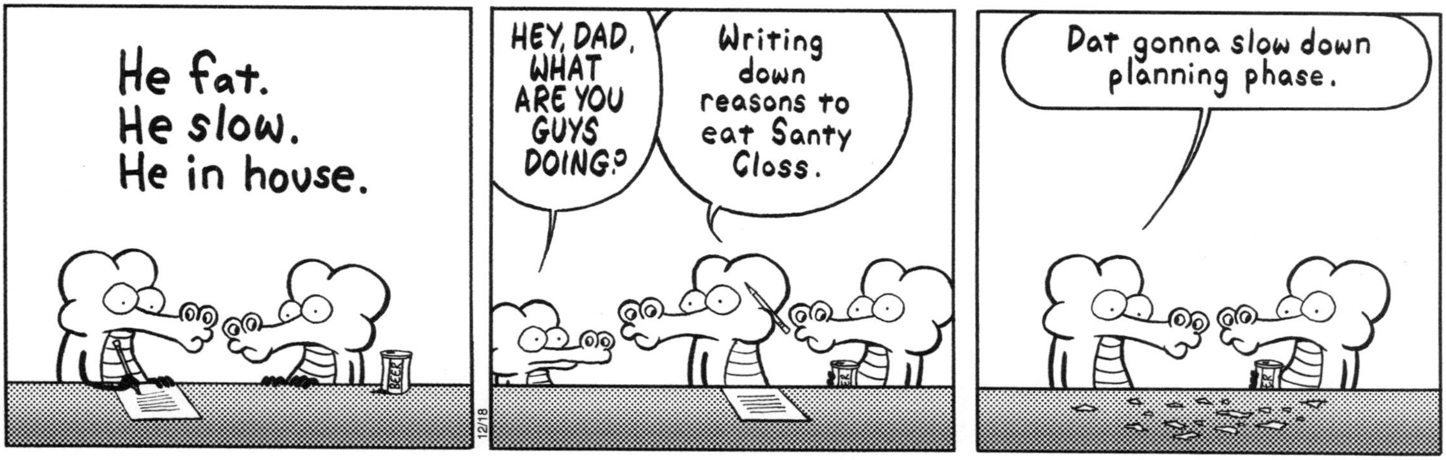
He fat.
He slow.
He in house.
12/18
HEY, DAD, WHAT ARE YOU GUYS DOING?
Writing down reasons to eat Santy Closs.
Dat gonna slow down planning phase.

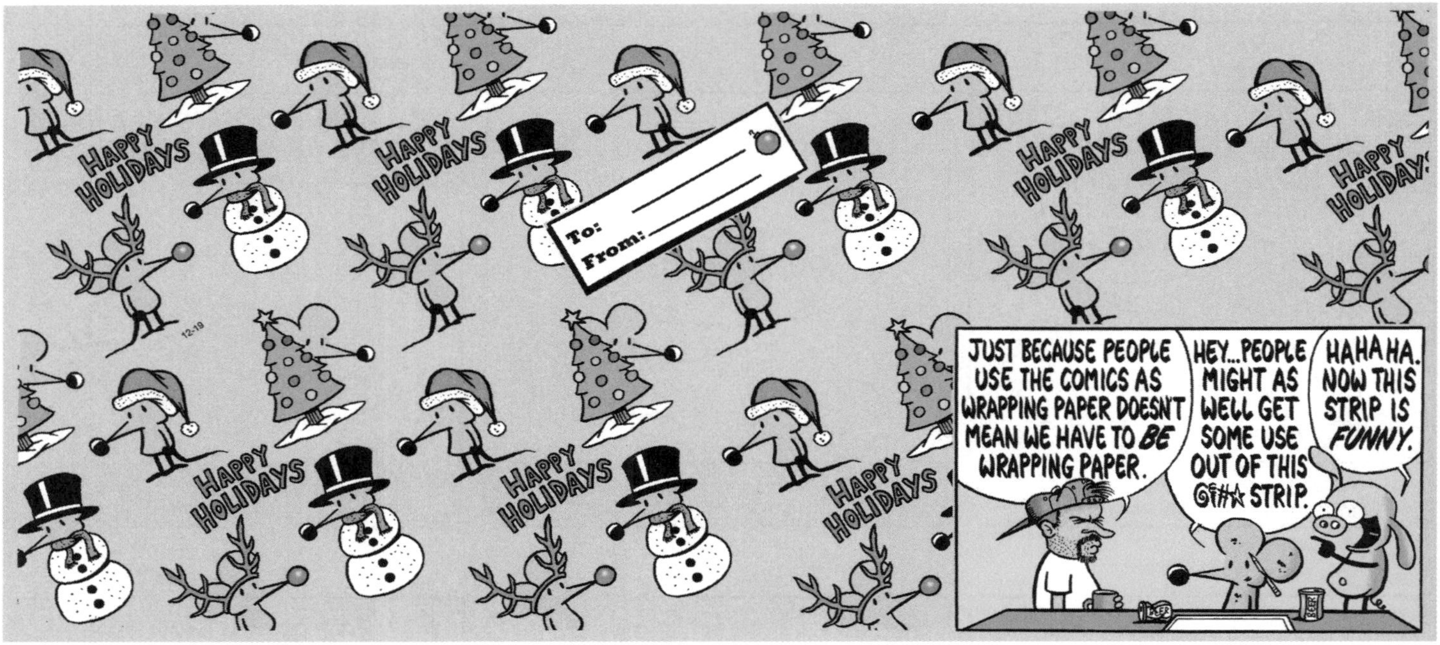
HAPPY HOLIDAYS
To:
From:
12-19
JUST BECAUSE PEOPLE USE THE COMICS AS WRAPPING PAPER DOESN'T MEAN WE HAVE TO *BE* WRAPPING PAPER.
HEY...PEOPLE MIGHT AS WELL GET SOME USE OUT OF THIS @$#☆ STRIP.
HAHAHA. NOW THIS STRIP IS *FUNNY*.

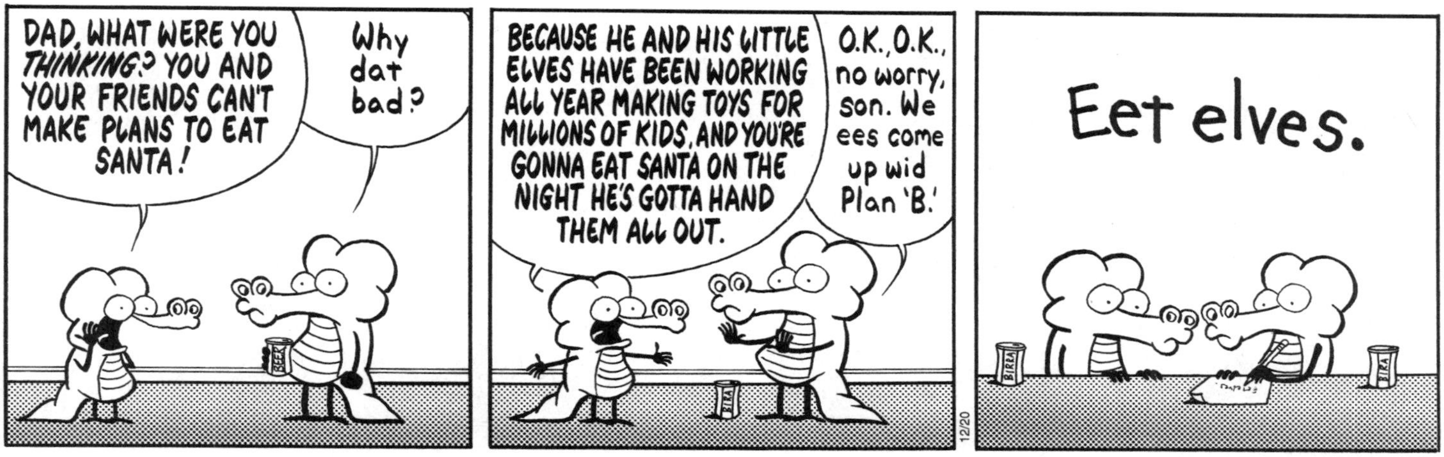
DAD, WHAT WERE YOU *THINKING*? YOU AND YOUR FRIENDS CAN'T MAKE PLANS TO EAT SANTA!
Why dat bad?
BECAUSE HE AND HIS LITTLE ELVES HAVE BEEN WORKING ALL YEAR MAKING TOYS FOR MILLIONS OF KIDS, AND YOU'RE GONNA EAT SANTA ON THE NIGHT HE'S GOTTA HAND THEM ALL OUT.
O.K., O.K., no worry, son. We ees come up wid Plan 'B.'
Eet elves.

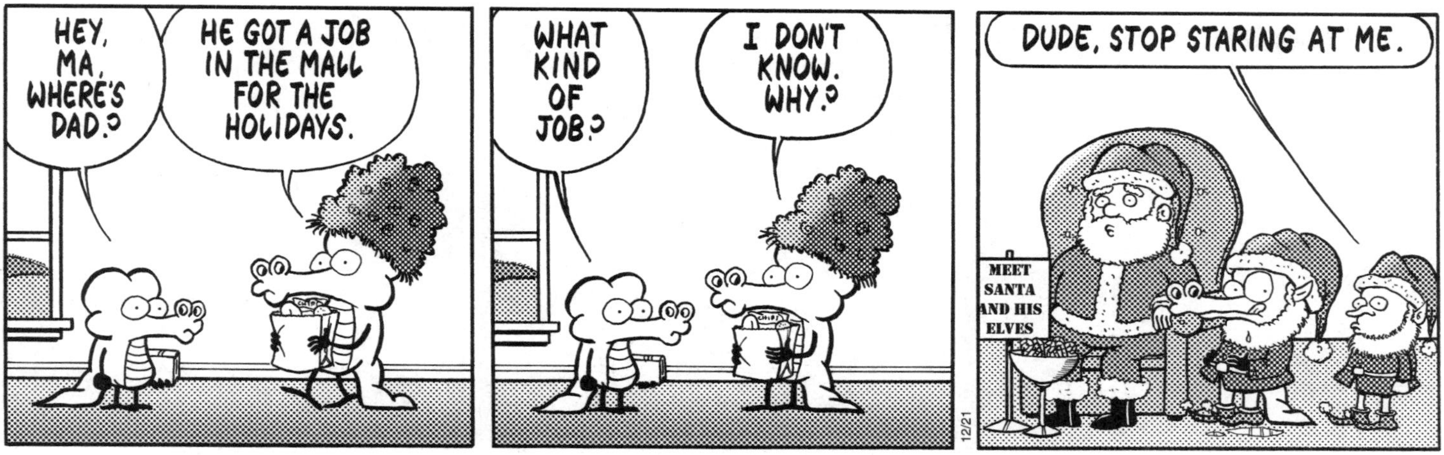
HEY, MA, WHERE'S DAD?
HE GOT A JOB IN THE MALL FOR THE HOLIDAYS.
WHAT KIND OF JOB?
I DON'T KNOW. WHY?
DUDE, STOP STARING AT ME.
MEET SANTA AND HIS ELVES

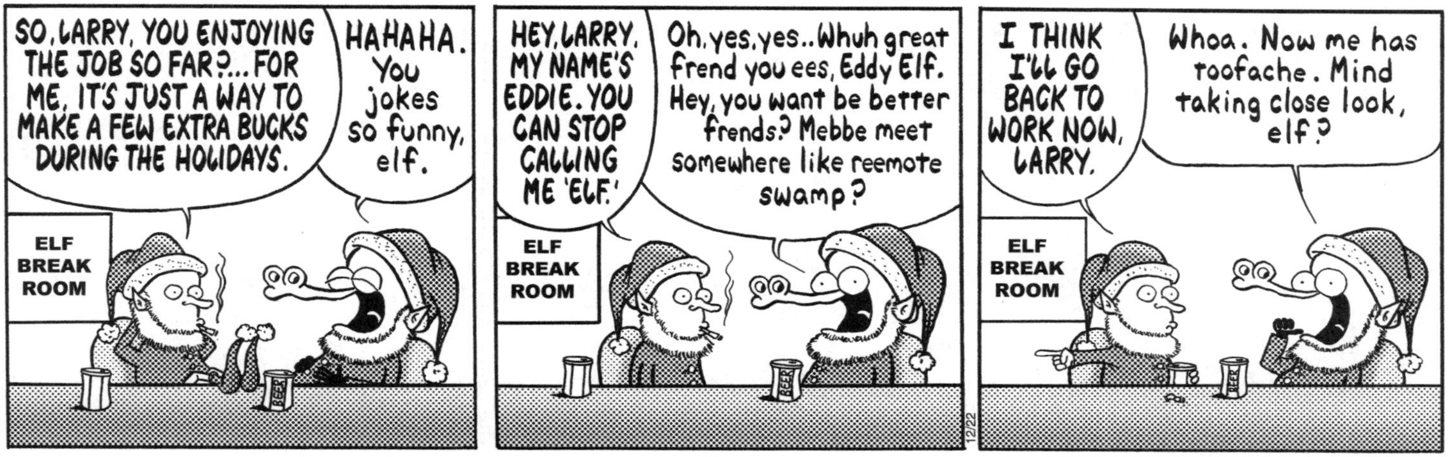
ELF BREAK ROOM
SO, LARRY, YOU ENJOYING THE JOB SO FAR?... FOR ME, IT'S JUST A WAY TO MAKE A FEW EXTRA BUCKS DURING THE HOLIDAYS.
HAHAHA. You jokes so funny, elf.
ELF BREAK ROOM
HEY, LARRY, MY NAME'S EDDIE. YOU CAN STOP CALLING ME 'ELF.'
Oh, yes, yes.. Whuh great frend you ees, Eddy Elf. Hey, you want be better frends? Mebbe meet somewhere like reemote swamp?
ELF BREAK ROOM
I THINK I'LL GO BACK TO WORK NOW, LARRY.
Whoa. Now me has toofache. Mind taking close look, elf?

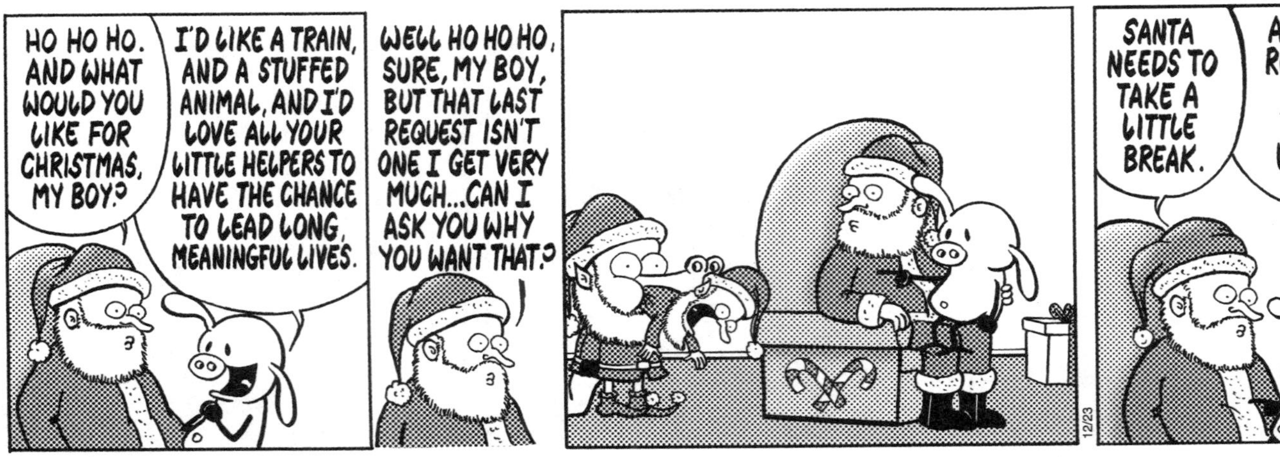
HO HO HO. AND WHAT WOULD YOU LIKE FOR CHRISTMAS, MY BOY?
I'D LIKE A TRAIN, AND A STUFFED ANIMAL, AND I'D LOVE ALL YOUR LITTLE HELPERS TO HAVE THE CHANCE TO LEAD LONG, MEANINGFUL LIVES.
WELL HO HO HO, SURE, MY BOY, BUT THAT LAST REQUEST ISN'T ONE I GET VERY MUCH...CAN I ASK YOU WHY YOU WANT THAT?
12/23
SANTA NEEDS TO TAKE A LITTLE BREAK.
AND YOUR REINDEERS... I'D LIKE THEM TO LIVE, TOO.

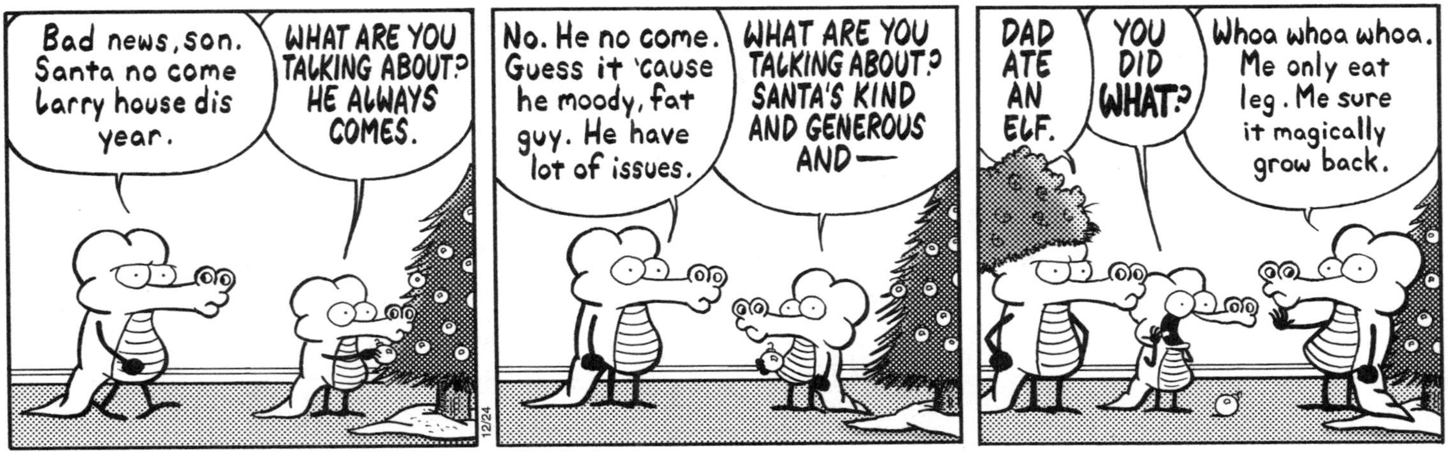
Bad news, son. Santa no come Larry house dis year.
WHAT ARE YOU TALKING ABOUT? HE ALWAYS COMES.
12/24
No. He no come. Guess it 'cause he moody, fat guy. He have lot of issues.
WHAT ARE YOU TALKING ABOUT? SANTA'S KIND AND GENEROUS AND—
DAD ATE AN ELF.
YOU DID WHAT?
Whoa whoa whoa. Me only eat leg. Me sure it magically grow back.

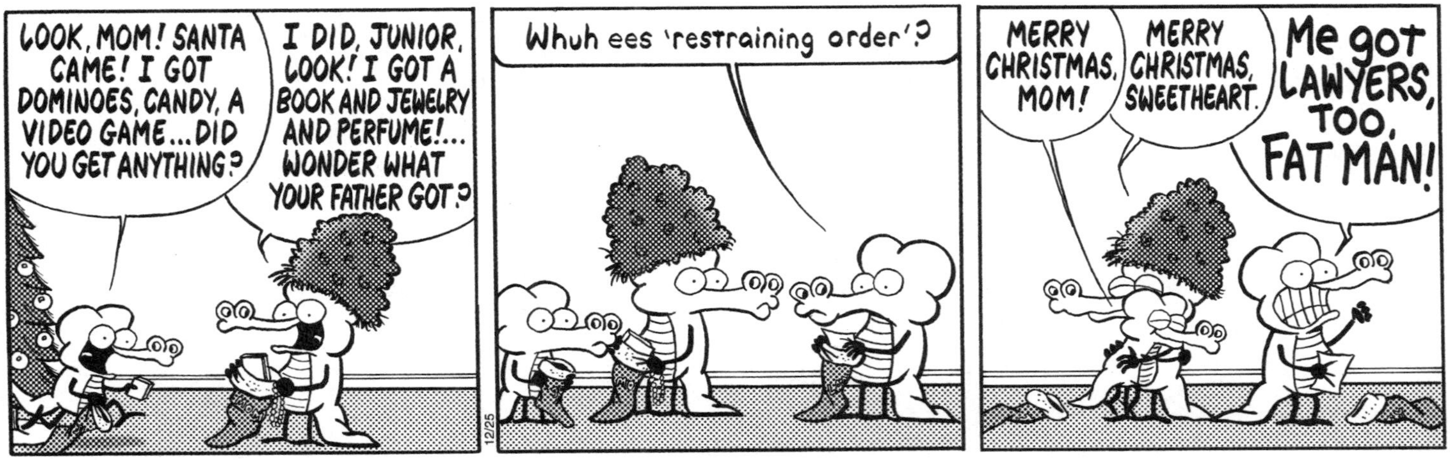
LOOK, MOM! SANTA CAME! I GOT DOMINOES, CANDY, A VIDEO GAME...DID YOU GET ANYTHING?
I DID, JUNIOR. LOOK! I GOT A BOOK AND JEWELRY AND PERFUME!... WONDER WHAT YOUR FATHER GOT?
12/25
Whuh ees 'restraining order'?
MERRY CHRISTMAS, MOM!
MERRY CHRISTMAS, SWEETHEART.
Me got LAWYERS, TOO, FAT MAN!

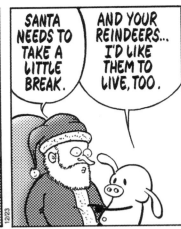

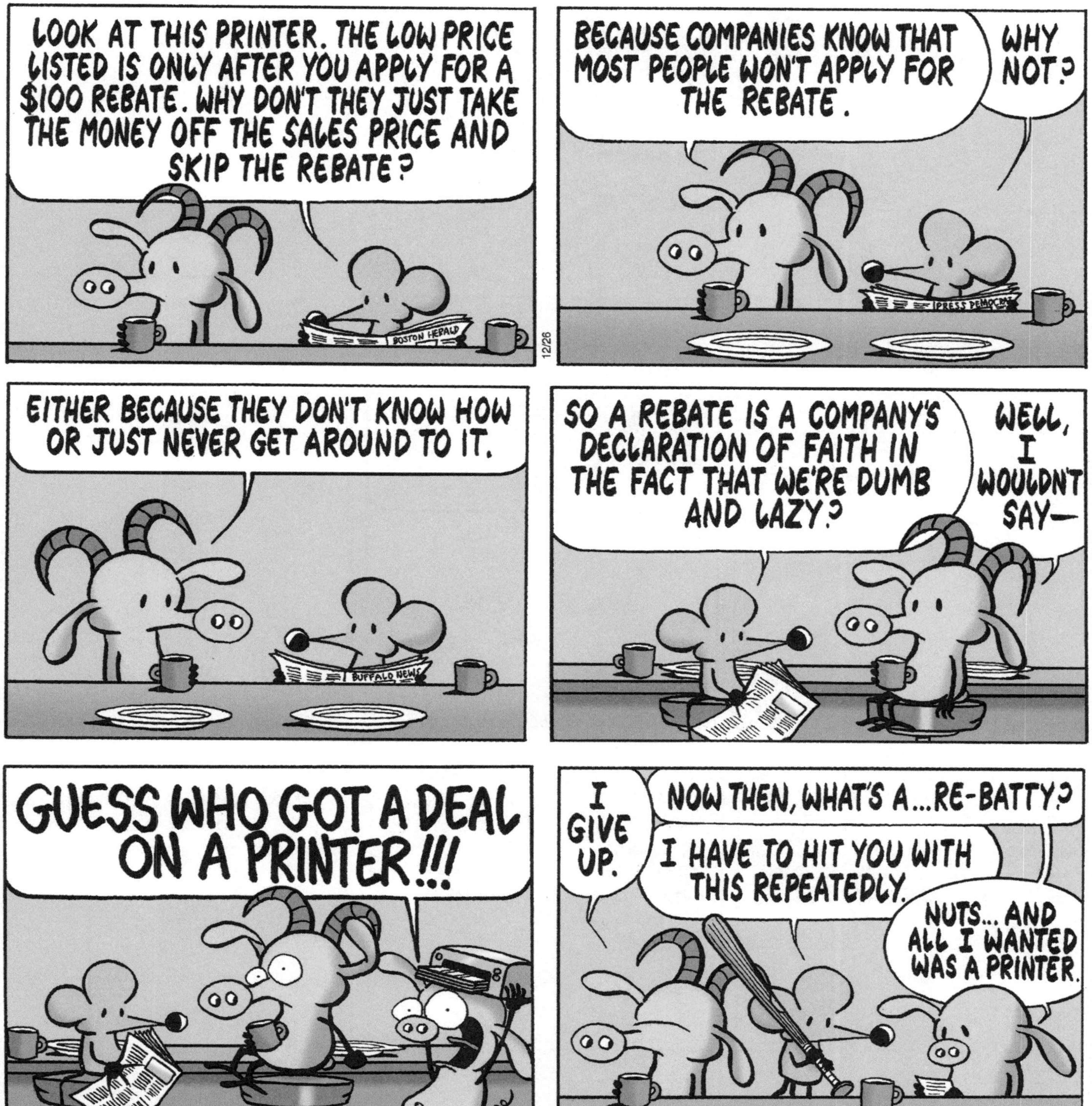

LOOK AT THIS PRINTER. THE LOW PRICE LISTED IS ONLY AFTER YOU APPLY FOR A $100 REBATE. WHY DON'T THEY JUST TAKE THE MONEY OFF THE SALES PRICE AND SKIP THE REBATE?
BOSTON HERALD
12/26
BECAUSE COMPANIES KNOW THAT MOST PEOPLE WON'T APPLY FOR THE REBATE.
WHY NOT?
PRESS DEMOCRAT
EITHER BECAUSE THEY DON'T KNOW HOW OR JUST NEVER GET AROUND TO IT.
BUFFALO NEWS
SO A REBATE IS A COMPANY'S DECLARATION OF FAITH IN THE FACT THAT WE'RE DUMB AND LAZY?
WELL, I WOULDN'T SAY—
GUESS WHO GOT A DEAL ON A PRINTER!!!
I GIVE UP.
NOW THEN, WHAT'S A...RE-BATTY?
I HAVE TO HIT YOU WITH THIS REPEATEDLY.
NUTS... AND ALL I WANTED WAS A PRINTER.

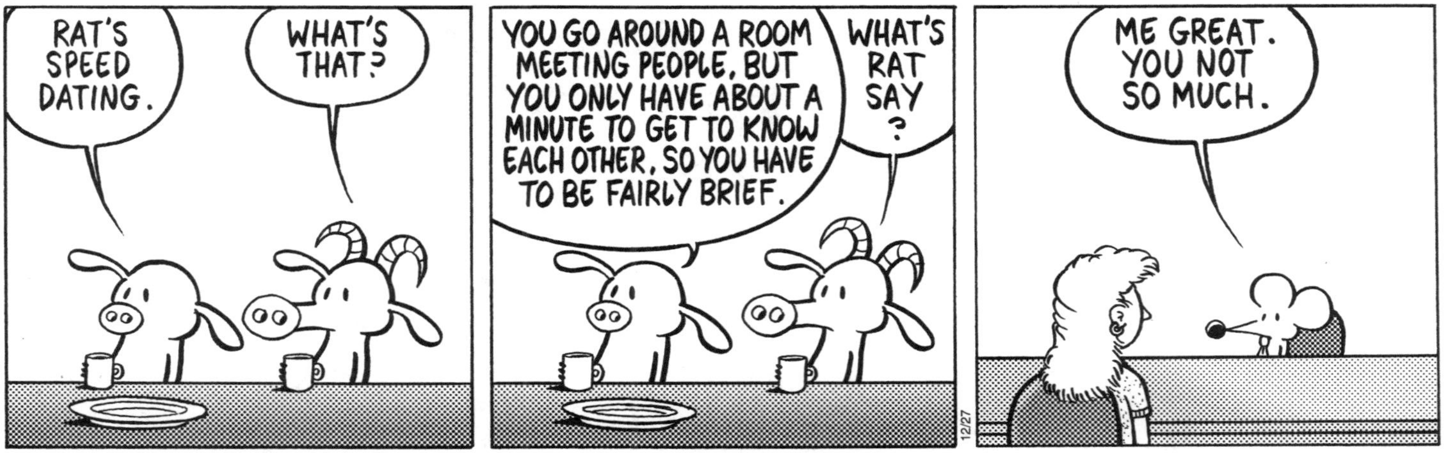
RAT'S SPEED DATING.
WHAT'S THAT?
YOU GO AROUND A ROOM MEETING PEOPLE, BUT YOU ONLY HAVE ABOUT A MINUTE TO GET TO KNOW EACH OTHER, SO YOU HAVE TO BE FAIRLY BRIEF.
WHAT'S RAT SAY?
ME GREAT. YOU NOT SO MUCH.
12/27

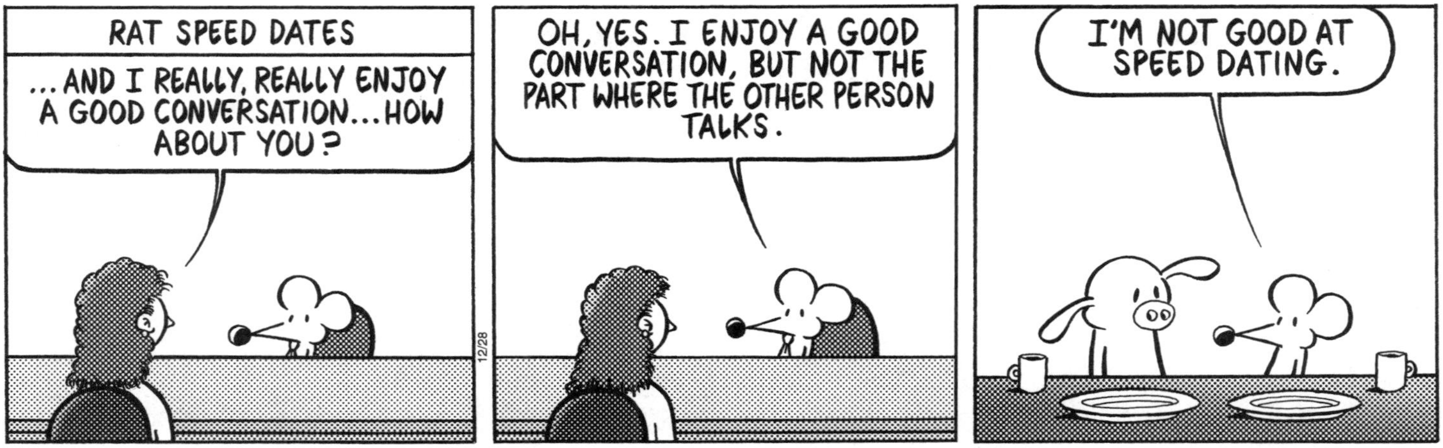
RAT SPEED DATES
... AND I REALLY, REALLY ENJOY A GOOD CONVERSATION... HOW ABOUT YOU?
OH, YES. I ENJOY A GOOD CONVERSATION, BUT NOT THE PART WHERE THE OTHER PERSON TALKS.
I'M NOT GOOD AT SPEED DATING.
12/28

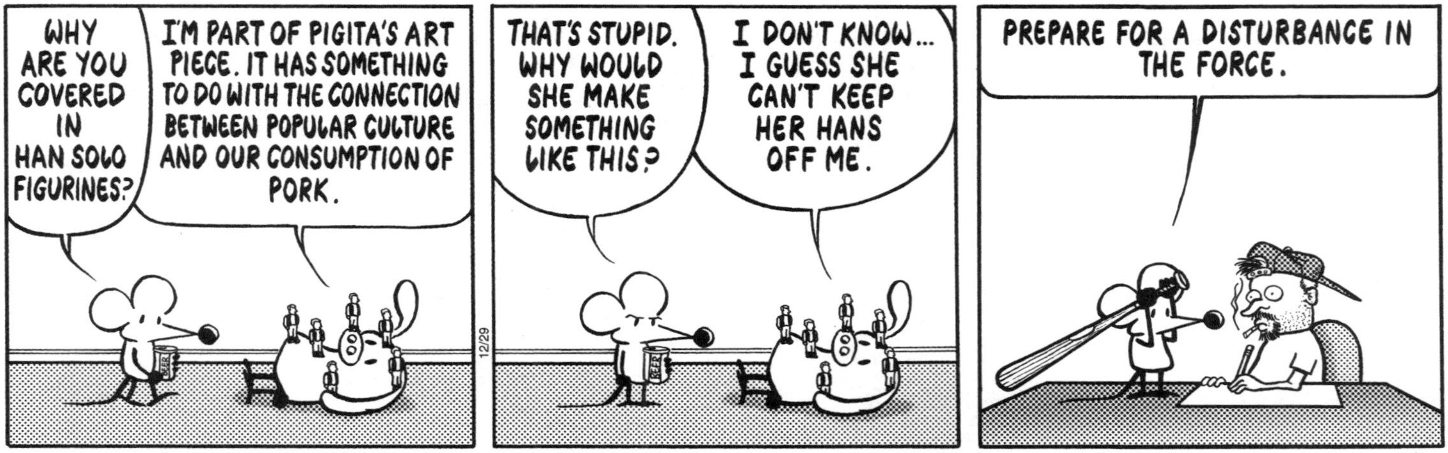
WHY ARE YOU COVERED IN HAN SOLO FIGURINES?
I'M PART OF PIGITA'S ART PIECE. IT HAS SOMETHING TO DO WITH THE CONNECTION BETWEEN POPULAR CULTURE AND OUR CONSUMPTION OF PORK.
THAT'S STUPID. WHY WOULD SHE MAKE SOMETHING LIKE THIS?
I DON'T KNOW... I GUESS SHE CAN'T KEEP HER HANS OFF ME.
PREPARE FOR A DISTURBANCE IN THE FORCE.
12/29

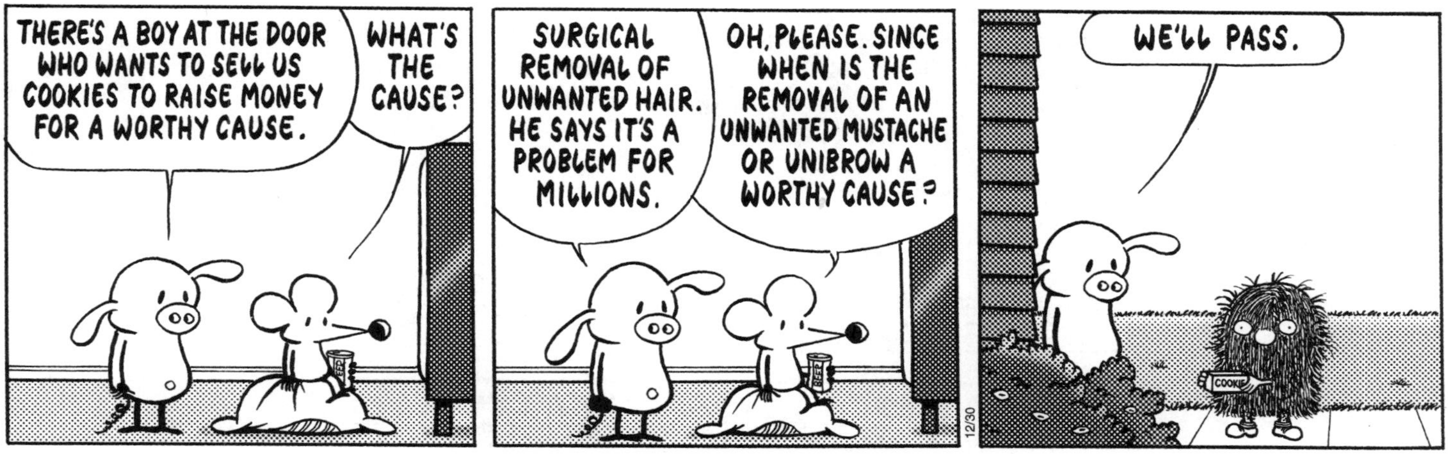
THERE'S A BOY AT THE DOOR WHO WANTS TO SELL US COOKIES TO RAISE MONEY FOR A WORTHY CAUSE.
WHAT'S THE CAUSE?
SURGICAL REMOVAL OF UNWANTED HAIR. HE SAYS IT'S A PROBLEM FOR MILLIONS.
OH, PLEASE. SINCE WHEN IS THE REMOVAL OF AN UNWANTED MUSTACHE OR UNIBROW A WORTHY CAUSE?
12/30
WE'LL PASS.
COOKIE

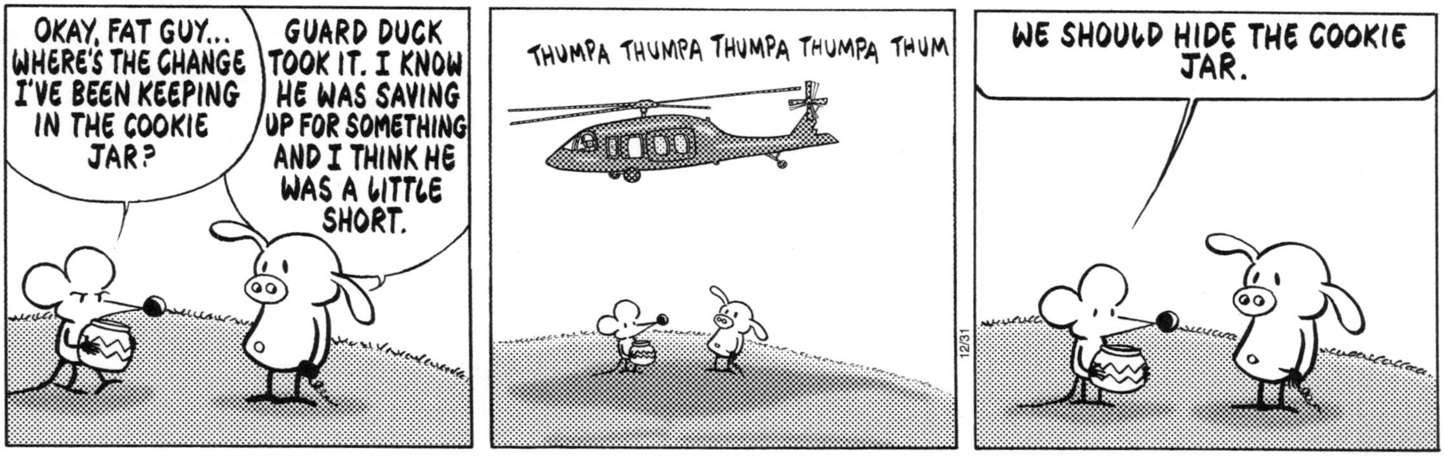
OKAY, FAT GUY... WHERE'S THE CHANGE I'VE BEEN KEEPING IN THE COOKIE JAR?
GUARD DUCK TOOK IT. I KNOW HE WAS SAVING UP FOR SOMETHING AND I THINK HE WAS A LITTLE SHORT.
THUMPA THUMPA THUMPA THUMPA THUM
12/31
WE SHOULD HIDE THE COOKIE JAR.

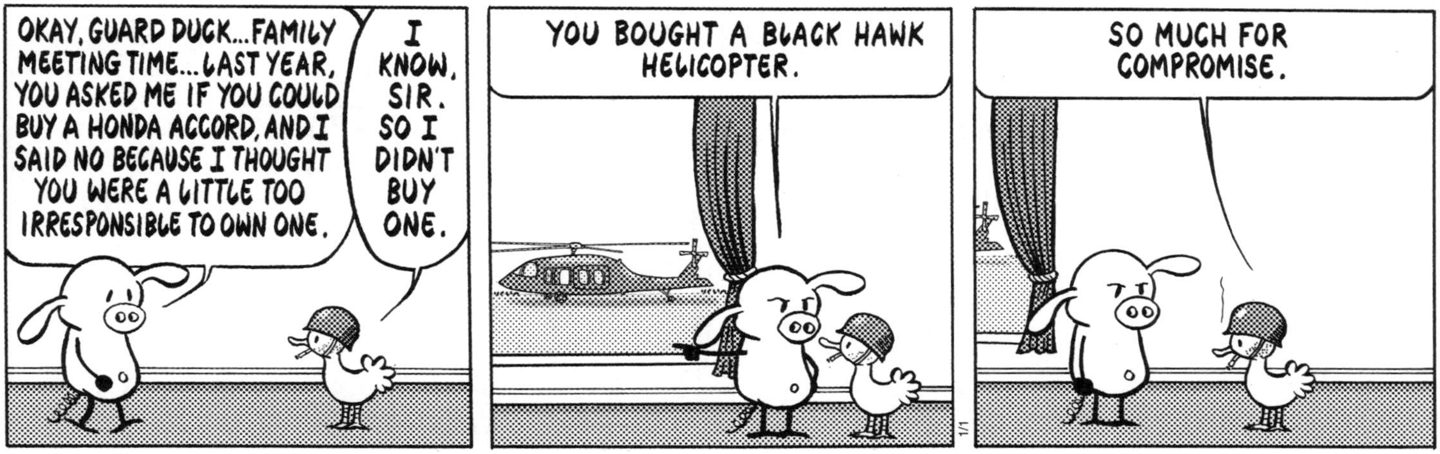
OKAY, GUARD DUCK...FAMILY MEETING TIME...LAST YEAR, YOU ASKED ME IF YOU COULD BUY A HONDA ACCORD, AND I SAID NO BECAUSE I THOUGHT YOU WERE A LITTLE TOO IRRESPONSIBLE TO OWN ONE.
I KNOW, SIR. SO I DIDN'T BUY ONE.
YOU BOUGHT A BLACK HAWK HELICOPTER.
1/1
SO MUCH FOR COMPROMISE.

WHATCHA WATCHING?
FOOTBALL. RAVENS AGAINST THE STEELERS. I'VE GOT A HUNDRED BUCKS ON THE STEELERS.
WHAT THE @☆!☆ ARE YOU DOING?
I JUST WANTED SOME POPCORN.
I DON'T CARE ABOUT THE POPCORN. YOU MOVED THE @$!#☆# BOWL.
SO?
SO WHEN MY TEAM BEGAN ITS COMEBACK, THE BOWL WAS RIGHT THERE. THE BOWL NEEDS TO REMAIN RIGHT THERE.
THERE?
THERE.
THERE?
YOU MOVED THE BEER! YOU MOVED THE BEER!!
AHHHHH! WHERE'S IT GO? WHERE'S IT GO?
PITTSBURGH FUMBLES. RAVENS WIN.
HAPPY?
I WILL FLY TO PITTSBURGH AND APOLOGIZE TO EACH AND EVERY ONE OF THEM!!

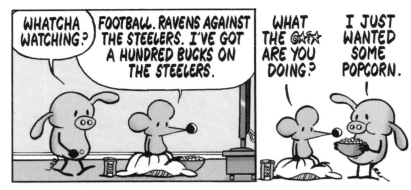

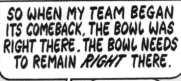

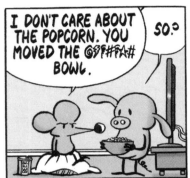

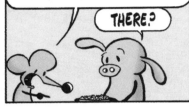

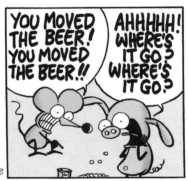

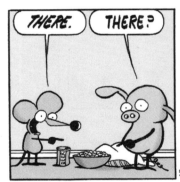

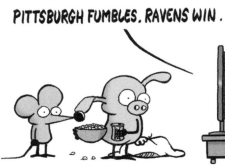

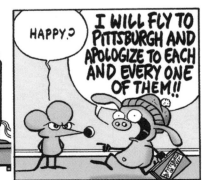

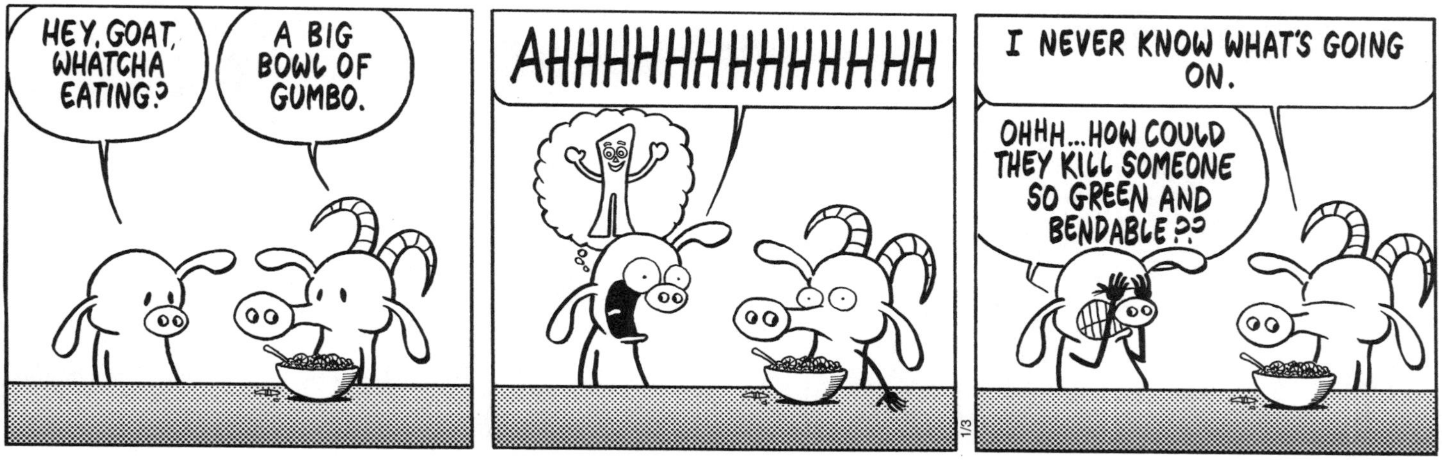
HEY, GOAT, WHATCHA EATING?
A BIG BOWL OF GUMBO.
AHHHHHHHHHHHHHH
I NEVER KNOW WHAT'S GOING ON.
OHHH...HOW COULD THEY KILL SOMEONE SO GREEN AND BENDABLE?!?
1/3

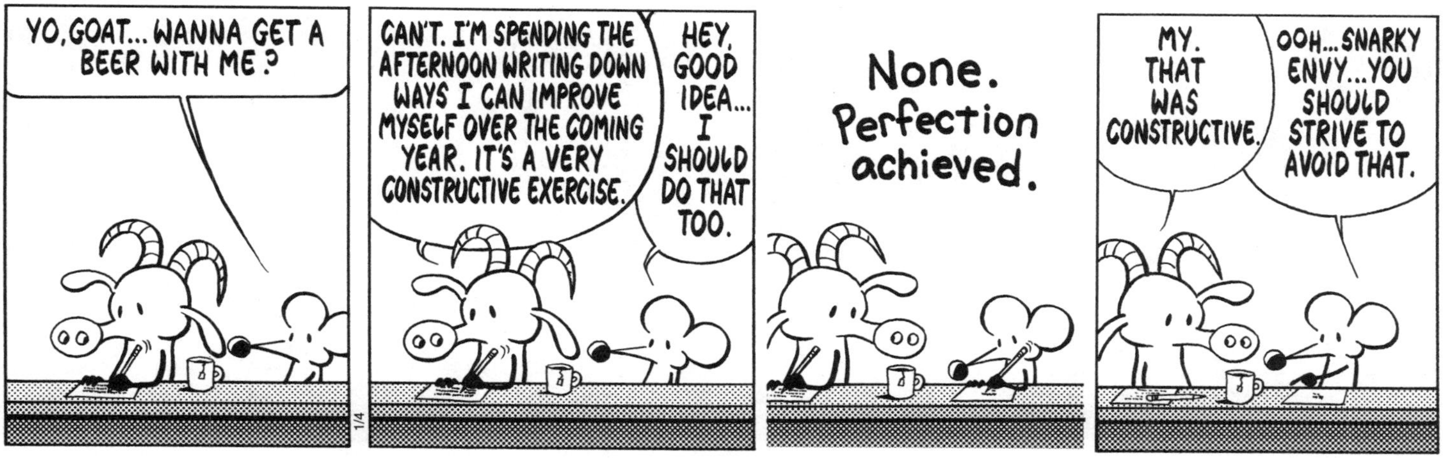
YO, GOAT... WANNA GET A BEER WITH ME?
CAN'T. I'M SPENDING THE AFTERNOON WRITING DOWN WAYS I CAN IMPROVE MYSELF OVER THE COMING YEAR. IT'S A VERY CONSTRUCTIVE EXERCISE.
HEY, GOOD IDEA... I SHOULD DO THAT TOO.
None. Perfection achieved.
MY. THAT WAS CONSTRUCTIVE.
OOH... SNARKY ENVY... YOU SHOULD STRIVE TO AVOID THAT.
1/4

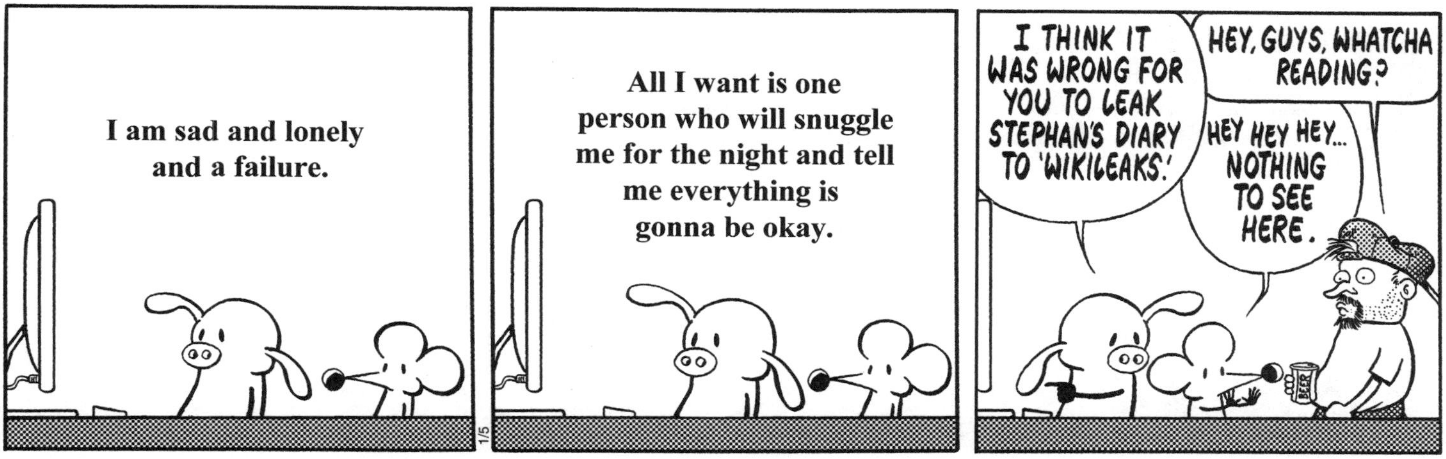
I am sad and lonely and a failure.
All I want is one person who will snuggle me for the night and tell me everything is gonna be okay.
I THINK IT WAS WRONG FOR YOU TO LEAK STEPHAN'S DIARY TO 'WIKILEAKS.'
HEY, GUYS, WHATCHA READING?
HEY HEY HEY... NOTHING TO SEE HERE.
1/5

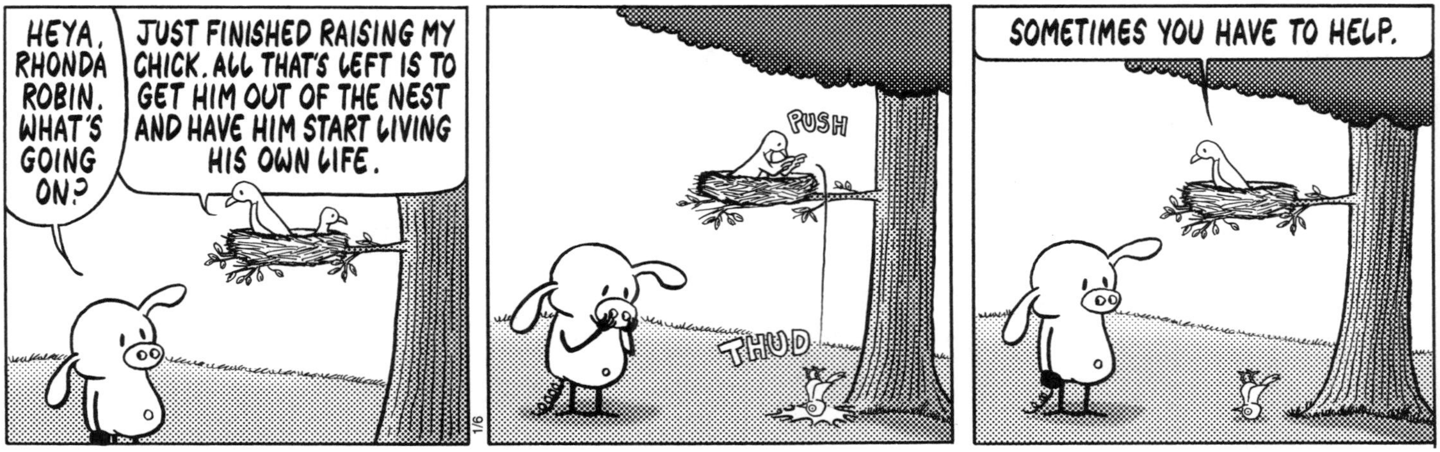
HEYA, RHONDA ROBIN. WHAT'S GOING ON?
JUST FINISHED RAISING MY CHICK. ALL THAT'S LEFT IS TO GET HIM OUT OF THE NEST AND HAVE HIM START LIVING HIS OWN LIFE.
1/6
PUSH
THUD
SOMETIMES YOU HAVE TO HELP.

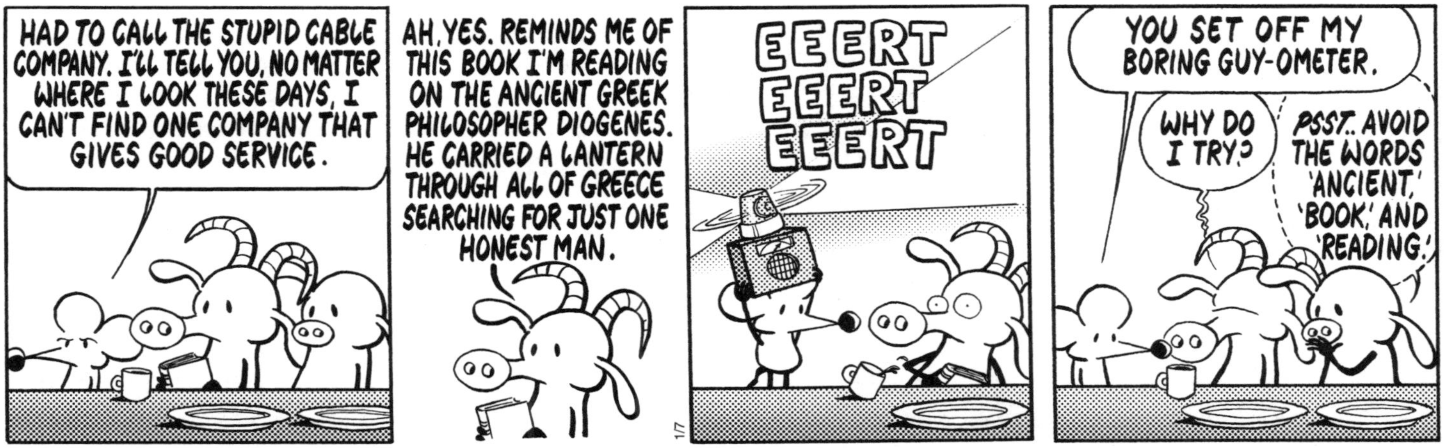
HAD TO CALL THE STUPID CABLE COMPANY. I'LL TELL YOU, NO MATTER WHERE I LOOK THESE DAYS, I CAN'T FIND ONE COMPANY THAT GIVES GOOD SERVICE.
AH, YES. REMINDS ME OF THIS BOOK I'M READING ON THE ANCIENT GREEK PHILOSOPHER DIOGENES. HE CARRIED A LANTERN THROUGH ALL OF GREECE SEARCHING FOR JUST ONE HONEST MAN.
1/7
EEERT
EEERT
EEERT
YOU SET OFF MY BORING GUY-OMETER.
WHY DO I TRY?
PSST.. AVOID THE WORDS 'ANCIENT,' 'BOOK,' AND 'READING.'

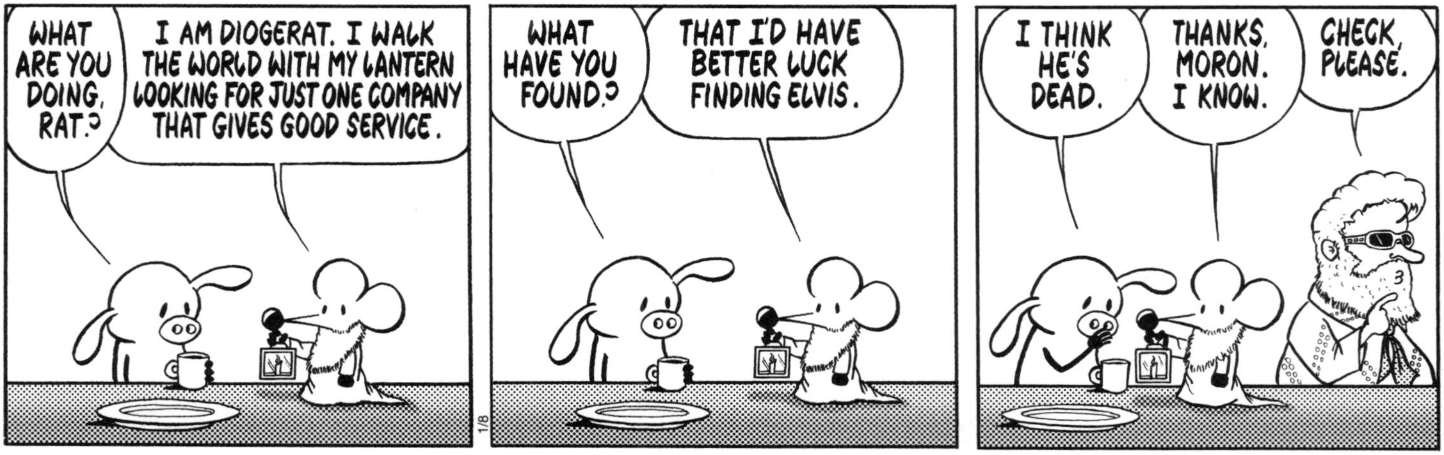
WHAT ARE YOU DOING, RAT?
I AM DIOGERAT. I WALK THE WORLD WITH MY LANTERN LOOKING FOR JUST ONE COMPANY THAT GIVES GOOD SERVICE.
1/8
WHAT HAVE YOU FOUND?
THAT I'D HAVE BETTER LUCK FINDING ELVIS.
I THINK HE'S DEAD.
THANKS, MORON. I KNOW.
CHECK, PLEASE.

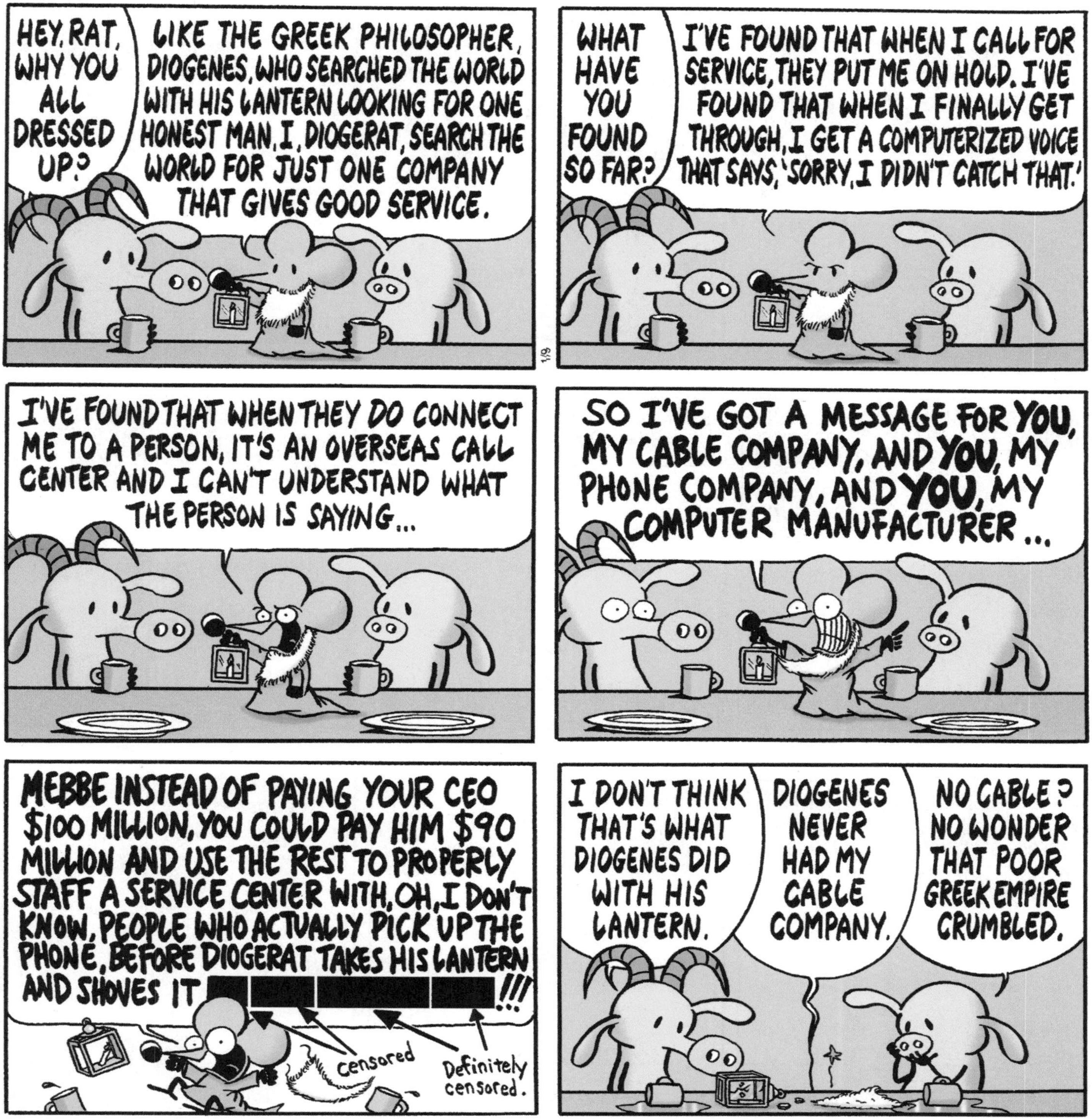
HEY, RAT, WHY YOU ALL DRESSED UP?
LIKE THE GREEK PHILOSOPHER, DIOGENES, WHO SEARCHED THE WORLD WITH HIS LANTERN LOOKING FOR ONE HONEST MAN, I, DIOGERAT, SEARCH THE WORLD FOR JUST ONE COMPANY THAT GIVES GOOD SERVICE.
WHAT HAVE YOU FOUND SO FAR?
I'VE FOUND THAT WHEN I CALL FOR SERVICE, THEY PUT ME ON HOLD. I'VE FOUND THAT WHEN I FINALLY GET THROUGH, I GET A COMPUTERIZED VOICE THAT SAYS, 'SORRY, I DIDN'T CATCH THAT.'
I'VE FOUND THAT WHEN THEY DO CONNECT ME TO A PERSON, IT'S AN OVERSEAS CALL CENTER AND I CAN'T UNDERSTAND WHAT THE PERSON IS SAYING...
SO I'VE GOT A MESSAGE FOR YOU, MY CABLE COMPANY, AND YOU, MY PHONE COMPANY, AND YOU, MY COMPUTER MANUFACTURER...
MEBBE INSTEAD OF PAYING YOUR CEO $100 MILLION, YOU COULD PAY HIM $90 MILLION AND USE THE REST TO PROPERLY STAFF A SERVICE CENTER WITH, OH, I DON'T KNOW, PEOPLE WHO ACTUALLY PICK UP THE PHONE, BEFORE DIOGERAT TAKES HIS LANTERN AND SHOVES IT [redacted]!!!
Censored
Definitely censored.
I DON'T THINK THAT'S WHAT DIOGENES DID WITH HIS LANTERN.
DIOGENES NEVER HAD MY CABLE COMPANY.
NO CABLE? NO WONDER THAT POOR GREEK EMPIRE CRUMBLED.

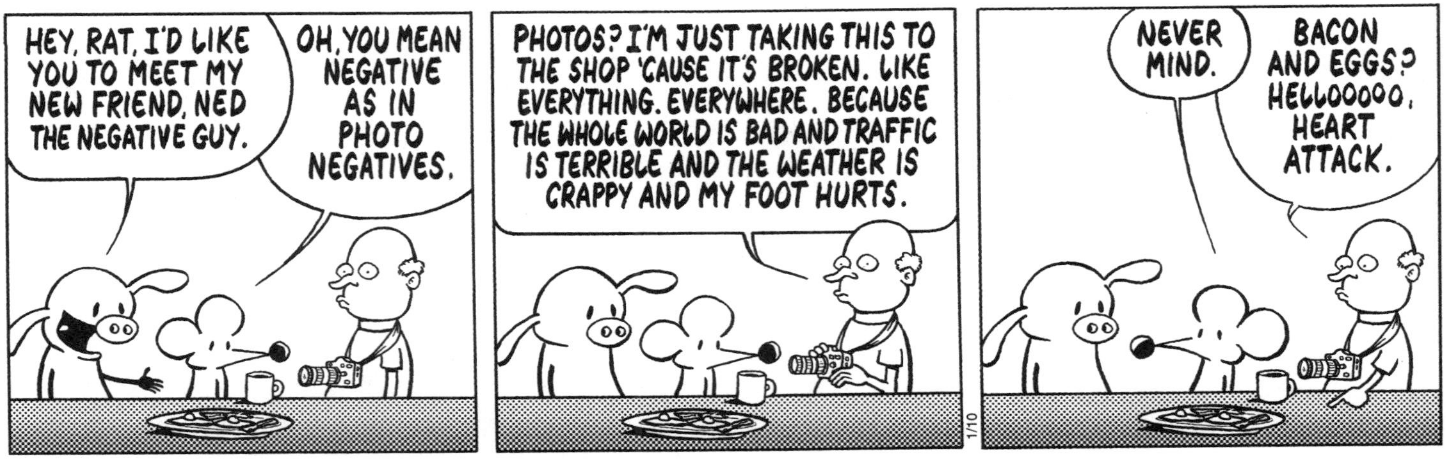
HEY, RAT, I'D LIKE YOU TO MEET MY NEW FRIEND, NED THE NEGATIVE GUY.
OH, YOU MEAN NEGATIVE AS IN PHOTO NEGATIVES.
PHOTOS? I'M JUST TAKING THIS TO THE SHOP 'CAUSE IT'S BROKEN. LIKE EVERYTHING. EVERYWHERE. BECAUSE THE WHOLE WORLD IS BAD AND TRAFFIC IS TERRIBLE AND THE WEATHER IS CRAPPY AND MY FOOT HURTS.
NEVER MIND.
BACON AND EGGS? HELLOOOOO. HEART ATTACK.
1/10

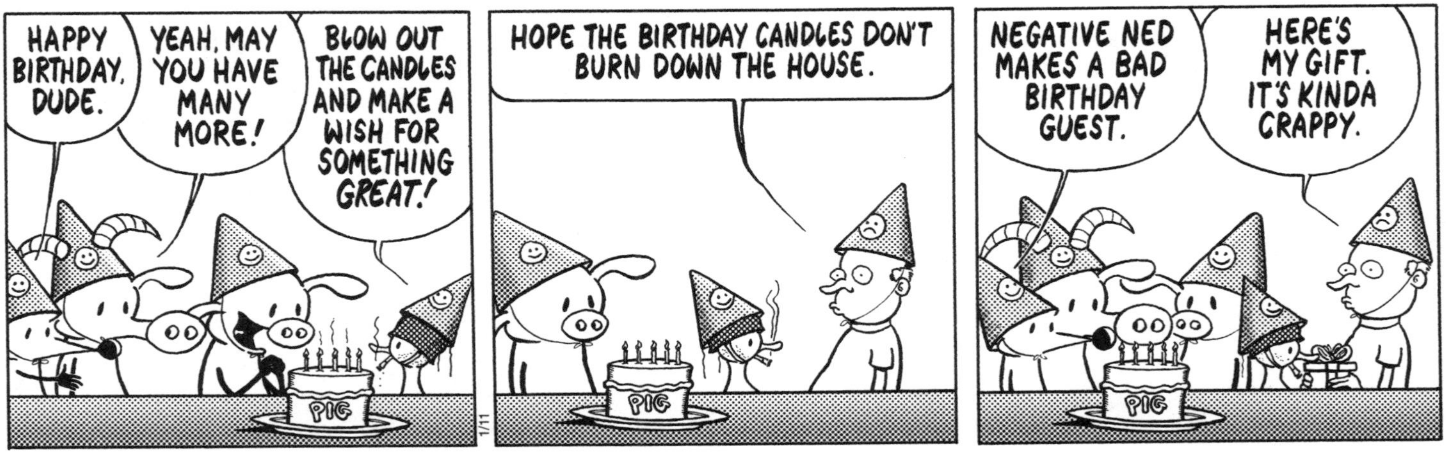
HAPPY BIRTHDAY, DUDE.
YEAH, MAY YOU HAVE MANY MORE!
BLOW OUT THE CANDLES AND MAKE A WISH FOR SOMETHING GREAT!
PIG
1/11
HOPE THE BIRTHDAY CANDLES DON'T BURN DOWN THE HOUSE.
PIG
NEGATIVE NED MAKES A BAD BIRTHDAY GUEST.
HERE'S MY GIFT. IT'S KINDA CRAPPY.
PIG

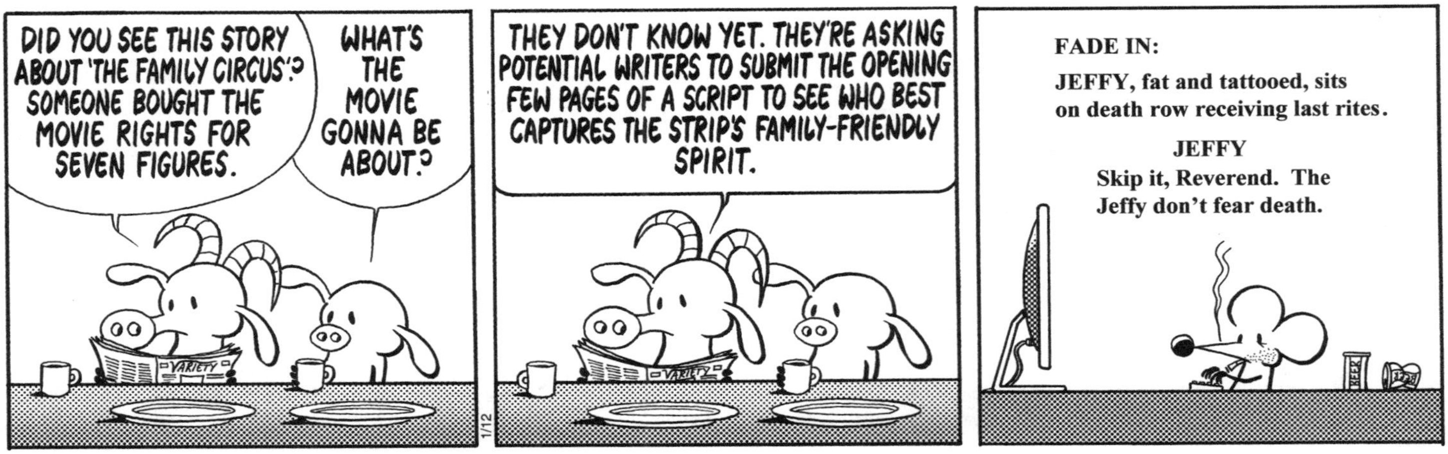
DID YOU SEE THIS STORY ABOUT 'THE FAMILY CIRCUS'? SOMEONE BOUGHT THE MOVIE RIGHTS FOR SEVEN FIGURES.
WHAT'S THE MOVIE GONNA BE ABOUT?
VARIETY
1/12
THEY DON'T KNOW YET. THEY'RE ASKING POTENTIAL WRITERS TO SUBMIT THE OPENING FEW PAGES OF A SCRIPT TO SEE WHO BEST CAPTURES THE STRIP'S FAMILY-FRIENDLY SPIRIT.
VARIETY
FADE IN:
JEFFY, fat and tattooed, sits on death row receiving last rites.
JEFFY
Skip it, Reverend. The Jeffy don't fear death.
BEER

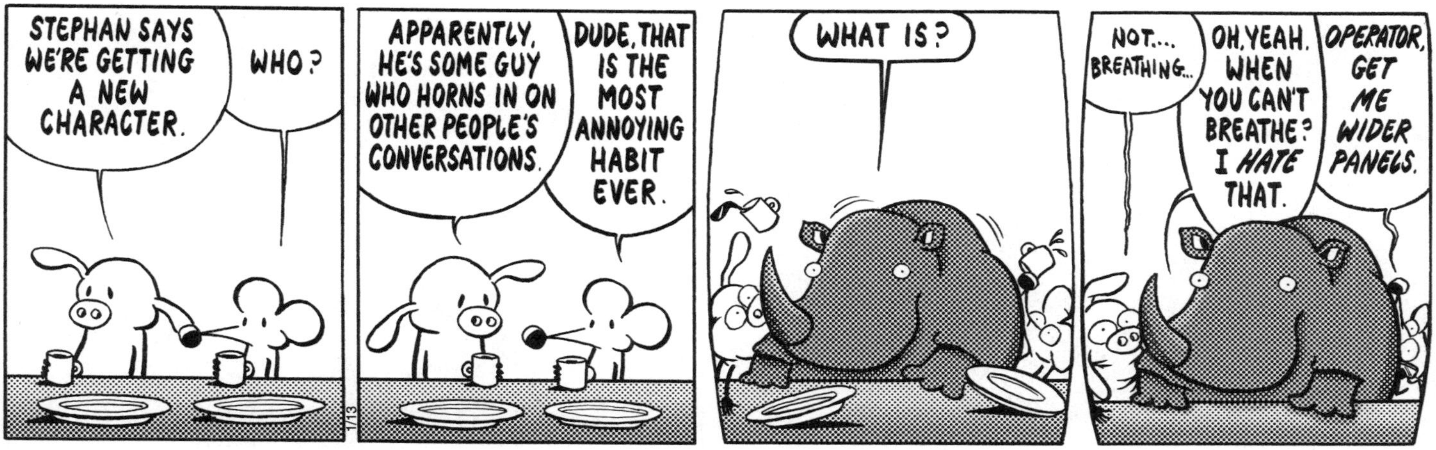
STEPHAN SAYS WE'RE GETTING A NEW CHARACTER.
WHO?
1/13
APPARENTLY, HE'S SOME GUY WHO HORNS IN ON OTHER PEOPLE'S CONVERSATIONS.
DUDE, THAT IS THE MOST ANNOYING HABIT EVER.
WHAT IS?
NOT.... BREATHING...
OH, YEAH. WHEN YOU CAN'T BREATHE? I HATE THAT.
OPERATOR, GET ME WIDER PANELS.

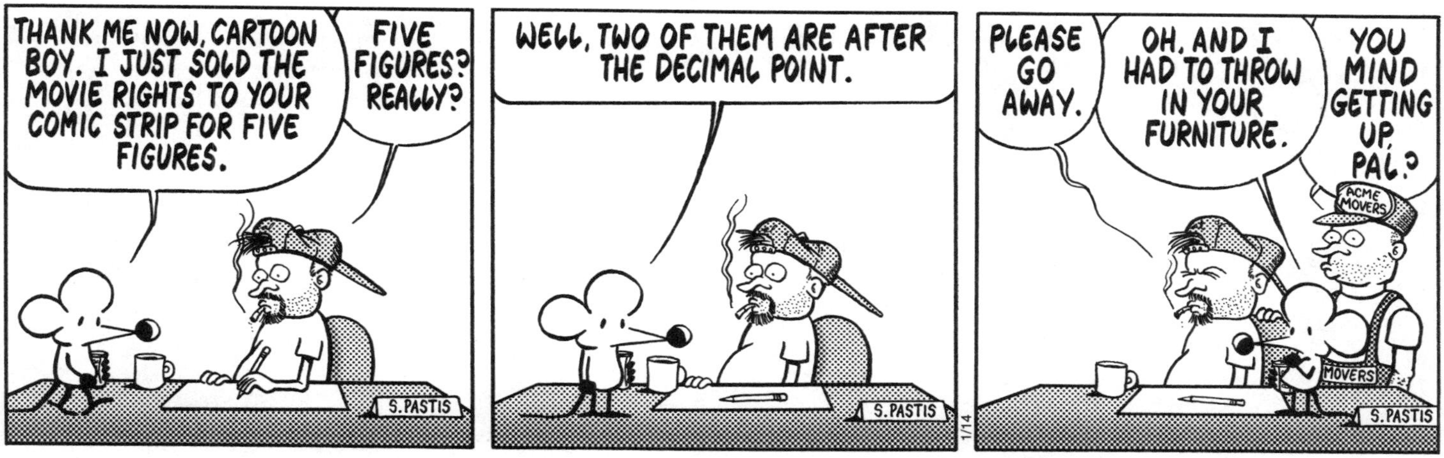
THANK ME NOW, CARTOON BOY. I JUST SOLD THE MOVIE RIGHTS TO YOUR COMIC STRIP FOR FIVE FIGURES.
FIVE FIGURES? REALLY?
S. PASTIS
WELL, TWO OF THEM ARE AFTER THE DECIMAL POINT.
S. PASTIS
1/14
PLEASE GO AWAY.
OH, AND I HAD TO THROW IN YOUR FURNITURE.
YOU MIND GETTING UP, PAL?
ACME MOVERS
MOVERS
S. PASTIS

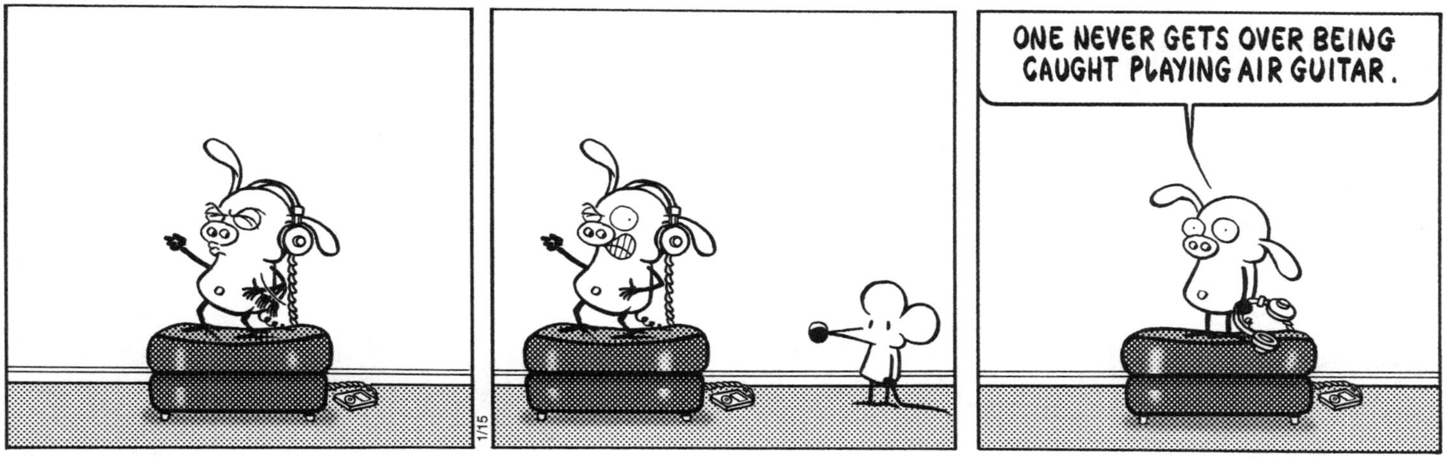
1/15
ONE NEVER GETS OVER BEING CAUGHT PLAYING AIR GUITAR.

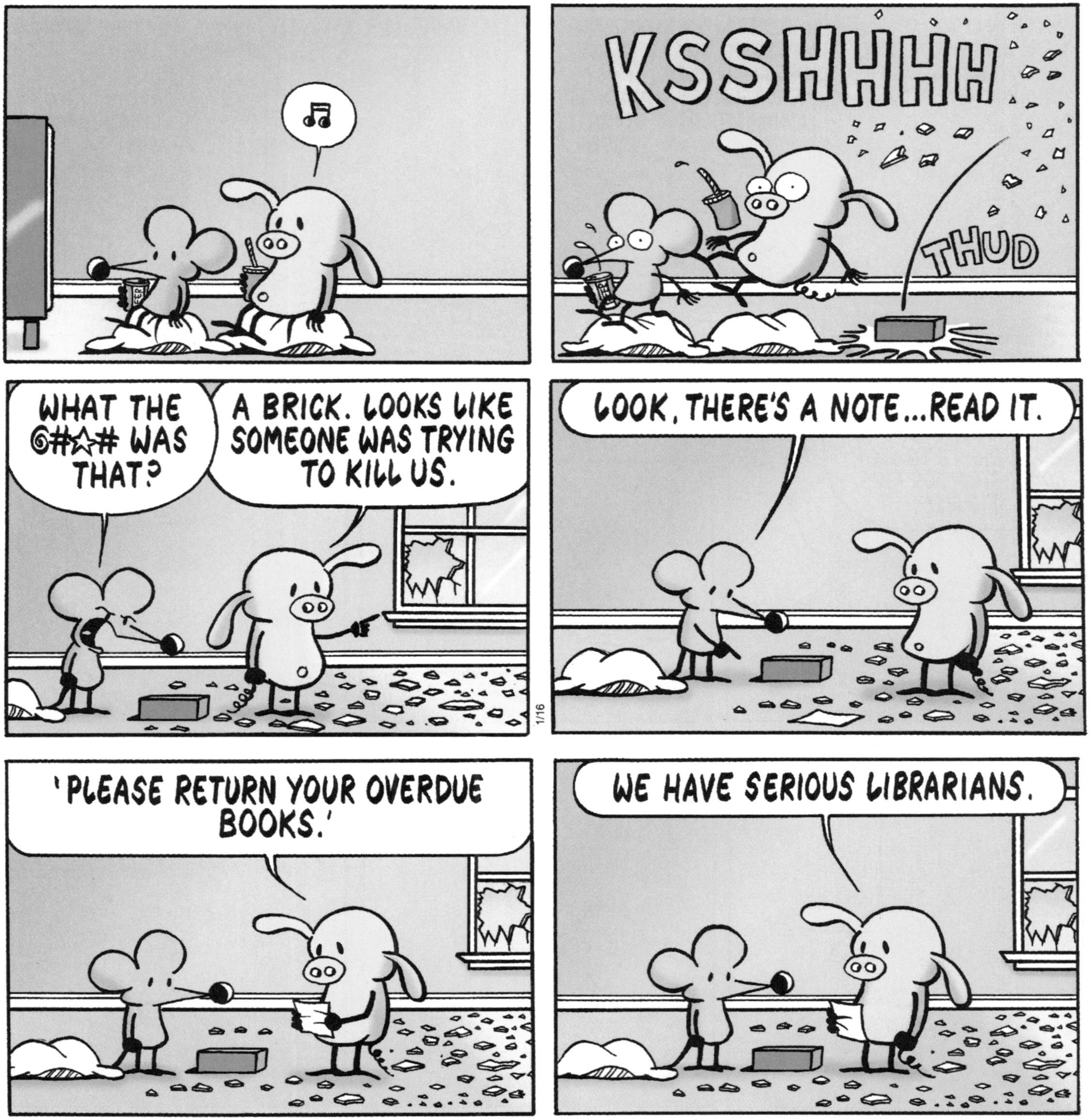
KSSHHHH
THUD
WHAT THE @#☆# WAS THAT?
A BRICK. LOOKS LIKE SOMEONE WAS TRYING TO KILL US.
1/16
LOOK, THERE'S A NOTE...READ IT.
'PLEASE RETURN YOUR OVERDUE BOOKS.'
WE HAVE SERIOUS LIBRARIANS.

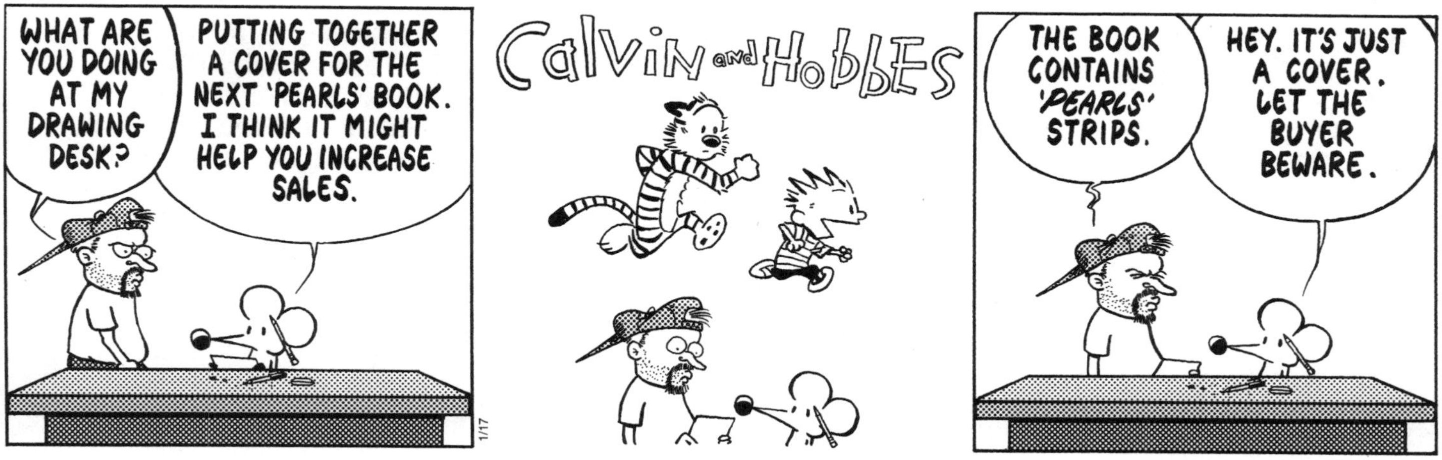
WHAT ARE YOU DOING AT MY DRAWING DESK?
PUTTING TOGETHER A COVER FOR THE NEXT 'PEARLS' BOOK. I THINK IT MIGHT HELP YOU INCREASE SALES.
Calvin and Hobbes
THE BOOK CONTAINS 'PEARLS' STRIPS.
HEY. IT'S JUST A COVER. LET THE BUYER BEWARE.
1/17

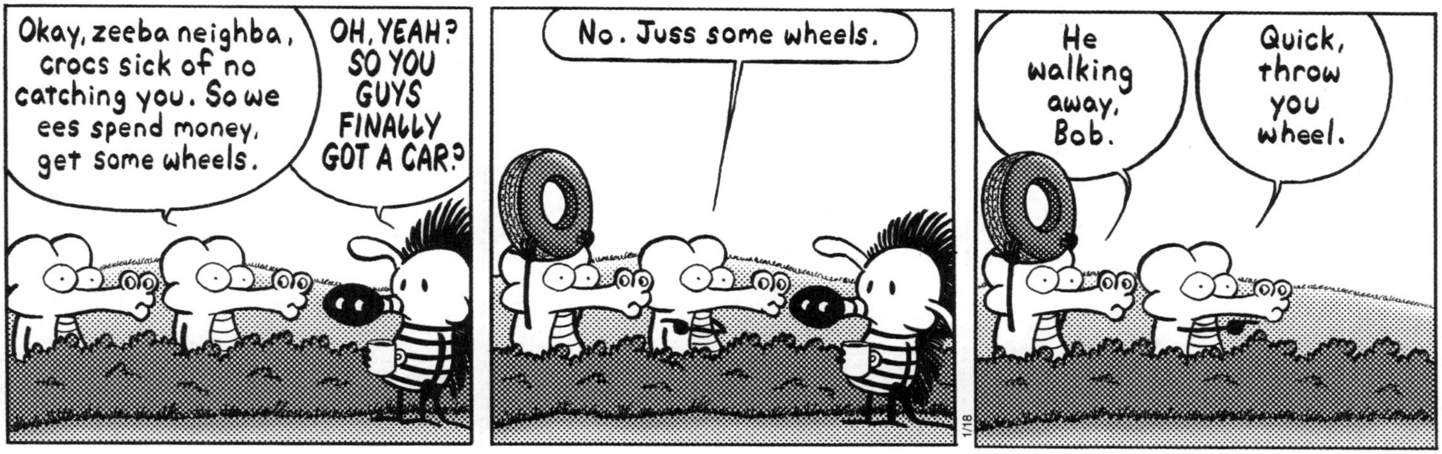
Okay, zeeba neighba, crocs sick of no catching you. So we ees spend money, get some wheels.
OH, YEAH? SO YOU GUYS FINALLY GOT A CAR?
No. Juss some wheels.
He walking away, Bob.
Quick, throw you wheel.
1/18

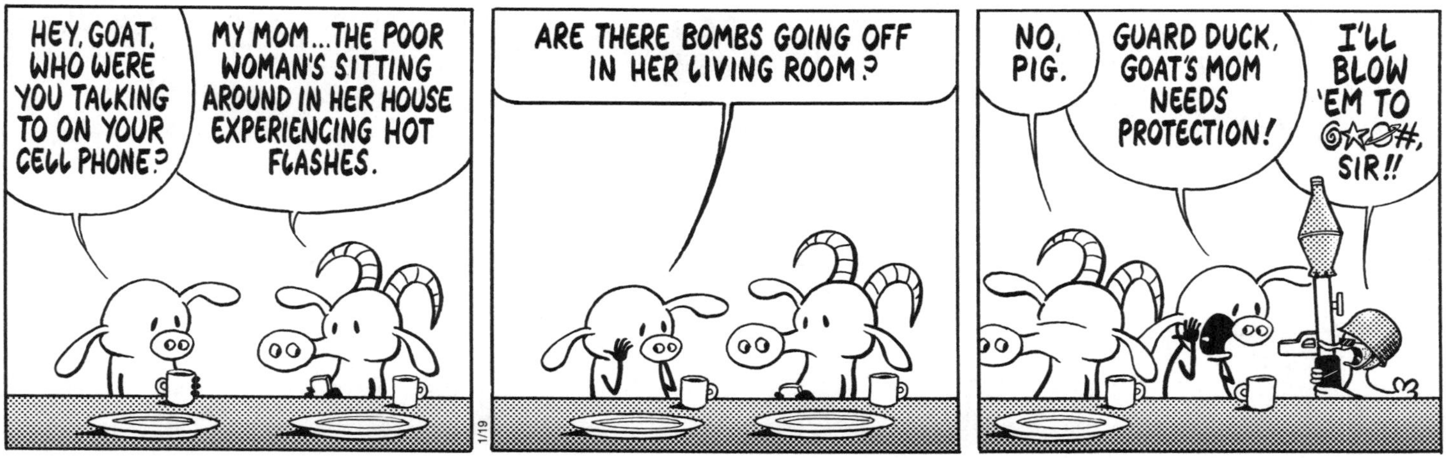
HEY, GOAT, WHO WERE YOU TALKING TO ON YOUR CELL PHONE?
MY MOM...THE POOR WOMAN'S SITTING AROUND IN HER HOUSE EXPERIENCING HOT FLASHES.
ARE THERE BOMBS GOING OFF IN HER LIVING ROOM?
NO, PIG.
GUARD DUCK, GOAT'S MOM NEEDS PROTECTION!
I'LL BLOW 'EM TO
SIR!!
1/19

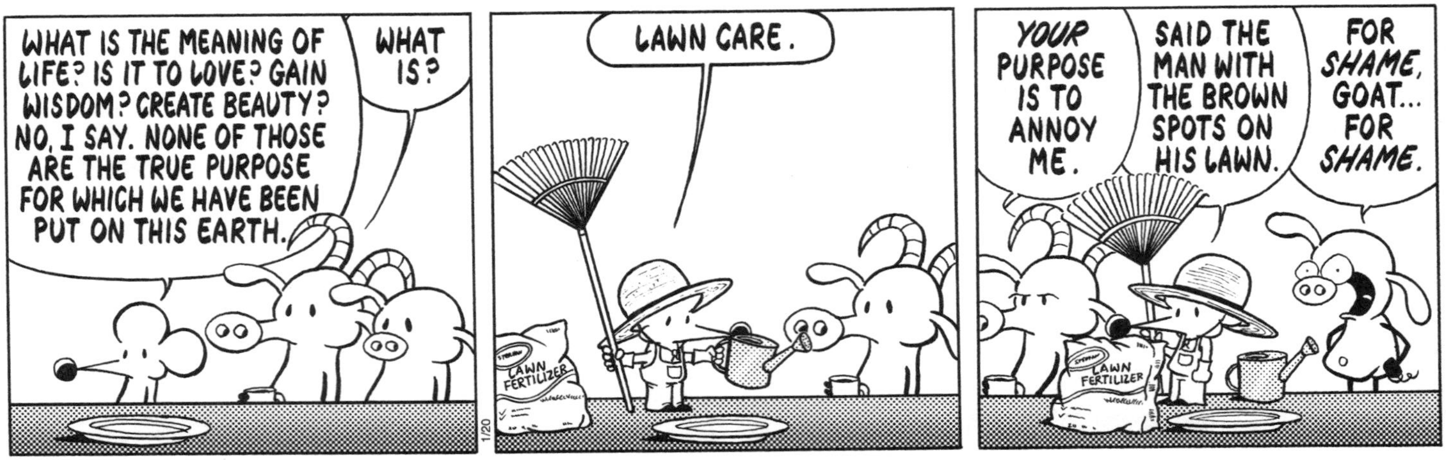
WHAT IS THE MEANING OF LIFE? IS IT TO LOVE? GAIN WISDOM? CREATE BEAUTY? NO, I SAY. NONE OF THOSE ARE THE TRUE PURPOSE FOR WHICH WE HAVE BEEN PUT ON THIS EARTH.
WHAT IS?
LAWN CARE.
LAWN FERTILIZER
YOUR PURPOSE IS TO ANNOY ME.
SAID THE MAN WITH THE BROWN SPOTS ON HIS LAWN.
FOR *SHAME*, GOAT... FOR *SHAME*.
1/20

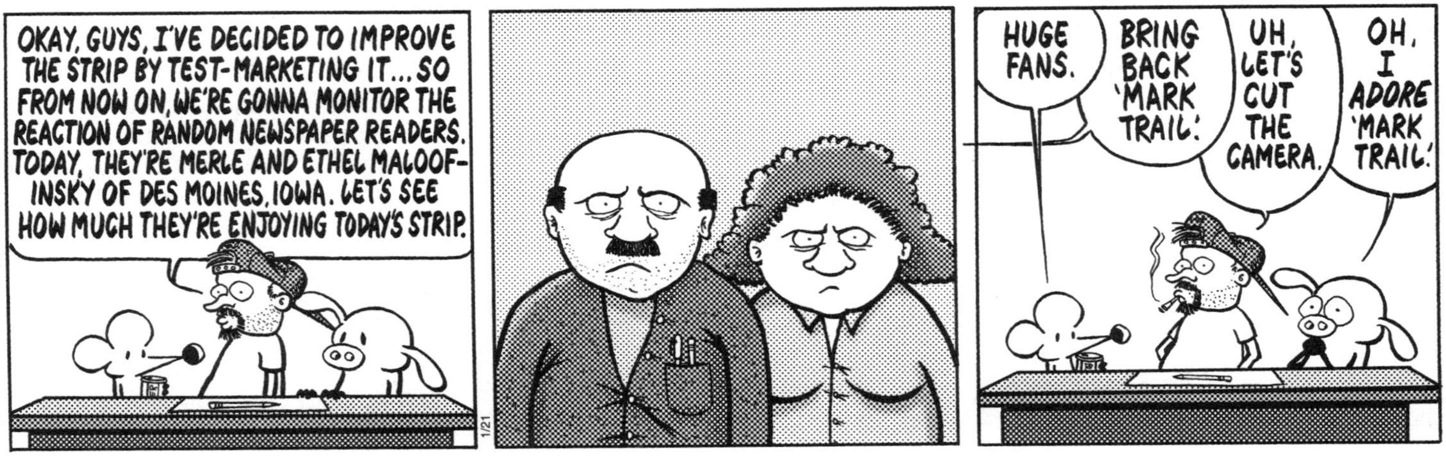
OKAY, GUYS, I'VE DECIDED TO IMPROVE THE STRIP BY TEST-MARKETING IT... SO FROM NOW ON, WE'RE GONNA MONITOR THE REACTION OF RANDOM NEWSPAPER READERS. TODAY, THEY'RE MERLE AND ETHEL MALOOFINSKY OF DES MOINES, IOWA. LET'S SEE HOW MUCH THEY'RE ENJOYING TODAY'S STRIP.
1/21
HUGE FANS.
BRING BACK 'MARK TRAIL.'
UH, LET'S CUT THE CAMERA.
OH, I *ADORE* 'MARK TRAIL.'

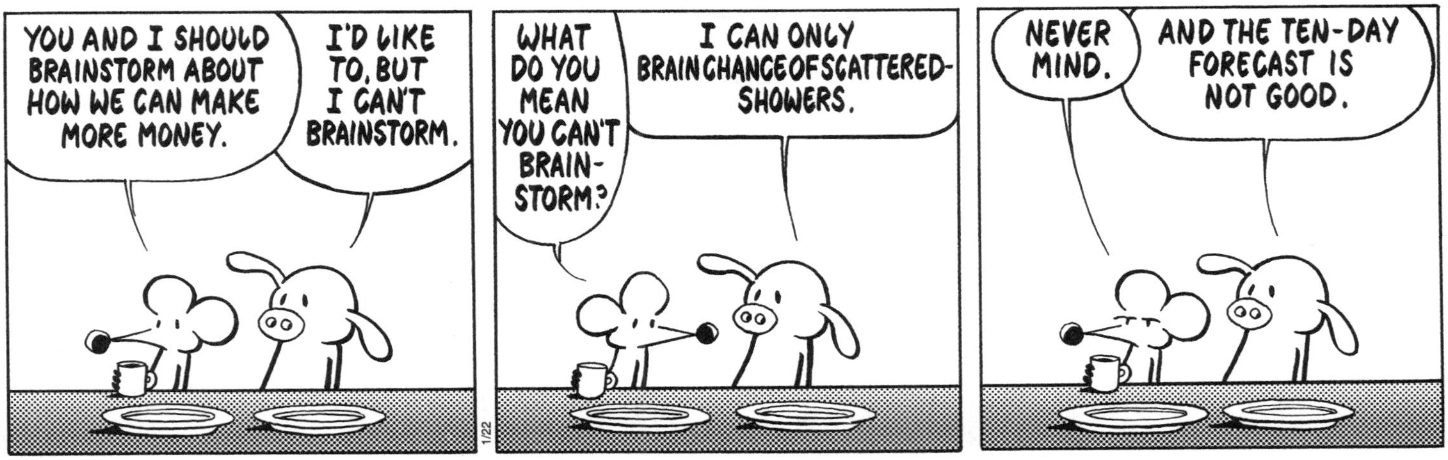
YOU AND I SHOULD BRAINSTORM ABOUT HOW WE CAN MAKE MORE MONEY.
I'D LIKE TO, BUT I CAN'T BRAINSTORM.
1/22
WHAT DO YOU MEAN YOU CAN'T BRAINSTORM?
I CAN ONLY BRAIN CHANCE OF SCATTERED-SHOWERS.
NEVER MIND.
AND THE TEN-DAY FORECAST IS NOT GOOD.

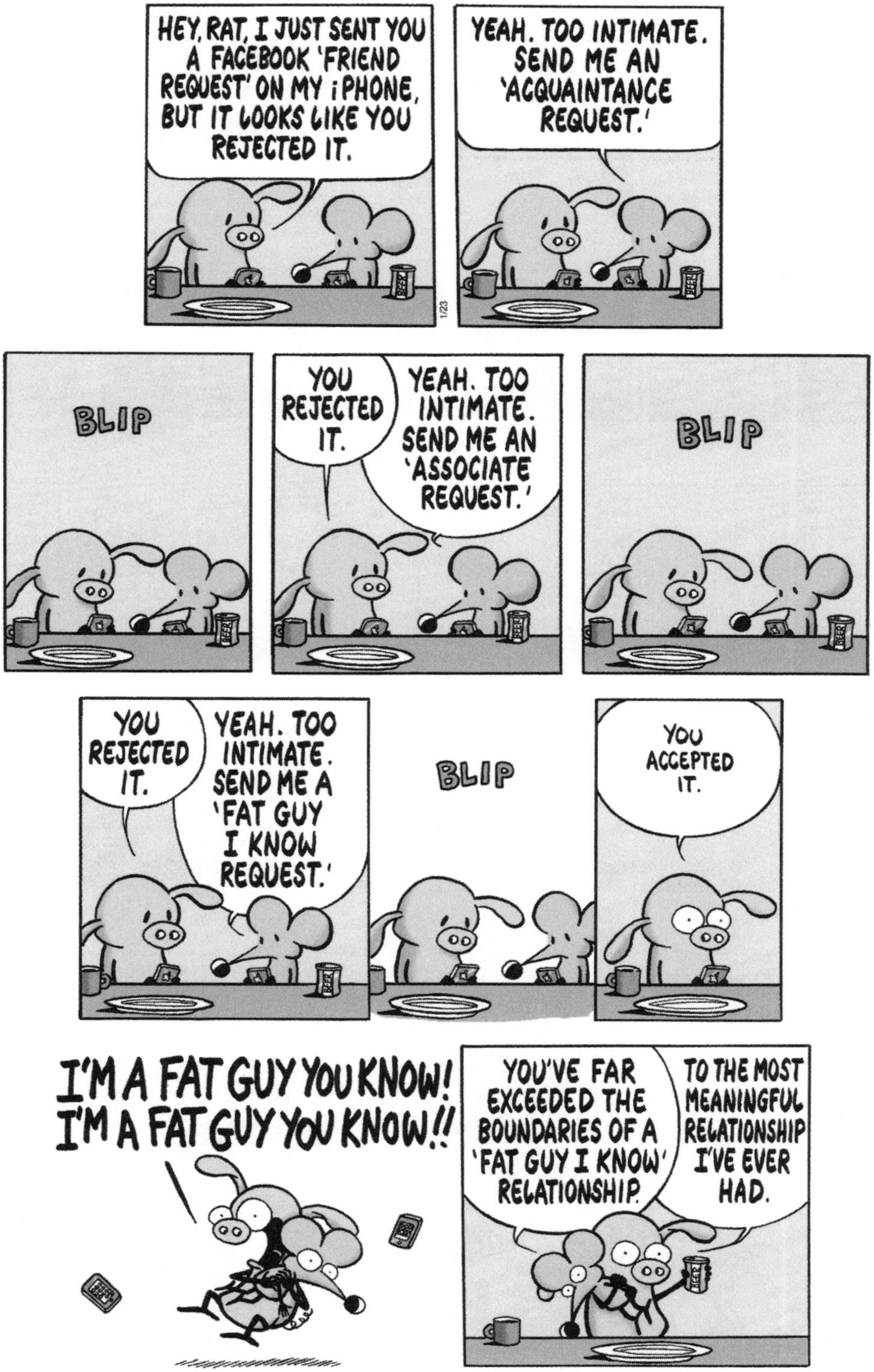
HEY, RAT, I JUST SENT YOU A FACEBOOK 'FRIEND REQUEST' ON MY iPHONE, BUT IT LOOKS LIKE YOU REJECTED IT.
BEER
1/23
YEAH. TOO INTIMATE. SEND ME AN 'ACQUAINTANCE REQUEST.'
BLIP
YOU REJECTED IT.
YEAH. TOO INTIMATE. SEND ME AN 'ASSOCIATE REQUEST.'
BLIP
YOU REJECTED IT.
YEAH. TOO INTIMATE. SEND ME A 'FAT GUY I KNOW REQUEST.'
BLIP
YOU ACCEPTED IT.
I'M A FAT GUY YOU KNOW! I'M A FAT GUY YOU KNOW!!
YOU'VE FAR EXCEEDED THE BOUNDARIES OF A 'FAT GUY I KNOW' RELATIONSHIP.
TO THE MOST MEANINGFUL RELATIONSHIP I'VE EVER HAD.

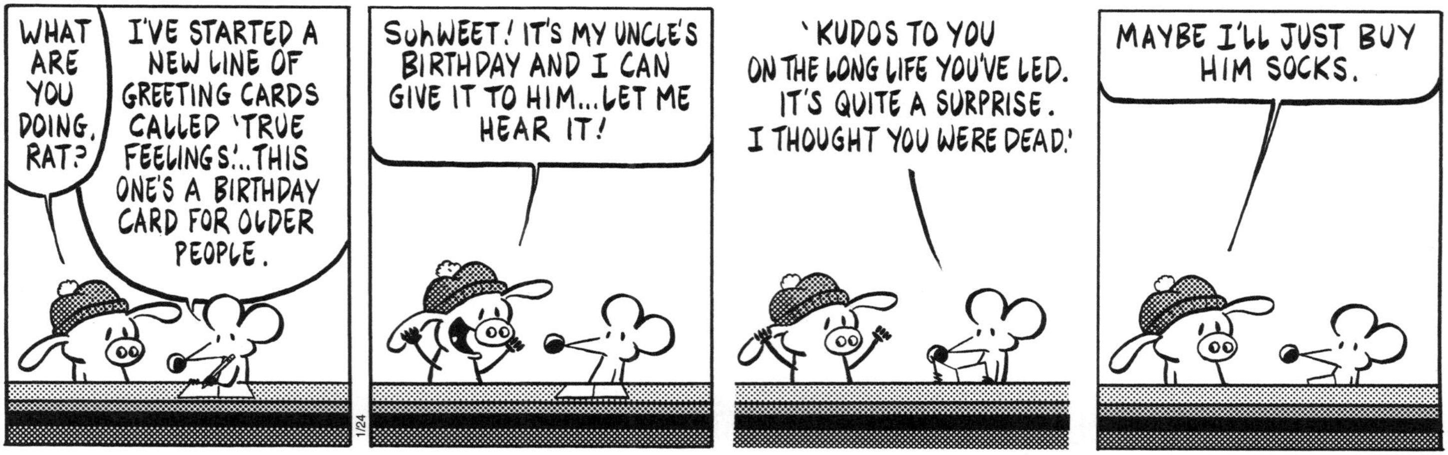
WHAT ARE YOU DOING, RAT?
I'VE STARTED A NEW LINE OF GREETING CARDS CALLED 'TRUE FEELINGS.'... THIS ONE'S A BIRTHDAY CARD FOR OLDER PEOPLE.
1/24
SUHWEET! IT'S MY UNCLE'S BIRTHDAY AND I CAN GIVE IT TO HIM... LET ME HEAR IT!
'KUDOS TO YOU ON THE LONG LIFE YOU'VE LED. IT'S QUITE A SURPRISE. I THOUGHT YOU WERE DEAD.'
MAYBE I'LL JUST BUY HIM SOCKS.

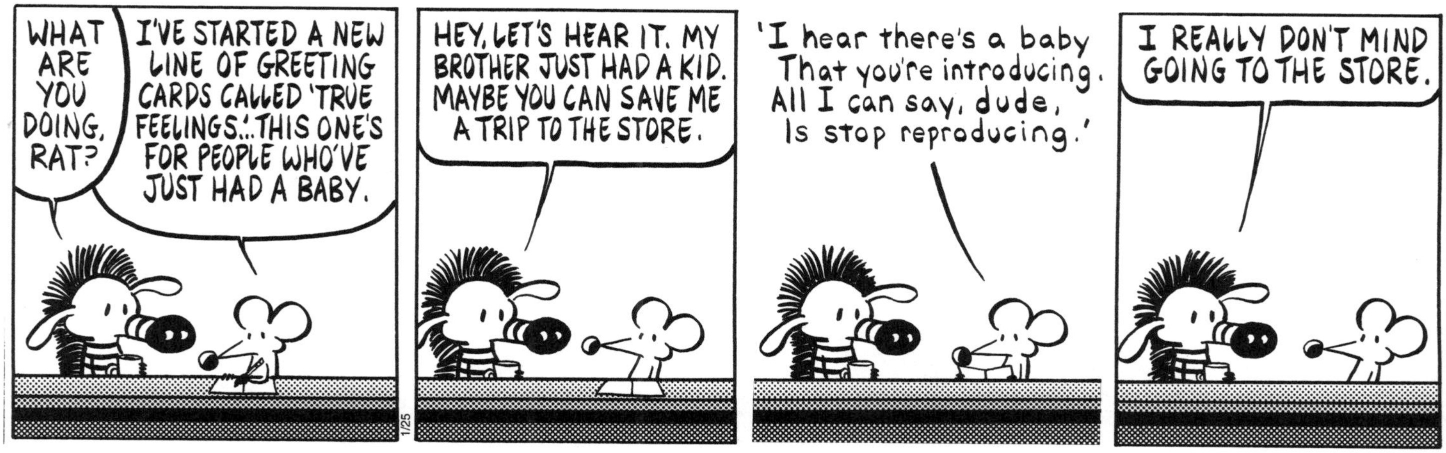
WHAT ARE YOU DOING, RAT?
I'VE STARTED A NEW LINE OF GREETING CARDS CALLED 'TRUE FEELINGS.'... THIS ONE'S FOR PEOPLE WHO'VE JUST HAD A BABY.
1/25
HEY, LET'S HEAR IT. MY BROTHER JUST HAD A KID. MAYBE YOU CAN SAVE ME A TRIP TO THE STORE.
'I hear there's a baby That you're introducing. All I can say, dude, Is stop reproducing.'
I REALLY DON'T MIND GOING TO THE STORE.

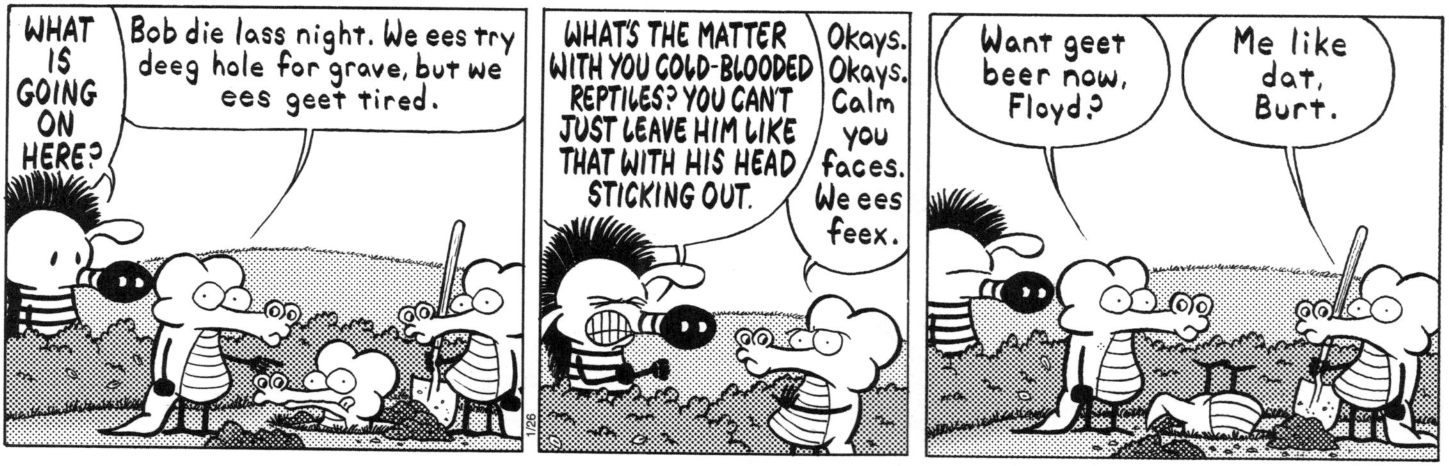
WHAT IS GOING ON HERE?
Bob die lass night. We ees try deeg hole for grave, but we ees geet tired.
1/26
WHAT'S THE MATTER WITH YOU COLD-BLOODED REPTILES? YOU CAN'T JUST LEAVE HIM LIKE THAT WITH HIS HEAD STICKING OUT.
Okays. Okays. Calm you faces. We ees feex.
Want geet beer now, Floyd?
Me like dat, Burt.

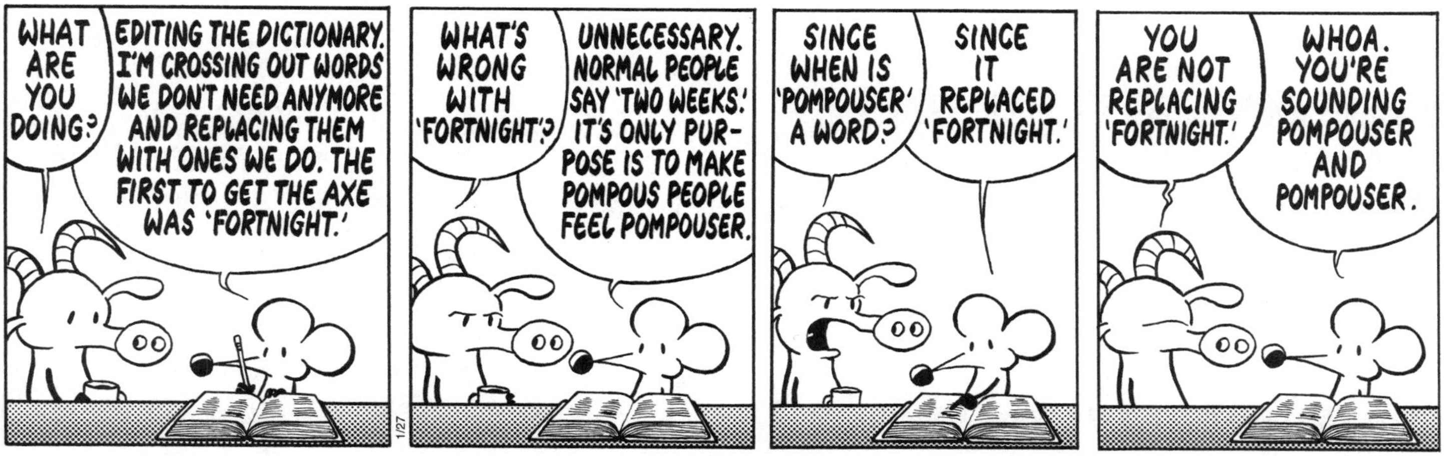
WHAT ARE YOU DOING?
EDITING THE DICTIONARY. I'M CROSSING OUT WORDS WE DON'T NEED ANYMORE AND REPLACING THEM WITH ONES WE DO. THE FIRST TO GET THE AXE WAS 'FORTNIGHT.'
1/27
WHAT'S WRONG WITH 'FORTNIGHT'?
UNNECESSARY. NORMAL PEOPLE SAY 'TWO WEEKS.' IT'S ONLY PURPOSE IS TO MAKE POMPOUS PEOPLE FEEL POMPOUSER.
SINCE WHEN IS 'POMPOUSER' A WORD?
SINCE IT REPLACED 'FORTNIGHT.'
YOU ARE NOT REPLACING 'FORTNIGHT.'
WHOA. YOU'RE SOUNDING POMPOUSER AND POMPOUSER.

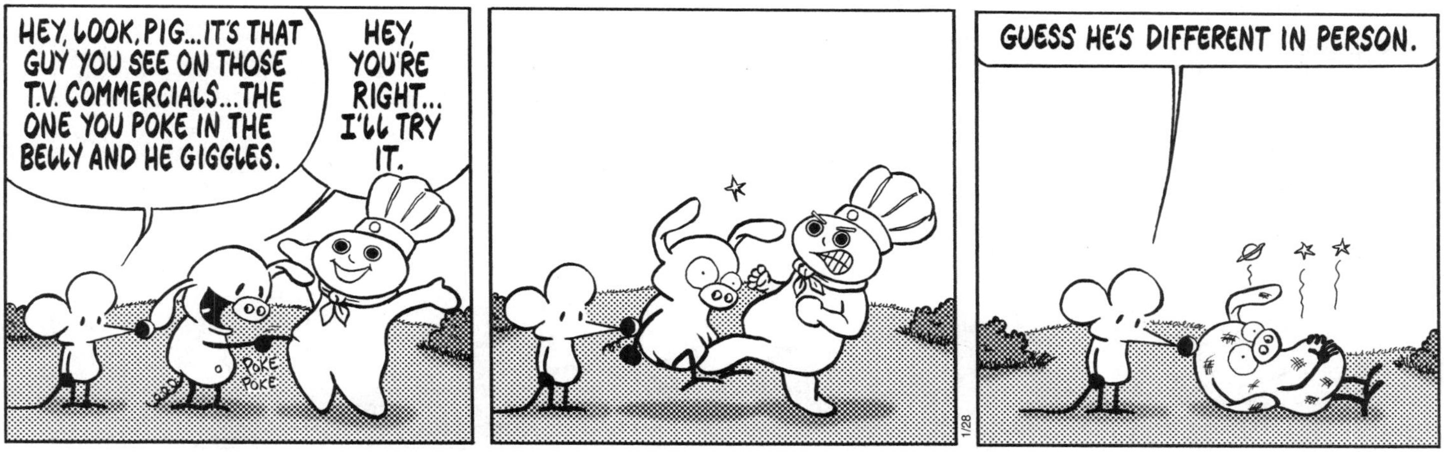
HEY, LOOK, PIG...IT'S THAT GUY YOU SEE ON THOSE T.V. COMMERCIALS...THE ONE YOU POKE IN THE BELLY AND HE GIGGLES.
HEY, YOU'RE RIGHT... I'LL TRY IT.
POKE POKE
1/28
GUESS HE'S DIFFERENT IN PERSON.

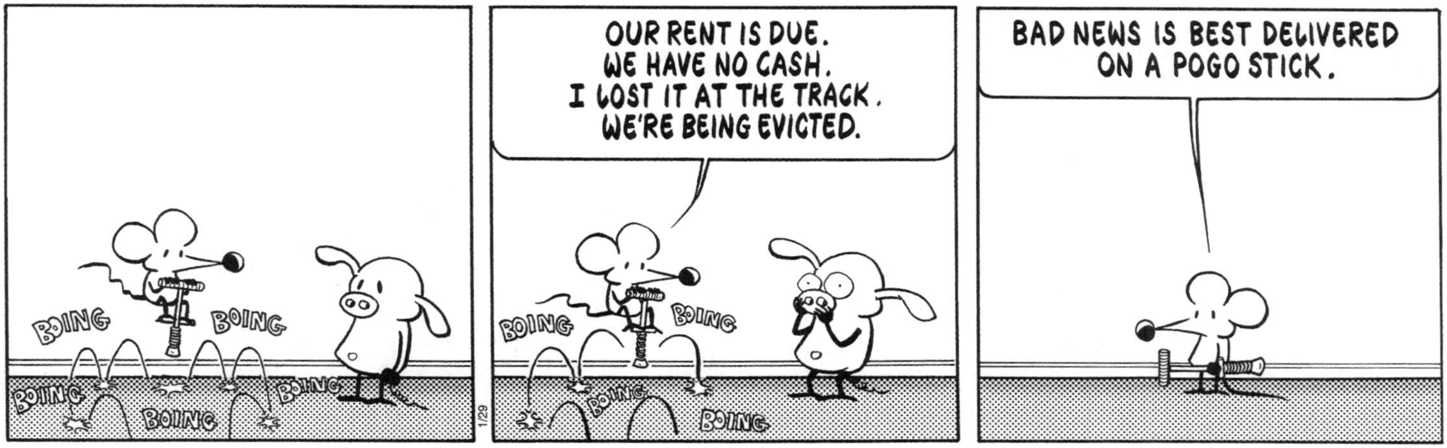
BOING
BOING
BOING
BOING
BOING
1/29
OUR RENT IS DUE. WE HAVE NO CASH. I LOST IT AT THE TRACK. WE'RE BEING EVICTED.
BOING
BOING
BOING
BOING
BAD NEWS IS BEST DELIVERED ON A POGO STICK.

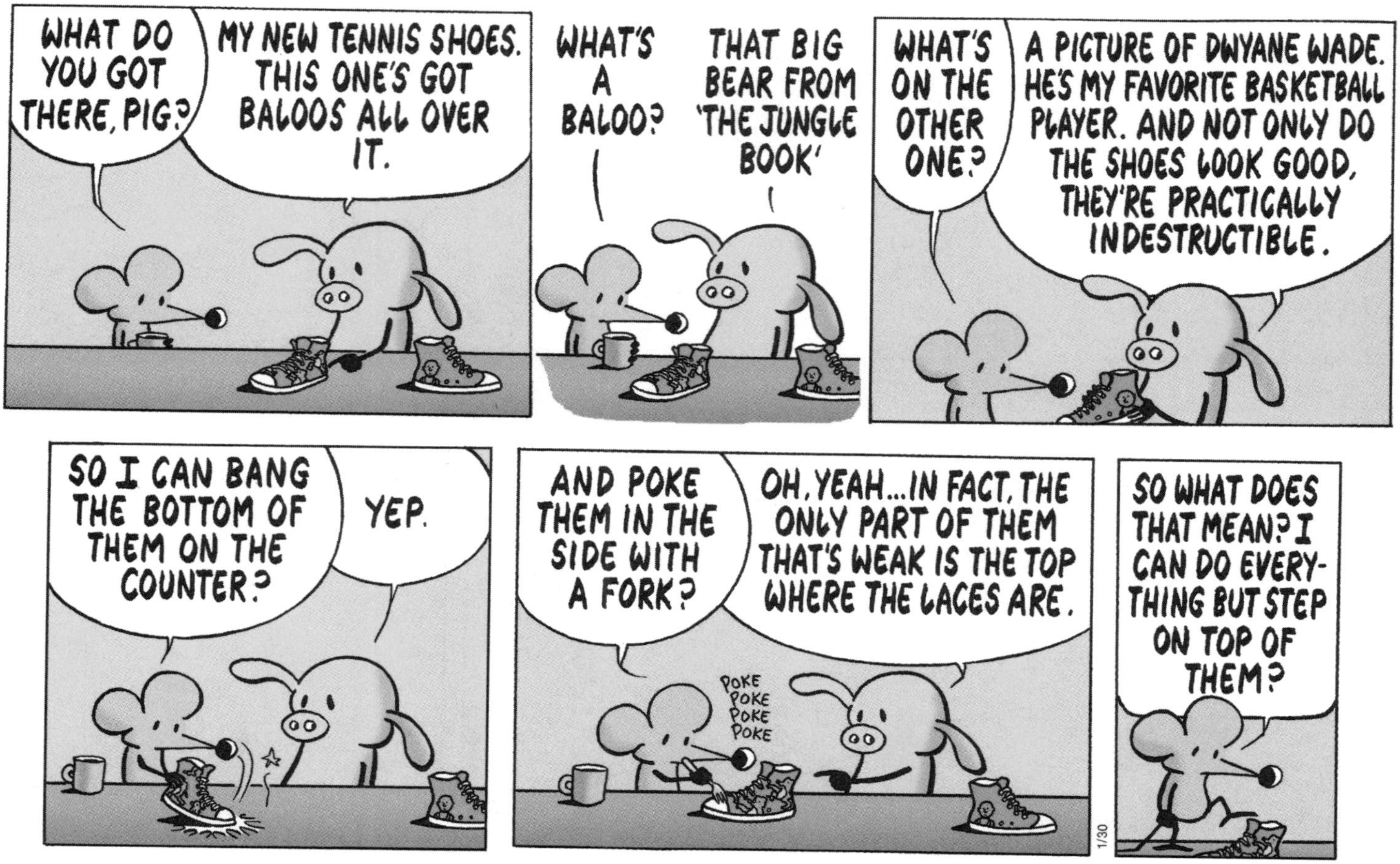
WHAT DO YOU GOT THERE, PIG?
MY NEW TENNIS SHOES. THIS ONE'S GOT BALOOS ALL OVER IT.
WHAT'S A BALOO?
THAT BIG BEAR FROM 'THE JUNGLE BOOK'
WHAT'S ON THE OTHER ONE?
A PICTURE OF DWYANE WADE. HE'S MY FAVORITE BASKETBALL PLAYER. AND NOT ONLY DO THE SHOES LOOK GOOD, THEY'RE PRACTICALLY INDESTRUCTIBLE.
SO I CAN BANG THE BOTTOM OF THEM ON THE COUNTER?
YEP.
AND POKE THEM IN THE SIDE WITH A FORK?
POKE POKE POKE POKE
OH, YEAH...IN FACT, THE ONLY PART OF THEM THAT'S WEAK IS THE TOP WHERE THE LACES ARE.
1/30
SO WHAT DOES THAT MEAN? I CAN DO EVERY-THING BUT STEP ON TOP OF THEM?

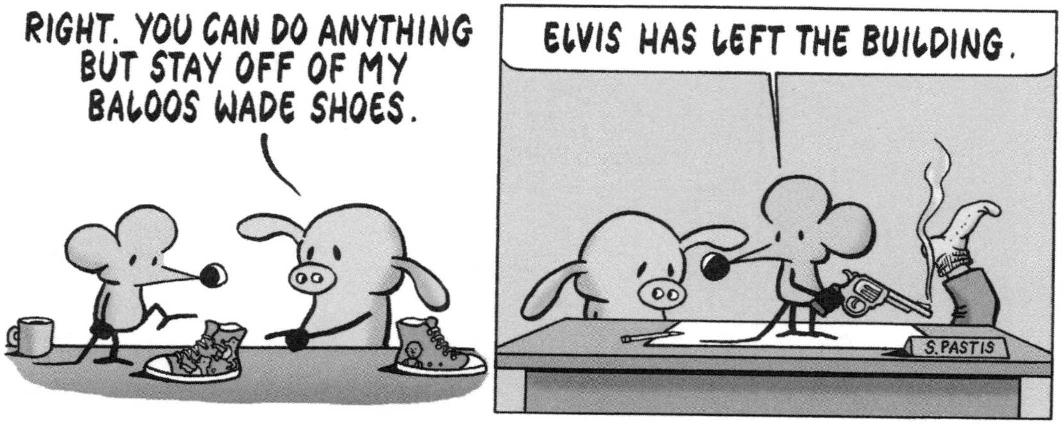
RIGHT. YOU CAN DO ANYTHING BUT STAY OFF OF MY BALOOS WADE SHOES.
ELVIS HAS LEFT THE BUILDING.
S. PASTIS

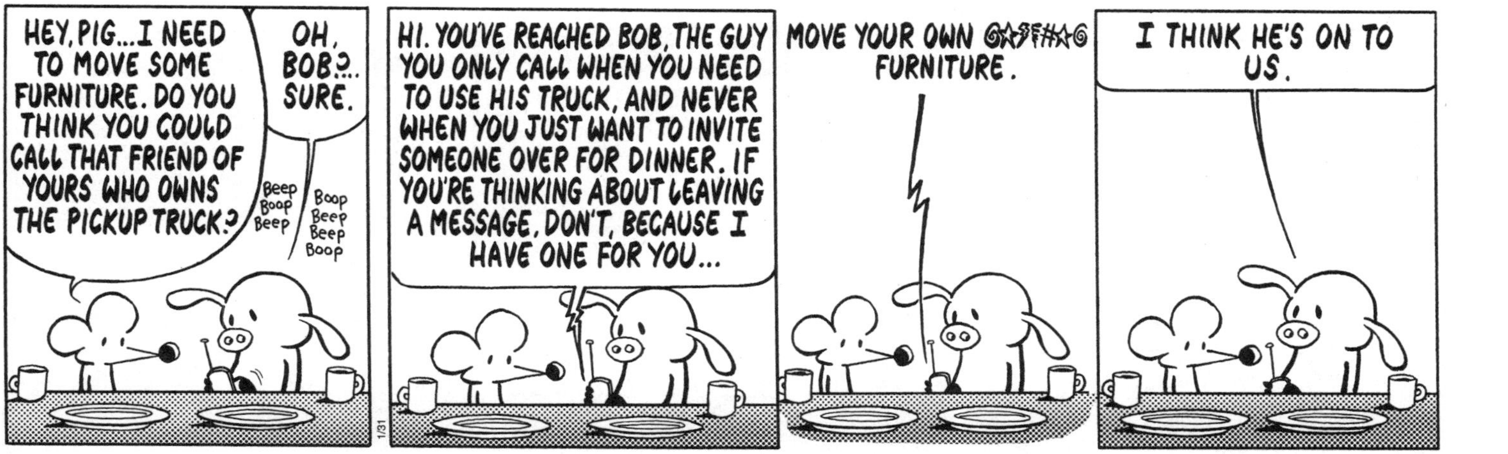
HEY, PIG...I NEED TO MOVE SOME FURNITURE. DO YOU THINK YOU COULD CALL THAT FRIEND OF YOURS WHO OWNS THE PICKUP TRUCK?
OH, BOB?... SURE.
Beep Boop Beep
Boop Beep Beep Boop
1/31
HI. YOU'VE REACHED BOB, THE GUY YOU ONLY CALL WHEN YOU NEED TO USE HIS TRUCK, AND NEVER WHEN YOU JUST WANT TO INVITE SOMEONE OVER FOR DINNER. IF YOU'RE THINKING ABOUT LEAVING A MESSAGE, DON'T, BECAUSE I HAVE ONE FOR YOU...
MOVE YOUR OWN FURNITURE.
I THINK HE'S ON TO US.

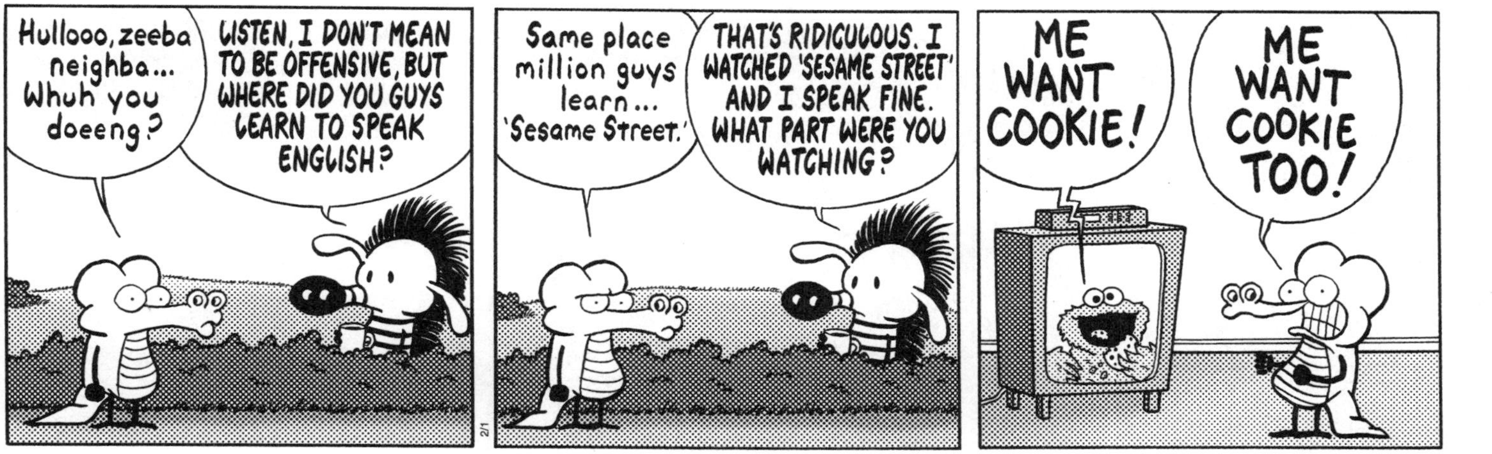
Hullooo, zeeba neighba... Whuh you doeeng?
LISTEN, I DON'T MEAN TO BE OFFENSIVE, BUT WHERE DID YOU GUYS LEARN TO SPEAK ENGLISH?
2/1
Same place million guys learn... 'Sesame Street.'
THAT'S RIDICULOUS. I WATCHED 'SESAME STREET' AND I SPEAK FINE. WHAT PART WERE YOU WATCHING?
ME WANT COOKIE!
ME WANT COOKIE TOO!

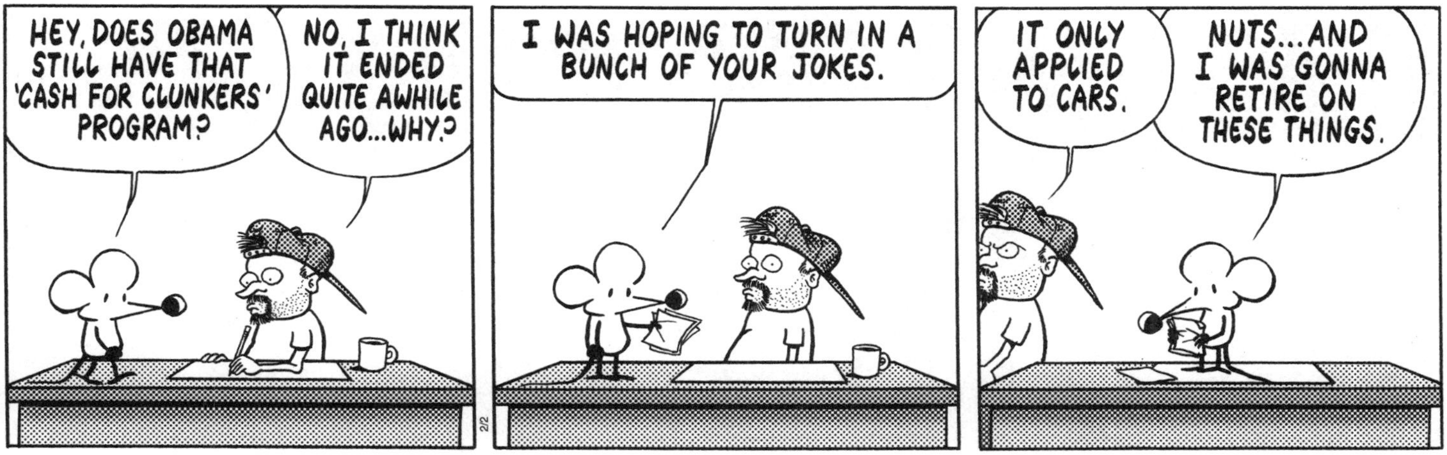
HEY, DOES OBAMA STILL HAVE THAT 'CASH FOR CLUNKERS' PROGRAM?
NO, I THINK IT ENDED QUITE AWHILE AGO...WHY?
2/2
I WAS HOPING TO TURN IN A BUNCH OF YOUR JOKES.
IT ONLY APPLIED TO CARS.
NUTS...AND I WAS GONNA RETIRE ON THESE THINGS.

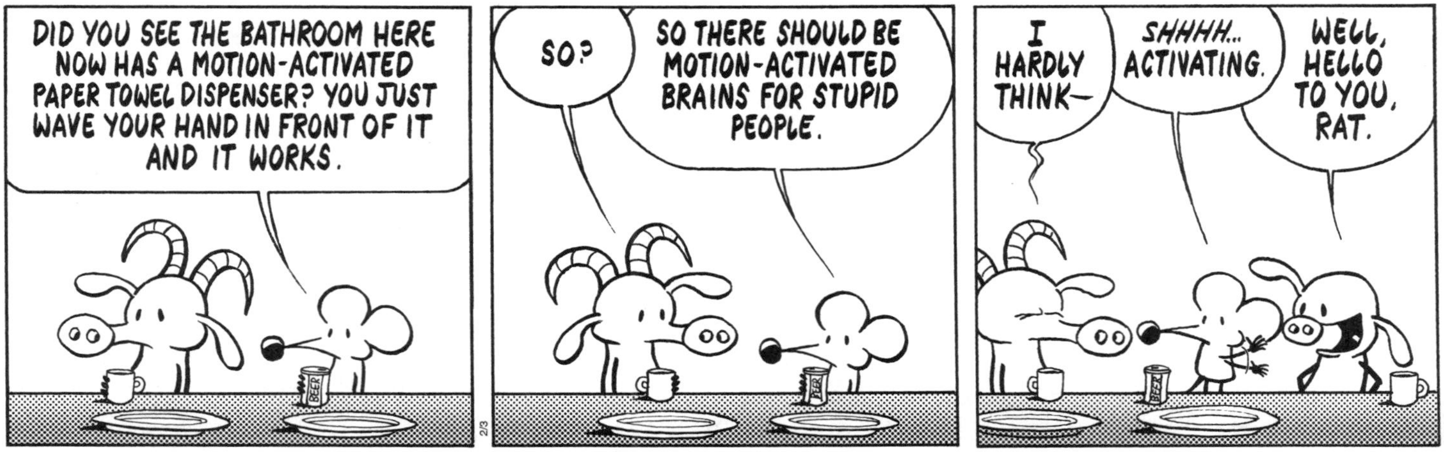
DID YOU SEE THE BATHROOM HERE NOW HAS A MOTION-ACTIVATED PAPER TOWEL DISPENSER? YOU JUST WAVE YOUR HAND IN FRONT OF IT AND IT WORKS.
SO?
SO THERE SHOULD BE MOTION-ACTIVATED BRAINS FOR STUPID PEOPLE.
I HARDLY THINK—
SHHHH... ACTIVATING.
WELL, HELLO TO YOU, RAT.

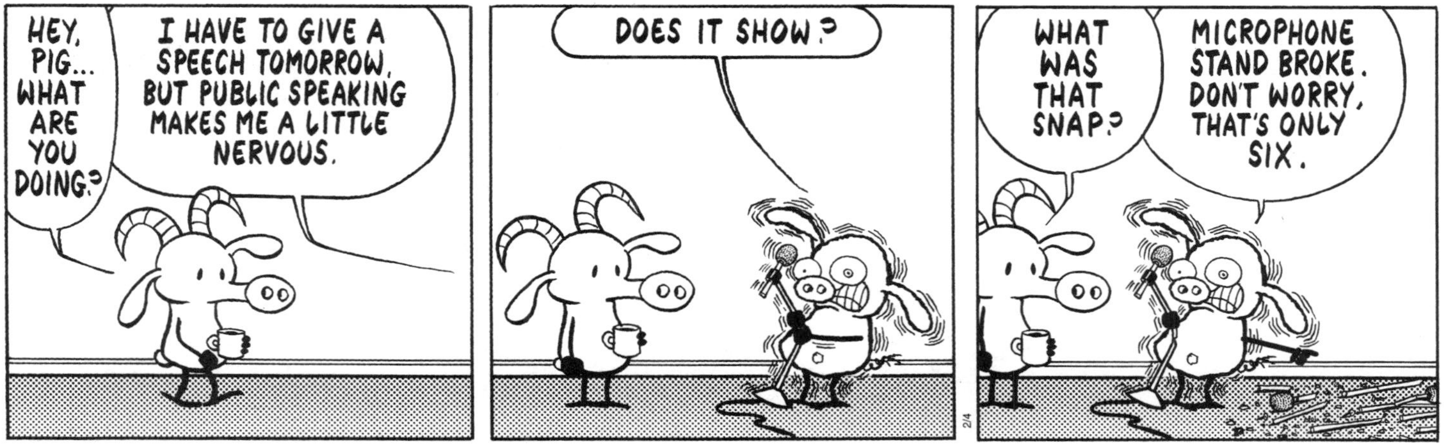
HEY, PIG... WHAT ARE YOU DOING?
I HAVE TO GIVE A SPEECH TOMORROW, BUT PUBLIC SPEAKING MAKES ME A LITTLE NERVOUS.
DOES IT SHOW?
WHAT WAS THAT SNAP?
MICROPHONE STAND BROKE. DON'T WORRY, THAT'S ONLY SIX.

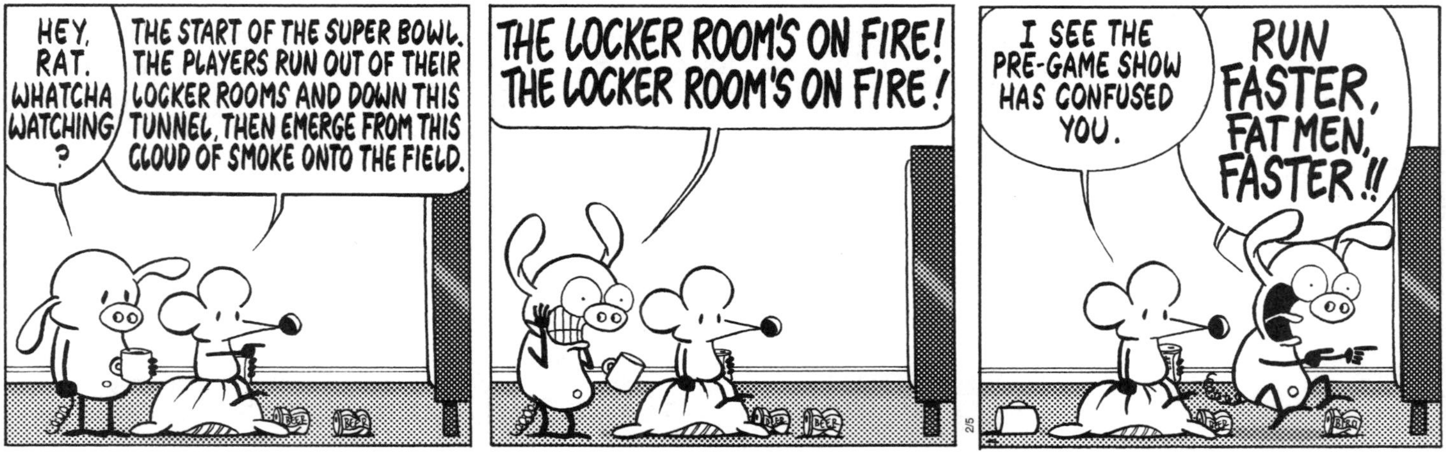
HEY, RAT. WHATCHA WATCHING?
THE START OF THE SUPER BOWL. THE PLAYERS RUN OUT OF THEIR LOCKER ROOMS AND DOWN THIS TUNNEL, THEN EMERGE FROM THIS CLOUD OF SMOKE ONTO THE FIELD.
THE LOCKER ROOM'S ON FIRE! THE LOCKER ROOM'S ON FIRE!
I SEE THE PRE-GAME SHOW HAS CONFUSED YOU.
RUN FASTER, FAT MEN, FASTER!!

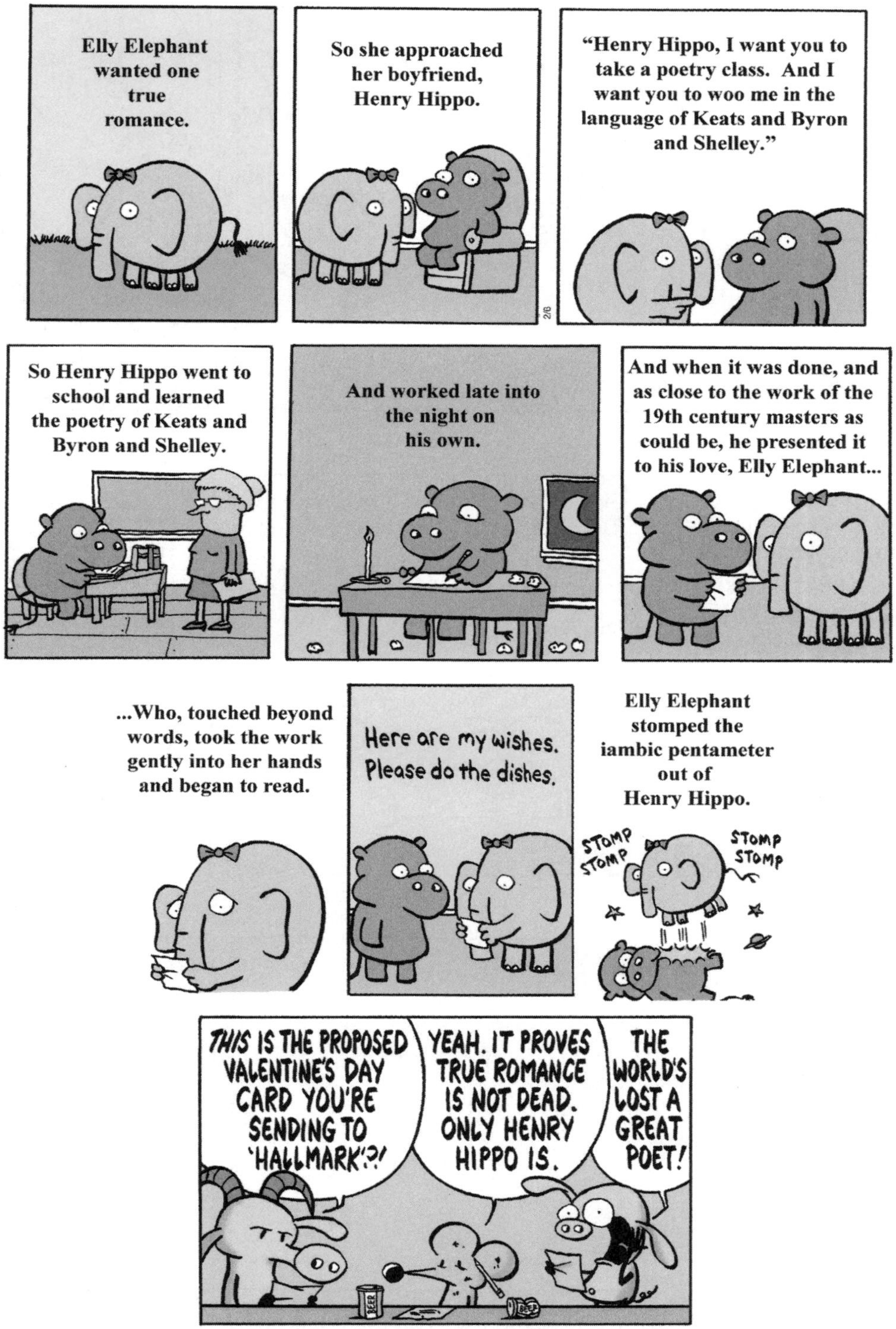

Elly Elephant wanted one true romance.
So she approached her boyfriend, Henry Hippo.
"Henry Hippo, I want you to take a poetry class. And I want you to woo me in the language of Keats and Byron and Shelley."
So Henry Hippo went to school and learned the poetry of Keats and Byron and Shelley.
And worked late into the night on his own.
And when it was done, and as close to the work of the 19th century masters as could be, he presented it to his love, Elly Elephant...
...Who, touched beyond words, took the work gently into her hands and began to read.
Here are my wishes. Please do the dishes.
Elly Elephant stomped the iambic pentameter out of Henry Hippo.
STOMP STOMP
STOMP STOMP
THIS IS THE PROPOSED VALENTINE'S DAY CARD YOU'RE SENDING TO 'HALLMARK'?!
YEAH. IT PROVES TRUE ROMANCE IS NOT DEAD. ONLY HENRY HIPPO IS.
THE WORLD'S LOST A GREAT POET!
BEER
BEER

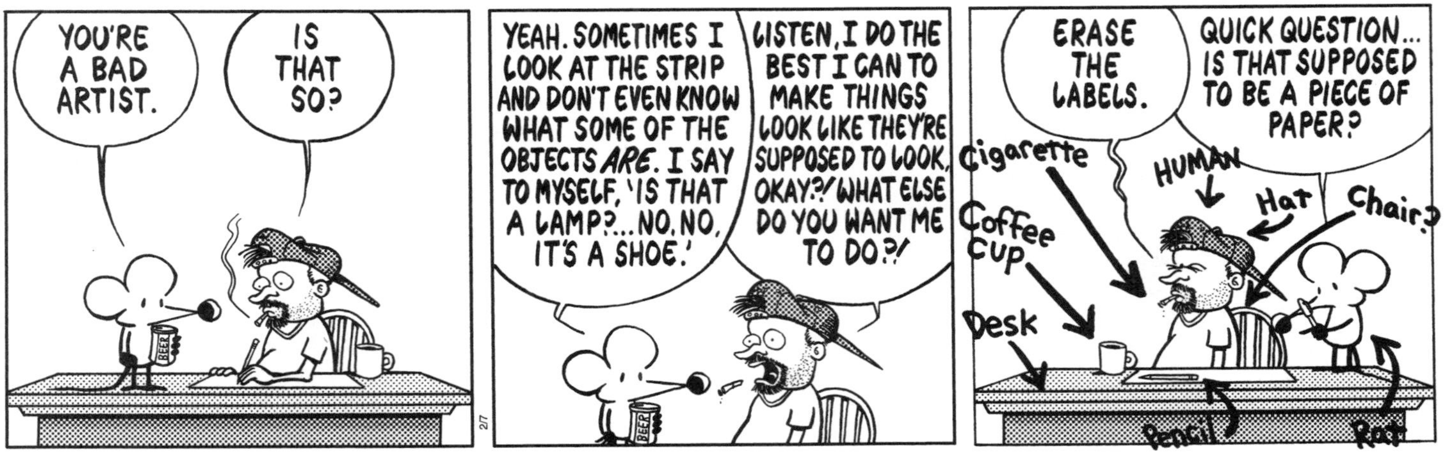
YOU'RE A BAD ARTIST.
IS THAT SO?
BEER
2/7
YEAH. SOMETIMES I LOOK AT THE STRIP AND DON'T EVEN KNOW WHAT SOME OF THE OBJECTS *ARE*. I SAY TO MYSELF, 'IS THAT A LAMP?... NO, NO, IT'S A SHOE.'
LISTEN, I DO THE BEST I CAN TO MAKE THINGS LOOK LIKE THEY'RE SUPPOSED TO LOOK, OKAY?! WHAT ELSE DO YOU WANT ME TO DO?!
BEER
ERASE THE LABELS.
QUICK QUESTION... IS THAT SUPPOSED TO BE A PIECE OF PAPER?
Cigarette
HUMAN
Hat
Chair?
Coffee Cup
Desk
Pencil
Rat

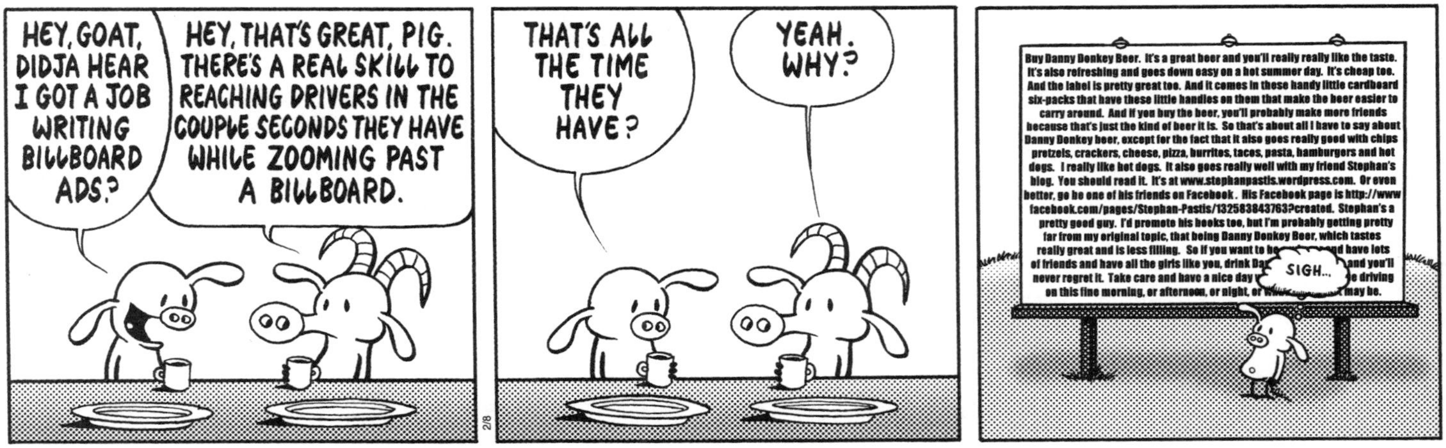
HEY, GOAT, DIDJA HEAR I GOT A JOB WRITING BILLBOARD ADS?
HEY, THAT'S GREAT, PIG. THERE'S A REAL SKILL TO REACHING DRIVERS IN THE COUPLE SECONDS THEY HAVE WHILE ZOOMING PAST A BILLBOARD.
2/8
THAT'S ALL THE TIME THEY HAVE?
YEAH. WHY?
Buy Danny Donkey Beer. It's a great beer and you'll really really like the taste. It's also refreshing and goes down easy on a hot summer day. It's cheap too. And the label is pretty great too. And it comes in these handy little cardboard six-packs that have these little handles on them that make the beer easier to carry around. And if you buy the beer, you'll probably make more friends because that's just the kind of beer it is. So that's about all I have to say about Danny Donkey beer, except for the fact that it also goes really good with chips pretzels, crackers, cheese, pizza, burritos, tacos, pasta, hamburgers and hot dogs. I really like hot dogs. It also goes really well with my friend Stephan's blog. You should read it. It's at www.stephanpastis.wordpress.com. Or even better, go be one of his friends on Facebook. His Facebook page is http://www facebook.com/pages/Stephan-Pastis/132583843763?created. Stephan's a pretty good guy. I'd promote his books too, but I'm probably getting pretty far from my original topic, that being Danny Donkey Beer, which tastes really great and is less filling. So if you want to be
d have lots of friends and have all the girls like you, drink Da
and you'll never regret it. Take care and have a nice day
e driving on this fine morning, or afternoon, or night, or
may be.
SIGH...

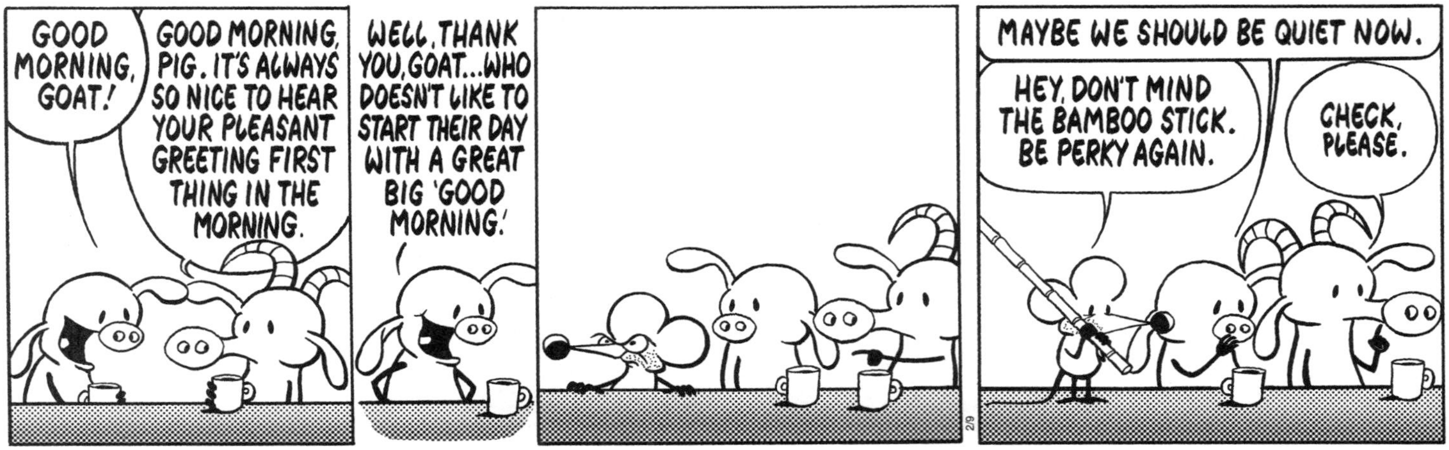
GOOD MORNING, GOAT!
GOOD MORNING, PIG. IT'S ALWAYS SO NICE TO HEAR YOUR PLEASANT GREETING FIRST THING IN THE MORNING.
WELL, THANK YOU, GOAT... WHO DOESN'T LIKE TO START THEIR DAY WITH A GREAT BIG 'GOOD MORNING.'
2/9
MAYBE WE SHOULD BE QUIET NOW.
HEY, DON'T MIND THE BAMBOO STICK. BE PERKY AGAIN.
CHECK, PLEASE.

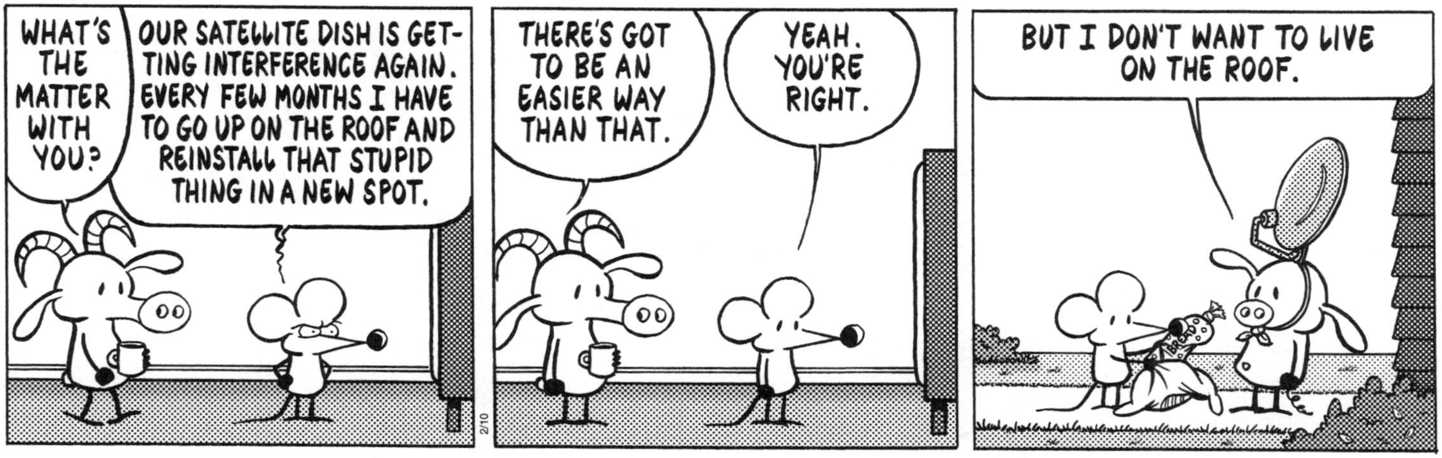
WHAT'S THE MATTER WITH YOU?
OUR SATELLITE DISH IS GETTING INTERFERENCE AGAIN. EVERY FEW MONTHS I HAVE TO GO UP ON THE ROOF AND REINSTALL THAT STUPID THING IN A NEW SPOT.
THERE'S GOT TO BE AN EASIER WAY THAN THAT.
YEAH. YOU'RE RIGHT.
BUT I DON'T WANT TO LIVE ON THE ROOF.

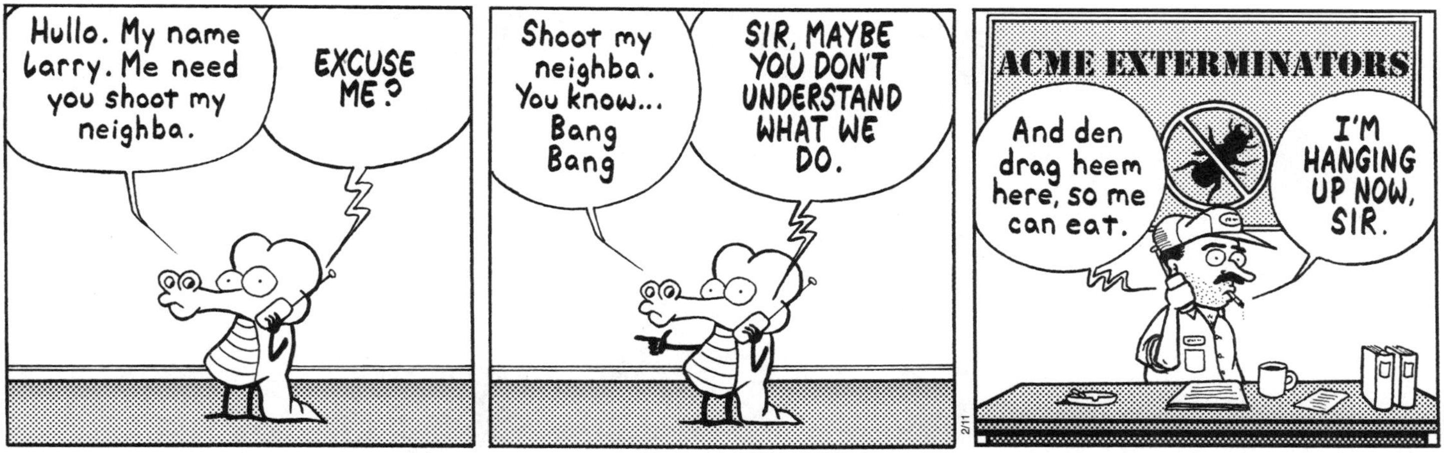
Hullo. My name Larry. Me need you shoot my neighba.
EXCUSE ME?
Shoot my neighba. You know... Bang Bang
SIR, MAYBE YOU DON'T UNDERSTAND WHAT WE DO.
ACME EXTERMINATORS
And den drag heem here, so me can eat.
I'M HANGING UP NOW, SIR.

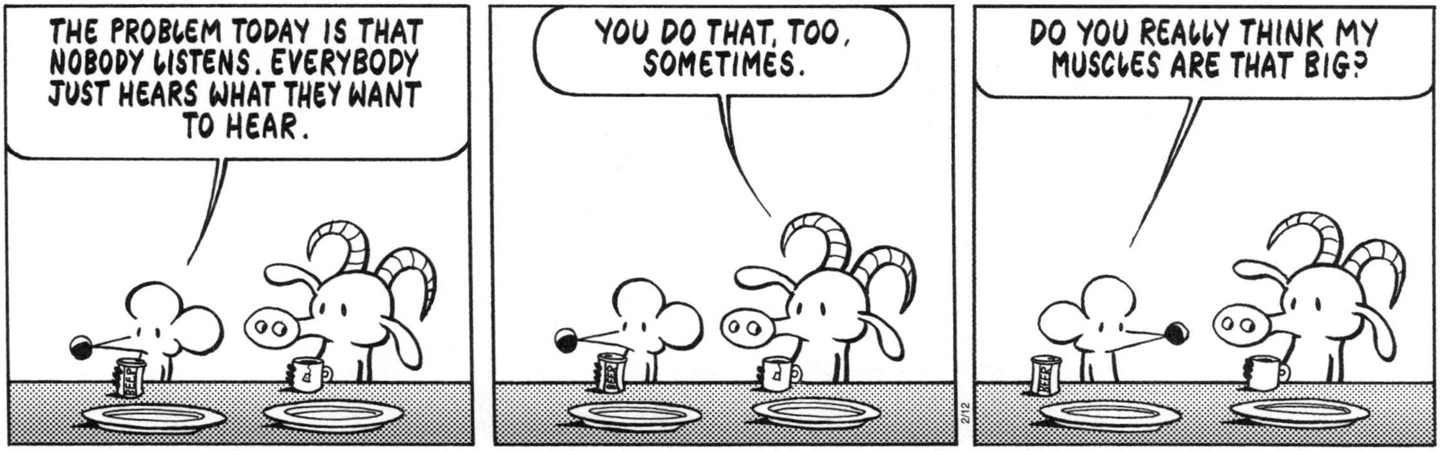
THE PROBLEM TODAY IS THAT NOBODY LISTENS. EVERYBODY JUST HEARS WHAT THEY WANT TO HEAR.
YOU DO THAT, TOO, SOMETIMES.
DO YOU REALLY THINK MY MUSCLES ARE THAT BIG?

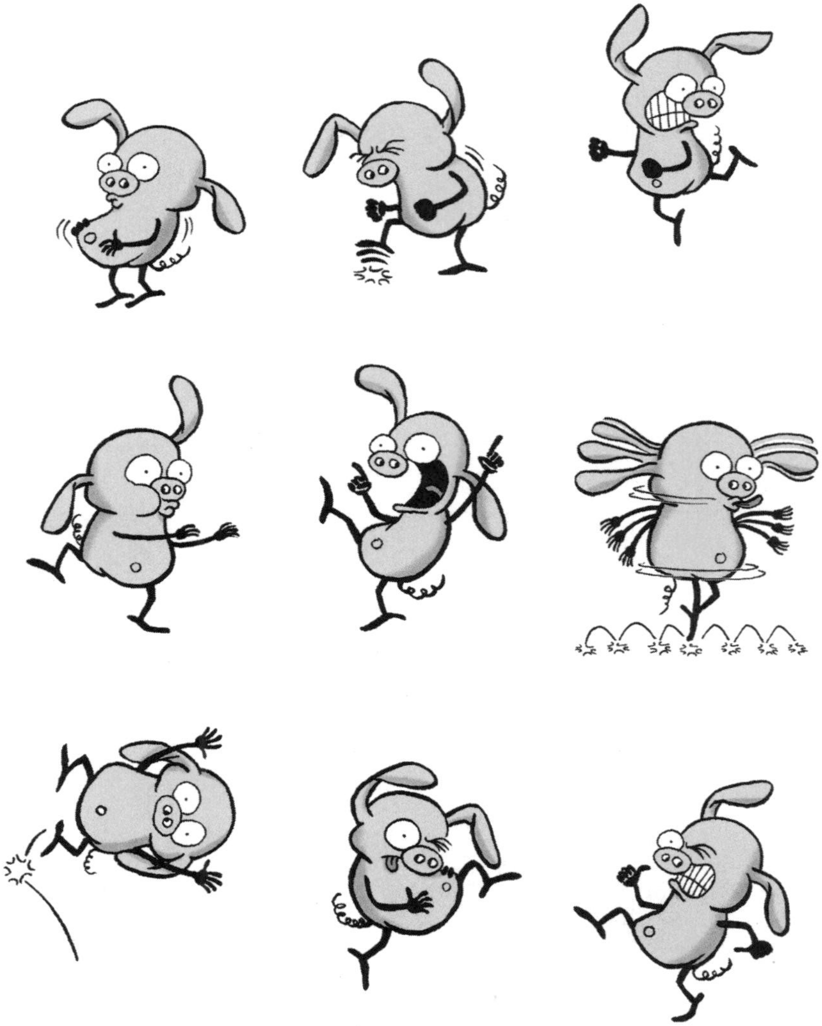

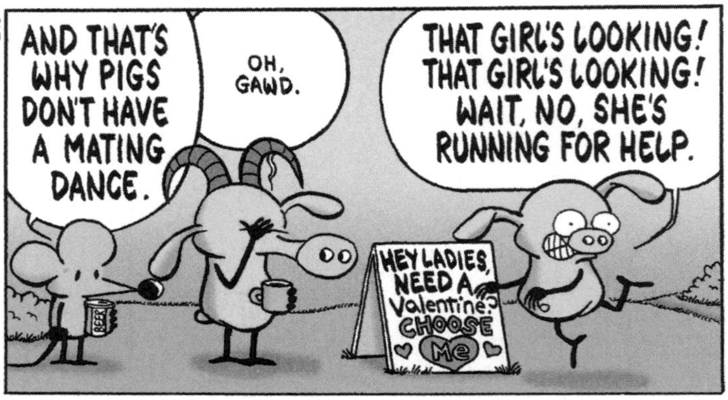
2/13
AND THAT'S WHY PIGS DON'T HAVE A MATING DANCE.
OH, GAWD.
THAT GIRL'S LOOKING! THAT GIRL'S LOOKING! WAIT, NO, SHE'S RUNNING FOR HELP.
BEER
HEY LADIES, NEED A Valentine? CHOOSE Me

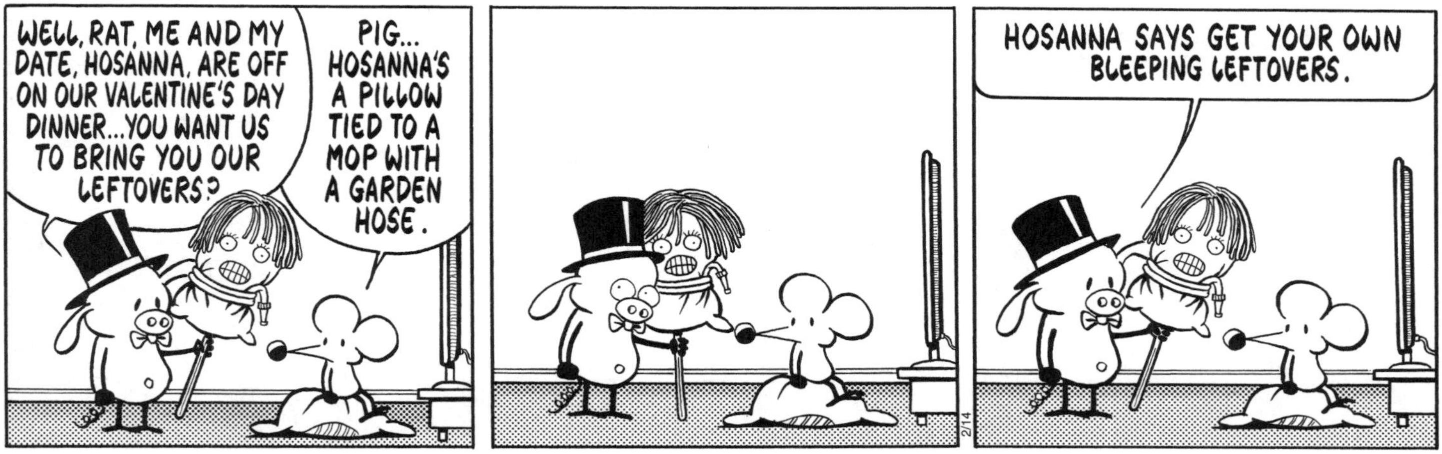
WELL, RAT, ME AND MY DATE, HOSANNA, ARE OFF ON OUR VALENTINE'S DAY DINNER...YOU WANT US TO BRING YOU OUR LEFTOVERS?
PIG... HOSANNA'S A PILLOW TIED TO A MOP WITH A GARDEN HOSE.
HOSANNA SAYS GET YOUR OWN BLEEPING LEFTOVERS.
2/14

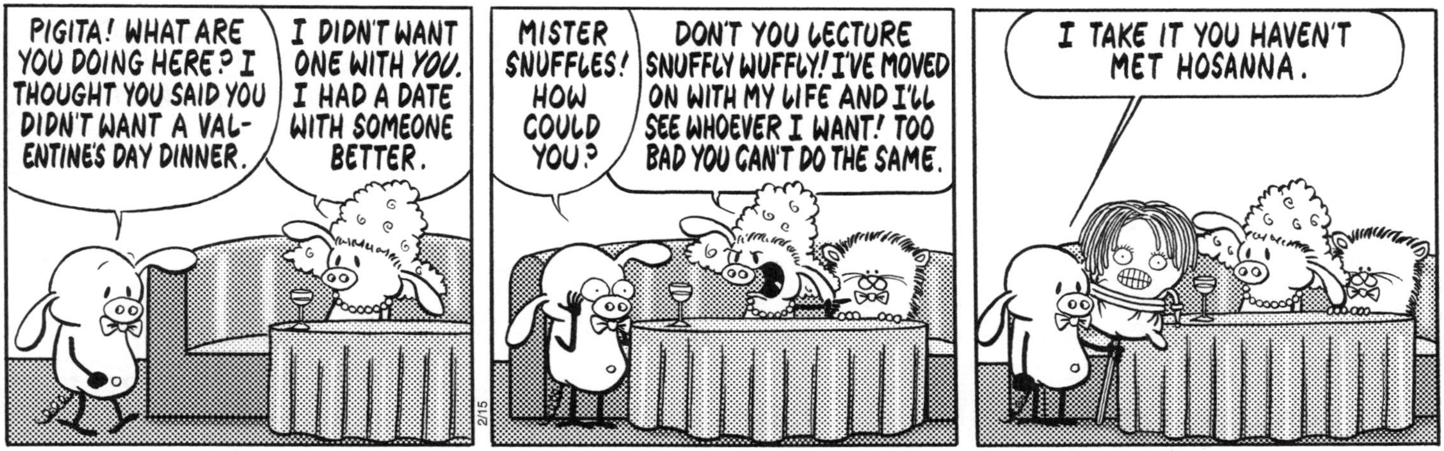
PIGITA! WHAT ARE YOU DOING HERE? I THOUGHT YOU SAID YOU DIDN'T WANT A VALENTINE'S DAY DINNER.
I DIDN'T WANT ONE WITH *YOU*. I HAD A DATE WITH SOMEONE BETTER.
2/15
MISTER SNUFFLES! HOW COULD YOU?
DON'T YOU LECTURE SNUFFLY WUFFLY! I'VE MOVED ON WITH MY LIFE AND I'LL SEE WHOEVER I WANT! TOO BAD YOU CAN'T DO THE SAME.
I TAKE IT YOU HAVEN'T MET HOSANNA.

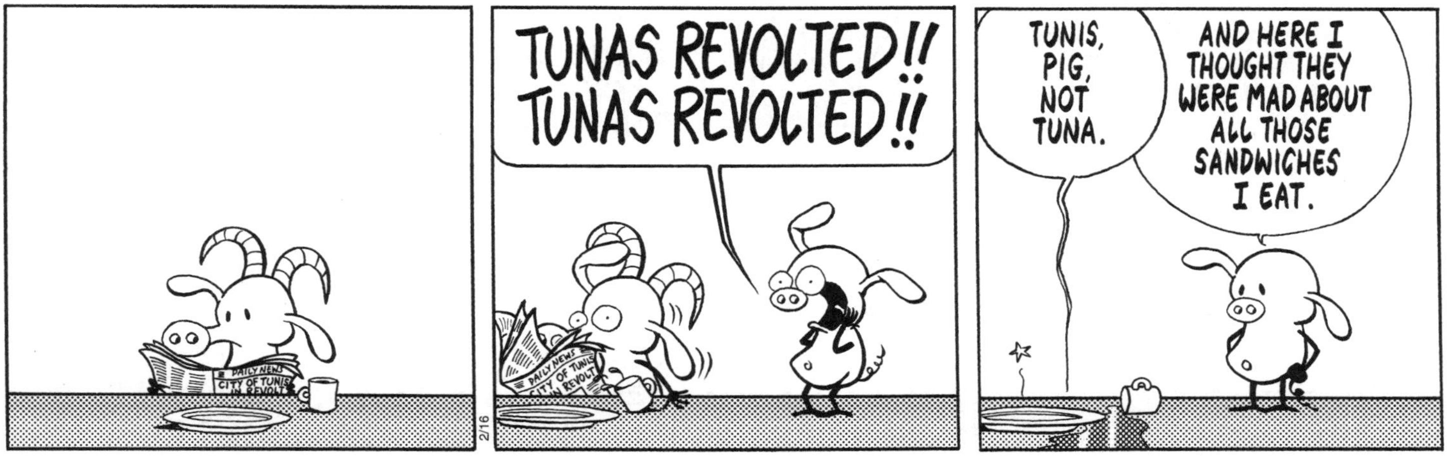
DAILY NEWS
CITY OF TUNIS IN REVOLT
2/16
TUNAS REVOLTED!! TUNAS REVOLTED!!
TUNIS, PIG, NOT TUNA.
AND HERE I THOUGHT THEY WERE MAD ABOUT ALL THOSE SANDWICHES I EAT.

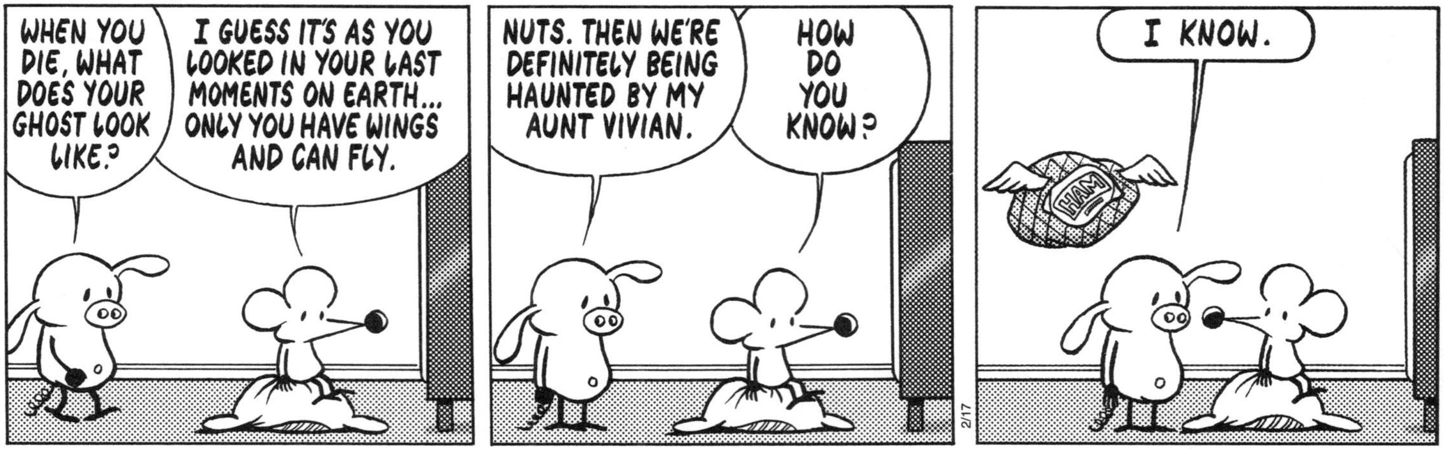
WHEN YOU DIE, WHAT DOES YOUR GHOST LOOK LIKE?
I GUESS IT'S AS YOU LOOKED IN YOUR LAST MOMENTS ON EARTH... ONLY YOU HAVE WINGS AND CAN FLY.
NUTS. THEN WE'RE DEFINITELY BEING HAUNTED BY MY AUNT VIVIAN.
HOW DO YOU KNOW?
I KNOW.
HAM
2/17

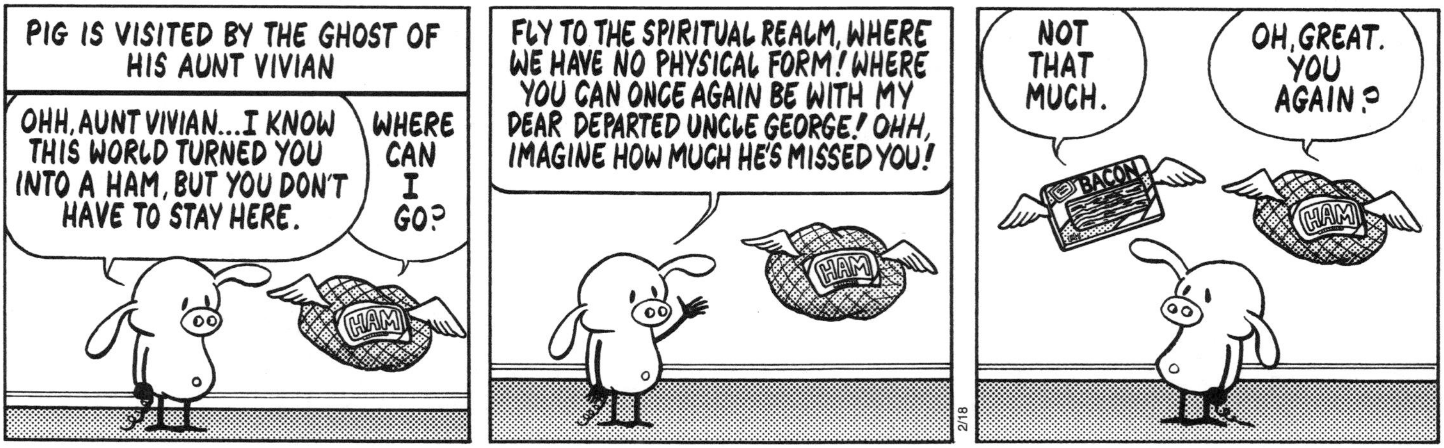
PIG IS VISITED BY THE GHOST OF HIS AUNT VIVIAN
OHH, AUNT VIVIAN...I KNOW THIS WORLD TURNED YOU INTO A HAM, BUT YOU DON'T HAVE TO STAY HERE.
WHERE CAN I GO?
FLY TO THE SPIRITUAL REALM, WHERE WE HAVE NO PHYSICAL FORM! WHERE YOU CAN ONCE AGAIN BE WITH MY DEAR DEPARTED UNCLE GEORGE! OHH, IMAGINE HOW MUCH HE'S MISSED YOU!
NOT THAT MUCH.
OH, GREAT. YOU AGAIN?
BACON
HAM
2/18

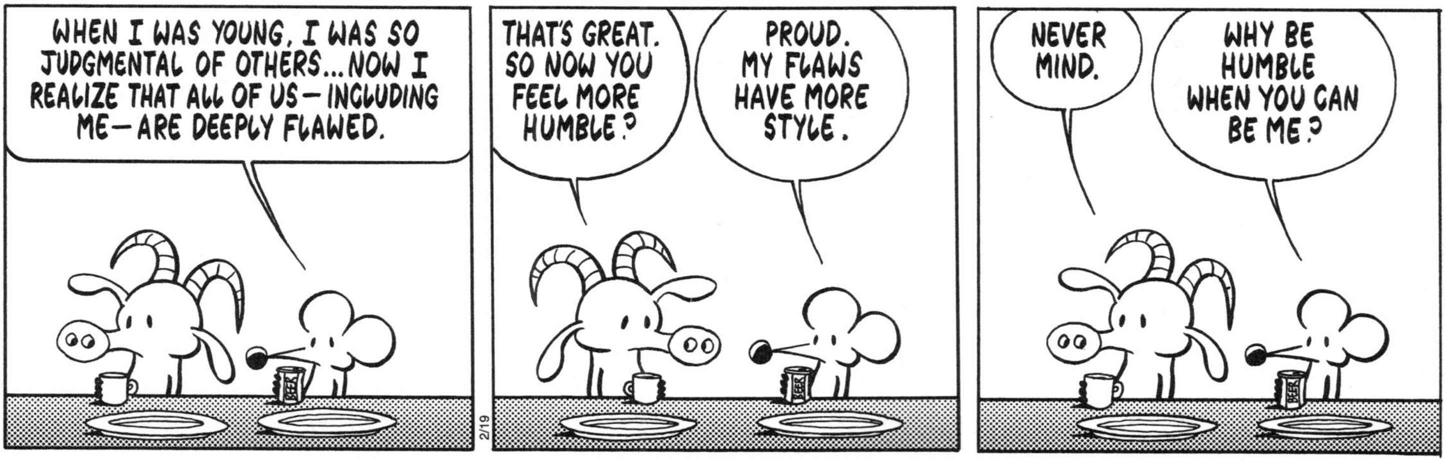
WHEN I WAS YOUNG, I WAS SO JUDGMENTAL OF OTHERS...NOW I REALIZE THAT ALL OF US—INCLUDING ME—ARE DEEPLY FLAWED.
THAT'S GREAT. SO NOW YOU FEEL MORE HUMBLE?
PROUD. MY FLAWS HAVE MORE STYLE.
NEVER MIND.
WHY BE HUMBLE WHEN YOU CAN BE ME?
BEER
2/19

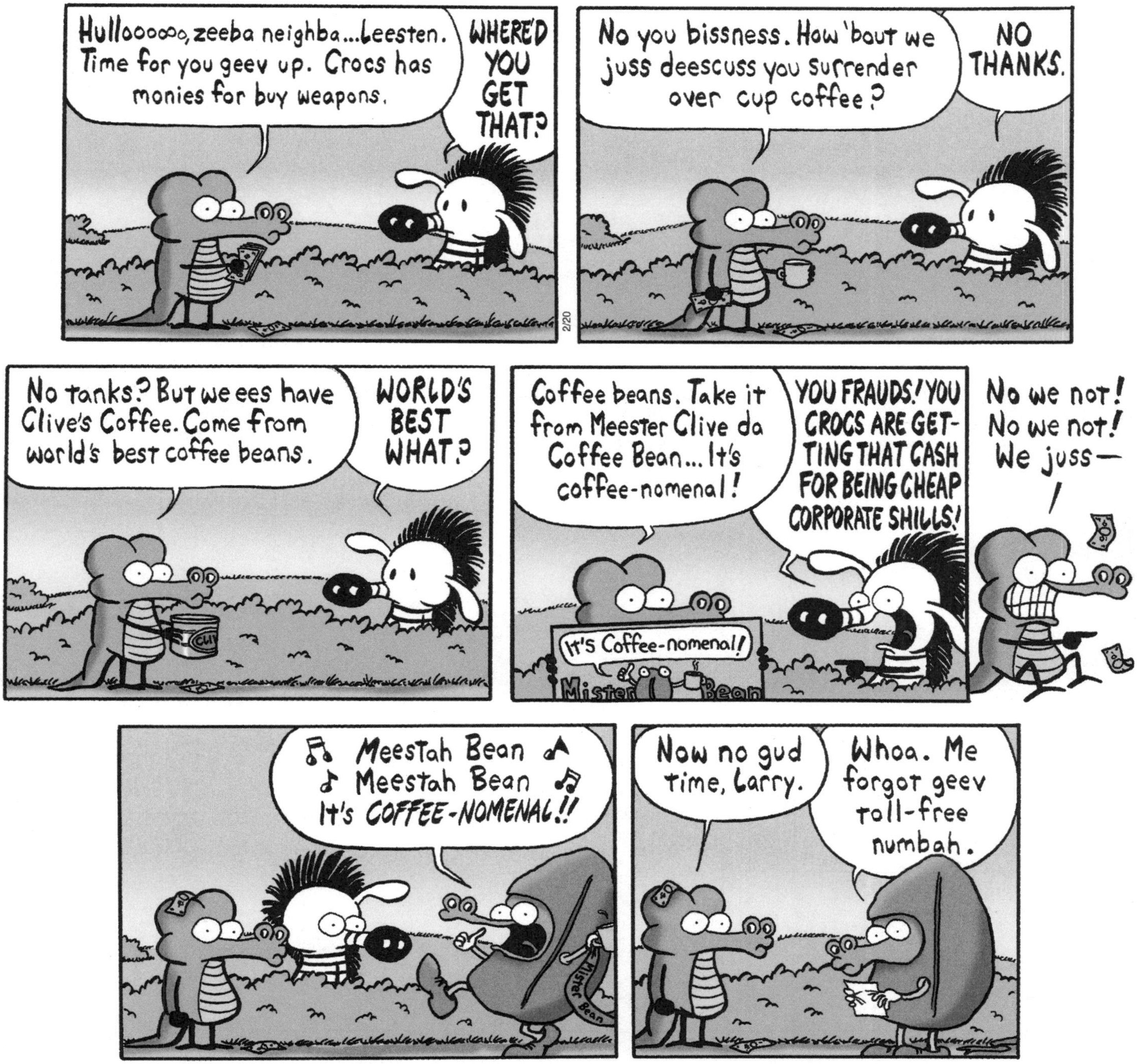
Hulloooooo, zeeba neighba...Leesten. Time for you geev up. Crocs has monies for buy weapons.
WHERE'D YOU GET THAT?
2/20
No you bissness. How 'bout we juss deescuss you surrender over cup coffee?
NO THANKS.
No tanks? But we ees have Clive's Coffee. Come from world's best coffee beans.
WORLD'S BEST WHAT?
Coffee beans. Take it from Meester Clive da Coffee Bean... It's coffee-nomenal!
It's Coffee-nomenal!
Mister Bean
YOU FRAUDS! YOU CROCS ARE GETTING THAT CASH FOR BEING CHEAP CORPORATE SHILLS!
No we not! No we not! We juss—
Meestah Bean
Meestah Bean
It's COFFEE-NOMENAL!!
Mister Bean
Now no gud time, Larry.
Whoa. Me forgot geev toll-free numbah.

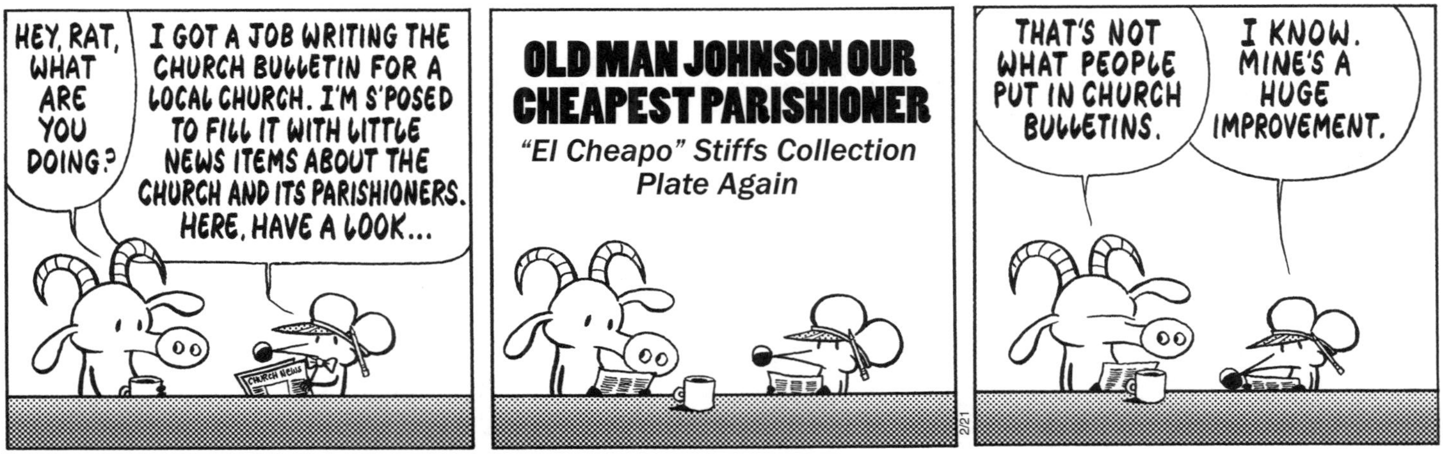
HEY, RAT, WHAT ARE YOU DOING?
I GOT A JOB WRITING THE CHURCH BULLETIN FOR A LOCAL CHURCH. I'M S'POSED TO FILL IT WITH LITTLE NEWS ITEMS ABOUT THE CHURCH AND ITS PARISHIONERS. HERE, HAVE A LOOK...
CHURCH NEWS
OLD MAN JOHNSON OUR CHEAPEST PARISHIONER
"El Cheapo" Stiffs Collection Plate Again
2/21
THAT'S NOT WHAT PEOPLE PUT IN CHURCH BULLETINS.
I KNOW. MINE'S A HUGE IMPROVEMENT.

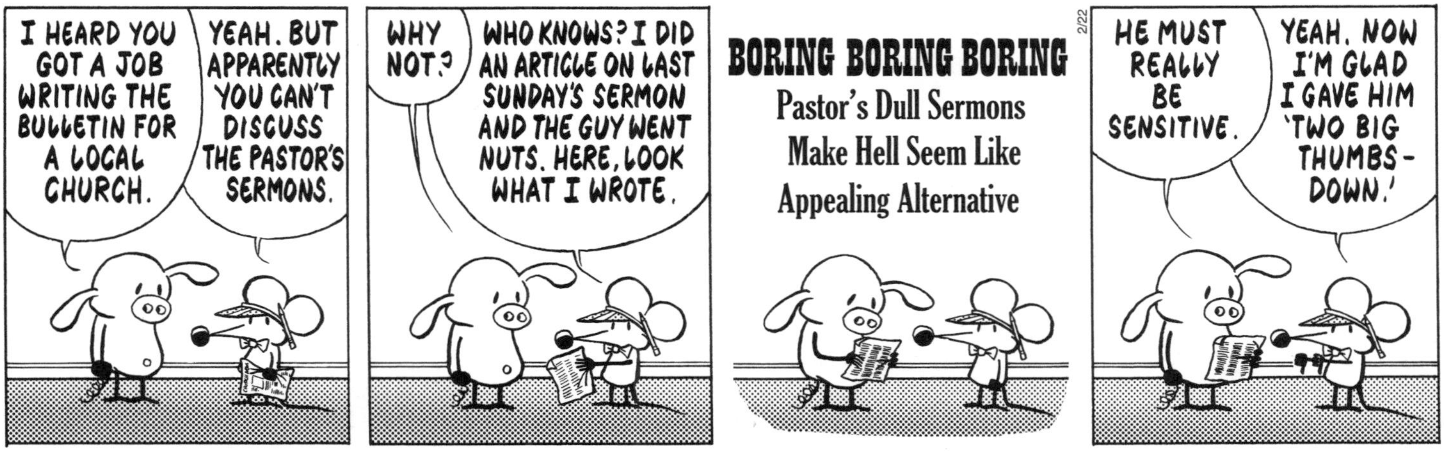
I HEARD YOU GOT A JOB WRITING THE BULLETIN FOR A LOCAL CHURCH.
YEAH. BUT APPARENTLY YOU CAN'T DISCUSS THE PASTOR'S SERMONS.
WHY NOT?
WHO KNOWS? I DID AN ARTICLE ON LAST SUNDAY'S SERMON AND THE GUY WENT NUTS. HERE, LOOK WHAT I WROTE.
BORING BORING BORING
Pastor's Dull Sermons Make Hell Seem Like Appealing Alternative
2/22
HE MUST REALLY BE SENSITIVE.
YEAH. NOW I'M GLAD I GAVE HIM 'TWO BIG THUMBS-DOWN.'

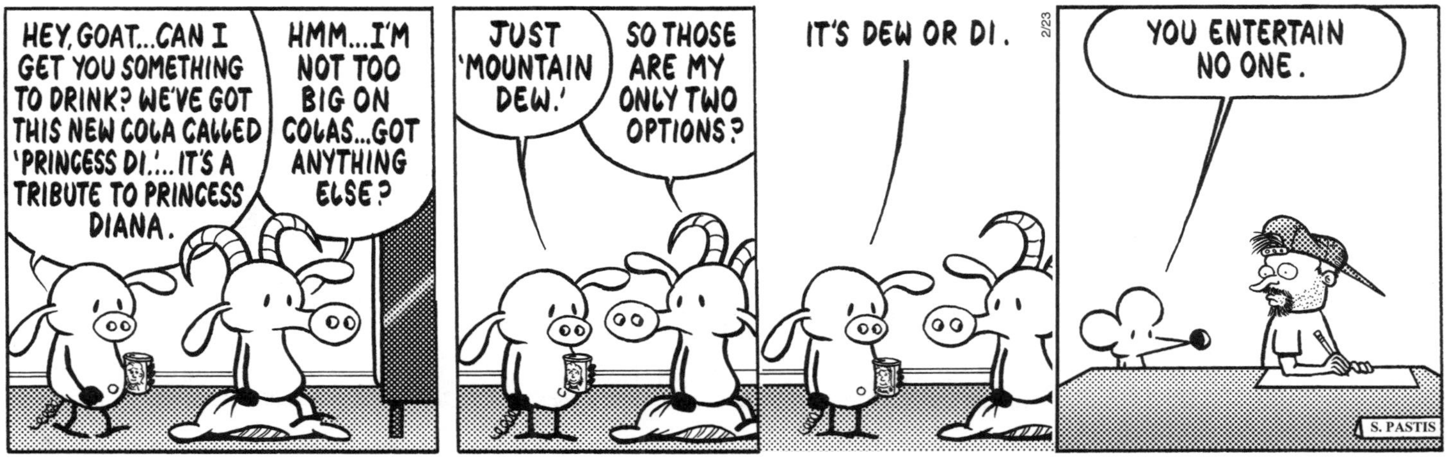
HEY, GOAT...CAN I GET YOU SOMETHING TO DRINK? WE'VE GOT THIS NEW COLA CALLED 'PRINCESS DI.'... IT'S A TRIBUTE TO PRINCESS DIANA.
HMM...I'M NOT TOO BIG ON COLAS...GOT ANYTHING ELSE?
JUST 'MOUNTAIN DEW.'
SO THOSE ARE MY ONLY TWO OPTIONS?
IT'S DEW OR DI.
2/23
YOU ENTERTAIN NO ONE.
S. PASTIS

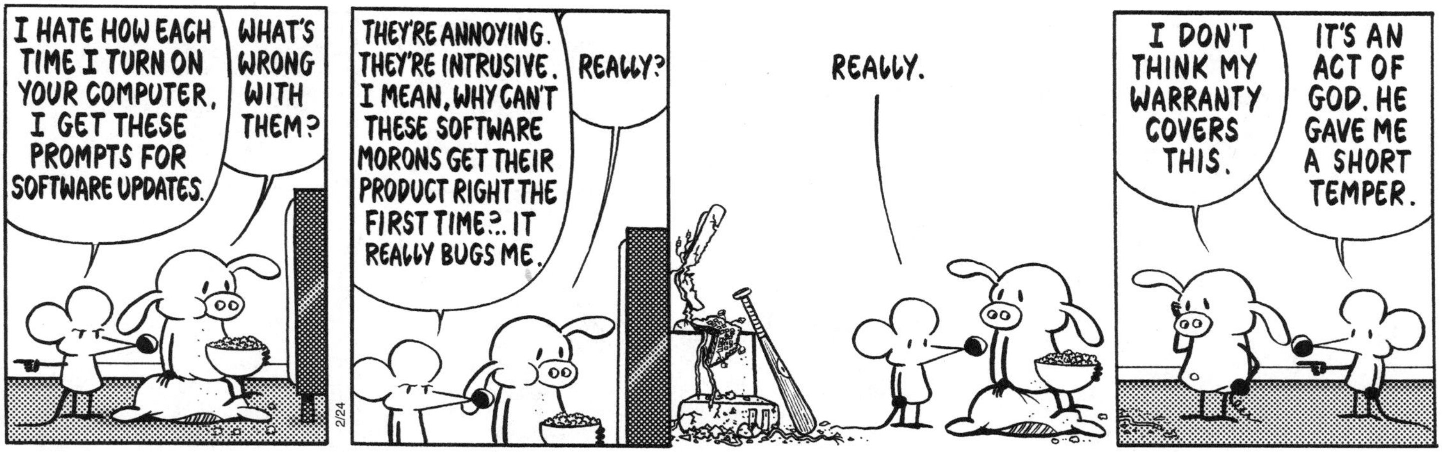
I HATE HOW EACH TIME I TURN ON YOUR COMPUTER, I GET THESE PROMPTS FOR SOFTWARE UPDATES.
WHAT'S WRONG WITH THEM?
2/24
THEY'RE ANNOYING. THEY'RE INTRUSIVE. I MEAN, WHY CAN'T THESE SOFTWARE MORONS GET THEIR PRODUCT RIGHT THE FIRST TIME?.. IT REALLY BUGS ME.
REALLY?
REALLY.
I DON'T THINK MY WARRANTY COVERS THIS.
IT'S AN ACT OF GOD. HE GAVE ME A SHORT TEMPER.

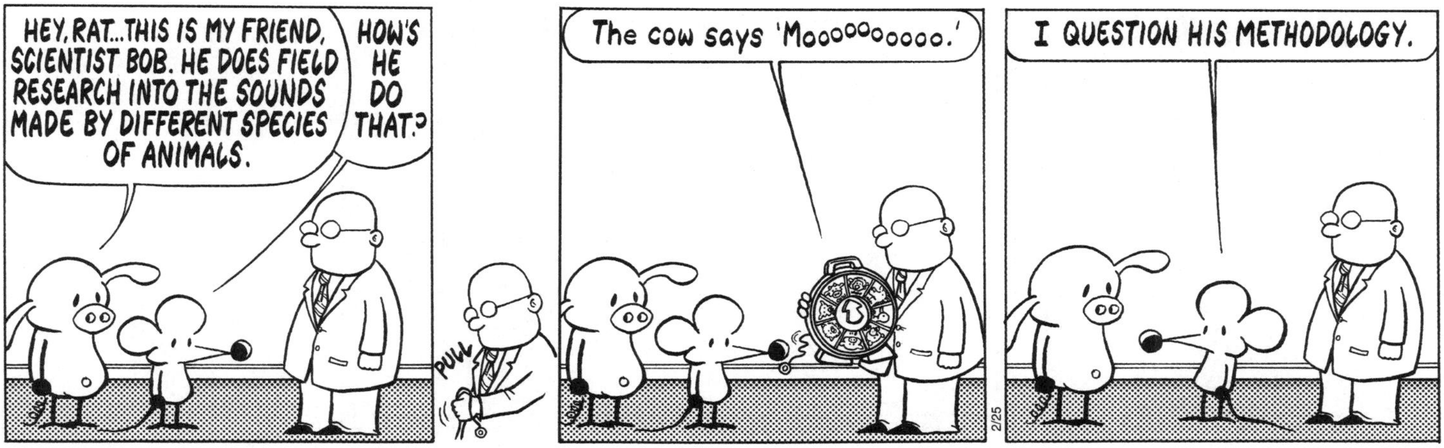
HEY, RAT...THIS IS MY FRIEND, SCIENTIST BOB. HE DOES FIELD RESEARCH INTO THE SOUNDS MADE BY DIFFERENT SPECIES OF ANIMALS.
HOW'S HE DO THAT?
PULL
The cow says 'Mooooooooo.'
2/25
I QUESTION HIS METHODOLOGY.

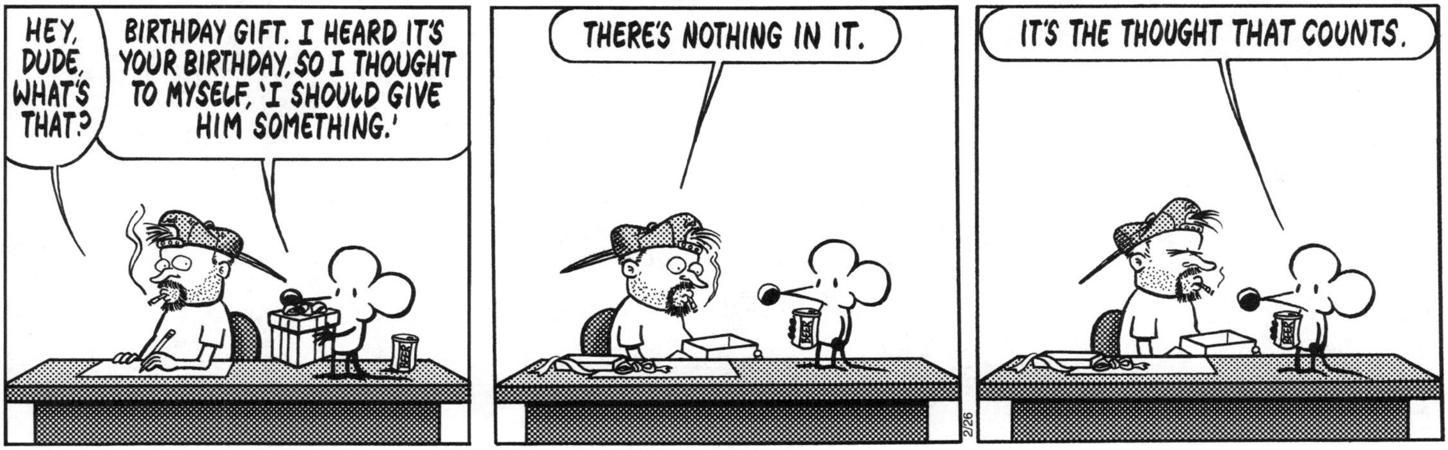
HEY, DUDE, WHAT'S THAT?
BIRTHDAY GIFT. I HEARD IT'S YOUR BIRTHDAY, SO I THOUGHT TO MYSELF, 'I SHOULD GIVE HIM SOMETHING.'
THERE'S NOTHING IN IT.
2/26
IT'S THE THOUGHT THAT COUNTS.

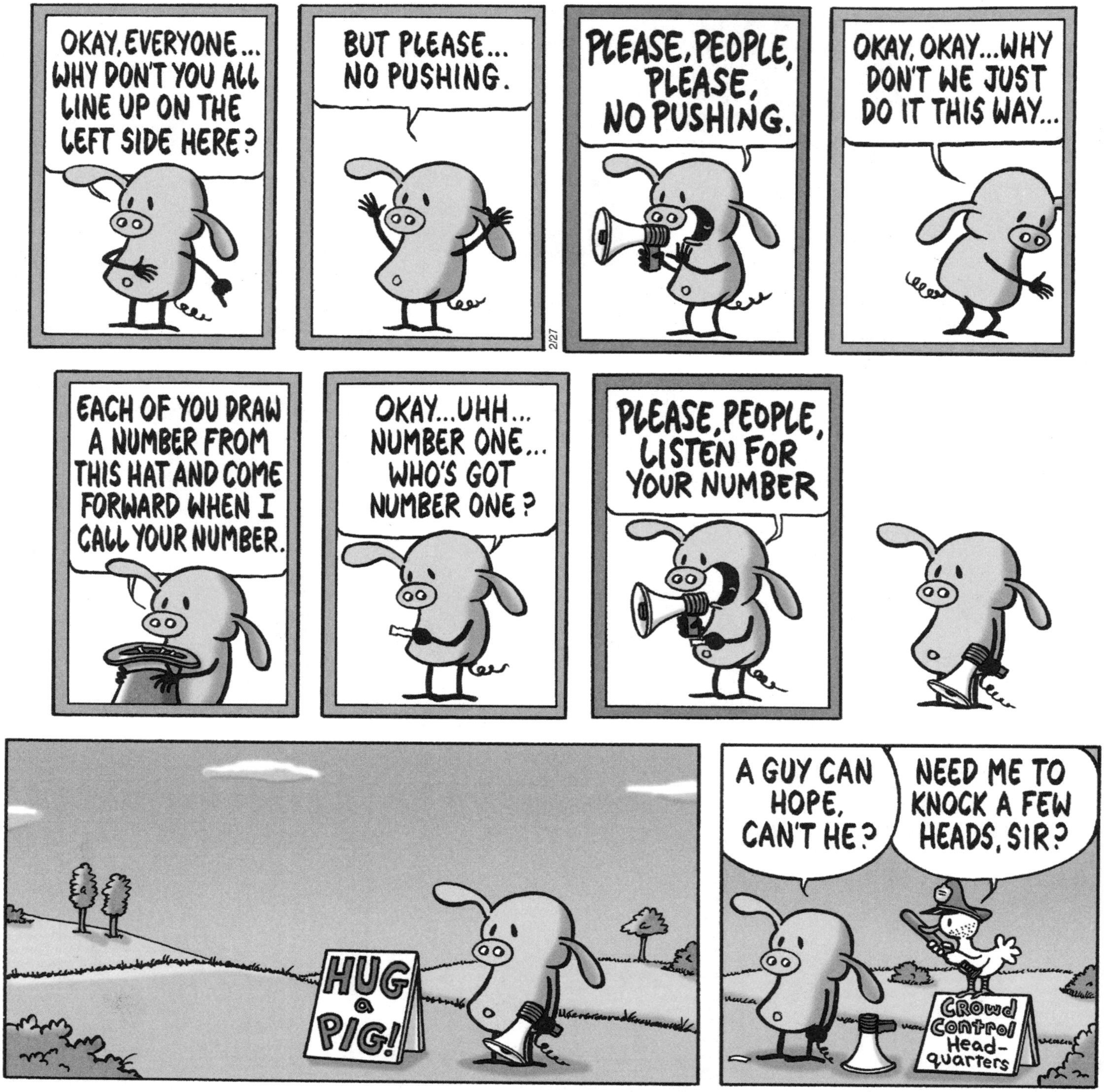
OKAY, EVERYONE... WHY DON'T YOU ALL LINE UP ON THE LEFT SIDE HERE?
BUT PLEASE... NO PUSHING.
PLEASE, PEOPLE, PLEASE, NO PUSHING.
OKAY, OKAY...WHY DON'T WE JUST DO IT THIS WAY...
EACH OF YOU DRAW A NUMBER FROM THIS HAT AND COME FORWARD WHEN I CALL YOUR NUMBER.
OKAY...UHH... NUMBER ONE... WHO'S GOT NUMBER ONE?
PLEASE, PEOPLE, LISTEN FOR YOUR NUMBER
HUG a PIG!
A GUY CAN HOPE, CAN'T HE?
NEED ME TO KNOCK A FEW HEADS, SIR?
Crowd Control Head-quarters